Industrial Communications and Networks

Industrial Communications and Networks

Edited by Sharon Garner

CLANRYE INTERNATIONAL
www.clanryeinternational.com

Clanrye International,
750 Third Avenue, 9th Floor,
New York, NY 10017, USA

ISBN: 978-1-63240-635-4

Cataloging-in-Publication Data

Industrial communications and networks / edited by Sharon Garner.
    p. cm.
Includes bibliographical references and index.
ISBN 978-1-63240-635-4
1. Industrial electronics. 2. Telecommunication. 3. Telecommunication systems--Industrial applications.
4. Mobile communication systems. 5. Communication in management. I. Garner, Sharon.
TK7881.I53 2017
621.381--dc23

For information on all Clanrye International publications
visit our website at www.clanryeinternational.com

Printed in the United States of America.

Contents

Permissions

List of Contributors

Index

Preface

Wireless communications are the primary means of industrial communications. They facilitate faster and accurate communication as well as transfer of data for varied purposes. The ever growing need of advanced technology is the reason that has fueled the research in this field in recent times. This book brings forth some of the most innovative concepts and elucidates the unexplored aspects of industrial communications and networks. It is appropriate for students seeking detailed information in this area as well as for experts. In this book, using case studies and examples, constant effort has been made to make the understanding of the difficult concepts of industrial communications as easy and informative as possible, for the readers.

The researches compiled throughout the book are authentic and of high quality, combining several disciplines and from very diverse regions from around the world. Drawing on the contributions of many researchers from diverse countries, the book's objective is to provide the readers with the latest achievements in the area of research. This book will surely be a source of knowledge to all interested and researching the field.

In the end, I would like to express my deep sense of gratitude to all the authors for meeting the set deadlines in completing and submitting their research chapters. I would also like to thank the publisher for the support offered to us throughout the course of the book. Finally, I extend my sincere thanks to my family for being a constant source of inspiration and encouragement.

Editor

Information theory based performance analysis and enhancement of Safety applications and cluster design in VANET

Zhongyi Shen *,1, Xin Zhang[1], Meng Zhang[1], Zhihao Chen[1], Weijia Li[1], Hongyu Sun[1]

[1]School of Information and Communication Engineering Beijing University of Posts and Telecommunications
PO Box93, 10 XiTuCheng Rd, HaiDian, Beijing, CHINA

Abstract

Safety applications in vehicular ad hoc network (VANET) are handled by broadcast to disseminate safety related messages, due to lack of stable topology. The mobility of vehicles leads to significant performance degradation, especially in dense and dynamic scenarios. This paper presents an information theory based mobility model to determine the theoretical amount of information for VANET safety applications. The new mobility model considers the safety distance and vehicle's status. Analysis results are helpful in reducing redundant information and gaining more insight for system design. Based on the model, an adaptive algorithm to derive the optimal data rate is proposed. In addition, an adaptive control channel interval (CCI) algorithm is applied in cluster forming to improve stability of cluster topology. Numerical simulations based on NS-3 show that algorithms proposed can improve the performance dramatically, and the effectiveness of the safety requirements is guaranteed.

Keywords: Mobility, information theory, cluster, vehicular ad hoc network (VANET), Dedicated Short-Range Communication (DSRC)

1. Introduction

The VANET is a self-organizing network that works on vehicular communications. New technologies like Dedicated Short-Range Communications (DSRC) are in support of advanced vehicular safety applications to improve traffic efficiency for vehicular transportation. Growing attention from researchers and transportation industry has been driven by DSRC technology which employs IEEE 802.11p and IEEE 1609 standards for its capability to improve the traffic safety via various safety applications, through vehicle-to-vehicle (V2V) and vehicle-to infrastructure (V2I) communications.

*Corresponding Author. E-mail: szy823804813@bupt.edu.cn

The work in this paper is sponsored by 111 Project of China under Grant No. B08004, "the Fundamental Research Funds for the Central Universities" with 2014ZD03-02 and Project 61471066 supported by NSFC.

The core of the DSRC-based applications are safety applications, including periodic broadcast and emergency message dissemination which are used for cooperative collision avoidance (CCA), and it's the primary motivation for deploying DSRC. Periodic broadcast messages containing safety information such as position, velocity etc. are disseminated among vehicles with DSRC-based equipment, and the message received form DSRC-equipped neighbors can be used to locate the vehicle in a collision threat or in blind spot. An emergency message will be send when accidents like collision or a sudden brake are detected. The U.S. Department of Transportation (DOT) has estimated that vehicle-to-vehicle (V2V) communication based on DSRC can address up to 82% of all crashes in the United States involving unimpaired drivers, potentially saving thousands of lives and billions of dollars [1].

The U.S. Federal Communications Commission allocated 75MHz of licensed spectrum in the 5.9 GHz band for DSRC [2], and the spectrum is divided in to seven 10-MHz channels, including a control channel (CCH) for control message and safety related applications, and six service channels (SCH) which will be used for non-safety applications. In order to ensure that all the control messages and safety messages won't be missed, DSRC devices will follow a synchronization procedure. A synchronization interval comprises a CCH interval, followed by a SCH interval. During the CCH interval, devices will tune to the CCH for safety applications and service announcement, and the SCH offered will be indicated. To handle time-critical safety applications, the broadcast mode is considered to be a highly appropriate technique for safety messages dissemination [3]. In this paper, safety-related information will be broadcast at a certain frequency, and a broadcast-based retransmission mechanism [4] is introduced to improve reliable of event-driven emergency message dissemination.

The mobility of vehicles determined by the density, velocity and drivers' behaviors is an essential part in analyzing VANET applications. The rapidly changing network topology resulting from the uncertainty of the vehicle's state can exercise a great influence on system performance. At high density scenario, there are a large amount of devices in the transmission range of each vehicle, which will leads to significant performance degradation of IEEE 802.11p Carrier Sense Multiple Access (CSMA) and serious channel congestion [5]. The latency and low reliability resulting from the channel congestion and packets collision in medium access control (MAC) Layer will impact the broadcast based safety applications. Due to lack of request-to-send/clear to- send (RTS/CTS) process in IEEE 802.11p broadcast mode, the reliability of the transmission of event-driven emergency messages will decrease.

Numerous congestion control algorithms in MAC layer have been proposed to improve the performance in dense and high mobility situation. Rate control schemes have been investigated extensively when the fixed beacon frequency which is broadcasted every 100ms may result in a large number of collisions, especially in high density networks. But seldom has the mobility of vehicles been considered, the influences of safety applications associated with the reduction of data rate. Clustering is another effective approach to increase the VANET capacity. Cluster members will perform in a non-competitive manner controlled by a cluster head. The main challenge in clustering is to maintain the stability of cluster with the rapid change of the vehicle's states. The high-frequency change of VANET topology will introduce high overhead and low throughput, and it will need more time for the access process.

This paper proposes a new mobility analytical model, taking into consideration the probability of the change of motion in different density and velocity, which can reflect the mobility of vehicles more realistically. Then

a novel information theory based rate control algorithm is introduced to obtain the theoretical optimum of messages rate to reduce redundant broadcast messages on the premise of the reliability of security under different scenarios. Entropy will be used in the rate control algorithm to measure the uncertainty based on the probabilistic model we derived. Based on the mobility model, a cluster-based adaptive CCI algorithm is proposed to derive the optimum amount of information needed to maintain the stability of clusters theoretically. The algorithm is employed in a more flexible cluster-based system designing considered the mobility of vehicles. Simulation results show that the proposed rate control algorithm can enhance the performance of DSRC system and make a good trade-off between the safety requirements and system performance in terms of delay and packet loss rate, aggravated by redundant broadcast messages which have little effects on safety applications, and the adaptive CCI algorithm shows significant gain in maintaining the stability of clusters by introduced a more flexible cluster design in various scenarios. The cluster can adopt a more suitable size to reduce the frequent network topology change. The main contributions of the algorithm is deriving accurately the relationship between the vehicle's mobility and CCI of cluster-based system to improve the stability, and the specific clustering methods are not discussed in this paper.

The rest of the paper is organized as follows. Section 2 reviews related work. Section 3 describes the mobility analytical model. In Section 4, the information theory based rate control algorithm is described along with the theoretical derivation based on the mobility model we proposed. In Section 5, the cluster-based adaptive CCI algorithm is given based on the mobility analysis. Simulation results are given in Section 6 to verify the performance and accuracy of algorithms proposed, and Section 7 presents the conclusion.

2. Related work

The MAC layer congestion issues have been investigated extensively. Numerous theoretical and simulation-based analyses show the impact of high density on latency and packet successful reception rate [6],[7]. A centralized approach and a distributed approach are proposed in [8] to adapt the window size without considering the mobility of vehicles. The study in [9] illustrates that high traffic of periodic broadcast messages may reduce the resource availability for the emergency messages. A Markov model is used in the article to analyze the dissemination delay of event-driven emergency messages in the presence of low-priority periodic messages, but no specific algorithm is proposed to determine a good tradeoff to improve the performance and the mobility of vehicles is overlooked. [10] describes a DSRC congestion control scheme, based on maximizing channel throughput via distributed control of the safety message rate. Hafeez et al. in [6] propose a mobility model considering the threshold distance to avoid collision in different vehicle density indicated by a Poisson arrival queue. In [11], an adaptive rate control algorithm is proposed, which takes into account the prediction deviation of the motion of nearby vehicles. The broadcast will be deferred when the predicted positions satisfy the feasibility condition in consecutive slots. Few works have been done to consider the threshold distance in mobility models. Hafeez in [6] introduces the threshold distance in the initial distribution of vehicles, but the state of each vehicle is considered to be constant and independent. The majority of studies of congestion control in safety-related message focus on the performance improvement of delay and throughput. There have been no studies to explore the theoretical optimum of messages rate control on the premise of the reliability of security.

For the problems in terms of low reception ratio, high delay, and channel congestion of IEEE 802.11p which have been studied extensively in [12–15]. Considerable cluster-based protocols have been proposed to improve the performance in VANET. The authors in [16] proposed a cluster-based scheme using the contention-free MAC within a cluster and the contention-based IEEE 802.11 MAC among cluster-head vehicles with two transceivers operating on different channels armed by each vehicle. The TDMA used in the system needs strict synchronization among all vehicles. Moreover, the status change due to the vehicle's mobility is neglected. A distributed multichannel and mobility-aware cluster-based MAC (DMMAC) protocol is proposed in [17]. Vehicles will send different types of message to form cluster and update their safety information. To guarantee all cluster members send their safety messages successfully during the CCI which is fixed as 100ms, the communication range will be decreased to reduce the members in the cluster in high density scenarios, which will lead to frequent change of VANET topology, and the structure of clusters will become unstable in real traffic. The majority of studies of cluster-based algorithms do not consider the impact on the stability of clusters introduced by the mobility of vehicles, and the exploration on the theoretical amount of information needed to maintain the stability of clusters is neglected in existing cluster-based system design.

3. Mobility model

Modeling the mobility of vehicles realistically is an essential and challenge task since the movement of the vehicle is determined by many factors such as the traffic density, the vehicles velocity and driving habits. Most related researches on vehicles mobility model neglect or simplify the changing status of vehicles caused by the traffic condition, driver's behavior. And the motion status is considered unchanged and independent throughout the entire process, which is unrealistic. In this paper, a new mobility model is proposed, considering the probability of status changes in different scenarios.

The proposed mobility model is based on a one-way one-lane highway scenario, which can be extended to other more complicated scenarios. Since the transmission range is much larger than the wide of the road, the highway scenario is abstracted into a 1-D model. Vehicles will follow the direction of the road with a speed uniformly distributed between V_{min} and V_{max} [18]. The Poisson process is widely adopted as a sufficiently accurate assumption for modeling the vehicle arrival process in the highway scenario [3]. Vehicles in the highway scenario follow Poisson point process with density β (in terms of vehicles per meter), and the vehicles spacing satisfies the exponential distribution. The probability distribution function (pdf) of vehicles spacing S is given as

$$f(s) = \beta e^{-\beta s}, s > 0. \tag{1}$$

The safety distance D_s is taken into account, which is determined by the current speed V and the reaction time T_r. And the safety distance is given as

$$D_s = V \times T_r. \tag{2}$$

To avoid collision caused by a sudden stop from the vehicle in front, the driver will decelerate when the distance from the vehicle ahead is detected smaller than the safety distance. At an arbitrary point in time, to find the probability that the vehicle will decelerate to keep a safety distance, the distributions of vehicle's density and speed are assumed constant is a certain period of time compared with the time of the communication process. Because the density and the speed are independent, the probability that the vehicle will decelerate at an arbitrary point in time can be described as

$$P_d = \iint\limits_{s < T_r \times V} f(s) \frac{1}{V_{max} - V_{min}} ds dv$$
$$= \frac{e^{-\beta T_r}(e^{-V_{min}} - e^{-V_{max}})}{\beta T_r (V_{max} - V_{min})}. \tag{3}$$

The probability of deceleration in a poor traffic condition with dense traffic and high speed is derived in (3), which means that the vehicles dynamic states are frequently changed, consistent with the actual traffic situation. On the contrary, a vehicle prefers to remain the current state when the traffic condition is good. In the case that a vehicle won't decelerate, it will remain the current speed or accelerate with the probability of $1 - P_d$. In this situation, the probability of accelerate is assumed to be proportional to P_d, which means that the probability of acceleration will increase with P_d in a good traffic condition, and will decrease when P_d is high. Based on the assumption and analysis above, the probability of acceleration can be written as

$$P_a = P_d(1 - P_d). \tag{4}$$

And the probability that a vehicle remains the current state is

$$P_r = 1 - P_d - P_a. \tag{5}$$

From (3), (4) and (5), it's clear that vehicles are more likely to accelerate or decelerate in the high-density and high-speed scenario, which means the vehicle's status will change frequent in mess road conditions for security.

Based on the analysis above, the motion of a vehicle is divided in time slots of Δt, during which the state of the vehicle is assumed to remain. The state can be changed at the beginning of a new time slot with the probability derived in the mobility model. To simplify the analysis, the acceleration is assumed to be a fixed value. Then the probability distribution of acceleration of the vehicle in the n_i slot based on (3), (4) and (5) is

$$a = \begin{cases} a, & P_a \\ 0, & P_r \\ -a, & P_d \end{cases} \tag{6}$$

The speed of the vehicle at the end of the n_i slot is

$$V_i = V_{i-1} + a_i \Delta t. \tag{7}$$

The distance the vehicle travels during the n_i slot can be written as

$$S_i = V_{i-1}\Delta t + \frac{1}{2}a_i \Delta t^2. \tag{8}$$

At the starting point t_0, the vehicle locates at X_0 with the speed V_0. Substituting the speed in the reference point t_0, the speed of the vehicle at the end of the n_i slot is given as

$$V_i = V_{i-1} + a_i \Delta t$$
$$= V_0 + \sum_{k=1}^{i} a_k \Delta t. \tag{9}$$

And the total distance in $N\Delta t$ from t_0 is

$$S_{N\Delta t} = \sum_{i=1}^{N} S_i$$
$$= \sum_{i=1}^{N} V_{i-1}\Delta t + \frac{1}{2}a_i \Delta t^2. \tag{10}$$

Substituting (9) in (10), we have

$$S_{N\Delta t} = \sum_{i=1}^{N} (V_0 + \sum_{k=1}^{i-1} a_k \Delta t)\Delta t + \frac{1}{2}a_i \Delta t^2$$
$$= NV_0\Delta t + \sum_{i=1}^{N} (N-i)a_i \Delta t^2 + \frac{1}{2}a_i \Delta t^2 \tag{11}$$
$$= NV_0\Delta t + \sum_{i=1}^{N} (N-i+\frac{1}{2})a_i \Delta t^2.$$

4. Analytical model and information theory based control algorithm

The Basic Safety Message (BSM) format [19] is utilized in the periodic broadcast messages of DSRC safety applications. The safety related messages are transmitted over 300-500 meters, with a 6 Mbps data rate, and a 10 Hz message rate by default [20],[21]. The redundancy introduced by the fixed message rate scheme when the broadcast messages are excess to support safety applications will aggravate network traffic and increase the probability of packets loss and the packets delay, especially in dense and high-mobility conditions. The performance degradation can severely impact the time-critical safety applications.

In this section, an information theory based rate control algorithm is proposed based on the mobility model in section 3 to analyze the optimum rate control scheme in substance. The entropy will be utilized to measure the uncertainty of vehicles position caused by the distribution of spacing and the mobility of vehicles based on the probabilistic model we derived.

The time a state packet is received from the target vehicle serves as a reference point t_0, and the speed and the position can be obtained from the received packet. The total distance $S_{N\Delta t}$ in $N\Delta t$ from t_0 can be derived from (11).

Assume that no state broadcast packet is received from the target vehicle since t_0, so the position prediction at $N\Delta t$ is based on the safety information obtained from the most recently received packet at t_0. The predicted position of the vehicle at $N\Delta t$ is

$$\tilde{S}_{N\Delta t} = NV_0\Delta t. \tag{12}$$

Combining (10) and (11), the deviation of the prediction about the position of the vehicle at $N\Delta t$ is

$$S_{N\Delta t} - \tilde{S}_{N\Delta t} = \sum_{i=1}^{N} (N-i+\frac{1}{2})a_i \Delta t^2. \tag{13}$$

Because of the motion in every slot is independent, the deviation of prediction is composed of N independent variables as

$$S_{N\Delta t} - \tilde{S}_{N\Delta t} = \sum_{i=1}^{N} X_i \tag{14}$$

$$X_i = (N - i + \frac{1}{2})a_i \Delta t^2. \tag{15}$$

According to the Liapunov central limit theorem, the deviation of prediction is approximate normal distribution.

$$S_{N\Delta t} - \tilde{S}_{N\Delta t} = \sum_{i=1}^{N} X_i \sim N(\mu, \sigma^2). \tag{16}$$

where μ and σ^2 are summations of the mean and variance of each independent variable X_i. According to the probability distribution of the acceleration in (6), μ and σ^2 can be expressed as

$$\mu = \sum_{i=1}^{N} EX_i$$

$$= \sum_{i=1}^{N} (N - i + \frac{1}{2})a_i \Delta t^2 (P_a - P_d) \tag{17}$$

$$= \frac{N^2 a_i \Delta t^2 (P_a - P_d)}{2}.$$

$$\sigma^2 = \sum_{i=1}^{N} DX_i$$

$$= \sum_{i=1}^{N} P_a[(N - i + \frac{1}{2})a_i \Delta t^2]^2 + P_d[(N - i + \frac{1}{2})a_i \Delta t^2]^2$$

$$= \frac{(P_a + P_d)a^2 \Delta t^4 (4N^3 - N)}{12}. \tag{18}$$

From (16), (17) and (18), it is clear that the accuracy of prediction decreases with the number of time slots. To guarantee the performance of safety applications in vehicles positioning and collision warning, the threshold E_{th} of the deviation of position prediction is set as 0.5m based on the analysis in [22]. Therefore, the probability that the positioning deviation of the target vehicle is less than the threshold is given by

$$P\{|S_{N\Delta t} - \tilde{S}_{N\Delta t}| \le E_{th}\}$$
$$= \Phi(\frac{E_{th} - \mu}{\sigma}) - \Phi(\frac{-E_{th} - \mu}{\sigma}). \tag{19}$$

In this paper, we consider that ensuring the positioning deviation less than the threshold with 95% probability is acceptable. Based on the analysis above, we get

$$\Phi(\frac{E_{th} - \mu}{\sigma}) \approx \Phi(2). \tag{20}$$

$$\sigma_{th} \approx \frac{E_{th} - \mu_{th}}{2}. \tag{21}$$

To measure the uncertainty of the positioning deviation, the entropy of the uncertainty Y at $N\Delta t$ is

$$H(Y) = ln(\sigma_N \sqrt{2\pi e}) \tag{22}$$

where σ_N is the standard deviation of the distribution at $N\Delta t$.

From (20) and (21), the threshold of the entropy at $N\Delta t$ is $ln(\sigma_{th}\sqrt{2\pi e})$. Assume that a state packet is received at $N'\Delta t$ during t_0 to $N\Delta t$, the conditional entropy is

$$H(Y|X) = ln(\sigma_{Y|X}\sqrt{2\pi e}) \tag{23}$$

where $\sigma_{Y|X}$ is the standard deviation of the distribution at $N\Delta t$ when a state packet is received at $N'\Delta t$.

To satisfy the threshold of the entropy, we get the inequality

$$\sigma_{Y|X} \le \sigma_{th}. \tag{24}$$

$$\sigma_{Y|X}^2 = \sum_{i=1}^{N-N'} DX_i$$
$$= \frac{(P_a + P_d)a^2 \Delta t^4 [4(N - N')^3 - (N - N')]}{12}. \tag{25}$$

Substituting (25) in (24), the maximum transmission interval $(N - N')\Delta t$ under the given density and velocity distribution can be derived.

5. Analytical model and adaptive cluster-based CCI algorithm

Most cluster-based scheme in VANET use contention-free MAC method within a cluster and the contention-based MAC method among different clusters through the cluster-head. The selected cluster-head will collected safety information containing velocity, position.etc. within a CCI, and the aggregated message will be disseminated to cluster members and neighbor clusters. Due to the contention-free MAC method within a cluster, the cluster size have to be limited to allow all the members to transmit safety messages within a CCI successfully. In high-density scenarios, relevant algorithm is necessary to decrease the cluster range as to reduce the number of cluster members, otherwise, some messages will be missed for the capability deficit with lots of vehicles in the cluster range. Nevertheless, the frequent change of VANET topology will introduce high overhead and low throughput, and it will need more time for the access process.

The CCI of existing cluster-based schemes [16, 17] is set to 100ms as a constant value, in accordance with the beacon interval in IEEE 802.11p. The inflexible design will introduce redundant information and reduce the capability of clusters, particularly in high-density scenarios. In this section, analysis based on the mobility model is given to derive the theoretical relationship between the vehicle's mobility and cluster stability, and an adaptive cluster-based CCI algorithm is proposed to obtain the optimum CCI in different scenarios. The major contribution of the algorithm is to analysis the influence of mobility characters in VANET on cluster stability, while the specific clustering methods are not discussed in this paper.

The analysis model is built based on a one-way multilane highway segment. The movement of vehicles in each lane is considered to be independent. Assume that vehicles in the lane have been clustered in a certain method, which has no influence on the analyze model, and C_h and C_t are the head and tail of a valid cluster at t_0, when the cluster head is aware of all the members in the cluster. The velocity of C_h and C_t at t_0 is V_0^h and V_0^t, which follow uniform distribution in section 3. The total distance of C_h and C_t in $N\Delta t$ from t_0 based on (11) are

$$S_{N\Delta t}^h = NV_0^h\Delta t + \sum_{i=1}^{N}(N-i+\frac{1}{2})a_i^h\Delta t^2. \quad (26)$$

$$S_{N\Delta t}^t = NV_0^t\Delta t + \sum_{i=1}^{N}(N-i+\frac{1}{2})a_i^t\Delta t^2. \quad (27)$$

The change of the cluster range in $N\Delta t$ is

$$\begin{aligned}
&S_{N\Delta t}^h - S_{N\Delta t}^t \\
&= NV_0^h\Delta t - NV_0^t\Delta t + \sum_{i=1}^{N}(N-i+\frac{1}{2})a_i^h\Delta t^2 \\
&- \sum_{i=1}^{N}(N-i+\frac{1}{2})a_i^t\Delta t^2.
\end{aligned} \quad (28)$$

Let $U=NV_0^h\Delta t - NV_0^t\Delta t$, because V_0^h and V_0^t are independent from each other, the probability density function (PDF) of U is solved as

$$f(U)=\begin{cases} \dfrac{(V_{max}-V_{min})N\Delta t - U}{(V_{max}-V_{min})N\Delta t^2} & 0\leq U < (V_{max}-V_{min})N\Delta t \\ \dfrac{(V_{max}-V_{min})N\Delta t + U}{(V_{max}-V_{min})N\Delta t^2} & (V_{min}-V_{max})N\Delta t \leq U < 0. \end{cases} \quad (29)$$

From (28),we set

$$\begin{aligned}
X_{Joint} &= \sum_{i=1}^{N}(N-i+\frac{1}{2})a_i^h\Delta t^2 - \sum_{i=1}^{N}(N-i+\frac{1}{2})a_i^t\Delta t^2 \\
&= \sum_{i=1}^{N}X_i^h - \sum_{i=1}^{N}X_i^t.
\end{aligned} \quad (30)$$

Where $\sum_{i=1}^{N}X_i^h$ and $\sum_{i=1}^{N}X_i^t$ follow normal distribution. On account of the movements of C_h and C_t are independent. From(16),(17)and(18),it can be derived that X_{Joint} has a normal distribution as

$$X_{Joint} = \sum_{i=1}^{N}X_i^h - \sum_{i=1}^{N}X_i^t \sim N(2\mu, 2\sigma^2). \quad (31)$$

Where μ and σ is described in (17) and (18).

Based on the analysis above, the change of the cluster range in $N\Delta t$ is $U+X_{Joint}$. The structure of a cluster is considered to be changed when a member leave the range or a new vehicle fall within the cluster range. The cluster head has to update the information of cluster members to detect the leaving member or the vehicle applying to join the cluster. On the basis of the mobility model, it is considered that the structure change when the variation of the cluster range is greater than the vehicles spacing S which satisfies the exponential distribution in (1), and the cluster head is assumed in the centra of the cluster consistently. The probability that the variation of the cluster range is greater than the vehicles spacing is

$$\begin{aligned}
P_c &= P\{|U + X_{Joint}| \geq S\} \\
&= \iiint_{|U+X_{Joint}|\geq S} f(u,x,s)dudxds.
\end{aligned} \quad (32)$$

Where P_c is a function of N. To update the cluster member promptly and guarantee the security, the probability that the structure of the cluster remained $1 - P_c$ should greater than a threshold value P_{th}. When there is L lanes on the highway, the following inequality should be satisfied.

$$(1 - P_c)^L \geq P_{th}. \quad (33)$$

Substituting (32) in (33), the maximum update interval in different density and velocity is derived, which is considered as the adaptive CCI, varied in different scenarios. To verify superiority of the adaptive CCI algorithm, it is applied in DMMAC proposed in[17]. There are 4 types of messages in DMMAC, containing status, invitation and consolidated messages sent from cluster members or cluster head. The upper bound of transmission time is given in [17] as

$$(T_{avg})_{ub} = T_{cf} + [T_{mf}] + (2\beta R - 1)[T_m] + [T_{in}] + [T_{cl}]. \quad (34)$$

Where T_{cf}, T_{mf} and T_m are the transmission times of the first messages sent by the cluster head and members, and T_{in}, T_{cl} are the transmission times of invitation and the last message. To enable all cluster members to transmit successfully their safety messages during the CCI, authors describe the condition that

$$(T_{avg})_{ub} \leq \varphi \times CCI. \quad (35)$$

Analysis and simulation results in [17] illustrate that the cluster need to decrease the range to reduce the nodes within the cluster in order to satisfied (35). The transmission range decrease form 300m to

Table 1. Value of parameters used in Simulation

Parameter	Value
Length of highway segment	2000m
Vehicle's speed	80–120km/h
Vehicle's density	0.01–0.1vehicle/m
Frequency	5.9GHz
Packet size	100Bytes
Transmission power	50mW
Received power threshold	3.162e-13W
Noise floor	1.26e-14W
DIFS	$64\mu s$
Antennas gain	1
Reaction time	1s
Δt	100ms

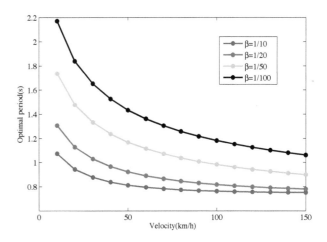

Figure 1. Optimal periods of the broadcast messages under different vehicle density and velocity distributions

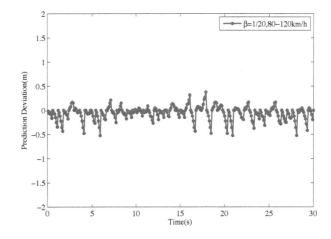

Figure 2. Prediction deviation with β=1/20,speed ranges from 80–120km/h

100m when the density reaches 0.25 vehicles/m. We apply the adaptive CCI algorithm proposed in this paper, the numerical results demonstrate the advantage over DMMAC in maintain the cluster size in high density scenarios to keep the stability of the cluster. Moreover, the redundancy is reduced to support other control messages. The numerical results is given in the simulation part.

6. Model validation and simulation

In this section, the theoretical results of the optimal periods under various conditions and the adaptive cluster-based CCI algorithm proposed in section 4 and section 5 are shown. The performance of the rate control scheme introduced in the paper is evaluated in terms of the accuracy of positioning, the packet loss rate and the average delay. The stability of the adaptive CCI algorithm in section 5 which is essential in clustering design is tested, compared with DMMAC in [17] and the CMCP in [16].

The well-known simulator NS3 [23] (version 3.22) is used to analyze the system's performance. The Nakagami propagation model is used in simulations, which is considered best for vehicular environment in many research [24], [25]. The simulation scenario is based on one-direction four-lane highway segment, with the velocity of vehicles ranges from 80-120 km/h, which is typical for highways. The simulation parameters are summarized in Table 1.

Figure 1 shows the optimal period of the broadcast messages which can be calculated from (24) and (25) under different vehicle density and velocity distributions. From the numerical results in Figure 1, it can be observed that the value of the broadcast period is significantly different under various conditions. The fixed rate control scheme can't meet the changing safety requirements and redundancy will be introduced in some circumstances.

Figure 2 shows the accuracy of the position prediction through the periodic broadcast messages with the rate control scheme we proposed. The motion of the vehicle is based on the mobility model in Section 3. The vehicles spacing satisfy the exponential distribution with $\beta = 0.05$, and the speed ranges from 80-120km/h as mentioned.

Figure 3 and Figure 4 show, respectively, the packet loss rate the packet delay versus vehicle density ranged from 0.01 to 0.1 vehicles/m in (1), with and without the entropy-based rate control algorithm. As is shown in Figure 3, the packets loss caused by collisions from neighboring vehicles and hidden terminals will become serious with the increase of vehicle density, which will leads to undesirable performance, particularly in dense vehicular environment. At the same time, vehicles will take longer time to access the channel to broadcast the state messages, and the packet delay increases with the increasing of vehicles density. The high packet loss rate and packet delay will be a disaster to safety

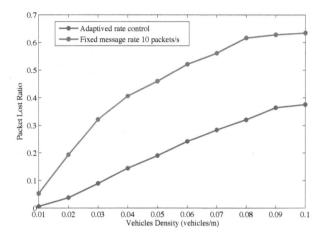

Figure 3. Packet loss rate versus vehicle's density

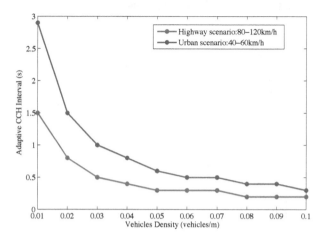

Figure 5. Adaptive CCI versus vehicle's density

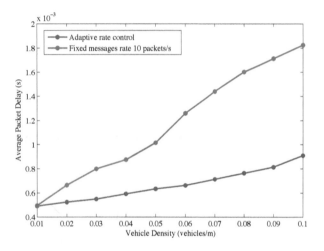

Figure 4. Packet delay versus vehicle's density

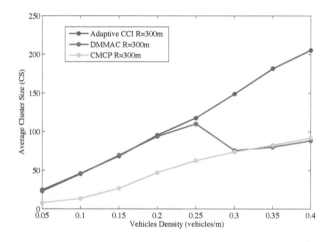

Figure 6. Cluster size versus vehicle's density

applications. Adapting the entropy-based rate control algorithm, the packet loss rate and packet delay are improved greatly, as is shown in the figure. It is obvious that the entropy-based rate control scheme outperforms fixed-rate and other rate control schemes not only for the improvements of network performance, but also the consideration to the safety requirements. The theoretical results of the adaptive cluster-based CCI in highway and urban scenarios are shown in Figure 5. Compared with the typical highway scenarios with the velocity ranging from 80-120km/h, vehicles in urban scenarios have more coincident and low speeds range from 40-60km/h. The threshold probability P_{th} is set as 90%. It can be seen that the value of the adaptive CCI is significantly different under various density, and clusters in urban scenarios have a longer CCI for a more coincident speed distribution, with means the structure of a cluster is less likely to change. The adaptive CCI algorithm has a more flexible CCI considering safety requirements compared with the fixed CCI in existing

works, and the redundancy is reduced to support other control messages.

Figure 6 shows the numbers of vehicles in the cluster range in different density compared with the DMMAC in [17] and the CMCP in [16]. It is clear that the cluster size in DMMAC has a abrupt change with the transmission switching to 100m when the density reaches 0.25 vehicles/m. The cluster stability will decrease when decreasing the communication range. Moreover, the frequent change of cluster range will introduce high overhead. Many vehicles have to wait for complicated procedures to access the channel again due to the sudden change of the cluster range. It can be observed that the adaptive cluster-based CCI can improve the capability of clusters and the safety requirements are guaranteed at the same time.

7. Conclusions

In this paper, a new mobility model has been presented in which the change of motion under various vehicle densities and speeds is considered. Entropy is used to describe the uncertainty of the vehicle position caused by the change of motions. An information theory based rate control algorithm is proposed to derive the optimum broadcast period. Adapting the rate control algorithm, vehicles are able to adjust the broadcast period of states messages to improve the performance of safety applications. Moreover, a theoretical model is proposed to analyze the stability of clusters considering the mobility of vehicles, and an adaptive cluster-based CCI algorithm is proposed to improve the stability of clusters in VANET. The adaptive cluster-based CCI can improve the capability of clusters to enhance the cluster stability and reduce redundant information compared with existing works. Simulation results in NS3 show that the proposed rate control algorithm can significantly reduce redundancy, thus reducing the packet delay and packet loss rate, and the accuracy of vehicle positioning is guaranteed at the same time. The adaptive cluster-based CCI shows a more flexible system design and the performance in maintain the cluster size. The information theory based analysis of measuring the uncertainty provides new insights on system design for novel networks with high mobility and high intelligence, and it can be applied in other heterogeneous networks like LTE-based vehicular communications in future works.

Acknowledgement. The authors would like to thank the experts from Qualcomm for their valuable comments.

References

[1] KENNEY, J.B. (2011) Dedicated short-range communications (dsrc) standards in the united states. *Proceedings of the IEEE* **99**(7): 1162–1182.

[2] COMMISSION, U.F.C. *et al.* (2003) R&o fcc 03-324,âř. *Dedicated Short Range Communications Report and Order* .

[3] YAO, Y., RAO, L. and LIU, X. (2013) Performance and reliability analysis of ieee 802.11 p safety communication in a highway environment. *Vehicular Technology, IEEE Transactions on* **62**(9): 4198–4212.

[4] BISWAS, S., TATCHIKOU, R. and DION, F. (2006) Vehicle-to-vehicle wireless communication protocols for enhancing highway traffic safety. *Communications Magazine, IEEE* **44**(1): 74–82.

[5] WU, X., SUBRAMANIAN, S., GUHA, R., WHITE, R.G., LI, J., LU, K.W., BUCCERI, A. *et al.* (2013) Vehicular communications using dsrc: challenges, enhancements, and evolution. *Selected Areas in Communications, IEEE Journal on* **31**(9): 399–408.

[6] HAFEEZ, K.A., ZHAO, L., MA, B. and MARK, J.W. (2013) Performance analysis and enhancement of the dsrc for vanet's safety applications. *Vehicular Technology, IEEE Transactions on* **62**(7): 3069–3083.

[7] EICHLER, S. (2007) Performance evaluation of the ieee 802.11p wave communication standard. In *Vehicular Technology Conference, 2007. VTC-2007 Fall. 2007 IEEE 66th*: 2199–2203.

[8] WANG, Y., AHMED, A., KRISHNAMACHARI, B. and PSOUNIS, K. (2008) Ieee 802.11p performance evaluation and protocol enhancement. In *Vehicular Electronics and Safety, 2008. ICVES 2008. IEEE International Conference on*: 317–322.

[9] KHABAZIAN, M., AÏSSA, S. and MEHMET-ALI, M. (2013) Performance modeling of safety messages broadcast in vehicular ad hoc networks. *Intelligent Transportation Systems, IEEE Transactions on* **14**(1): 380–387.

[10] BANSAL, G. and KENNEY, J.B. (2013) Controlling congestion in safety-message transmissions: A philosophy for vehicular dsrc systems. *Vehicular Technology Magazine, IEEE* **8**(4): 20–26.

[11] NGUYEN, H.H. and JEONG, H.Y. (2013) Adaptive beacon rate control algorithm for vehicular ad-hoc networks. In *Ubiquitous and Future Networks (ICUFN), 2013 Fifth International Conference on* (IEEE): 652–653.

[12] GALLARDO, J.R., MAKRAKIS, D. and MOUFTAH, H.T. (2009) Performance analysis of the edca medium access mechanism over the control channel of an ieee 802.11p wave vehicular network. *Communications .icc.ieee International Conference on* : 1 – 6.

[13] TORRENT-MORENO, M., MITTAG, J., SANTI, P. and HARTENSTEIN, H. (2009) Vehicle-to-vehicle communication: Fair transmit power control for safety-critical information. *IEEE Transactions on Vehicular Technology* **58**(7): 3684–3703.

[14] HASSAN, M.I., HAI, L.V. and SAKURAI, T. (2010) Performance analysis of the ieee 802.11 mac protocol for dsrc with and without retransmissions. In *2013 IEEE 14th International Symposium on "A World of Wireless, Mobile and Multimedia Networks" (WoWMoM)*: 1–8.

[15] NG, S.C., ZHANG, W., ZHANG, Y., YANG, Y. and MAO, G. (2011) Analysis of access and connectivity probabilities in vehicular relay networks. *Selected Areas in Communications, IEEE Journal on* **29**(1): 140–150.

[16] SU, H. and ZHANG, X. (2007) Clustering-based multichannel mac protocols for qos provisionings over vehicular ad hoc networks. *IEEE Transactions on Vehicular Technology* **56**(6): 3309 – 3323.

[17] HAFEEZ, K.A., ZHAO, L., MARK, J.W., SHEN, X. and NIU, Z. (2013) Distributed multichannel and mobility-aware cluster-based mac protocol for vehicular ad hoc networks. *Vehicular Technology, IEEE Transactions on* **62**(8): 3886–3902.

[18] HAFEEZ, K.A., ZHAO, L., LIAO, Z. and MA, B. (2010) Impact of mobility on vanets' safety applications. In *Global Telecommunications Conference (GLOBECOM 2010), 2010 IEEE* (IEEE): 1–5.

[19] COMMITTEE, D. *et al.* (2009), Dedicated short range communications (dsrc) message set dictionary.

[20] KENNEY, J.B., BANSAL, G. and ROHRS, C.E. (2011) Limeric: a linear message rate control algorithm for vehicular dsrc systems. In *Proceedings of the Eighth ACM international workshop on Vehicular inter-networking* (ACM): 21–30.

[21] CONSORTIUM, C.V.S.C. *et al.* (2005) Vehicle safety communications project: task 3 final report: identify

intelligent vehicle safety applications enabled by dsrc. *National Highway Traffic Safety Administration, US Department of Transportation, Washington DC* .

[22] SHLADOVER, S.E. and TAN, S.K. (2006) Analysis of vehicle positioning accuracy requirements for communication-based cooperative collision warning. *Journal of Intelligent Transportation Systems* **10**(3): 131–140.

[23] Ns-3 network simulator, http://www.nsnam.org. [Online;Available:].

[24] SCHMIDT-EISENLOHR, F., TORRENT-MORENO, M., MITTAG, J. and HARTENSTEIN, H. (2007) Simulation platform for inter-vehicle communications and analysis of periodic information exchange. In *Wireless on Demand Network Systems and Services, 2007. WONS'07. Fourth Annual Conference on* (IEEE): 50–58.

[25] TALIWAL, V., JIANG, D., MANGOLD, H., CHEN, C. and SENGUPTA, R. (2004) Empirical determination of channel characteristics for dsrc vehicle-to-vehicle communication. In *Proceedings of the 1st ACM international workshop on Vehicular ad hoc networks* (ACM): 88–88.

2

Cloud Based Mobile Network Sharing: A New Model

Malla Reddy Sama*,1, Yvon Gourhant1 and Lucian Suciu1

1 Orange Labs, France

Abstract

The tradition network sharing models on existing mobile architecture is a challenging for the mobile operator to cope the future competitive market while increasing average revenue per user. In fact, to sustain the future data tsunami, the operators are already investing in their network. However, they are not yet capturing their investments. The average revenue per user has declined. Moreover, the static and rapid commoditization of network equipments and service provisioning are pushing the mobile operators' to adopt different strategies such as networking sharing in the access and core network for to reduce OPEX and CAPEX. In this paper, we proposed new models for mobile operators to share their network through cloud platform (e.g. pay-as-you-go) in order to open new business strategies and to reduce CAPEX and OPEX. On the other hand, this proposal also cops the future data tsunami and introduces more flexibility, elasticity and on-demand features to the LTE/EPC architecture.

Keywords: LTE/EPC, Cloudification, Infrastructure sharing, MVNO and Emerging Markets.

1. Introduction

New market liberalization developments around the world and growing mobile data traffic drive; dramatic and fundamental technological changes the telecom sector landscape. After dramatic changes in mobile phones and new innovations in the mobile network, LTE/EPC (Long Term Evolution/Evolved Packet Core) is a perfect example for this liberation changes in telecom sector. These enormous successes of the telecom industries in worldwide, the current architecture imposes challenges for mobile operators in order to introduce new business model for increasing the revenue and to cope the future data tsunami [1]. For example, the mobile operators has been struggling to cope with the increasing data demands of new devices like tablets, smartphones and their rich applications like multimedia services. However, they are not been able to take full advantages of the higher transmission technology like LTE. Among the key reason for this shortfall is the custom equipment, static network equipment behavior and computationally heavy protocols are ultimately leading to high CAPEX and increasing network operational cost.

In addition, the current LTE/EPC architecture was not designed with enough flexibility in mind. Its components like eNB, MME, SGW and PGW are based on custom hardware and need to be statically provisioned and configured [2]. Indeed, these components are too expensive, vendor lock-in, too complicated to manage and change their behavior. Consequently, the network architecture does not come with enough flexible and extensible features. The network is typically dimensioned based on the load foreseen at the peak hours. For example, to increase the network capacity and configure new functions, it requires the deployment of new entities in specific network sites and to integrate them smoothly in the existing network. Hence, the operation of such a static and device-centric network management is a costly, cumbersome and time-consuming process [3]. Unfortunately, this state-of-affairs has remained true for well over two decades. In fact, the operators are prohibited to change any software function or implement any new functions in the network entity. Often, the operator have to wait for a vendor to put it in plan in their proprietary products. Significantly, this will put greater strain on network operators because it may increase the OPEX.

On the other hand, the mobile operators are facing a strong competition environment. A recent study shows that the operators' revenues are decreasing exponentially and faces "end of profit" sometime before mid-2015 [4]. In fact, the cost to build, upgrade and operate the network is becoming too expensive while the revenue is not growing at the same rate. In addition to this, mobile data traffic has been growing at an unprecedented rate over the last few years [5], while the ARPU (Average Revenue Per User) is decreasing slowly ([6], [7]). This will impact the ability to build out new networks and offer new services. In this predication, the mobile operators must rethink about their solution in order to reduce cost and to maintain profitability and growth as well as to provide better services to the end users.

On these grounds, network operators should investigate new solutions to manage the dynamic nature of future traffic in a cost-efficient manner. There have been studies ([8], [9], [10] and [11]) and standardization bodies such as ONF Wireless & Mobile group [13] and ETSI NFV [12] that address the challenge caused by mobile data traffic increase in LTE/EPC architectures and highlighted the immediate need for the reduction of network costs both OPEX and CAPEX. For instance, in [11], the authors explored OpenFlow as an architecture for eNode B virtualization and infrastructure sharing between operators. Thus, the operators recognize the opportunity to tap into advanced technologies such as server virtualization, efficient traffic management, and automation tools in order to reduce overall operating cost and provide Quality of Experience (QoE) adapted to user needs.

A trend consists of sharing infrastructure between operators (passive infrastructure sharing or even RAN sharing) in order to reduce costs ([14], [15]). But unfortunately, it reduces also revenues and decrease network competition between operators. Outsourcing passive infrastructure to Tower Co, network management to equipment vendors, or even IT management to IT vendors is another current trend [16]. But it reduces the knowledge on troubleshooting and the control on the network evolutions. Infrastructure sharing and outsourcing may be combined through a joint venture. This is a possible solution for emerging markets but we suggest applying them only to the access network because the core network has a lower cost than access but much more intelligence needed for feeding competition. Therefore, we suggest looking at other ways to mutualize the core network for reducing its cost but still keeping the control by operators and the competition between them.

2. LTE/EPC Architecture

The LTE/EPC architecture aims at providing seamless internet connectivity between UE and EPC. The EPC has a flat, all-IP architecture with separation of control plane and data plane. The architecture is composed of the Evolved Universal Terrestrial Radio Access Network (E-UTRAN) and the EPC core as shown in Fig. 1. The E-UTRAN handles the radio communications between the UE and the EPC and has one component only, the evolved base stations, called eNodeB (eNB). The base station that is communicating with a UE is known as its serving eNB. Each eNB connects with the EPC by means of the S1 interface and it can also be connected

to nearby eNB by the X2 interface, which is mainly used for signaling and packet forwarding during handover.

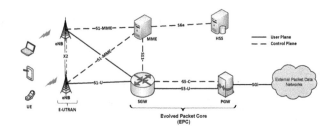

Figure 1. The LTE/EPC architecture

The EPC consists in four network elements namely Serving Gateway (SGW), PDN Gateway (PGW), Mobility Management Entity (MME), and Home Subscriber Server (HSS) [17]. The UE connects to eNB, the eNB directs data traffic to SGW and PGW in a GTP tunnel and for the control traffic it directs to MME. The MME acts as the manager of the network connectivity and it plays an important role in LTE/EPC architecture. In fact, the MME is the main signaling node in the EPC. It is responsible for UE authentication and authorization, UE session setup, and intra-3GPP mobility management. The SGW and PGW are responsible for data forwarding, IP mobility and QoS control at the data plane. The PGW communicates with the outside world (i.e. PDN Network), using SGi interface. Each packet data network is identified by an access point name (APN). The QoS level that should be affected to each bearer is decided by the PGW. The MME is connected to SGW by means of S11 interface. The SGW is connected to PGW by means of S5 interface.

2.1. Existing sharing models and cloud based solutions

In mature mobile markets revenue growth is limited or total industry revenue may even decline. In this situation, the only way to grow cash flow is to reduce an Operating Expenditure (OPEX) and also a future Capital Expenditure (CAPEX). Infrastructure sharing between the Mobile Network Operators (MNOs) and Mobile Virtual Network Operators (MVNOs) are the primary and well know model to reduces the both OPAEX and CAPEX. For instance, the network sharing between AT&T and T-Mobile in USA [18], 3G RAN sharing between T-Mobile & 3 in UK, Vodafone & 3 in Sweden, and Orange & Vodafone in Spain. This significant sharing translates into 43% saving in CAPEX and 49% in OPEX [19]. In addition, the estimated CAPEX savings on infrastructure sharing in the Middle East and Africa region amount to $ 8 billion [20]. The MVNOs are an important player for infrastructure sharing and also bring business for MNOs. In addition, the MVNOs markets are growing faster and estimated CAGR of MVNO subscriber is 10% over the next five years [21]. In fact, MVNOs requires the lowest investments (sharing infrastructure with MNOs (i.e. access network)) and also requires very short time to enter into the market.

On the other hand, a new trend started to reduce OPEX and also future CAPEX such as virtualization and cloud based network (i.e. C-RAN and vEPC). The estimated virtualization and mobile cloud to be a $400 Million Market by 2018 [23]. The main idea of virtualization and cloud technology is to runs the appliances on high volume servers instead of running on dedicated proprietary hardware (i.e. vendor depended physical monolithic devices) [12]. For instance, the C-RAN project by China Mobile is to centralize all BBUs, layer 2 and layer 3 functions and estimated the reduction of both OPEX and CAPEX will be 53% and 30% including energy and maintains of the network [24] and pooling the base band units [25].

3. Cloud based Mobile Network

Moving the mobile network into the cloud platforms, create the opportunity for the mobile operators to move towards a completely different network paradigm, where network entities functions such as BBU, MME, SGW and PGW are implemented by applications running on IT hardware being part of a cloud infrastructure. All these functions are bound to a specific location and dynamically scale up/down based on time-based requirements. For instance, some of functions can scale down while moving active workload to another same function in the same location or in a different cloud center, without causing any service interruption to the users [26]. In addition, present static functionality of entities can be more dynamic implementation based on time of the day.

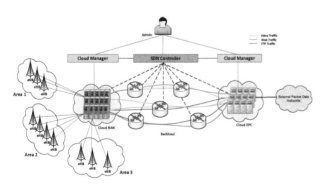

Figure 2. Cloud based mobile network

The Fig. 2 shows the proposed cloud based mobile network. The cloud RAN connects to different eNode Bs in pools on one side and on the other side, it connects to cloud EPC. The data and control traffic from

UE goes to appropriate EPC cloud through backhaul. This cloud infrastructure managed by their cloud manager and backhaul which include switches and routes are managed by the software defined networking (SDN) controller. The admin views and program the network through control platform such as cloud manager and SDN controller using Graphical user interface (GUI)/Application programming interface (API) interfaces and admin can also command the network to change the network behavior or change the entity location or allocate more resource to specific site.

The control platform entities such as cloud manager and SDN controller have an interface between each other. These interfaces exchange the messages, if any changes in the network behavior or any network entity scale up/down in cloud especially in the cloud EPC. For example, if any entity in cloud EPC is relocated to another location within same cloud or other cloud near to user location for better QoE. In this case, the controllers will steer dynamically the active sessions to new cloud site without any interruption.

3.1. Cloud RAN

The Cloud RAN (C-RAN) is composed of a centralized software-based Base Band Units (BBUs) and distributed low-cost remote radio heads (RRHs) plus antennas which are located at the remote site such as eNB. The RRH converts the digital baseband signals from BBU and it composed of RF devices (AMP) and signal processing units including digital to analog converter [27]. The BBU is responsible for digital baseband signal processing and it is the termination point for IP packet and baseband signaling as shown in Fig. 3a. For instance, the baseband signals are received from remote cell sites are demodulated and IP packets are transmitted to the EPC. The BBU and remote cell site unit connected with each other using an optical standard interface CPRI (Common Public Radio Interface) [28].

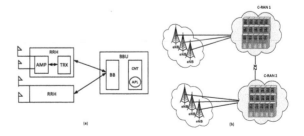

Figure 3. (a). eNB architecture, (b) Each cloud platform connected with other cloud platform by using X2 interfaces.

In the C-RAN platform, based on traffic volume that a BBU can handle, it can control one or more RRH units. In addition to this, in the cloud platform power consumed by air conditioning and number of equipment room at sites can be reduced significantly ([29], [30]). On the other hand, this centralized BBUs can scale up/down for maximizing the resources. For instance, if an operator wants to increase the network capacity, in traditional way, the operator will increases the capacity by installing a new cell site including all RAN equipment like BBUs, RRUs, etc. In C-RAN case, the operator only need to deploy the antenna and RRU, and connect to the BBU pool in the cloud platform. The operator only need to upgrade the BBU pools hardware, when the network processing capacity increases. In addition, any upgrades in the radio interface can be done easily by using software defined radio [31]. Consequently, the operators can benefit in terms of OPEX and CAPEX, and also decrease the carbon emission by reducing energy (by switch-offing selected base station during nights [32]) and the number base stations. In addition, the centralized approach improves the efficiency of base stations under dynamic load management and it taps the new business opportunities in terms of sharing with multiple operators.

3.2. Cloud EPC

Cloud EPC is composed of all EPC components such as MME, SGW, PGW and HSS. These components still maintain the same standard interfaces between them in order to conform to the 3GPP standard. These components can be composed into a single service function (SF) including MME, SGW and PGW or it can be independent functions. In our case, we assumed that each component is composed into a single function (virtual machine) and this function run on top of dedicated hardware in the cloud platform as shown in Fig. 4a. The VM manager lies between VMs and hardware, and acts like a hypervisor between software and hardware.

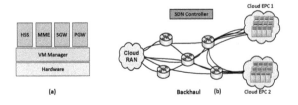

Figure 4. (a) Dedicated hardware running EPC components in the VMs, (b) Traffic steering between the cloud EPCs using SDN controller during VM images moves between the clouds.

In the cloud platform, it is important to transfer the context of the users or virtual image file from one cloud location to another location for to optimize the network efficiency and also decrease the load when it is in overload. In EPC case, there is a need to transfer the active or idle users profile information from a cloud

location to another better location which is near to user location (see Fig. 4b) (the data transfer can be done like [33]). For instance, in existing EPC components, in overload situation it's very difficult to reduce the load because of its static behavior of each component. Indeed, the 3GPP also proposed an inappropriate solution on balancing the load between the components [17]. In the cloud platform, the cloud manager always track the each virtual machines load. If any function is overloaded, then cloud manager immediately deploys the new virtual machine and moves the active users to newly deployed function. In this case, the active users' context will transfer from old VM to newly deployed VM without interrupting the active sessions (similar to [34]). The VM deployment can be at same location or also another location. However, this depends on the UE location and available resources in the cloud. In fact, the deployment will be near to UE location to reduce the latency.

The SDN controller manages the backhaul network based on information received from the cloud managers [35]. For instance, if an EPC component image moved from one cloud center to another cloud center, the SDN controller dynamically steer active traffic to the new location using the OpenFlow protocol. The OpenFlow protocol is an initial protocol that applies the SDN concept. It enables a remote software-based controller to manage the connected OpenFlow switches through a well-defined "forwarding instruction set" [36]. Significantly, the cloud EPC moving from today's mostly static deployments to highly dynamic network implementations such as dynamically provisioning and configuration.

3.3. Cloud Manager

The cloud manager can make decisions about the usage of virtual resources. These decision is based on all parameters (i.e. tenant policies, location of users/data centre) and acts towards the carbon copy (cc) to execute them. The cloud manager will configure the SFs during the scaling in/out. For instance, executing SF in the network, the manager will trigger existence of this SF with other SFs, in order to route the traffic.

The monitoring function in cloud manager will monitor and predictions about the bandwidth requested in a certain geographical area at a certain time by an aggregated group of users. Indeed, the manager will be the responsible entity to initial configuration of each SFs including basic networking and configuring of service parameters such as 3GPP LTE/EPC parameters (like identifiers, QoS policies, PCRF parameter, etc).

4. Cloud Based Mobile Network Sharing Models

The network infrastructure sharing is an alternative solution for mobile operators' to reduce the CAPEX and

OPEX. The infrastructure sharing in cloud networks move the telecom into a completely different network paradigm, where operators can deploy the network components based on-demand from the tenant, it can be short term or long term sharing. The main players for mobile network sharing are between the operators' or with the MVNOs.

4.1. Pay As You Go

Infrastructure sharing between operators undoubtedly leads to a reduction of the investment made by each operator involved in the network sharing process. Indeed, present network sharing models are purely static and fixed resources. For instance, the mobile operator (tenant) makes an service level agreement (SLA) with infrastructure owner (i.e. mobile operators owns the infrastructure) for a fixed amount of usage such as bandwidth and fixed time period e.g. for one year. Based on the SLA, the owner designs their network based on the load foreseen in the peak hours. The network design based on custom hardware and need to be statically provisioned and configured [37]. Consequently, the network architecture does not come any elasticity and on-demand features. For example, the BBUs are deployed in cell site based on peak load and SLA. This deployment is static and custom hardware, and very difficult to increase the capacity based on traffic demand. In addition, it's difficult to optimize the resource during non-peak hours, this leads to the wastage of resources. These wastages are so costly and it directly influences the OPEX. On the other hand, in existing sharing models, the tenant cannot buy extra resource for a specific time period from the owner due to network static functionality and limited resources. Consequently, the end-user faces a poor QoE during peak hours.

The cloud based mobile network, the operator can share part of the network for specific time periods. For instance, any network equipment failure may occur in the network, let say SGW (serving gateway) in the LTE network. In this case, the operator can demand for a new SGW in a fraction of minutes from the cloud operator and configure with their network, instead of keeping network down for a period of time. After, the failure recovery, the allocated gateway releases and corresponding resource such as CPU and memory can be used for other services. The owner will charged the tenant based on used service resources, versus an entire infrastructure (i.e. the tenant will as he/she used the resource like Pay-as-you-go [38]). This model will introduces the new business strategies such as short-term sharing (i.e. an hour based on demand).

4.2. RAN-as-a-Service (RANaaS)

The RANaaS models taps the new business paradigm for mobile operators. In fact, over the decade, the sharing the access network while maintaining control logic inside the RAN controller of each operator independently of one another. This type of solution can be difficult to optimize the resource during non-peak hours, which can be leads to the wastage of resources ([39], [40]). The RANaaS will make it possible to make an efficient usage of datacenter resources, through the dynamic deployment of the required resources. Hence, it is possible for a MNOs (cloud service providers) to provide RAN in an on-demand and elastic way.

In RANaaS model, the tenant can be initiate to execute RAN nodes in particular cell site for specific period of time. For instance, due to unexpected events (e.g. football games, public strikes, etc) in particular location, the tenant needs extra resource on those specific locations, in order to avoid congestions/failures in the network. The tenant can demand extra resource (i.e. BBUs and RRUs) for particular cell sites for specific period of time. The owner will initiate the tenant requirement in specified cell site, the cloud manager configure these requirements and execute into the network. For example, the cloud manager will execute new BBUs and RRUs for specific cell site in the cloud and configure these units with the network including networking with tenant core network.

After completion of requirements, provided resources to tenant will be released and charged for usage of resources and these resources can be used for other services.

4.3. EPC-as-a-Service

The cloudification of the EPC creates the opportunity for the MNOs and MVNOs to move to a completely different network paradigm, where the network functions that used to be implemented on physical boxes deployed in specific Points of Presence (PoPs), become workloads running on top of a cloud infrastructure.

The cloud service providers (CSP) will provide the EPC entities as a service (i.e. HSS, MME, SGW and PGW as a service), run on a virtualized environment, which is implemented as workloads on a cloud platform (similar to cloud network). For instance, a CSP can integrated the functions by combining services provided by MVNOs and build a specific cloud-based MVNO network in the cloud platform. By this, the MVNO can benefit on low CAPEX and OPEX on their business instead of building their own physical network (i.e. low CAPEX and OPEX for building and maintaining application server, billing units and core equipments, etc.).

5. Analysis of Mobile network investments and Advantages of sharing models

Mobile operators aggressive pursuit of lean business models has led to an evolution, turning to infrastructure sharing as a viable option [41]. Investment on

Table 1. CAPEX analysis for mobile network [44].

Parameters	Estimated CAPEX (%)
Building, Rigging and Materials	42
eNode B	15
Network Testing	12
Site Acquisition and Design	10
Power	10
Backhaul	6
Spares	3
Router Pricing	2

Table 2. OPEX analysis for mobile network [19].

Parameters	Estimated OPEX (%)
Network Operations Center (NOC)	17
Field Services	23
Transmission lease management - Leased Line (LL) fees	12
Network planning and engineering - ongoing planning	3
Spares and logistics	4
IT infrastructure and application - applications management	4
3rd party care contracts - HW / SW maintenance	4
3rd party care contracts - Multi-vendor repair	1
Other 3rd party contracts - electrical power and fuel	3
NOC operations TAC2 support	4
Testbed	1
(Ongoing) network optimization	2
Site lease/rental	12
Transmission lease management - Microwave (MW) frequency fees	2
Site infrastructure management - site maintenance	4
Site infrastructure management - other site-related costs for leased sites	0.5
Site infrastructure management - other site-related costs for owned sites	0.5
Other 3rd party contracts - roaming management	2
Other	1

ever-changing technologies and increasing competition between global and virtual operators, has been pushing mobile operators towards new ways of business strategies and low cost network maintenance. Significantly, the saving can be transfer to upgrade their networks and providing better roll out and coverage to end-users.

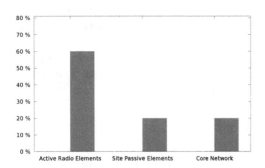

Figure 5. Mobile network deployment investment

Total deployment investment of mobile network can be divided as shown in Fig. 5. Here, the highest investment will be on active elements such as antenna, feeder cable, base station (i.e. eNode B), RAN, transmission system installed in base stations, mobile network equipment, and access node switches, it can be 60% of total investment. The remaining investment on passive elements and core network. The investment on passive elements such as physical sites, buildings, shelters, towers, power supply, and battery backup [42] will be 20% and remaining 20% on core network. Table. 1 shows an CAPEX on individual elements.

Table. 2 shows a typical individual OPEX on mobile network. In emerging and developing countries, this values may varies due to poor infrastructure facilities. In fact, emerging countries has a history of unreliable power supply and frequent cut-outs. African countries less covered by public grid most of the telecom operators depends on diesel generators and solar energy [43]. Diesel generators cause main disadvantages like increase the maintenance and transport to the station

especially in rural areas. Significantly, it directly influence on operational expenditures.

Cloud based mobile network sharing between the operators or virtual operators undoubtedly leads to a reduction of the investment and operational expenditure. Fig. 6 shows the investment saving in cloud based network. In cloud based network sharing will reduces roughly 50% of total investment. In fact, the operators or MVNOs will rent the resource based on requirement and pay for usage of resources. It is true that, the cloud service provider investment reduction will varies due to building the infrastructure. However, the service provider will benefit from other operators by selling the services, this benefits may overcome the total investments in future. For the clients (other operators/ MVNOs), 50% of total investment on active elements (total investment shown in Fig. 5) will apparently reduces. For example, the client no need to invest on access node switches and some RAN elements like BBUs and RRUs, etc. The client can share these elements with cloud provider based on requirement dynamically. Similarly, with the passive and core network elements, in passive element we can benefit more (i.e. 60%) and required less investments. For instance, cloud based sharing no need to invest on building physical site, rents and shelters, etc.

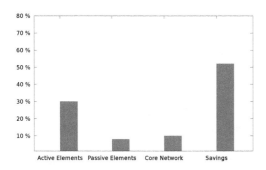

Figure 6. Investment savings in cloud–based mobile network.

In cloud based mobile network, the operational expenditure such as site rental, the fees for leased lines, microwave links, and site infrastructure management represent the site-related costs, electricity and fuel will be reduces roughly 70 - 80%. For example, the client will need less sites, sharing transmission links, installing less equipment and less human investment for management, etc.

6. Implementation and Discussions

Fig. 7 illustrate the cloud based mobile network testbed architecture. To provide realistic testbed, we used a software based mobile network entities provided by Fraunhofer FOKUS OpenEPC [45]. OpenEPC is a reference implementation of 3GPP's Evolved Packet Core (EPC) (Releases 11 and 12) developed by the Fraunhofer FOKUS competence center Next Generation Network Infrastructures (NGNI).

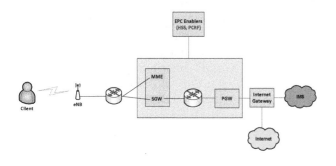

Figure 7. Implemented LTE/EPC architect OpenEPC.

In this emulation, each modules of LTE/EPC such as MME, SGW, PGW, eNB, HSS and UE are running

in each virtual machine. All these VMs are running in single Linux based machine. KVM (Kernel-based Virtual Machine) is used as a hypervisor between the VMs [46] in kernel. All the VMs are with same configuration such as 500MB RAM and 20 GB hard drive and each running with Ubuntu 12.04 operating system.

To validate cloud based network, we performed a test to find out the latency of OpenEPC network with compared to direct internet network. We generated normal IP traffic such as ping traffic between OpenEPC network and google DNS server (8.8.8.8) and also Hypertext Transfer Protocol (HTTP) traffic towards Internet. Similarly, we generated same traffic with direct Internet access network (i.e. without OpenEPC). The test results are in Fig. 8. It clearly shows that, OpenEPC network will have more latency then direct internet access network. This is due to the LTE/EPC network will have an extra IP overhead with GTP tunneling in the user plane nodes (i.e. the tunneling between eNB and SGW, and between SGW and PGW ([47], [48])). When UE generated traffic, the traffic is tunneled in eNB and forwarded to the SGW. Similarly, the SGW will tunnel the same traffic and forwarded to PGW. Due to this encapsulation and decapsulation of GTP tunnels in user plane, the round trip time in LTE/EPC network in increasing compared with direct internet access network. Interestingly, the IP traffic latency (see Fig. 8a) is more than the HTTP traffic (see Fig. 8b). However, this latency is totally depends on the selection of paths and location of servers. In fact, the both the servers are located in same location (i.e. USA) and they selected the different paths. However, the latency of LTE/EPC network is around 22ms for IP traffic and 20ms for HTTP traffic, and these latencies are acceptable for a audio and video conversation. Based on IMT-2000 performance and Quality of Service requirements, this latency is acceptable (the maximum one-way transfer delay that human perception can tolerate is 400 ms [49]).

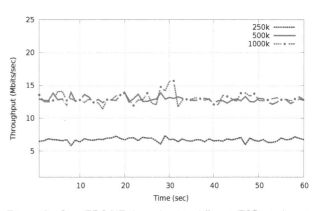

Figure 9. OpenEPC UE throughput in different TCP window size

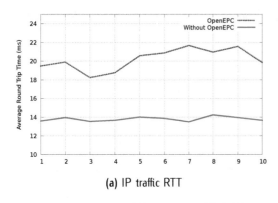

(a) IP traffic RTT

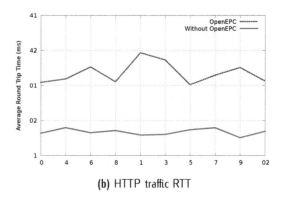

(b) HTTP traffic RTT

Figure 8. Average RTT between LTE/EPC network using OpenEPC and direct internet access network.

Fig. 10 and 9 depicts the evaluation of throughput in OpenEPC network. The Fig. 10 shows the throughput evolution in UDP traffic (i.e. can be see as VOIP traffic which is also an UDP) with respect normal Internet access network. On the other hand, Fig. 9 shows the throughput in different TCP window size such as 250k, 500k and 100k. For all this evaluation, we used traffic generator tool such as Iperf [50], which is able to generate TCP and UDP traffics with multiple parallel connections. The Iperf client running in th OpenEPC UE generates the TCP/UDP traffic towards the server which is connected to PGW. When increasing the TCP window size the throughput also increases. However, after the saturation state, evenif the incremental in the window size the trhoughput will not increase. Similarly, in the OpenEPC network, above 1000k window size, the throughput is the approximately same. However, this throughput is acceptable for the normal internet connection, which is normally required minimum 1Mbits/sec [51]. In fact, we believe, the same OpenEPC runs in high volume servers in cloud, the performances are much better and the latency will be reduces to 10ms.

which is less than the limited bandwidth (in Fig. 10). For better comparison, we evaluated the same test in normal internet network, where throughput is around 9.5 Mbits/sec which is also less than the limited bandwidth. However, this throughput is acceptable for the high quality video and VOIP services [51].

This implementation can be a mirror of cloud based mobile network. The main advantages of this cloud based mobile network, the network can be easy scale in/out based on demand and introduces flexibility and elasticity nature to the network. For instance, the VM images OpenEPC of each LTE/EPC nodes can be easily transfer from one data center to other data center and scale in during demand. The VMs migration process is out of scope of this paper. The test results shows, the latency is acceptable in IP and HTTP traffic case and also voice and video traffic (which is UDP traffic) is 30ms which is also acceptable then the specifie time (i.e. end-to-end 150ms, including access network) using this cloud based network.

7. Challenges

The cloud based mobile network sharing imposes some technical challenges for operators.

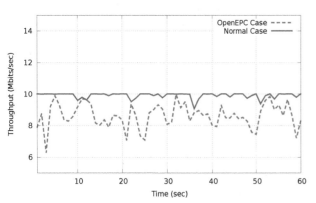

Figure 10. UE throughput for UDP traffic where bandwidth is limited to 10 Mbits

Similarly, the UDP traffic is generated by the Iperf client in OpenEPC where bandwidth is limited to 10Mbits/sec. The throughput is around 8.5 average

- The major challenges in the cloud RAN are to decrease the bandwidth usage between the antenna and the BBU in order to carry baseband signaling. For example, it requires 10 Gpbs transmission rate to run a eight antenna LTE with 20 MHz [24]. On the other hand, centralizing the BBUs and distributing the radio heads require a ubiquitous fiber network which is a cost effective solution. It can be solved by using microwave links for small configurations (low number of antenna, 5 or 10MHz spectrum, and small distances) thanks to millimetrics waves bandwidth

- When a component changes the location from one cloud to another cloud, the transfer of the active content from to a new location will be a challenge for the cloud provider. In addition, scaling up/down VMs and configuring them with other VMs may cause performance issues like latency. For instance, when a MME scale ups, it has to wait until all the interfaces are established with other VMs such as S11, S1-MME, S6a. On the other hand, the load balancing between the VMs is another technical challenge. For example, when VMs scale up/down, the active traffic balancing with other VMs and tunnels encapsulation/decapsulation, etc. However, it can be possible to reuse an existing load balancer in data centers with extension to mobile network.

- In the sharing network, billing models and implement these models are challenging issues. For instance, each tenant (MNOs and MVNOs) will have their own SLAs with their users and also with cloud provider. In this case, all these SLAs as to be implemented in the network and real-time monitoring is needed. On the other hand, each tenant requires interfaces to monitor their resources and implement any new service into the network. However, this can be solved by providing interfaces with control platform but the cloud provider has to take care of viewing and managing tenant user profile only.

8. Conclusion and Perspectives

Infrastructure sharing offers compelling cost benefits to mobile operators and is therefore expected to become a major solution for future deployments. In this paper, we proposed a cloud based mobile network sharing model for LTE/EPC architecture. We believe this model shifts the network into new paradigm while opening up a range of new business models through which the mobile operators can increase the revenue and providing guarantee QoS for the end users. In addition, in this paper, we presented the total network sharing including the core network between the MNOs and MVNOs with low investments. This proposal is the first step towards a future cloud based mobile network and the next step of this work to be implement the total proposed architecture in the orange cloud and validate the sharing models and their functions.

This work has many perspectives. Firstly, to test the performance of OpenEPC in the cloud network. In addition, also need to develop an SDN controller to manage the back-haul network based on commands received from the cloud managers. Then, need to develop an new algorithms in the cloud manager and SDN controller in order to act dynamically based the VMs characteristics and also to increase the network performances. Finally, our proposal will be extended to non-3GPP access like WiFi which are connected to PGW via ePDG.

References

[1] Téhomas W.-H., "Allocating Radio Spectrum for the Mobile Data Tsunami", Engage Volume 13, Issue 2, July 2012.

[2] Carrier-Grade Virtualization for Telecom Service Providers, https://solutionexchange.vmware.com/store/content/carrier-grade-virtualization-for-telecom-\service-providers.

[3] Taleb, T.; Ksentini, A, "Follow me cloud: interworking federated clouds and distributed mobile networks," IEEE Network , vol.27, no.5, pp.12,19, September-October 2013.

[4] Tellabs "End of profit" study executive summary, White Paper, 2011. http://www.tellabs.com/markets/tlab_end-of-profit_study.pdf.

[5] Cisco white paper on mobile data traffic, "Cisco Visual Networking Index: Global Mobile Data Traffic Forecast Update 2012-17", 6 Feb 2013.

[6] GSMA Intelligence. https://gsmaintelligence.com/analysis/2011/03/european-mobile-arpu-falls-20/270/

[7] "Telecoms in emerging markets", straighttalk, Ovum, February 2009

[8] Tarik Taleb, Peer Hasselmeyer, and Faisal Ghias Mir, "Follow-Me Cloud: An OpenFlow-Based Implementation". In Proceedings of the 2013 IEEE International Conference on Green Computing and Communications and IEEE Internet of Things and IEEE Cyber, Physical and Social Computing Washington, DC, USA, 240-245.

[9] Taleb, T.; Ksentini, A, "An analytical model for Follow Me Cloud," 2013 IEEE Global Communications Conference (GLOBECOM), vol., no., pp.1291,1296, 9-13 Dec. 2013.

[10] Yasir Zaki, Liang Zhao, Carmelita Goerg, and Andreas Timm-Giel, "LTE mobile network virtualization", Journal Mobile Networks and Applications, August 2011.

[11] Venmani Philip and Yvon Gourhant and Djamal Zeghlache,"OpenFlow as an Architecture for e-Node B Virtualization", 2012 third International e-Infrastructure and e-Services for Developing Countries.

[12] Network Functions Virtualisation, An Introduction, Benefits, Enablers, Challenges & Call for Action, Introductory White Paper, October 22-24, 2012.

[13] ONF Wireless & Mobile Working group, Open Networking Foundation (ONF).

[14] Meddour, D.-E., Rasheed, T., & Gourhant, Y., "On the Role of Infrastructure sharing for Mobile Network Operators in Emerging Markets", The International Journal of Computer and Telecommunications Networking, Volume 55, Issue 7, 2011.

[15] Digital World Forum, "Low cost broadband access and infrastrucure", http://digitalworld.ercim.eu/wp3.html

[16] Patil, Sunil D., "Challenges in Outsourcing of Telecom Tower Management - System Integrators (SI) Perspective", Social Science Research Network (SSRN), December 18, 2012.

[17] 3GPP TS 23.401 Technical Specification Group Services and System Aspects; General Packet Radio Service (GPRS) enhancements for Evolved Universal Terrestrial Radio Access Network (E-UTRAN) access, (Release 10)

[18] Suzanne, C., "AT&T and T-Mobile network sharing for those in Sandy's path", NBC News, Oct. 31, 2012.

[19] Frisanco, T.; Tafertshofer, P.; Lurin, P.; Ang, R., "Infrastructure sharing and shared operations for mobile network operators From a deployment and operations view", IEEE NOMS Network Operations and Management Symposium, vol., no., pp.129,136, 7-11 April 2008

[20] Victor, F.; Chris, D.; Alphonse, R.; Shohinee, G., "Tower sharing in the Middle East and Africa: Collaborating in competition", The Delta Perspective, April 2009

[21] Berge Ayvazian., "Market Opportunities for B2C Fourth - Generation MVNOs", Heavy reading white paper, Oct 2012

[22] Copeland, R.; Crespi, N., "Modelling multi-MNO business for MVNOs in their evolution to LTE, VoLTE & advanced policy", 2011 15th International Conference on Intelligence in Next Generation Networks (ICIN) , pp.295,300, 4-7 Oct. 2011

[23] ABI Research, "SDN and Virtualization of Evolved Packet Core to be a $400 Million Market by 2018" https://www.abiresearch.com/press/sdn-and-virtualization-of-evolved-packet-core-to-b

[24] China Mobile,"C-RAN The Road Towards Green RAN", White Paper, China Mobile Research Institute, Oct 2011.

[25] Michelle Donegan, "China Mobile Steps Up Cloud RAN Efforts", European Editor, Light Reading Mobile, Mar 2012.

[26] Clark, Christopher and Fraser, Keir and Hand, Steven and Hansen, Jacob Gorm and Jul, Eric and Limpach, Christian and Pratt, Ian and Warfield, Andrew., "Live Migration of Virtual Machines", Proceedings of the 2nd Conference on Symposium on Networked Systems Design & Implementation - Volume 2, 2005

[27] Kimio, W.; Mamoru, M., "Outdoor LTE Infrastructure Equipment (eNodeB)", FUJITSU Sci. Tech. J., Vol. 48, No. 1, pp. 27-32, January 2012.

[28] Common Public Radio Interface (CPRI); Interface Specification, V4.2, Sept 2010.

[29] Namba, S.; Warabino, T.; Kaneko, S., "BBU-RRH switching schemes for centralized RAN", 7th International ICST Conference on Communications and Networking in China (CHINACOM), vol., no., pp.762,766, 8-10 Aug. 2012

[30] Sabella, D.; Rost, P.; Yingli Sheng; Pateromichelakis, E.; Salim, U.; Guitton-Ouhamou, P.; Di Girolamo, M.; Giuliani, G., "RAN as a service: Challenges of designing a flexible RAN architecture in a cloud-based heterogeneous mobile network," Future Network and Mobile Summit (FutureNetworkSummit), 2013 , vol., no., pp.1,8, 3-5 July 2013.

[31] Software defined radio. http://en.wikipedia.org/wiki/Software-defined_radio

[32] Sama, M.R.; Gupta, A.; Afifi, H.; Genet, M.G.; Jouaber, B., "Energy saving by Base Station pooling: A signaling framework", IFIP Wireless Days (WD), vol., no., pp.1,7, 21-23 Nov. 2012

[33] Duong, Hoa Hà and Demeure, Isabelle, "Data Sharing over Mobile Ad Hoc Networks", Proceedings of the 8th International Conference on New Technologies in Distributed Systems, USA, 2008.

[34] Liu, Ziyang and Hacigümüs, Hakan, "Online Optimization and Fair Costing for Dynamic Data Sharing in a Cloud Data Market", Proceedings of the 2014 ACM SIGMOD International Conference on Management of Data, USA, 2014.

[35] Staessens, D.; Sharma, S.; Colle, D.; Pickavet, M.; Demeester, P., "Software defined networking: Meeting carrier grade requirements," 18th IEEE Workshop on Local & Metropolitan Area Networks (LANMAN), vol., no., pp.1,6, 13-14 Oct. 2011

[36] Open Networking Foundation, OpenFlow Switch Specification, Version 1.3.1, 6 Sept 2012.

[37] Jain, R.; Paul, S., "Network virtualization and software defined networking for cloud computing: a survey," IEEE Communications Magazine, vol.51, no.11, pp.24,31, November 2013

[38] Ibrahim, S.; Bingsheng He; Hai Jin, "Towards Pay-As-You-Consume Cloud Computing," IEEE International Conference on Services Computing (SCC) , vol., no., pp.370,377, 4-9 July 2011.

[39] NGMN report, "Suggestions on Potential Solutions to C-RAN", Technical Report, the Next Generation Mobile Networks (NGMN) Alliance, Jan, 2013.

[40] F. Loizillon et. al. "Final results on seamless mobile IP service provision economics", TONIC project deliverable, October 2002.

[41] Passive Infrastructure Sharing in Telecommunications, KPMG Africa Limited, 2011.

[42] Tom, L.; Peter, E.; Michael, R., "Passive infrastructure sharing", Allen & Overy, white paper, 2012.

[43] "Power to the base stations - a modest proposition", http://www.balancingact-africa.com/news/en/issue-no-361/top-story/power-to-the-base-st/en

[44] Market Research Report: Emerging Market Opportunities, Analysis Mason, May 2010.

[45] "OpenEPC - Open Evolved Packet Core", Fraunhofer FOKUS. http://www.openepc.net/index.html

[46] "Kernel-based Virtual Machine", http://en.wikipedia.org/wiki/Kernel-based_Virtual_Machine

[47] "3GPP TS 29.274 Technical Specification Group Core Network and Terminals; 3GPP Evolved Packet System (EPS); Evolved General Packet Radio Service (GPRS) Tunnelling Protocol for Control plane (GTPv2-C); Stage 3, (Release 11), 2012-09".

[48] "3GPP TS 29.281 Technical Specification Group Core Network and Terminals; General Packet Radio System (GPRS) Tunnelling Protocol User Plane (GTPv1-U), (Release 9), 2010-06".

[49] Pierre, L.; Thierry, L., "Evolved Packet System (EPS) - The LTE and SAE Evolution of 3G UMTS", In John Wiley & Sons Ltd, France, 2008.

[50] Iperf, https://iperf.fr/

[51] Barb Gonzalez, "All About Internet Speed Requirements for Hulu, Netflix, and Vudu Movie Viewing".

3

Attribution of Cyber Attacks on Industrial Control Systems

Allan Cook[1], Andrew Nicholson[2], Helge Janicke[1], Leandros Maglaras[1,*], Richard Smith[1]

[1]Cyber Security Centre, De Montfort University, Leicester, LE1 9BH, UK
[2]Cyber Security Centre, WMG, University of Warwick, Coventry CV4 7AL, UK

Abstract

In order to deter or prosecute for cyber attacks on industrial control systems it is necessary to assign attribution to the attacker and define the type of attack so that international law enforcement agencies or national governments can decide on appropriate recourse. In this paper we identify the current state of the art of attribution in industrial control systems. We highlight the critical differences between attribution in enterprise networks and attribution in industrial networks. In doing so we provide a roadmap for future research.

Keywords: attribution, scada, industrial control systems, survey, cyber attacks

1. Introduction

Industrial Control Systems (ICS) are increasingly becoming the subject of computer network attacks [53]. These systems provide essential services for sovereign nations critical infrastructure, and as such these attacks represent a significant threat to the continued security of these countries [39]. ICS have performance and reliability requirements that may be considered unconventional by contemporary IT professionals. These requirements include the management of processes that, if not executed correctly, pose a significant risk to the health and safety of human lives, serious damage to the environment, as well as serious financial issues such as production losses that may have a negative impact on a nation's economy [72].

2. Contribution

We present the first survey of technical attribution techniques specifically in relation to ICS. Previous attack taxonomies used for contemporary attribution do not accommodate methods to integrate data from these cyber-physical systems (CPS). Our paper collates research into one self-containing attribution resource that is useful for new researchers to the field. We identify promising areas for future work, particularly that a combination of techniques offers the potential to build a probabilistic model that may improve overall attack attribution.

3. Motivations for Attribution in Critical National Infrastructure

In this paper we discuss fundamental aspects of attribution of cyber attacks when considering industrial control systems. To the best of our knowledge the information is disparate and not self-contained, hence providing motivation for our paper. We consider technical and non-technical issues including current legal precedent and standards that will shape future direction of this field.

The subject of attribution of cyber attacks targeted at industrial control systems (ICS) is an emerging issue. Zhu et al (2011) [84] describe how these systems are "deeply ingrained in the fabric of critical infrastructure", but subject to disruption or damage by cyber effects. They describe in particular, the potential for cyber-physical attacks, where the impact of cyber attacks can result in outcomes in the physical world. Miller and Rowe (2012) [47] described examples of these physical outcomes in a range of incidents between 1982 and 2012.

In order to prosecute in response to cyber attacks on industrial control systems it will be necessary to assign attribution to the attacker, and define the type of attack, so that international law enforcement agencies or national governments can decide on appropriate recourse. Attribution serves to act as a deterrent to future attacks, can provide the basis for interrupting attacks in progress and can support overall improvements to defensive techniques [32].

*Corresponding author. Email: leandros.maglaras@dmu.ac.uk

3.1. Defining Attribution

Attribution of cyber attacks lacks a universally accepted definition. Proposed definitions have often been limited in their approach, confining each to subsets of attribution. For example, definitions offered by Hunker et al [32] limits attribution to "any attribution technique that begins with the defending computer and recursively steps backward in the attack path towards the attacker". Wheeler et al [79] defined attribution as "determining the identity or location of an attacker or an attacker's intermediary".

3.2. Legal Requirements for Attribution

Before considering the techniques available for attack attribution it is necessary to understand the legal requirements for the prosecution of a cyber attack and the role that attribution plays.

Brenner [10] described the legal requirements for attribution as answering two fundamental questions; firstly, who carried out the attack and, secondly, what kind of an attack was it? The former assigns responsibility for committing an act, the latter assigns responsibility for responding to an attack. With regard to the responsibility for committing an act, Keyser [36] highlighted the adoption of the Council of Europe Convention on Cybercrime as the de facto standard for transnational cyber crime prosecution framework for Western European counties and the North Americas by harmonising local laws. He discussed Article 5 of the treaty, relating to "system interference"and its aim to prevent the intentional "hindering"of the functioning of a computer system by interfering with, or manipulating, computer data without right. It continued with a discussion of violations under the article and the requirement for a demonstration of *mens rea* (guilty mind), although he cites that the definition of intentional action remains an unresolved issue and has been treated differently in signatory countries. Therefore, simply tracing an attack on an ICS to its source will not necessarily result in sufficient evidence for a prosecution. Any technical facts must be supported by a motive or intent.

With regard to responsibility for responding to an attack, Brenner [10] touched upon national jurisdictions and the transnational nature of cyber crime. Keyser [36] described how cyber criminals and malicious actors either base their operations in counties outside of legal frameworks such as the Convention on Cybercrime, or route their traffic through such countries. Kohl [40] discussed how a response to a cyber attack then becomes a question of which country or law enforcement agency has the responsibility and authority to investigate, under which legal framework the perpetrators can be prosecuted, and which laws apply.

This transnational issue was explored more recently in the Tallinn Manual on the International Law Applicable to Cyber Warfare [64] when discussing the acts of a nation-state. Rule 6 described how a nation-state "bears international legal responsibility for a cyber operation attributable to it", but recognised that the location from which the attack took place does not necessarily define whether that nation-state is responsible. It described a scenario in which Nation-State A, under the instructions of Nation-State D created a botnet in Nation-State B to attack targets in Nation-State C (as illustrated in Figure 1). Under these conditions the Tallinn Manual defined that Nation-State B could not be held responsible for the attack, and that Nation-State D, from which the intent was derived, was attributable for the actions. The involvement of Nation-State A was discussed as a less well-defined area as it could not be presumed responsible based on the fact that the attack traffic originated from there. It again, required a measure of mens rea to determine legal responsibility.

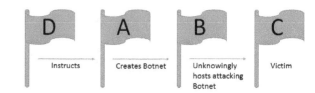

Figure 1. An illustration of the complexity of nation–state responsibility in attribution

It therefore becomes apparent that, in light of the ambiguities in international laws, methods of attributing the execution of an attack must include not only the technical reconstruction of the attack path to the source device, but also a means by which the intent of the perpetrator is elicited. Similarly, in order to support the decision of who should respond to an incident, a taxonomy of types of attack is required to allow an international understanding of the nature and impact of cyber effects. The significance of this assessment rises in priority if the industrial control system attack results in loss of life or significant impact on a nation-state.

In light of this risk, it is perhaps more practical to focus on deterrence rather than prosecution. Libicki [44], discussing cyberattacks in the context of cyberwarfare, argued "cyberattacks can be launched from literally anywhere, including cybercafes, open Wi-Fi nodes, and suborned third-party computers. They do not require rare or expensive machinery. They leave no physical trace. Thus, attribution is often guesswork. True, ironclad attribution is not necessary for deterrence as long as attackers can be persuaded that their actions may provoke retaliation. Yet some proof may be necessary given (1) that the attacker may believe it can shake the retaliator's belief that it got attribution right by doing nothing different ("who, me?") in response to retaliation, (2) that mistaken attribution makes new enemies, and (3) that neutral observers may need to be convinced that retaliation is not aggression"[44].

While reporting of security breaches is on the rise [33], little data is available to identify the sources of such attacks. The problem of attribution of cyber effects in general is a well documented issue, yet little has emerged from academic or industry research to satisfy the legal requirements for accuracy to support prosecution of the attack originators [15]. The techniques available to attackers to obfuscate their location and route to target introduce too much uncertainty in a court of law, or at the least to act as a deterrent [27].

4. Challenges of ICS Attribution

Attribution of cyber attacks in ICS environments is a significant challenges when compared with attribution of cyber attacks in enterprise environments. In this section we begin by identifying those differences and what this means for attribution.

4.1. Attribution and Architecture

ICS differ from traditional IT architectures in that they are generally not all IP-enabled, and incorporate a number of proprietary or industry-specific protocols based upon serial or bus communications. Even when IP is used, the performance requirements necessitated the use of modified IP stacks or optimised routers that limit the level of auditing and inspection available. These protocols are deployed at differing layers of the architecture and often require gateways for interoperability [24]. This heterogeneous communications environment services a number of measurement and control devices, and are often in service for 10-20 years [49] [4] running the same operating systems, and operate with limited computing capacity, designed for performance and reliability rather than security [12] [83].

4.2. Enterprises and Industrial Control Systems

ICS is a general term that encompasses a family of process automation technologies, including Supervisory Control and Data Acquisition (SCADA) systems and Distributed Control Systems (DCS). These control systems use Programmable Logic Controllers (PLC) or similar Remote Terminal Units (RTU) and Intelligent Electronic Devices (IED) to manage electromechanical equipment in either local or distributed environments. Their application covers a range of industrial sectors

Table 1. PLC vs. General-Purpose Computer [60] [20]

PLC	Computer
Ruggedised design for industrial environments	Designed mainly for data processing and calculation
Ability to operate in high temperatures and humidity	Limited environmental range
High immunity to signal noise	Optimised for speed
Integrated proprietary command interpreter	Support for multiple development environments
Limited memory	Significant and expandable memory
Optimised for single-thread processing	Multitasking capability

and critical infrastructures such as electricity generation and distribution, water treatment and supply, oil refining, food production and logistics [51]. These control systems provide automation and process control of the systems that provide the reliable flow of products and services necessary for the security and operations of industrialised nation-states [48].

As an example of the differences between ICS and conventional enterprise IT, Table 1 compares a PLC to a generalised IT computer.

When considering the diversity of industrial control systems it is helpful to have a common framework in which to model the common aspects of such systems, and the levels of process hierarchy that exists. Williams [81] described the Purdue model, a reference architecture for control hierarchy that has become the standard within ICS [84]. It described six levels within an organisation managing an industrial control system, as illustrated in Figure 2.

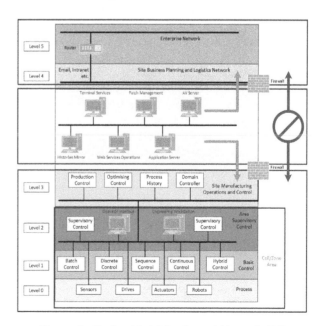

Figure 2. Purdue Model for Control Hierarchy[18]

Level 5 describes the corporate or enterprise network of an organisation running its business management applications and services. Internet access exists within this layer. **Level 4** shows the services to manage the planning, scheduling and logistics of the operations. **Level 3** encompasses the management of the day-to-day industrial operations of the facility, including production scheduling, quality assurance, process optimisation etc. **Level 2** provides supervisory control of the equipment involved in the overall industrial process. **Level 1** encapsulates the control of individual devices and equipment involved in discrete elements of the overall process (PLC, RTU, IED etc.) **Level 0** includes the devices, sensors and associated equipment performing the industrial process.

Whilst the Purdue reference model is not used to govern ICS implementations, it reflects the general architectural principles adopted whereby the control of industrial equipment is managed in a layered hierarchy that is logically, if not physically, separated from the management of the industrial facility and its business processes. Importantly, it defines the areas of an industrial control architecture where IP-based protocols transition to legacy serial communications.

4.3. Importance of ICS Artifacts for Attribution

In the case of a cyber attack on an ICS it is likely that there will be some real-world physical manifestation of the misuse. In the worst cases this could result in damage, injury, environmental impact or loss of life. In these instances, where it is probable that some legal or regulatory investigation would be required, the importance of attribution artefacts increases. It would be necessary to identify whether the behaviour of the ICS was caused by an error in facility operations, a failure of a safety device, or whether the processes and devices were maliciously manipulated to achieve the end result.

These artefacts, ideally, should be in a form whereby their authenticity can be guaranteed and track traffic and ICS commands through the entire operational process, ensuring end-to-end integrity. This assurance should include the logs of the devices and components that controlled the industrial equipment involved.

5. Review of Attribution Taxonomies

Studies into the spectrum of attribution techniques for attacks on ICS are limited at present. A taxonomy of attribution techniques for cyber attacks by Nicholson et al [52] provides an overview of the technical options available and classifies their attributed and practicalities. An initial investigation into attribution in SCADA systems, also by Nicholson et al [51], investigates five known attribution techniques and discusses their viability within an ICS environment.

Researchers have surveyed individual technical approaches to attribution, including; traceback - where the traffic from a target device is recursively stepped-back through its routing path to its originating source, and honeypots - where vulnerable software and services are hosted in order to allow activities to be monitored. Kuznetsov et al [42] evaluated four traceback approaches. Their criteria evaluated the number of packets required, complexity, robustness and ease of deployment. They found that current approaches are at a disadvantage as they need a large number of attack packets and require changes to Internet infrastructure. Kuznetsov et al [42] concluded that a better solution would be to embed traceback functionality within key Internet devices. Belenky and Ansari [6] proposed a framework for evaluating IP traceback systems. Their criteria for traceback qualities includes effects of partial deployment, processing and bandwidth overhead, memory requirements and scalability. They find that no traceback scheme is able to meet each criteria. Strayer [73] produced a taxonomy of stepping stone detection techniques. [26] evaluated five traceback techniques; Probabilistic Packet Marking (PPM), ICMP Traceback (iTrace), Deterministic Packet Marking(DPM), Source-Path Isolation Engine (SPIE) and a hybrid CenterTrack approach, classifying by factors such as computational overhead and robustness. Hamadeh and Kesidis [30] authored a taxonomy of Internet Traceback techniques, separating the problem into IP traceback, traceback across stepping stones, and worm traceback. Vincent and Raja [76] published a survey of IP traceback mechanisms, specifically looking at overcoming DoS attacks by using two types of IP traceback techniques; Packet Marking and Packet Logging, with an exploration of a hybrid of them both.

These taxonomies and surveys focus on specific families of techniques, which are each one category within the field of technical attribution, and therefore are limited in their approach when considering attribution holistically, these surveys miss important techniques when not accounting for all of them. Wheeler and Larsen [79] were the first to classify the landscape of technical attribution techniques and thus critique their combined merits. A number of taxonomies followed this approach. For example,Thing et al [74] reviewed a number of attribution techniques in the context of adaptive responses to DoS attacks. Blakely also considered traceback as a mechanism to identify cyber attackers by feature analysis [9].

The intent of an attack was explored by Duggan [19] and included an assessment of attacker capability. The research proposed a set of six generic threat actor profiles and their level of proficiency over seven characteristics, those being; available funding, determination, stealth, physical access to the target, software development skills, the perceived time it would take to develop an effect, and finally the size of the organisation required to develop the effect. Barnum [5] described a more detailed model of capability. In this taxonomy the seven characteristics essentially decomposed to a lower level of granularity. Barnum also included an impact severity. Miller and Rowe [47], in a survey of SCADA and critical infrastructure incidents, included an impact of the attack, citing the outcomes of cyber effects on ICS as including disruption, distortion, destruction, disclosure or death. Fleury et al [23] do not cover motivation or intent, but proposed a framework based on an "attack-vulnerability-damage"(AVD) model.

Zhu et al (2011) [82] described a taxonomy of cyber attacks on SCADA systems and introduced the esoteric nature of ICS to the various methods of attack that these systems face. The research explained the focus on data integrity and availability within such systems, with a perceived reduced need (at least in the past) for confidentiality. It went on to offer examples of various attack surfaces and vectors, but did not offer a repeatable model for categorising and analysing attacks.

These taxonomies and surveys focus on specific families of techniques, which are each one category within the field of technical attribution, and therefore are limited in their approach when considering attribution holistically, these surveys miss important techniques when not accounting for all of them. Wheeler and Larsen [79] were the first to classify the landscape of technical attribution techniques and thus critique their combined merits. A number of taxonomies followed this approach. For example,Thing et al [74] reviewed a number of attribution techniques, as did Blakely [9].

None of the individual taxonomies reviewed offer the level of detail required in order to adequately define the intent, capability, level of exploitation and impact of an attack on an ICS, but there is merit in considering a fusion of various elements of them all in order to create a model of sufficient robustness to support an international definition of the outcome of an attack to allow agreement on ways and means to allocate responsibility and resources to investigate.

5.1. ICS and Attribution Problem Catalogue

As none of the taxonomies reviewed offer the level of detail required, it is therefore necessary to review individual tecniques. In order to assess the usefulness of an attribution technique to ICS we require a set of criteria by which the technique's effectiveness can be judged. The characteristics below have been used to measure the effectiveness of each attribution method in the context of an industrial system.

Performance: The ability to provide attribution functions without degrading ICS performance.

Reliability: The ability to provide attribution functions without adversely affecting the operating and safety processes of the ICS facility.

Extent: The ability to monitor traffic from originating source to the final end ICS device, including all protocol transformations en route, to provide a full picture of network behaviour.

Coherence: The ability to cross-reference traffic with ICS device behaviours through the synchronisation of device logs to permit inspection of command execution.

Identification: The ability to identify the attacker from behaviours or technical signatures.

Intent: The ability to determine the purpose of the attack, whether successful or otherwise, to provide suitable evidence and mens rea in order to support a prosecution.

5.2. Review of Attribution Techniques

Traceback. Traceback is a class of methods that encompasses techniques by which the traffic from a target device is recursively stepped-back through its routing path to its originating source device [63]. Figure 3 shows three paths that represent possible attack paths from suspected attackers. Traceback creates an attack graph showing the intermediate devices that the attack passed through.

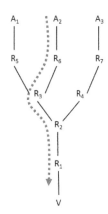

Figure 3. Theoretical Attack Graph [63]

Kuznetsov et al [42] aggregated the significant research in this area into three distinct approaches and evaluated their practicality. The first category included manual methods of traffic tracing, and required the routing device to support input debugging as well as constraining the period of analysis to the duration of the attack itself. The second category spanned logging techniques, whereby routers persist information about the traffic they have encountered. These were described as impractical due to the storage requirements of such a mechanism. One variant, however, the Source Path Isolation Engine (SPIE) techniques of Snoeren et al [68], capable of tracing the route of a single packet through SPIE-compliant routers, could trace the addressed storage issues by only collecting hashes of the packets. While this reduced the storage overhead, Gao and Ansari [26] highlight that the computational requirements increased as a consequence. The third category included the various methods of probabilistic packet marking (PPM), and ICMP traceback (iTrace).

PPM, originally proposed by Savage et al [63], and extended by Song and Perrig [70] and Belinky and Ansari [6], used packet marking to sample a number of packets with path data so that should a target device receive a sufficient volume of such packets it could reconstruct the entire path back to the source. Marking information is stored in unused or infrequently used packet header fields, such as the 16-bit Identification field. Savage et al [63] suggest that 75 packets would be sufficient when the path length is 10 and the number of attackers is small. When the number of attackers is large, this technique becomes ineffective; thousands of packets are required and convergence time increases.

Song and Perrig [70] proposed Advanced and Authenticated Marking Schemes (AMS and AMS II). AMS advances upon the work of Savage et al by compressing entire traceback data into the Identification field. AMS II introduced authentication so that each router used a unique secret key to mark packets. Despite these modifications, the technique still remained weak against distributed denial of service attacks (DDoS) and spoofing. Goodrich [29] proposed Randomize-and-Link which aimed to counter these weaknesses. This technique used large checksums to link packets across a wide spectrum meaning an attacker's chance of spoofing was minimised. Finally, Belenky and Ansari [6] proposed Deterministic Packet Marking (DPM), which aimed to stop spoofing and allow low packet quantity.

iTrace, first proffered by Bellovin et al [7], generated out-of-band ICMP messages containing the same IP destination address as well as the IP header of the traced packet. It also included the IP address of the incoming and outgoing interfaces. As long as the target victim device received enough of these messages it could reconstruct the attack path, although this was reliant on the proper handling of ICMP traffic at all stages of the traffic route. Kim et al [37] highlighted the dependency on this method on correct BGP routing paths, and the inadequacies of BGP authentication and monitoring of changes. They proposed an augmented iTrace method whereby AS-PATH and link connectivity data was also

included in the message in order to facilitate correct validation of routing through autonomous systems.

Traceback methods typically require a modification to the network infrastructure over which they will operate, and it is questionable how cost-effective this would be given the scale of the modern Internet. More important, however, is that all traceback techniques, including a hybrid model proposed by Korkmaz et al [41], fail to address the nature of contemporary, multi-stage attacks described by Clark and Landau [14] whereby intermediary devices are coerced by malware to infiltrate one computer to use as a platform to attack a second etc., in an ongoing process of originator obfuscation. At best, they will only attribute the attack to a coerced device.

Traceback techniques suffer from a number of problems that mean deployment in the Internet environment is unlikely. Traceback techniques provide direct artefacts such as the source IP address, however since IP addresses may be associated with compromised machines, this is of little use. It is only useful if the owner of the IP address endpoint is willing to fully cooperate and allow forensic investigation of their machine(s). Traceback is intrusive, requiring infrastructure changes for deployment and packet/router modifications, additional traffic or additional storage and processing requirements. Furthermore, the onus of who should manage these aspects is unclear. Finally, traceback techniques may introduce new attack vectors. For example, packet logging produces additional traffic and could cause a DDoS attack in itself.

Traceback is considered against our assessment criteria below:

Performance: Traceback functions require mechanisms to capture and analyse traffic, sometimes including router modification. This would introduce a level of latency that is likely to be unacceptable to an ICS operator.

Reliability: Traceback functions would require he introduction of new elements in the ICS safety chain that would require certification, and would probably not be certified to operate within known boundaries.

Extent: Currently traceback mechanisms only support IP traffic. ICS include a number of non-IP-based protocols that existing approaches would not support.

Coherence: Currently traceback only focuses on traffic, not associated log analysis.

Identification: Without modification of the infrastructure of the internet, traceback would not provide a means by which end-to-end traffic could be accurately monitored.

Intent: Whilst the purpose of the traffic could be assessed, traceback does not currently provide a suitable evidence chain for a prosecution.

Honeypots. Honeypots approach the issue of attribution of attacks differently to Traceback methods, by observing an attack in situ. A honeypot is a system, or set of systems, where vulnerable software and services are hosted in order to allow activities to be monitored and logged.

Franz and Pothamsetty (2004) [57], created the first publicly acknowledged SCADA honeypot. Their goal was to determine the feasibility of building a software framework to simulate a variety of industrial networks and devices. They found that there was a general lack of information relating to SCADA vulnerabilities and attacks. A technical deliverable was produced, a SCADA honeypot based on a low interaction honeypot, Honeyd. Honeyd simulated many network protocols such as HTTP, SMTP and FTP. Honeyd could be extended to simulate more network protocols using simple scripts. Franz and Pothamsetty created scripts to simulate the SCADA functionality of a Modicon Quantum device with HTTP, FTP, Telnet and Modbus services. They also created a Java applet, "StatusApplet.java", which could be accessed via a web server and simulated the status of a SCADA field device. The technical implementation of this honeynet was primitive and at a proof of concept stage. Subsequently little effort was placed on concealing the honeypot status. For example, the action event on the HTML forms reads 'action="honeyd-feedback.py"', an indicator that the SCADA system is actually a honeypot.

Researchers at Digital Bond expanded upon the work of Franz and Pothamsetty when they released two VMWare virtual images [77]. One image contained a SCADA honeypot based on Franz and Pothamsetty's work and another image contained Honeywall to monitor activity, collect data and prevent outbound connections from compromised honeypots. Digital Bond also included their Quickdraw rules, a collection of Snort intrusion detection system (IDS) preprocessors and plugins specifically for SCADA protocols. What made this work unique was that the Honeywall image could be placed in front of either the SCADA honeypot or a real non-production PLC. The latter configuration was important because it enabled a physical SCADA device to be used as a honeypot.

In the following year Rrushi and Campbell [61] continued the trend of using real devices when they proposed "reactor mirage theory". Their proposal aimed to use deception to detect intrusions against the nuclear power sector. Their prototype made active decisions to draw adversaries towards a honeypot which used real industrial devices as honeypots. By populating the environment with deceptive systems they increased the possibility of an adversary targeting a non-production system. Similarly, by using real devices as deception systems and creating simulated activity, Modbus protocol traffic, they increased realism and decreased the possibility of an adversary discovering that they are interacting with a honeypot. Despite these benefits, the costs associated with deploying many real devices for deception purposes is high and any increase of network traffic directly or indirectly on a production SCADA network should be approached with close scrutiny.

In another academic proposal in 2009, Valli [75] described a SCADA forensics framework which combined the Snort IDS with two low interaction honeypots; Honeyd and Nepenthes. The idea was to replay known SCADA exploits in a controlled lab to create network IDS rules which would then influence configurations for the two honeypots. However, it is unclear if this initial proposal received further attention.

Dacier et al [17] considered attribution in their study of low-interaction honeypots to differ from that of traceback, i.e. "determining the identity or location of an attacker or an attacker's intermediary". Instead they approached the issue in terms of defining a series of "attack events" that were observed to model the attackers' modus operandi. Attack events comprised a series micro attack events that occurred during observed periods of time, which were then analysed to attempt to establish connections between them in order to form an aggregate of activity into a "Misbehaving Cloud"(MC). The paper illustrated various means to correlate the observed activities into such MCs at an attack level, thus demonstrating the attack techniques, but did not apply this to a wider analysis of the data advertised on the honeypots and the correlation between the attack method and the ultimate aim of the attacker. Pouget and Dacier [58] attempted to address this in a later paper that used clustering algorithms to analyse the data captured by a honeypot and presented methods to identify the root causes of attacks, stating that "identifying the root causes is a prerequisite for a better understanding of malicious activity". The results however, did not propose a framework in which to attempt to assess the attacker's intent.

Spitzner [71] highlighted the limitations of honeypots due to the narrow field of view available to them, and that it only allows a focus on attacks against specific targets (i.e. the honeypot). He highlighted that while the data capture can be very rich, it does not encompass all of the surrounding behaviour that may occur outside of the honeypot that may indicate the wider events associated with an attack.

In order to try and address this issue, Wagener et al [78] adopted high-interaction, self-adapting honeypots that introduced simulated failures into the interactions to repeatedly attract attackers and lure them into revealing as much information about themselves as possible. The study noted that attackers showed a level of determination to achieve their perceived objectives and that "we assume that attackers are rational and follow a specific goal during attacks", implying a further focus on modus operandi.

The SCADA honeypot proposals discussed so far focused on the assumption that attacks are network borne. In 2012 students at Bonn University in Germany, led by Sebastian Poeplau, created Ghost USB, a honeypot which emulates USB devices to counter the threat of malware that propagated by removable media [56]. Currently, Ghost USB supports 32bit Windows XP/7 and is supported by the Honeynet Project. The project has obvious uses for SCADA systems; Stuxnet was presented as a use case for Ghost USB, since the malware propagated by USB devices connected to SCADA engineer workstations. This tool could be deployed on production systems with little cost and is readily available.

Wilhoit [80] attempted to address the attribution of attacks specifically against ICS by employing a set of honeypots that advertised themselves as an operational system with PLCs attached. The honeypot architecture ran the BeEF framework (Browser Exploitation Framework Project) [3] to embed a script into web pages that was executed every time an attacker compromised the site authentication. The script determined the geographical location of the attacker, as well as capturing statistical information. The study managed to identify the locations of the attackers, and made a high-level assessment of the perceived intent of the attacks, stating that if "an attack was targeted in nature, for instance, but did not compromise the operation of a target ICS device, the attackers' motivation could be espionage or information gathering. If an attack, however, compromised the operation of a target ICS device, depending on how badly it was affected then the motivation could be considered destructive in nature". There would be merit in considering this research in the context of the Miller and Rowe [47] taxonomy.

Most recently the Honeynet Project has announced and released Conpot, which aims to simplify the process of setting up SCADA honeypots [59]. Conpot currently supports Modbus and SNMP, however the developers intend to add support for other protocols. The tool simulates the Siemens S7-200 PLC. Conpot feeds into HPFeeds, a data sharing platform which is used by a number of the Honeynet Project honeypots.

Performance: Honeypots can be deployed so that they do not introduce additional links in a process chain, and if properly located, can avoid impact on existing operations.

Reliability: Honeypots can be deployed away from critical systems and networks to avoid impacting operational processes.

Extent: Honeypots could simulate serial or bus connected devices, or perhaps have some physically attached, but they would not necessarily provide a representative architecture in a complex environment.

Coherence: Honeypots only provide a view of attack behaviour from the device itself, and by its nature encourages the attacker to that device. Wider situational awareness of other malicious activities is not maintained.

Identification: As the attacker is encouraged towards particular devices, repeat activities can be identified and recorded, and mechanisms deployed to increase the level of confidence of attribution.

Intent: The purpose of the attack on they honeypot device will become apparent, however the legal issues of entrapment are yet to be addressed in this matter.

Digital Forensics Techniques. Digital Forensics is a broad subject which involves the recovery, acquisition and investigation of digital evidence. In traditional IT domains commercial tools such as EnCase [69] and FTK [1] and open source tools such as Sleuthkit and Autopsy [67] are used to acquire, analyse, and report on digital evidence. These tools tend to be specific to x86 and x64 processor architectures and targeted towards file systems, such as FAT, NTFS and popular operating systems, such as Windows and Linux.

Forensics in a SCADA environment could identify attribution data to identify perpetrators. In the SCADA network segment and field device segments there are a broad range of devices which may store a wealth of digital evidence. However, SCADA systems come with a unique set of challenges for forensic analysis. For example, the standard forensic procedure for taking a bit-for-bit disk acquisition involves switching off a system, connecting the hard disk to a write blocker and acquisition system and then waiting for the acquisition to complete. Switching off a SCADA system which monitors and controls critical infrastructure is unlikely to be an option. One way to mitigate this issue is to have fail over systems. However, this is costly and if the fail-over system is a duplicate of the original system, it might be infected in exactly the same way.

The diversity of devices that a forensic investigator can encounter in the SCADA environment is far wider than that of the traditional IT domain. Traditional IT systems have a lifespan of a couple of years, perhaps 10 at most, whilst ICS will typically remain in service for 20 years [49] [4]. However, as PLCs and other SCADA devices continue to move towards commercial off-the-shelf hardware and software, the forensic analysis of SCADA systems becomes standardised and therefore simpler.

Among the diverse devices found in SCADA environments is the Historian, which is essentially a database management system (DBMS). It collects a wealth of data to enable auditing, trend analysis and anomaly detection. As a DBMS, traditional database forensics techniques should be suitable for these devices. However, unlike the historian, many of these devices encountered are unlikely to have persistent memory. It is true that "most process control systems were not built to track their processes, but merely to control them"[50]. For example, the Siemens S7-300 PLC uses a micro memory card (MMC) for storage [66] which ranges from 64KB to 8MB, while integrated CPU memory for this device ranges from 32KB to 2MB.

With this absence of persistent memory, researchers have proposed the use of another technique from the traditional IT domain to SCADA; live forensics. In live forensics data acquisition takes place while the system is operational. In traditional IT systems, tools are used to capture running processes, RAM memory, browsing history and more, in the order of volatility. Performing live forensics on an operational machine in a SCADA environment prompts significant challenges; accidentally causing the machine to crash could be catastrophic. Ahmed et al [2] discusses this issue and suggests using fail over systems to allow for live forensic analysis to take place. Another challenge is that post-incident the investigator is competing with recovery efforts which will most likely destroy evidence. There is also clearly a logistics concern when performing SCADA forensics. Field devices could be located many miles away, perhaps on different continents, or perhaps in difficult to reach places, such as on the ocean floor. Physically reaching these devices may not be possible.

Forensics is primarily a practitioner-led field with research taking place as and when it is required. In a recent effort to outline a research agenda for this field, SCADA forensics was identified as a predominant theme [50]. The following points were identified as near future research for forensics in SCADA systems:

1. Collection of evidence in the absence of persistent memory.

2. Hardware-based capture devices for control systems network audit trails.

3. Honeypots for control systems as part of the investigatory process.

4. Radio frequency forensics.

5. Intrusion detection systems for control systems.

Digital Forensics techniques are considered for applicability against our criteria as below:

Performance: Forensic techniques require mechanisms to record behaviour which may degrade performance.

Reliability: The requirement for additional monitoring will have a performance impact on devices not scaled to support facilities beyond their original scope. Additionally, the process may also require compromised devices to be taken out of service in order to facilitate an analysis.

Extent: The lack of support for proprietary devices and operating systems limits the scope of its applicability.

Coherence: If all elements of an ICS could be deployed with forensic tools, the possibility for an end-to-end analysis of attack behaviour increases.

Identification: The ability to identify the attacker from behaviours or technical signatures would depend on the capabilities of the overall suite of forensic tools deployed, their ability to integrate to a coherent time source and operate in proprietary environments. This currently limits the scope of its deployment.

Intent: Forensic tools would support the identification of targeted devices, and may add weight to other evidential means, but by themselves they do not provide attribution suitable for taking forward a prosecution.

Network Forensics. Another field of forensics used in traditional IT systems is network forensics. This field primarily involves two stages: collecting network messages and analysing network messages. Existing infrastructure such as switches and routers can be configured to collect messages, or extra equipment can be deployed, such as a network tap device. By logging messages to files, analysis can take place during an attack or post-attack. During analysis of network traffic, attribution data can be found, such as connection source, time of connection, commands that were sent and payload data.

Collection of data is relatively straightforward. An organisation must identify points in the network where they wish to collect network data. Mahmood et al [45] describes traditional network analysis problems and network sniffer deployment in a SCADA environment. An area that will require further consideration is when traditional communication channels other than Ethernet are used, such as RS232 and radio link. Specialist sniffers will be required in this instance. Traffic should be stored in known network capture formats, such as PCAP. Wireshark, a popular network sniffer and packet analyser tool, already has dissectors for some SCADA protocols, including Modbus [34],

DNP3 [16] and FINS [55], a proprietary protocol, however there are many SCADA protocols that are not supported.

Full packet capture in a traditional IT system can cause problems due to the high volume and large packet size. In a SCADA environment traffic volume is generally much lower and message sizes are much smaller. Message content is likely to be significantly less diverse, as content is machine generated and not user generated. This results in network collection devices requiring less storage and processing power, meaning that organisations can make savings or deploy more devices.

Of course, similar to traceback, network forensics will only be able to identify attacks that use network communications as a vehicle for attack. Those that use removable media will not be visible.

Network Forensics techniques are assessed against our criteria as follows:

Performance: Many ICS protocols are optimised for performance. The introduction of devices into the communications chain will require significant testing to prove it will not increase latency.

Reliability: Significant testing will be required to ensure that the introduction of devices will not impact the boundary conditions of the system.

Extent: The lack of support for proprietary protocols and non-IP bearers limits the scope of its applicability.

Coherence: Network forensics, offer the ability to capture wider attack behaviour as it extends beyond individual devices. However, the lack of support for non-IP protocols and bearers limits its utility.

Identification: Behaviours across the network would allow for attack tools and techniques to be analysed for commonalities.

Intent: Network forensics would, if deployed across all elements of the ICS, provide a means to ascertain the intent of the attack.

Malware Analysis. Malware, in its various forms; virus, worm, trojan, adware, spyware, back doors and rootkits, may be analysed to identify characteristics which could be used as an attribution data source. Malware analysis in the traditional IT domain can be split into two areas: behavioural analysis and code analysis.

Behavioural analysis examines the way that malware interacts with the environment. Malware might make changes to the registry, create new processes, hide files, execute other binaries, contact command-and-control servers, cover tracks by deleting evidence of its modifications (as Stuxnet did), disable security protections, record user interaction (e.g. keylogging), harvest sensitive data, exfiltrate data, attempt to update, pivot to other systems, establish back doors and more. A controlled sandbox environment is usually created to examine this behaviour. Virtual machines are commonly used for this task as they can be quickly reset with snapshot/roll-back functionality. A wide range of tools are available to analyse malware behaviour in the traditional IT domain, such as the Microsoft Windows SysInternals suite [46]. The investigator can change the sandbox environment to illicit a response from malware. Examples of change include:

1. Introducing new services, files and removable media.

2. Introducing Internet connectivity.

3. Browsing websites, sending and receiving e-mail.

4. Inputting passwords and other sensitive information.

The response, or lack of response, helps to identify what the malware does. The process of behavioural analysis can be automated with tools such as CWSandbox [62] which monitors Windows system calls made by malware. Behaviour analysis tools and environments are fairly limited to operating systems used in traditional IT environments e.g. Windows and Linux; they do not support the firmware found on SCADA PLCs and RTUs. Ahmed et al. (2012) [2] identified that SCADA simulation environments should be created, possibly by Universities and industry partners, and this would certainly help to rectify this issue.

Code analysis is concerned with examining the code that makes up the malware. Source code for malware might be available, although it is unlikely. If by chance it is then source code analysis can take place. Otherwise, reverse engineering and debugging take place. Reverse engineering involves restoring the malware's binary machine code to human-readable assembly code, using tools such as IDA Pro [31] and OllyDbg [54]. These tools are particularly effective at reversing binaries compiled for x86, x64 and ARM CPU architectures. The code can then be executed in a debugger to step through the instructions, inspect register contents, identify embedded strings and set breakpoints to determine the malware's functionality.

Practitioners used reverse engineering against the Stuxnet malware [21]. They identified clues in the code, such as binary compile times, suspicious variable names, registry keys that appear to be dates and directory names that might be biblical names. Some or all of these clues could have been false flags; data that was purposely crafted to implicate another entity as the malware authors. Symantec consulted the expertise of established SCADA practitioners in order to understand the effects that the Stuxnet malware had on the Siemens PLCs. This again highlights the diverse skill sets required for the SCADA environment and the necessity for security professionals to work closely with SCADA engineers. Code analysis was also used to identify re-use of code and libraries; Stuxnet, Flame and Duqu were identified as having shared code.

Malware Analysis techniques are reviewed against our standard criteria below:

Performance: As malware analysis occurs after an infection has been discovered, and takes place in an environment away from operational systems, the process has no impact on ICS performance.

Reliability: Similarly, the offline analysis has no impact on safety processes.

Extent: The propagation of the malware can be determined if it leaves a persistent footprint, although it does not necessarily provide evidence of a targeted progression through systems and devices.

Coherence: Malware analysis provides limited opportunities to cross-reference traffic and behaviours.

Identification: The reverse-engineering of malware may highlight commonalities in coding techniques, naming conventions and other identifiable features.

Intent: The functionality of the malware can be assessed as to its purpose, and from that its likely targets.

Intelligence-led Attribution. A number of non-technical investigatory techniques may offer alternative or complementary approaches to assigning attribution to a cyber attack. For the purposes of this survey these have been categorised as âĂŸintelligence-ledâĂŹ techniques.

As technical attribution techniques offer limited and varying degrees of actionable data. Carr [11] proposed that the "one thing you can count on is that someone has to pay for the necessities of virtual combat. Therefore, one sound strategy in any cyber investigation is to follow the money trail created by the necessary logistics of organizing a cyber attack – domain registration, hosting services, acquisition of software, bandwidth, and so on."He highlighted that although false identities are often used when registering and acquiring services, the increased use of social media and the increasing size of individual and corporate digital footprints allows for a forensic examination of online presence and identity may reveal such deceptions. Gantz et al [25] estimated that approximately 45GB of data existed for every person on the planet. They also discussed the analysis of âĂŸdigital shadowsâĂŹ, that ambient

content data created by traffic cameras, use of ATMs, online transactions etc.

An analysis of alleged Chinese computer attack behaviour [13] resulting from a reported seven years of covert observation offered an insight into the scale and complexity of attacks on ICS. Targets included transportation, navigation, engineering, food and agriculture, chemicals, energy, aerospace and mining - all areas where industrial control systems were likely to be used. Its attribution of the observed attack behaviour to China was based upon a mix of technical measures and intelligence data gathering and analysis. In particular, the report focused on commonalities between attack methods, consistencies in naming conventions and comparative analysis of malware.

Both Fireeye [22] and Shivraj [65] described the consistency in attack behaviour observed from common sources. Fireeye leveraged their position as a supplier of commercial security products to gather and analyse APT callback traffic and events in order to establish patterns of behaviour and command and control traffic. Shivraj [65] defined the stages of contemporary APT behaviour with a focus on SCADA attacks and illustrated how common malware approaches can be applied to ICS targets with limited alteration required, at least at the early stages of an attack. The combined findings of both papers could be potentially combined to provide an indication of attack attribution and a tangible assessment of where the target is in the attack cycle, and therefore what preventative measures may be appropriate as a consequence.

Langner [43], in his investigation of the Stuxnet malware, was unable to provide any substantive evidence to attribute the originator of the code, but did find significant indicators as to the evolution of the software and its intended effects. In particular, he highlighted the level of industrial process and control system knowledge required to develop the malware, and speculated as to the high level of testing that would have been required to prove the payload prior to its release. The necessity for the malware to traverse the traditional IT layers of the target environment before its compromise of the industrial control system to damage the physical elements of the system under control gave rise to a complex piece of software. Langner [43] believed that to develop Stuxnet required nation-state resources. Although he provided no irrefutable evidence for this, he presented a compelling argument based on the complexity of the development undertaken. Knake [38], took a more pragmatic and empirical view when testifying to the US House of Representatives on the cyber threat, stating that at the uppermost level of threat, that of a nation-state, the issue of attribution is simplified as "there are a limited number of actors capable of carrying out such attacks."It is perhaps worth considering the requisite capability of an actor when attempting to assign attribution to a covert attack.

This concept of nation-state capability was extended by Geers et al [28] in an attempt to characterise the motivations and nature of state-sponsored cyber attacks. In a discussion of cyberwarfare, the paper proposed that "[a] cyber attack is best understood not as an end in itself, but as a potentially powerful means to a wide variety of political, military, and economic goals."In this context, an analysis of the intent of an attack would perhaps elucidate which nation-state(s) would benefit from the outcome of the attack, and from this we could derive motive. While not an attribution method in itself, it would allow for an investigation into attribution to be focused on likely perpetrators.

In a post-Stuxnet analysis, Bencsáth et al [8] undertook comparative analyses of malware in their investigation of the Duqu, Flame and Gauss executables. The report highlighted that Duqu shared "striking similarities with Stuxnet"and proposed that there were indications that the three malware tools were part of the same family, suggesting at least a partial common source.

Accepting that there are inherent problems with absolute attribution of cyber attacks, Kalutarage et al [35] proposed a probabilistic approach based on Bayesian methods. The methodology divided the problem into two smaller domains; evidence fusion and aggregation (described as "accumulation"), and the subsequent analysis (described as the "anomaly definition"). The accumulation allowed for the incorporation and use of many Bayesian approaches and prepared the anomaly definition to allow the analysis of attacker activity patterns within a series of node profiles. The data used in the experimentation came from a series of logging techniques and appeared to be entirely IP-based. However, there appeared to be nothing in the methodology that would preclude the use of serial data or historian records from an ICS. In the context of intelligence-led attribution analyses, there may be some valuable research to be undertaken in the field of probabilistic attribution.

Performance: As intelligence-led analysis requires no specific hardware or software to be deployed into the ICS, it has no impact.

Reliability: As above, no changes to the operational systems are required.

Extent: Without technical means, the level of penetration of an attack cannot be determined.

Coherence: The process does not determine how the attack was achieved.

Identification: An analysis of tools, techniques and methods of known malicious actors can be used to determine a subset of possible attack originators.

Intent: A broad analysis of the attack can allow non-technical impacts of the attack to be considered, including financial losses, reputational impact etc., and an assessment of who would gain as a result of the attack.

6. Summary of Attribution Techniques

Table 2 summarises the review of the attribution techniques by assigning a value of low, medium or high that refers to the techniques ability to support the chosen assessment criteria. A value of 1, 2 or 3 is assigned respectively, allowing an overall assessment to be produced (out of a possible total of 18).

7. Conclusions

This study has identified few publications on the subject of the attribution of attacks on industrial control systems, and none where the problem has been explored to any significant depth. Technical research on the related subject of IP traceback has highlighted that while the research areas are maturing, the techniques do not address the multi-stage nature of contemporary cyber attacks and only serve to identify the device from which the attack was launched. Honeypots offer a potentially richer dataset from which to analyse the source of an attack, and begin to look for repeated patterns of behaviour, but relies on an organisation being prepared to leave devices open to exploitation by malicious actors in order to obtain this information. Few of the publications reviewed provided a detailed analysis of the nature of industrial protocols, particularly those not based on IP, and the need to integrate logging and monitoring data into any attribution mechanism in order to assess the entire attack chain.

The international legal frameworks for dealing with cyber attacks appear fragmented and do not lend themselves to addressing transnational malicious activities. In order to prosecute for such behaviours it is necessary to identify the human, or group of humans, responsible for the attack. Technical attribution cannot achieve this. In order to prosecute, or in the extreme case of cyberwarfare, to retaliate, it is necessary to determine mens rea. This intent cannot be defined by technical means alone, nor can it be determined absolutely. Alongside the technical means that can be applied during or after an attack, there are a number of intelligence-led investigatory methods and techniques than can be adopted to determine the motivations and capability of an attacker, along with their previous

Table 2. Summary of Attribution Technique Assessment.

	Traceback	Honeypots	Digital Forensics	Network Forensics	Malware Analysis	Intelligence Led
Performance	Low	High	Low	Low	High	High
Reliability	Low	High	Low	Low	High	High
Extent	Low	Medium	Low	Medium	Medium	Low
Coherence	Low	Medium	Medium	Medium	Low	Low
Identification	Low	Medium	Medium	High	Medium	High
Intent	Low	Low	Low	High	High	High
TOTAL	6	13	8	12	14	14

modus operandi, in order to present a probabilistic picture of the originator of the attack.

8. Future Research Opportunities

This study suggests that further research into the end-to-end chain of attacks on industrial control systems, covering all elements of their architecture, is required to allow comprehensive attack taxonomies to be defined and applied. This study also suggests there is merit in research into a methodology that encompasses both technical and non-technical techniques to form a probabilistic model of attribution.

References

[1] AccessData. Forensic toolkit (ftk). http://accessdata.com/solutions/digital-forensics/forensic-toolkit-ftk, Accessed 01/01/2016.

[2] Irfan Ahmed, Sebastian Obermeier, Martin Naedele, and Golden G Richard III. Scada systems: Challenges for forensic investigators. *Computer*, (12):44–51, 2012.

[3] W Alcorn. Browser exploitation framework (beef). *Online at http://beefproject. com*, 2013.

[4] Rafael Ramos Regis Barbosa. *Anomaly detection in SCADA systems: a network based approach*. University of Twente, 2014.

[5] S Barnum. Common attack pattern enumeration and classification (capec) schema description. *Cigital Inc, http://capec. mitre. org/documents/documentation/CAPEC_Schema_Description_v1*, 3, 2008.

[6] Andrey Belenky and Nirwan Ansari. Ip traceback with deterministic packet marking. *IEEE communications letters*, 7(4):162–164, 2003.

[7] Steven Michael Bellovin, Marcus Leech, and Tom Taylor. Icmp traceback messages. 2003.

[8] Boldizsár Bencsáth, Gábor Pék, Levente Buttyán, and Mark Felegyhazi. The cousins of stuxnet: Duqu, flame, and gauss. *Future Internet*, 4(4):971–1003, 2012.

[9] Benjamin A Blakely. Cyberprints: Identifying cyber attackers by feature analysis. 2012.

[10] Susan W Brenner. "At Light Speed": Attribution and response to cybercrime/terrorism/warfare. *The Journal of Criminal Law and Criminology*, pages 379–475, 2007.

[11] Jeffrey Carr. *Inside cyber warfare: Mapping the cyber underworld*. " O'Reilly Media, Inc.", 2011.

[12] Nicholas B Carr. *Development of a tailored methodology and forensic toolkit for industrial control systems incident response*. PhD thesis, Monterey, California: Naval Postgraduate School, 2014.

[13] Mandiant Intelligence Center. Apt1: Exposing one of chinaâĂŹs cyber espionage units. *Mandian. com*, 2013.

[14] David D Clark and Susan Landau. The problem isn't attribution: it's multi-stage attacks. In *Proceedings of the Re-architecting the Internet Workshop*, page 11. ACM, 2010.

[15] Paul Cornish, David Livingstone, Dave Clemente, and Claire Yorke. *Cyber security and the UK's critical national infrastructure*. Chatham House, 2011.

[16] Ken Curtis. A dnp3 protocol primer. *DNP User Group*, pages 1–8, 2005.

[17] Marc Dacier, Van-Hau Pham, and Olivier Thonnard. The wombat attack attribution method: some results. In *Information Systems Security*, pages 19–37. Springer, 2009.

[18] Paul Didier, Fernando Macias, James Harstad, Rick Antholine, Scott A Johnston, Sabina Piyevsky, Mark Schillace, Gregory Wilcox, Dan Zaniewski, and S Zuponcic. Converged plantwide ethernet (cpwe) design and implementation guide. *CISCO Systems and Rockwell Automation*, pages 252–253, 2011.

[19] David Patrick Duggan. *Generic threat profiles*. United States. Department of Energy, 2005.

[20] K. Erickson. Programmable logic controllers: Hardware, software architecture. https://www.isa.org/standards-publications/isa-publications/intech-magazine/2010/december/automation-basics-programmable-logic-controllers-hardware-software-architecture, 2010.

[21] Nicolas Falliere, Liam O Murchu, and Eric Chien. W32. stuxnet dossier. *White paper, Symantec Corp., Security Response*, 5, 2011.

[22] FireEye. The advanced cyber attack landscape. https://www2.fireeye.com/WEB2013ATLReport.html, 2013.

[23] Terry Fleury, Himanshu Khurana, and Von Welch. Towards a taxonomy of attacks against energy control systems. In *Critical Infrastructure Protection*, pages 71–85. Springer, 2008.

[24] Brendan Galloway and Gerhard P Hancke. Introduction to industrial control networks. *Communications Surveys & Tutorials, IEEE*, 15(2):860–880, 2013.

[25] John F Gantz and Christopher Chute. The diverse and exploding digital universe: An updated forecast of worldwide information growth through 2011. IDC, 2008.

[26] Zhiqiang Gao and Nirwan Ansari. Tracing cyber attacks from the practical perspective. *Communications Magazine, IEEE*, 43(5):123–131, 2005.

[27] Kenneth Geers. The challenge of cyber attack deterrence. *Computer Law & Security Review*, 26(3):298–303, 2010.

[28] Kenneth Geers, Darien Kindlund, Ned Moran, and Rob Rachwald. World war c: Understanding nation-state motives behind todayâĂŹs advanced cyber attacks. Technical report, Technical report, FireEye, 2014.

[29] Michael T Goodrich. Efficient packet marking for large-scale ip traceback. In *Proceedings of the 9th ACM Conference on Computer and Communications Security*, pages 117–126. ACM, 2002.

[30] Ihab Hamadeh and George Kesidis. A taxonomy of internet traceback. *International Journal of Security and Networks*, 1(1-2):54–61, 2006.

[31] Hex-Rays. What is ida all about? https://www.hex-rays.com/products/ida/, Accessed 01/01/2016.

[32] Jeffrey Hunker, Bob Hutchinson, and Jonathan Margulies. Role and challenges for sufficient cyber-attack attribution. *Institute for Information Infrastructure Protection*, 2008.

[33] ICS-CERT. Ics-cert year in review - 2012. Online, 2012.

[34] National Instruments Inc. The modbus protocol in-depth. http://www.ni.com/white-paper/52134/en/, Accessed 13/12/2014.

[35] Harsha K Kalutarage, Siraj Shaikh, Qin Zhou, Anne E James, et al. Sensing for suspicion at scale: A bayesian approach for cyber conflict attribution and reasoning. In *Cyber conflict (CYCON), 2012 4th international conference on*, pages 1–19. IEEE, 2012.

[36] Mike Keyser. Council of europe convention on cybercrime, the. *J. Transnat'l L. & Pol'y*, 12:287, 2002.

[37] Eunjong Kim, Dan Massey, and Indrajit Ray. Global internet routing forensics. In *Advances in Digital Forensics*, pages 165–176. Springer, 2005.

[38] Robert K Knake. Untangling attribution: Moving to accountability in cyberspace. *Prepared Statement before the Subcommittee on Technology and Innovation, Committee on Science and Technology, Hearing: Planning for the Future of Cyber Attack*, 2010.

[39] Eric D Knapp and Joel Thomas Langill. *Industrial Network Security: Securing critical infrastructure networks for smart grid, SCADA, and other Industrial Control Systems*. Syngress, 2014.

[40] Uta Kohl. Eggs, jurisdiction, and the internet. *International and comparative law quarterly*, 51(03):556–582, 2002.

[41] Turgay Korkmaz, Chao Gong, Kamil Sarac, and Sandra G Dykes. Single packet ip traceback in as-level partial deployment scenario. *International Journal of Security and Networks*, 2(1-2):95–108, 2007.

[42] Vadim Kuznetsov, Helena Sandstrom, and Andrei Simkin. An evaluation of different ip traceback approaches. In *Information and Communications Security*, pages 37–48. Springer, 2002.

[43] Ralph Langner. To kill a centrifuge. *Langner Group*, 2013.

[44] Martin C Libicki. *Cyberdeterrence and cyberwar*. Rand Corporation, 2009.

[45] Abdun Naser Mahmood, Christopher Leckie, Jiankun Hu, Zahir Tari, and Mohammed Atiquzzaman. Network traffic analysis and scada security. In *Handbook of Information and Communication Security*, pages 383–405. Springer, 2010.

[46] Microsoft. Windows sysinternals. https://technet.microsoft.com/en-gb/sysinternals/bb545021.aspx, Accessed 01/01/2016.

[47] Bill Miller and Dale Rowe. A survey scada of and critical infrastructure incidents. In *Proceedings of the 1st Annual conference on Research in information technology*, pages 51–56. ACM, 2012.

[48] John Moteff and Paul Parfomak. Critical infrastructure and key assets: definition and identification. DTIC Document, 2004.

[49] Martin Naedele. Addressing it security for critical control systems. In *40th Annual Hawaii International Conference on System Sciences*. IEEE, 2007.

[50] Kara Nance, Brian Hay, and Martin Bishop. Digital forensics: defining a research agenda. In *System Sciences, 2009. HICSS'09. 42nd Hawaii International Conference on*, pages 1–6. IEEE, 2009.

[51] Andrew Nicholson, Helge Janicke, and Tim Watson. An initial investigation into attribution in scada systems. In *Proceedings of the 1st International Symposium on ICS & SCADA Cyber Security Research 2013*, pages 56–65. BCS, 2013.

[52] Andrew Nicholson, Tim Watson, Peter Norris, Alistair Duffy, and Roy Isbell. A taxonomy of technical attribution techniques for cyber attacks. In *European Conference on Information Warfare and Security*, page 188. Academic Conferences International Limited, 2012.

[53] Cabinet Office. The uk cyber security strategy–protecting and promoting the uk in a digital world, 2011.

[54] OllyDbg.de. Ollydbg. http://www.ollydbg.de/, Accessed 01/01/2016.

[55] Omron. Fins command technical guide. http://downloads.omron.us/, 2012.

[56] Sebastian Poeplau and Jan Gassen. A honeypot for arbitrary malware on usb storage devices. In *Risk and Security of Internet and Systems (CRiSIS), 2012 7th International Conference on*, pages 1–8. IEEE, 2012.

[57] Venkat Pothamsetty and Matthew Franz. Scada honeynet project: Building honeypots for industrial networks, 2008.

[58] Fabien Pouget, Marc Dacier, et al. Honeypot-based forensics. In *AusCERT Asia Pacific Information Technology Security Conference*, 2004.

[59] The Honeynet Project. Conpot. https://www.honeynet.org/node/1047, November 2013.

[60] F. Rios-Gutierrez. Overview of programmable logic controllers. http://www.d.umn.edu/ snorr/ece4951s7/Lect4.pdf,, 2007.

[61] Julian Rrushi and Roy Campbell. Detecting cyber attacks on nuclear power plants. In *Critical Infrastructure Protection II*, pages 41–54. Springer, 2008.

[62] sandbox.org. Understanding the sandbox concept of malware identification. www.cwsandbox.org, Accessed 01/01/2016.

[63] Stefan Savage, David Wetherall, Anna Karlin, and Tom Anderson. Practical network support for ip traceback. In *ACM SIGCOMM Computer Communication Review*, volume 30, pages 295–306. ACM, 2000.

[64] Michael N Schmitt. *Tallinn manual on the international law applicable to cyber warfare.* Cambridge University Press, 2013.

[65] Anant Shivraj. Cyber threat evolution with a focus on scada attacks. Online, May 2011.

[66] Siemens. Which memory cards can you use with an s7-300 cpu? https://support.industry.siemens.com/cs/document/ 19102565/which-memory-cards-can-you-use-with-an- s7-300-cpu?dti=0&lc=en-WW, July 2013.

[67] sleuthkit.org. Open source digital forensics. http://www.sleuthkit.org/, Accessed 01/01/2016.

[68] Alex C Snoeren, Craig Partridge, Luis A Sanchez, Christine E Jones, Fabrice Tchakountio, Stephen T Kent, and W Timothy Strayer. Hash-based ip traceback. In *ACM SIGCOMM Computer Communication Review*, volume 31, pages 3–14. ACM, 2001.

[69] Guidance Software. Encase forensic v7 overview. https://www2.guidancesoftware.com/products/Pages/encase- forensic/overview.aspx, Accessed 01/01/2016.

[70] Dawn Xiaodong Song and Adrian Perrig. Advanced and authenticated marking schemes for ip traceback. In *INFOCOM 2001. Twentieth Annual Joint Conference of the IEEE Computer and Communications Societies. Proceedings. IEEE*, volume 2, pages 878–886. IEEE, 2001.

[71] Lance Spitzner. *Honeypots: tracking hackers*, volume 1. Addison-Wesley Reading, 2003.

[72] Keith Stouffer, Joe Falco, and Karen Scarfone. Guide to industrial control systems (ics) security. *NIST special publication*, pages 800–82, 2011.

[73] W Timothy Strayer, Christine E Jones, Isidro Castineyra, Joel B Levin, and Regina Rosales Hain. An integrated architecture for attack attribution. *BBN Technologies*, 10, 2003.

[74] Vrizlynn LL Thing, Morris Sloman, and Naranker Dulay. Adaptive response system for distributed denial-of- service attacks. In *Integrated Network Management, 2009. IM'09. IFIP/IEEE International Symposium on*, pages 809– 814. IEEE, 2009.

[75] Craig Valli. Scada forensics with snort ids. 2009.

[76] Shweta Vincent and J Immanuel John Raja. A survey of ip traceback mechanisms to overcome denial-of-service attacks. In *Proceedings of the 12th international conference on Networking, VLSI and signal processing*, pages 20–22, 2010.

[77] Susan Marie Wade. Scada honeynets: The attractiveness of honeypots as critical infrastructure security tools for the detection and analysis of advanced threats. 2011.

[78] Gérard Wagener, Alexandre Dulaunoy, Thomas Engel, et al. Self adaptive high interaction honeypots driven by game theory. In *Stabilization, Safety, and Security of Distributed Systems*, pages 741–755. Springer, 2009.

[79] David A Wheeler and Gregory N Larsen. Techniques for cyber attack attribution. Technical report, DTIC Document, 2003.

[80] Kyle Wilhoit. The scada that didnâĂŹt cry wolf. *Trend Micro Inc., White Paper*, 2013.

[81] Theodore J Williams. The purdue enterprise reference architecture. *Computers in industry*, 24(2):141–158, 1994.

[82] Bonnie Zhu, Anthony Joseph, and Shankar Sastry. A taxonomy of cyber attacks on scada systems. In *Internet of things (iThings/CPSCom), 2011 international conference on and 4th international conference on cyber, physical and social computing*, pages 380–388. IEEE, 2011.

[83] Bonnie X Zhu. Resilient control and intrusion detection for scada systems. Technical report, DTIC Document, 2014.

[84] Quanyan Zhu, Craig Rieger, and Tamer Bacsar. A hierarchical security architecture for cyber-physical systems. In *Resilient Control Systems (ISRCS), 2011 4th International Symposium on*, pages 15–20. IEEE, 2011.

4

Surfing the Internet-of-Things: Lightweight Access and Control of Wireless Sensor Networks Using Industrial Low Power Protocols

Zhengguo Sheng[1,2], Chunsheng Zhu[2,*] and Victor C. M. Leung[2]

[1]Department of Engineering and Design, University of Sussex, UK
[2]Department of Electrical and Computer Engineering, The University of British Columbia, Canada

Abstract

Internet-of-Things (IoT) is emerging to play an important role in the continued advancement of information and communication technologies. To accelerate industrial application developments, the use of web services for networking applications is seen as important in IoT communications. In this paper, we present a RESTful web service architecture for energy-constrained wireless sensor networks (WSNs) to enable remote data collection from sensor devices in WSN nodes. Specifically, we consider both IPv6 protocol support in WSN nodes as well as an integrated gateway solution to allow any Internet clients to access these nodes. We describe the implementation of a prototype system, which demonstrates the proposed RESTful approach to collect sensing data from a WSN. A performance evaluation is presented to illustrate the simplicity and efficiency of our proposed scheme.

Keywords: Internet-of-things, IPv6, RESTful, wireless sensor netorks

1. Introduction

In recent years, the Internet-of-things (IoT) has emerged as an important research focus of both industry and academia. The concept of IoT can be traced back to the pioneering work done by Kevin Ashton in 1999 [1] on using radio frequency identification (RFID) tags in supply chain management. Soon after, this term became popular and is well known as a new type of communication system in which the Internet is extended to the physical world via wireless sensor networks (WSNs) [2].

With the rapid development of IoT technologies in the past few years, a wide range of intelligent and tiny sensing devices have been massively deployed in a variety of vertical applications, and several major standardization alliances or forums have emerged based on the interests of technology developments and commercial markets. Generally, sensing devices are constrained by limitations in energy resources (battery power), processing and storage capability, radio communication range and reliability, etc., and yet their deployment must satisfy the real-time nature of applications under little or no direct human interactions. Over the past decades, the research community has invested substantial efforts to develop networking systems called WSNs that meet the challenges stated above. With large-scaled deployments of WSNs and their interconnection into the global IoT, a new ecosystem supporting ubiquitous deployment of smart applications has been formed.

Technically speaking, current IoT solutions can be categorized as non-IP based or IP based solutions. Most off-the-shelf solutions belong to the former, especially those from some well-known standard alliances, such as ZigBee [3], Z-Wave [4], INSTEON [5] and WAVE2M [6]. However, most of these non-IP solutions are isolated within their own verticals, which hinder the

★This work was supported by the Natural Sciences and Engineering Research Council of Canada (NSERC), the NSERC DIVA Strategic Research Network, the ICICS/TELUS People & Planet Friendly Home Initiative at The University of British Columbia, TELUS and other industry partners.
*Corresponding author. Email: cszhu@ece.ubc.ca

global IoT development due to incompatibility across heterogeneous communication systems.

Motivated by the fact that the Transmission Control Protocol (TCP)/Internet Protocol (IP) suite is the de-facto standard for computer communications in today's networked world, IP based solutions could be the future for networks that form the IoT [7]. In order to tackle the technical challenges, such as extensive protocol overheads against memory and computational limitations of sensor devices, the Internet Engineering Task Force (IETF) has taken the lead to develop and standardize communication protocols for resource constrained devices, including Routing Protocol for Low Power and Lossy Networks (RPL) [8], and Constrained Application Protocol (CoAP) [9]. Besides, the IP Smart Object Alliance (IPSO) [10] also actively promotes the use of IP version 6 (IPv6) embedded devices for machine-to-machine (M2M) applications. Although it is still in its early stage to be commercialized, there are already a substantial number of IP-based WSN solutions supported by growing availability of products and systems.

To promote organic-growth of IoT systems, open technologies are preferred for integration into IoT, and IPv6-based solutions are promising. In order to well-maintain sensor devices as well as facilitate the efficient development of IoT applications, e.g., to monitor the performance of sensor devices and send commands to sensor nodes, trusted-entities in an IoT system should be provided with a reliable and efficient way to remotely monitor and control WSNs without consuming significant resources. We take an approach based on the Representational State Transfer (REST) paradigm [11] whereby a lightweight web server can be embedded in resource constrained sensor devices. In essence, not only can the proposed method integrate IoT devices into the network, but also connect them to the "web".

The following summarizes our contributions and key results:

- We present an implementation of the full IPv6 protocol stack on WSN nodes to enable wireless connectivity among sensor devices. Specifically, the 6LowPAN/IPv6/RPL/UDP/CoAP protocol stack has been deployed on WSN nodes employing the IEEE 802.15.4 radio platform.

- We integrate IEEE 802.15.4 connectivity into an open-platform gateway and implement the Hypertext Transfer Protocol (HTTP)-CoAP proxy using OpenWrt, an open-source operating system based on Linux in the gateway to realize remote access from any IP terminal to IPv6 sensor devices.

- We propose two alternative access methods to enable REST based applications with sensor devices. In the direct access method, the user can directly visit any sensor devices by sending CoAP request, whereas for the proxy access method, the user can use the normal HTTP requests to access sensor devices, but the gateway needs to help convert the HTTP requests to CoAP requests and vise versa.

The remainder of this paper is organized as follows. A survey of related works is provided in Section 2. The implementation of the RESTful protocol stack in WSNs is introduced and analyzed in Section 3. The prototype implementation of the remote access schemes is presented in Section 4 and performance evaluation results are shown in Section 5. Finally, concluding remarks are given in Section 6.

2. Related Works

Recent technology trends in the Web Services (WS) are primarily focused on two different architectures, namely Big WS (or WS-*) and RESTful WS. Cesare *et al.* in [12] compare these two architectures and argue that the RESTful WS can create a loosely coupled system that is better suited for simple and flexible integration scenarios, whereas WS-* can provide more advanced quality-of-service support for enterprise-class applications.

Many recent works are dedicated to the development of REST-style IoT systems to enable easy access from application servers to wireless sensor devices, since the REST-style device would not require any additional application programming interface (API) or descriptions of resources/functions. REST is a general architectural design style for developing lightweight WS to access resources over the Internet using standard protocols. It provides a design concept that all the objects in the Internet are abstracted as resources. Each resource corresponds to a unique identity. Through a general interface, all the operations on a resource do not change its identity as they are stateless. REST-style can make applications as sharable, reusable and loose coupling services. The uniform operation and interaction mechanisms on resources can help developers or decision makers to quickly react to market changes.

Weijun *et al.* in [13] propose an adaptation layer to integrate RESTful WS infrastructures, which can enable connectivity of embedded devices with mobile Internet applications. Vlad in [14] proposes a resource discovery mechanism based on RESTful principles, which enables a plug and play experience in web of things. Dominique *et al.* in [15] and [16] also propose a RESTful mechanism to integrate wireless energy monitors with application servers to build mashup applications. However, most of the embedded devices considered in the above works are not IP based, which means that a multiprotocol translation gateway is needed. As discussed in [2], network protocol translation can bring more complexity than just a packet format conversion, which usually involves semantics translations between different mechanisms and logics for routing, quality of service, security, etc.

There are some recent papers focusing on the implementation of IPv6 protocol stacks on various hardware platforms. Thomas *et al.* in [17] demonstrate an intelligent container testbed in which CoAP is implemented on the embedded operating system TinyOS [18]. Moreover, a couple of other implementations of CoAP are also available on the Contiki platform [19]-[21]. However, most of these implementations are only for the purpose of connectivity evaluations on different operation platforms and usually assume that a virtual gateway, which is usually a IEEE 802.15.4 USB dongle connected to a personal computer (PC), is mounted as a root node to collect upstream packets from leaf nodes.

Different to the above works, our contribution in this paper is that we consider both IPv6 protocol implementation on sensor devices as well as an integrated gateway solution to allow any normal Internet device (e.g., PC and smart phone) to access an IPv6 sensor device. Specifically, we integrate real-world things into the existing web by turning real objects into RESTful resources that can be retrieved directly using HTTP.

3. A RESTful Protocol Stack for WSN

We employ the IPv6 based protocol stack for WSNs. Some protocols within this stack, which have been developed for resource constrained networks, are introduced as follows.

3.1. 6LoWPAN

From the very beginning, IPv6 has been selected by IETF as the only choice to support wireless communications in IoT. Its key features such as universality, extensibility and stability, etc., have been designed to overcome many known problems in the existing version of IP, i.e., IP version 4, and therefore IPv6 is expected to be widely adopted for the future Internet. To develop a standard that enables IP connectivity in resource constrained WSNs, the 6LoWPAN working group [22] was established to work on protocol optimization of IPv6 over networks built on top of IEEE 802.15.4 [23]. Specifically, the 6LoWPAN protocol considers how to integrate IPv6 with the medium access control (MAC) and physical (PHY) layers of IEEE 802.15.4.

In fact, there are two key challenges to run IPv6 over the IEEE 802.15.4 network. On the one hand,

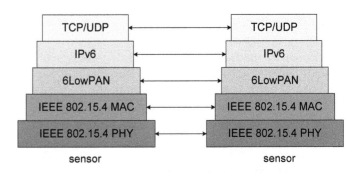

Figure 1. The position of 6LoWPAN in the IPv6 protocol stack

the maximum frame size supported by IEEE 802.15.4 is only 127 Bytes. Considering that significant header overheads are occupied by layered protocols (e.g., MAC layer header, IPv6 header, security header and transmission layer), the payload size available for the application layer is very limited. On the other hand, since the minimum value of maximum transmission unit (MTU) specified by IPv6 is 1280 Bytes (RFC 2460), if MTU supported by the under layer (i.e., IEEE 802.15.4) is smaller than this value, the data link layer must fragment and reassemble data packets. In order to address these issues, 6LoWPAN incorporates an adaptation layer right above the data link layer to fragment large IPv6 packets into small pieces required by the under layer and reassemble them at the receiving end. Moreover, 6LoWPAN specifies stateless compression methods for IP header in order to reduce the overhead of IPv6. The position of 6LoWPAN in the IPv6 protocol stack is shown in Figure 1.

Note that the fundamental purpose of header compression methods is to remove the redundant information from the header by using compression encoding schemes. Although the IPv6 header takes 40 Bytes, most of information bits can be compressed in the link layer. The compression methods for each field of IPv6 header are as follows:

1. Version (4 bits): The value is 6. It can be omitted in the IPv6 network.

2. Traffic Class (8 bits): It can be compressed by compression encoding methods.

3. Flow label (20 bits): It can be compressed by compression encoding methods.

4. Payload Length (16 bits): It can be omitted because the length of IP header can be obtained through the Payload Length field in the MAC header.

5. Next Header (8 bits): It can be compressed by compression encoding methods if the next header is assumed to be one of UDP, ICMP, TCP or extended header.

6. Hop Limit (8 bits): This is the only field that cannot be compressed.

7. Source Address (128 bits): It can be compressed by omitting the prefix or Interface Identifier (IID).

8. Destination Address (128 bits): It can be compressed by omitting the prefix or IID.

In order to implement the stateless compression on IPv6 header, the 6LoWPAN working group has specified two compression algorithms: LOWPAN_HC1 (RFC4944) [24] and LOWPAN_IPHC (RFC6282) [25]. HC1 algorithm is applicable to networks using link-local addresses. The prefix of a node's IPv6 address is fixed as FE80::/10 and IDD can be obtained via the MAC address. Since this algorithm cannot efficiently compress global/routable addresses or broadcast addresses, it cannot be used to connect a 6LoWPAN with the Internet. LOWPAN_IPHC, however, is proposed to improve the efficiency of compressing routable addresses.

Both LOWPAN_HC1 and LOWPAN_IPHC define an 8-bit dispatch field after the MAC header. Its possible values as shown in Table I determine the specific format of the type-specific header and algorithm. For example, if the first 8 bits is 01000010, the following filed is the header corresponding to the LOWPAN_HC1 algorithm; if the first 3 bits is 011, the following field is the header corresponding to the LOWPAN_IPHC algorithm.

Table 1. 6LoWPAN dispatch field

Type	Header type
00 xxxxxx	NALP - Not a LoWPAN frame
01 000001	IPv6 - Uncompressed IPv6 Addresses
01 000010	LOWPAN_HC1 - LOWPAN_HC1 compressed IPv6
...	Reserved
01 010000	LOWPAN_BC0 - LOWPAN_BC0 broadcast
...	Reserved
01 XXXXXX	IPv6 header compressed by LOWPAN_IPHC
01 000000	ESC-There are others subsequent header
10 xxxxxx	MESH - Mesh Header
11 000xxx	FRAG1- Fragmentation Header (first)
11 100xxx	FRAGN - Fragmentation Header (subsequent)

The dispatch field is immediately followed by the type-specific header, which consists of some indicating bits. The indicating bits indicate specific compression schemes for IPv6. Readers can refer to RFC4944 for more details.

In addition to stateless IPv6 header compression, 6LoWPAN also includes other relevant standards including schemes supporting mesh routing, simplified IPv6 neighbour discovery protocol, use cases and routing requirements. In summary, the 6LoWPAN working group provides the fundamental of IETF on IoT communications.

3.2. RPL

IETF Routing over Lossy and Low-power Networks working group (RoLL) was established in February 2008. It focuses on routing protocol design and is committed to standardize the IPv6 routing protocol for lossy and low power networks (LLN). Its tasks start with the routing requirements of various application scenarios. So far, the routing requirements of four application scenarios have been standardized, i.e., Home Automation (RFC5826), Industrial Control (RFC5673), Urban Environment (RFC5548) and Building Automation (RFC 5867).

In order to develop suitable standards for LLN, RoLL first provides an overview of existing routing protocols for wireless sensor networks. The literature [26] analyzes the characteristics and shortcomings of the relevant standards and then discusses the quantitative metrics for constructing routing in the routing protocol. RFC6551 [27] introduces two kinds of quantitative metric: node metrics including node state, node energy and hop count, and link metrics including throughput, latency, link reliability, expected transmission count (ETC) and link colour object. In order to assist dynamic routing, nodes can incorporate objective functions to determine the rule for path selection based on the quantitative metrics.

Based on the results of routing requirements and quantitative static link metrics, RoLL has developed a routing protocol for LLN (RPL) as specified in RFC6550 [28]. RPL supports three kinds of traffic flows including point-to-point (between devices inside the LLN), point-to-multipoint (from a central control point to a subset of devices inside the LLN) and multipoint-to-point (from devices inside the LLN towards a central control point). RPL is a distance-vector routing protocol, in which nodes construct a Directed Acyclic Graph (DAG) by exchanging distance vectors. Through broadcasting routing constraints, the DAG root node (i.e., central control point) filters out the nodes that do not meet the constraints and select the optimum paths according to the metrics.

3.3. CoAP

CoAP, as specified by the IETF Constrained RESTful Environments working group (CoRE) [9], is a specialized web transfer protocol for resource constrained nodes and networks. CoAP conforms to the REST

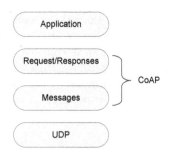

Figure 2. CoAP protocol stack

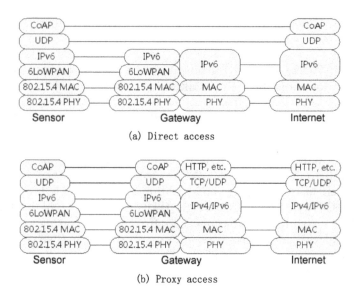

style. It abstracts all the objects in the network as resources. Each resource corresponds to a unique Universal Resource Identifier (URI), based on which the resources can be operated upon in a stateless manner using commands including GET, PUT, POST, DELETE and so on.

Strictly speaking, CoAP is not a HTTP compression protocol. On the one hand, CoAP realizes a subset of HTTP functions and is optimized for constrained environments. On the other hand, it offers features such as built-in resource discovery, multicast support and asynchronous message exchanges.

Unlike HTTP, CoAP utilizes a datagram-oriented transport protocol underneath, such as UDP. In order to ensure reliable transmissions over UDP, CoAP introduces a two-layer structure as shown in Figure 2. The messaging sublayer is used to deal with asynchronous interactions using UDP. Specifically, there are 4 kinds of CoAP messages:

1. Confirmable (CON): ACK is needed.

2. Non-confirmable (NON): ACK is not needed.

3. Acknowledgment (ACK): To represent that a Confirmable message is received.

4. Reset (RST): To represent that a Confirmable message is received but can't be processed.

The Request/Response interaction sublayer is used to transmit resource operation requests and the request/response data. As a summary, CoAP has the following features:

- Constrained web protocol fulfilling M2M requirements.

- Asynchronous message exchanges.

- Low header overhead and parsing complexity.

- URI and Content-type support.

- Simple proxy and caching capabilities.

- Built-in resource discovery.

Figure 3. Direct access vs. Proxy access

- UDP binding with optional reliability supporting unicast and multicast requests.

- A stateless HTTP-CoAP mapping, allowing a proxy to provide access to CoAP resources via HTTP in a uniform way and vice versa.

3.4. HTTP–CoAP protocol implementation

Applying REST-style network structure in WSN can largely facilitate connection between WSN and the Internet. By applying CoAP protocol on wireless sensors devices, Internet services can access WSNs as resources directly or via gateway as a proxy. Basically, there are two methods to enable remote access from an Internet client to a sensor device.

Direct access. Direct access means that the an Internet user accesses a WSN through a gateway that only implements protocol conversions between the IPv6 network layer and 6LoWPAN, but does not process the upper layers protocols (e.g., CoAP). As an example shown in Figure 3 (a), a sensor node in WSN can be accessed through an IPv6 address and the gateway only needs to implement conversion between IPv6 and 6LoWPAN, which significantly reduces the processing overhead.

Proxy access. Proxy access means that an Internet user accesses a WSN through a proxy that can convert an incompatible data format from outside networks into a WSN compatible data format. For example, in our case, the proxy can have functions of protocol conversion from a HTTP request to a CoAP request, and vice versa, payload conversion and blockwise segmentation of large data packets (e.g., those representing an image), etc.

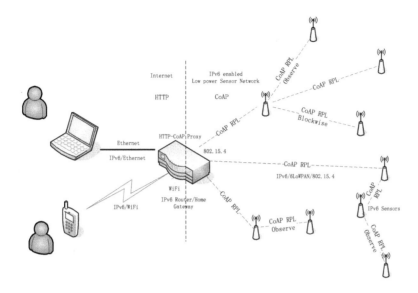

Figure 4. System Architecture

The advantage of this method is that current Internet services can easily access WSN resources without any changes, because of the existence of the proxy gateway. Moreover, since low power sensor nodes cannot support TCP efficiently, the proxy mechanism can buffer and process the requests to avoid TCP time out. However, the protocol conversion increases the complexity of the gateway and thereafter affects communication efficiency. Figure 3 (b) illustrates the protocol conversion between HTTP and CoAP via a gateway.

4. Prototype Implementation

In this section, we present our prototype to illustrate the implementation of the RESTful access methods to IPv6 wireless sensor devices, considered as the representative of future embedded devices in IoT. A RESTful gateway supports both IEEE 802.11 Wi-Fi and IEEE 802.15.4 interfaces for communications. The web resources in sensor devices are accessible through the RESTful APIs. The system architecture is shown in Figure 4, where a PC acts as a client to retrieve sensor resources via the RESTful gateway.

4.1. Sensor node

We deploy wireless sensor devices to monitor air temperature and humidity, detect movements and take photos. All these sensors are equipped with the same ATmega1284P MCU and AT86RF231 radio transceiver to support 250kbps data transmissions at 2.4GHz using the IEEE 802.15.4 protocol. To support IPv6 connectivity, all the sensor devices run the Contiki v2.6 operating system and incorporate 6LowPAN, IPv6 and RPL protocols on top of IEEE 802.15.4. The web

Figure 5. A snapshot of sensor platform

service running on the sensor devices relies on the application protocol CoAP. A snapshot of the sensor platform is illustrated in Figure 5 and the detailed technical specifications are shown in Table II.

4.2. RESTfull Gateway

To ease access from Internet applications to sensor resources, especially for those Internet users without CoAP support, we integrate IEEE 802.15.4 connectivity into an open-platform gateway and port the HTTP-CoAP proxy implementation to the OpenWrt, the operation system of the gateway, to realize remote access from an ordinary IP terminal to an IPv6 sensor device. Figure 6 gives the hardware architecture of the RESTful gateway, which technical specifications are provided in Table III.

The HTTP-CoAP (HC) proxy provides translation and mapping between HTTP and CoAP protocol. CoAP can be directly mapped to HTTP, because CoAP actually implements a subset of HTTP functions. The mapping is performed only at the Request/Response interaction sublayer of the CoAP protocol and is invisible to the

Table 2. Technical specifications of sensor device

	Parameters	Note
CPU Performance		
Internal storage	128KB	
External storage	16KB	
EEPROM	4KB	
Serial communication	UART / USART	TTL Transmission Level
A/D converter	10-bit ADC	8 channels, 0-3V input
Other Interfaces	Digital I/O, I2C,SPI	
Maximum Current	18mA	Work mode
	2uA	Sleep mode
RF transceiver		
Frequency band	2400-2485MHz	ISM global free band
Data rate	250Kbps/ 1000Kbps/ 2000Kbps	
RF power	3.2 dBm	
Receiving sensitivity	-104 dBm	
Adjacent Channel Suppression	36 dBc	+5M Channel bandwidth
	34 dBc	-5M Channel bandwidth
Outdoor transmission	≥ 300m	
Indoor transmission	≥ 10m	
Maximum Current	12mA	Receiving Mode
	14mA	Tx -3dBm
Extended interface	51 pins	

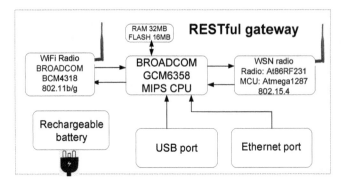

Figure 6. Hardware architecture of gateway

Table 3. Technical specifications of gateway

	Parameters	Note
CPU frequency	300MHz	
RAM	32MB	
Flash	16MB	
Serial communication	UART / USART	TTL Transmission Level
A/D converter	10-bit ADC	8 channels, 0-3V input
USB HOST	2	
RJ45	4	
WiFi	1	IEEE 802.11abg
OS	OpenWrt	v12.09-beta2
Protocol	IPv6, IPv4	

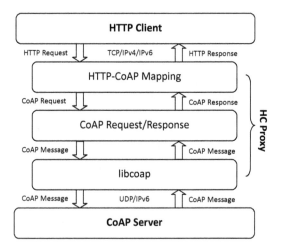

Figure 7. Interaction process of HC proxy

messaging sublayer. There are two kinds of mapping: CoAP-to-HTTP and HTTP-to-CoAP. In our case, we only realize HTTP-to-CoAP mapping, which is implemented by specifying CoAP-URI as the request address for transmitting HTTP request to the HTTP-CoAP proxy. Note that compared to CoAP-to-HTTP mapping, HTTP-to-CoAP mapping is more complex since it is necessary to determine whether to ignore the content or report an error by checking unsupported HTTP request methods, response codes, content-types and options.

In our prototype gateway, the HC proxy is implemented based on libcoap [29] which is an open-source C-Implementation of CoAP and conforms to GPL v2 or higher licenses.

The interaction process of the HC proxy is shown in Figure 7. Specifically, for each of the HC proxy layers, we have the following implementations:

libcoap layer. libcoap implements the CoAP messaging sublayer based on UDP. It defines CoAP message structure and methods to operate CoAP messages.

CoAP Request/Response layer. The CoAP Request/Response layer implements the function of the Request/Response interaction sublayer in Figure 2 by encapsulating the data structure and methods relevant to CoAP Requests and Responses. It is responsible to transmit CoAP requests in the form of CoAP messages through the messaging sublayer and generate CoAP response based on received CoAP messages. Because CoAP messaging sublayer adopts unreliable UDP, certain issues need to be solved in order to implement a reliable transmission, including CoAP message acknowledgement, message retransmission for timeout, message process, asynchronous message process and segmented message process, etc. The following code header is provided to illustrate the implementation of CoAP Request/Response.

```
1  /* request.h */
2
3  typedef struct {
4    unsigned char msgtype;
5    method_t method;
6    coap_list_t *optlist;
7    str proxy;
8    unsigned short proxy_port;
9    str payload;
10   int ready;
11   char lport_str[NI_MAXSERV]
12   coap_uri_t uri;
13   int flags;
14   coap_block_t block;
15   unsigned int wait_seconds;      /*
         default timeout in seconds */
16   coap_tick_t max_wait;           /*
         global timeout (changed by
         set_timeout()) */
17   unsigned int obs_seconds;       /*
         default observe time */
18   coap_tick_t obs_wait; /* timeout for
         current subscription */
19  } coap_request_t;
20
21  void coap_request_method(coap_request_t
       *request, char *arg);
22  void coap_request_uri(coap_request_t *
       request, char *arg);
23  int coap_request_proxy(coap_request_t *
       request, char *arg);
24  void coap_option_content_type(
       coap_request_t *request, char *arg,
       unsigned short key);
25  int coap_option_blocksize(coap_request_t
       *request, char *arg);
26  void coap_option_subscribe(
       coap_request_t *request, char *arg);
27  void coap_option_token(coap_request_t *
       request, char *arg);
28  int coap_send_request(coap_request_t *
       request, void *context);
```

```
29
30  void coap_init_request(coap_request_t *
       request);
31  void coap_register_request_handler(int
       (*handler)(coap_pdu_t *pdu, void *
       context));
32  void coap_register_request_data_handler(
       int (*handler)(const unsigned char
       *data, size_t len, void *context));
```

HTTP-CoAP mapping layer. This layer implements mappings from HTTP requests to CoAP requests and vice versa. When converting a HTTP request to a CoAP request, the HC proxy needs to convert the HTTP request method, URI, header/option and payload, respectively. If a proxy encounters an error, it has to generate the corresponding error response. The C function defined for handing the HTTP-CoAP mapping is also provides as follows.

```
1  int coap_response_map_code(int code);
2  char* coap_response_map_content_type(int
       content_type);
3
4  BOOL coap_proxy_handler(SOCKET
       localwebuser, char *szLineBuffer,
       int nLineBuffer)
```

5. Performance Evaluations

In this section, we provide evaluation results of the prototype system. Especially, we experimentally evaluate the performance over the prototype system at two layers: the routing layer where the round trip times (RTTs) and packet loss rates of multi-hop transmissions in the WSN are measured and the application layer where web resources of sensor devices are retrieved using RESTful methods.

5.1. System configuration

Our prototype system is composed of three different sensor devices, one HC proxy gateway and one PC for the tests. In order to ease the setup of WSN in a multi-hop fashion, we manually assign IPv6 addresses for the sensor devices as follows:

Camera sensor	2001:2::19
Humidity & temperature sensor	2001:2::14
Approach detecting sensor	2001:2::16

We deploy the prototype system in an open office area. The HC proxy gateway and sensor devices are connected wirelessly via IEEE 802.15.4 over channel 26. The PC client is connected to the gateway through the Wi-Fi link. The network topology is built with a maximum number of 2 hops, where the camera

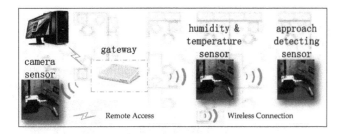

Figure 8. Network topology of prototype system

```
Routes [6 max]
2001:2::14/128 (via fe80::14)
2001:2::16/128 (via fe80::14)

---------

Connected to 192.168.1.1
```

(a) Routing table

```
Ping statistics for 2001:2::14:
Approximate round trip times in milli-seconds:
    Minimum = 16ms, Maximum = 126ms, Average = 24ms
```

(b) RRTs from one-hop sensor device

```
Ping statistics for 2001:2::16:
Approximate round trip times in milli-seconds:
    Minimum = 37ms, Maximum = 212ms, Average = 43ms
```

(c) RRTs from two-hop sensor device

Figure 9. Routing table and RTTs evaluations

sensor and humidity&temperature sensor are directly connected to the gateway over single hops, and the approach detecting sensor is the leaf node of the humidity&temperature sensor and it is two hops away from the gateway. Figure 8 provides the network topology of the prototype system.

5.2. RTTs and Packet loss evaluations of RPL routing

Wireless sensor networks should be capable of forming multi-hop transmissions among peer sensor devices. In this evaluation, the RTTs and packet loss rate in a single-hop and multi-hop scenarios using RPL routing are measured. After setting up of the system, we use the simple ping commands to evaluate the RTTs from the PC client to the humidity&temperature sensor and approach detecting sensor, respectively. The payload size for each transmission packet is 32 bytes and the RTTs results are averaged over 100 measurements. Figure 9 (a) shows the routing table via the secure shell client. As can be seen from Figure 9 (b), for one-hop transmissions, the average RTTs is 24ms. When the routing extends to two hops, the results as shown in Figure 9 (c) are degraded to 43ms average RTTs.

To further evaluate the performance of a large scale network, we set up another test to evaluate the packet loss rate in a multi-hop environment. The test is carried out in an open office area with strong Wi-Fi background noise and lowest possible WSN radio frequency output power to ensure a multi-hop fashion, which makes a sensor device can only communicate to each other within around 30 cm.

A maximum number of 6 hops can be obtained by optimizing the communication system. To retrieve the onboard resources via GET request (i.e., < /.well-known/core >) over the same number of measurements, Table 4 shows the packet loss rate in a multi-hop scenario. We can observe that the packet loss rate increases dramatically with an increasing number of hops, because of severe environmental interference and channel congestions, etc. Moreover, additional configurations to ensure a multi-hop transmission, such as one way communication, low output power and RPL settings, also contribute to the high loss.

Table 4. Packet loss rate in a multiple-hop network

	Hop 2	Hop 3	Hop 4	Hop 5	Hop 6
Received	2020	1704	1173	1112	944
Lost	161	474	1003	1068	1234
Packet loss rate	7.38%	21.76%	46.09%	48.9%	56.65%

5.3. RESTful method to retrieve sensor resources

To illustrate IoT applications, we initiate a trial to 'GET' an image from the camera sensor device. Specifically, we use both proxy access and direct access methods to retrieve the sensor data via the gateway. Figure 10 (a) shows the proxy access result by sending a HTTP GET request along with the URI http://[2001:2::19]/camera. The HC proxy then converts the HTTP request to CoAP request and forwards the request to the camera sensor. As a comparison, Figure 10 (b) shows the direct access result by sending a CoAP request coap://[2001:2::19]:5683/camera directly from the CoAP browser [30] on the PC. Since the picture takes about 27 kBytes, which exceeds the payload size defined by the CoAP client, the CoAP protocol adopts the blockwise transfer by dividing the response into 64-Byte blocks in such a way that the web server can handle each block transfer separately, with no need for a connection setup or other server-side memory of previous block transfers. In summary, both methods show an acceptable performance.

(a) Proxy access using HTTP

(b) Direct access using CoAP

Figure 10. HTTP vs. CoAP methods

6. Conclusion

We have implemented the 6LowPAN/IPv6/RPL/CoAP protocol stack on an IEEE 802.15.4 radio platform to enable wireless sensor communications. Furthermore, by integrating IEEE 802.15.4 connectivity and HTTP-CoAP proxy into an open-platform gateway, we have realized remote access from any IP node to IPv6 sensor devices. We have presented performance evaluations, which have shown that the IP based solution is promising to drive IoT development. In the future work, we plan to design a more robust and reliable IP solution for IoT. Especially, how to deploy large scale networks with decent performance is a critical issue and we need to continue to optimize both hardware and software implementations. Moreover, other issues, such as device management and control of sensor devices, can also be explored via RESTful methods.

References

[1] ASHTON K. (2009) *That 'internet of things' thing*, RFID Journal.

[2] VASSEUR J.-P. and DUNKELS A. (2010) *Interconnecting smart objects with ip: The next internet*, Morgan Kaufmann.

[3] ZIGBEE ALLIANCE (2007) *Zigbee home automation public application profile*, IEEE J. Select. Areas Commun..

[4] Z-WAVE (2007) *Z-wave protocol overview*.

[5] DARBEE P. (2005) *Insteon: The details*.

[6] GARCIA-HERNANDO A. ET AL. (2008) *Problem solving for wireless sensor networks*, Springer.

[7] SHENG Z. and YANG S. and YU Y. and VASILAKOS A. and MCCANN J. and LEUNG K. (2013) *A survey on the IETF protocol suite for the internet of things: standards, challenges, and opportunities* in IEEE Wireless Communications Magazine, vol. 20, no. 6, pp. 91-98.

[8] IETF *Routing Over Low power and Lossy networks (roll)*, Available at: http://datatracker.ietf.org/wg/roll/charter.

[9] IETF *Constrained RESTful Environments (core)*, Available at: http://datatracker.ietf.org/wg/core/charter.

[10] IP SMART OBJECT ALLIANCE (IPSO) *Available at: http://www.ipso-alliance.org*.

[11] FIELDING R. T. (2000) *Architectural styles and the design of network-based software architectures*, Doctoral dissertation, University of California, Irvine, USA.

[12] PAUTASSO C. and ZIMMERMANN O. and LEYMANN F. (2008) *Restful web services vs. "big" web services: Making the right architectural decision*, in Proc. 17th International Conference on World Wide Web (WWW), pp. 805-814.

[13] QIN W. and LI Q. and SUN L. and ZHU H. and LIU Y. (2011) *Restthing: A restful web service infrastructure for mash-up physical and web resources* in Proc. IFIP 9th International Conference on Embedded and Ubiquitous Computing (EUC), pp. 197-204.

[14] STIRBU V. (2008) *Towards a restful plug and play experience in the web of things* in Proc. IEEE International Conference on Semantic Computing (ICSC), pp. 512-517.

[15] GUINARD D. (2009) *Towards the web of things: Web mashups for embedded devices* in Proc. Workshop on Mashups, Enterprise Mashups and Lightweight Composition on the Web (MEM 2009) in conjunction with 18th International Conference on World Wide Web (WWW).

[16] GUINARD D. and TRIFA V. and WILDE E. (2010) *A resource oriented architecture for the web of things* in Proc. Internet of Things (IOT), pp. 1-8.

[17] POTSCH T. and KULADINITHI K. and BECKER M. and TRENKAMP P. and GOERG C. (2012) *Performance evaluation of coap using rpl and lpl in tinyos* in Proc. 5th International Conference on New Technologies, Mobility and Security (NTMS), pp. 1-5.

[18] IYENGAR S. S. and PARAMESHWARAN N. and PHOHA V. V. and BALAKRISHNAN N. and OKOYE C. D. (2011) *Fundamentals of sensor network programming: Applications and technology*, Wiley-IEEE Press.

[19] DUNKELS A. and GRONVALL B. and VOIGT T. (2004) *Contiki - a lightweight and flexible operating system for tiny networked sensors* in Proc. 29th Annual IEEE International Conference on Local Computer Networks (LCN), pp. 455-462.

[20] KOVATSCH M. and DUQUENNOY S. and DUNKELS A. (2011) *A low-power coap for contiki* in Proc. IEEE 8th International Conference on Mobile Adhoc and Sensor Systems (MASS), pp. 855-860.

[21] SCHNWLDER J. and TSOU T. and SARIKAYA B. (2011) *Protocol profiles for constrained devices* Available at: www.iab.org/wp-content/IAB-uploads/.../Schoenwaelder.pdf.

[22] IETF *IPv6 over Low power WPAN (6lowpan)*, Available at: http://datatracker.ietf.org/wg/6lowpan/charter.

[23] IEEE COMPUTER SOCIETY (2003) *Ieee std. 802.15.4-2003*.

[24] MONTENEGRO G. and KUSHALNAGAR N. and HUI J. and CULLER D. *Transmission of ipv6 packets over ieee 802.15.4 networks*, RFC4944, available at: https://datatracker.ietf.org/doc/rfc4944/.

[25] HUI J. and THUBERT P. *Compression format for ipv6 datagrams over ieee 802.15.4-based networks*, RFC6282, available at: http://datatracker.ietf.org/doc/rfc6282/.

[26] LEVISI P. and TAVAKOLI A. and *Dawson-Haggerty S. Overview of existing routing protocols for low power and lossy networks*, Internet-Draft, available at: http://tools.ietf.org/html/draft-ietf-roll-protocols-survey-07.

[27] Vasseuri J. and Kim M. and Pister K. and Dejean N. and Barthel D. *Routing metrics used for path calculation in low-power and lossy networks*, RFC 6551, available at: http://datatracker.ietf.org/doc/rfc6551/.

[28] Winter T. and Thubert P. and Brandt A. and Hui J. and Kelsey R. and Levis P. and Pister K. and Struik R. and Vasseur J. and Alexander R. *Rpl: Ipv6 routing protocol for low-power and lossy networks*, RFC 6550, available at: http://datatracker.ietf.org/doc/rfc6550/.

[29] Bergmann O. *libcoap: C-implementation of coap*, Available at: http://libcoap.sourceforge.net.

[30] Copper (Cu) CoAP Browser *A firefox add-on to browse the internet of things*, Available at: https://github.com/mkovatsc/Copper.

5

Empirical analysis of IPv6 transition technologies using the IPv6 Network Evaluation Testbed

Marius Georgescu*, Hiroaki Hazeyama, Youki Kadobayashi, Suguru Yamaguchi

Nara Institute of Science and Technology, 8916-5 Takayama, Ikoma, Nara 630-0192, JAPAN

Abstract

IPv6 has yet to become more than a worthy successor of IPv4, which remains, for now, the dominant Internet Protocol. This is due to the complicated transition period through which the Internet will have to go, until IPv6 will completely replace IPv4. One of the challenges introduced by this transition is to decide which technology is more feasible for a particular network scenario. To that end, this article proposes the IPv6 Network Evaluation Testbed (IPv6NET), a research project whose ultimate goal is to obtain feasibility data in order to formulate a coherent, scenario-based IPv6 transition strategy. The paper presents the overview of IPv6NET, the testing methodology and empirical results for a specific network scenario. The presented empirical feasibility data includes network performance data such as latency, throughput, packet loss, and operational capability data, such as configuration, troubleshooting and applications capability.

Keywords: IPv6 transition, IETF IPv6 scenario, 464 scenario, Enterprise Networks, IPv6NET, Asamap, MAPe, MAPt, DSLite, 464XLAT

1. Introduction

Threatened by the limitations of IPv4, the Internet community turned to IPv6 as means to continue the expansion of the Internet. IPv6 uses a 128 bit address, extending the address space to $2^{128} \approx 3.4 \cdot 10^{38}$ unique IP addresses, enough for many years to come. However the appeal of IPv6 has diminished since 1998, mainly because it is not able to communicate directly with its predecessor, IPv4. This introduced the Internet community with a great challenge, namely the transition to IPv6, which is represented by the stages the Internet will have to undergo until IPv6 will completely replace IPv4.

Given the complexity of the current IPv4-dominated Internet, the transition to IPv6 will be a long and complex process. So far, only a small number of production networks are IPv6-capable. The APNIC Labs IPv6 deployment report[1] shows that only about 2% of the worldwide users have IPv6 connectivity. IPv6 transition scenarios have been researched within the IETF by the v6ops and Softwire Working Groups. The scenarios were dedicated to four main types of networks: ISP Networks[2], Enterprise Networks[3], 3GPP Networks[4] and Unmanaged Networks[5]. The IETF Next Generation Transition (ngtrans) Working Group has made many efforts to propose and analyze viable transition mechanisms. Many transition mechanisms have been proposed and implemented. All have advantages and disadvantages considering a certain transition scenario, but no transition mechanism can be considered most feasible for all the scenarios. This opens many research opportunities. One of which is a scenario-based analysis of IPv6 transition implementations, and represents the ultimate goal of our research.

In this article, we are proposing the IPv6 Network Evaluation Testbed (IPv6NET), which is dedicated to measuring the feasibility of transition mechanisms in a series of scenario-based network tests. As a study case, the article focuses on one of the scenarios, introduced by the IETF for Enteprise Networks in [3].The scenario targets enterprises using an IPv6-only core network technology, but with IPv4-capable nodes, which need to communicate over the IPv6 infrastructure.

The paper is organized as follows: section 2 presents related literature, section 3 introduces the IPv6NET concept and the testing methodology, in section 4 the empirical results are introduced, and the feasibility of the tested implementation is analyzed in relation to the specific scenario, section 5 discusses our approach and lastly section 6 states the conclusions and future work.

2. Related Work

There are a variety of articles dedicated to IPv6 transition experimental environments in current literature. They can be generally classified into closed environments and open environments. The closed environments are usually small scale, local environments, which are isolated from production networks or the Internet. In [6], two 6-over-4, and IPv6 in IPv4 tunneling implementations are tested and experimental performance results are analyzed, in comparison with a homogeneous IPv6-only network. In [7], the performance of Linux operating systems is evaluated in relation to an IPv4-v6 Configured Tunnel and a 6to4 Tunnel. Four workstations were employed to build the testbed. In [8], differences in bandwidth requirements for common network applications like remote login, web browsing, voice communication, database transaction, and video streaming are analyzed over 3 types of networks: IPv4-only, IPv6-only and a 6to4 tunneling mechanism. The environment was built using the OPNET simulator, which also served as the basis for the testbed presented in [9], dedicated to the performance analysis of transition mechanisms over a MPLS backbone. [10] evaluates the performance of DNS64 implementations, BIND9 and TOTD, running on OpenBSD and FreeBSD. A common trait of the above mentioned closed environments, is the thorough performance analysis, which resulted in quantifiable data such as CPU and memory utilization, throughput, end-to-end delay, jitter and execution time.

However, as [11] also underlines, before transition mechanisms are applied in a large scale environment, a systematic and quantitative performance analysis should be performed. This gets us to the second group of experimental environments, namely: open environments. They can be defined as experimental networks connected to a large scale production network or to the Internet. In [12], poor implementation and erroneous operations are identified in an dual-stack environment. A hotel Internet service is presented as a case study. Operational issues such as lack of path/peering, Bad TCP reaction or misbehaving DNS resolution are identified. [13] describes the lessons learned from deploying IPv6 in Google's heterogeneous corporate network. The report presents numerous operational troubles: the lack of dual-stack support of the customer-premises equipments (CPE), or the immature IPv6 support of operating systems and applications. One of their conclusions was that the IPv6 transition can affect every operational aspect in a production environment, hence interoperability considerations have to be made. In [14], experiences with IPv6-only Networks are presented. NAT64 and DNS64 technologies are tested in two open environments: an office and a home environment. Common applications such as web browsing, streaming, instant messaging, VoIP, online gaming, file storage and home control were tested. Application issues in relation to the NAT64/DNS64 technology are identified, for example Skype's limitation to connect to IPv6 destinations, or the lack of network operational diagnostics for certain standalone games. Experiences with IPv6-only Networks from previous WIDE Camp events in

[15] present a great deal of meaningful interoperability data such as IPv6 capability of OSes, applications and network devices. Many operational issues have been identified. Some examples are long fall-back routine, low DHCPv6 capability of certain OSes, lack of IPv6 support in some network devices, DNS64 overload, inappropriate AAAA replies or inappropriate selection of DNS resolvers. Considering these examples we can conclude that open environment testing has the potential of exposing interoperability issues, which can otherwise get overlooked.

Combing the advantages of the two testing methods can lead to a complete feasibility analysis. Hence we are considering both methods for testing.

3. Testing Methodology of IPv6NET

The IPv6 Network Evaluation Testbed (IPv6NET) is dedicated to quantifying the feasibility of IPv6 transition implementations in relation to a specific network scenarios. IPv6NET has two main components: the testing component and the infrastructure component. The testing component has the following building blocks: a specific network scenario, an associated network template and a test methodology. The infrastructure component is represented by the implementations under testing and the network test environment. As mentioned prior, we are considering building both closed and open environments.

The scenario targeted in this article was introduced by the IETF in [3] as Scenario 3. It is dedicated to an enterprise which decided to use IPv6 as the main protocol for network communications. Some applications and nodes, which are IPv4-capable would need to communicate over the IPv6 infrastructure. In order to achieve this, the Enterprise would need to apply an IPv6 transition technology, which would allow both protocols to coexist in the same environment. For simplicity, the technologies suitable for this specific scenario will be referred to as *464 technologies*.

3.1. IPv6NET Feasibility indicators and metrics

This subsection presents some clarifications regarding the semantics used for the methodology associated with IPv6NET throughout this paper. For the empirical feasibility analysis presented in this article, we are using the term *feasibility indicator* as a generic classifier for performance metrics. For closed environment testing, the proposed feasibility indicator was *network performance*. Network performance indicates the technical feasibility of each technology in relation to existing computer network standards. To quantify network performance, we have used well established metrics, such as *round-trip-delay*, *jitter*, *throughput* and *packet loss*. For open-environment testing, we have proposed *operational capability* as a feasibility indicator, which shows how a certain technology fits in with the existing environment or how it manages to solve operational problems. To the best of our knowledge, there are no associated metrics for operational feasibility of network devices in current literature. Consequently we have introduced the following three metrics:

- *configuration capability*: measures how capable a network implementations is in terms of contextual configuration or reconfiguration

- *troubleshooting capability*: measures how capable a network implementation is at isolating and identifying faults

- *applications capability*: measures how capable a device is at ensuring compatibility with common user-side protocols

Details about the measurement process for these three metrics, as well as other methodology and infrastructure details, are presented in the following subsections.

3.2. Closed environment

Infrastructure. The basic, small scale template for 464 technologies is composed of a set of network routers: a Customer Edge (CE) router which encapsulates/translates the IPv4 packets in IPv6 packets, and a Provider Edge (PE) router, which handles the decapsulation/translation from IPv6 back to IPv4. The IPv4-only backbone is used for forwarding the IPv4 traffic. The IPv6 traffic would be directly forwarded by the IPv6 backbone. The closed experiment's design, presented in Fig. 1a, follows the basic network template, including one Customer Edge (CE) machine and one Provider Edge (PE) machine.

Multiple technologies can be considered suitable for the 464 scenario: MAPe[16], MAPt[17], DSLite[18], 464XLAT[19], SA46T[20]. Some implementations supporting these technologies have been proposed. One of those is the Asamap vyatta distribution[21], which covers 4 of those technologies: MAPe, MAPt, DSLite and 464XLAT. Both 464 PE and 464CE machines have used as Operating System the Asamap vyatta distribution.

For the underlaying infrastructure, the closed experiment uses StarBED [22], a large scale general purpose network testbed, administered by the National Institute of Information and Communications Technology (NICT) of Japan. Four Cisco UCS C200 M2 servers were used for this experiment: two for the devices under test (DUT), 464 PE and 464 CE, and two for the testing platform. As hardware details, each computer used a dual Intel Xeon X5670 CPU and 49.152 GB of RAM. The testing platform computers have used Ubuntu 12.04.3 server as base operating system. The traffic was generated using the Distributed Internet

Traffic Generator (D-ITG) [23]. One of the computers performed the ITGSend function, generating the traffic, while the other ran the ITGRecv function, receiving the generated traffic.

Methodology. The experimental workload is represented by the amount of traffic inserted into the experimental network. We have considered the combinations of frame size and frame rates displayed in Table 1. These have been recommended in RFC5180, IPv6 Benchmarking Methodology for Network Interconnect Devices [24], as maximum frame rates × frame sizes for 10 Mbps and 100 Mbps Ethernet. For future tests we intend to expand to 1Gbps as well.

We have considered the following parameters as potentially affecting the network performance: the IP version, IPv4 and IPv6, the upper layers protocols, UDP and TCP, the IPv6 transition technology and the IPv6 transition implementation. A full factorial design was employed. As recommended by RFC2544 [25], the duration of each experiment was 60 seconds after the first timestamp is sent. Each test was repeated 20 times and the average of the recorded values was reported.

3.3. Open environment

Infrastructure. The open experiment topology, presented in Fig. 1b also follows the basic, small scale 464 network template. The major difference is that the testing platform is replaced by open up-link and down-link connections. We have built this type of environment as part of a bigger experimental network, which supplied Internet access to participants at the WIDE Camp 1309, a networking event, held between September 10 and September 13 2013, at Shinsu-Matsushiro Royal Hotel, Nagano, Japan. The 464 network consisted of two virtual machines, the Customer Edge machine (CE) and the Provider Edge machine (PE). The two machines have ran on a virtual environment consisting of a Dell PowerEdge R805, with the following hardware description: Six-Core AMD Opteron 2400 CPU and 8GB of RAM. For the hypervisor a Citrix XenServer 6.0 distribution was employed. Previous experiences with building and analyzing a similar 464 open environment are presented in [26]. The base implementation for all four tested transition technologies, MAPe, MAPt, DSLite, 464XLAT has been the Asamap vyatta distribution. On the up-link, the IPv4 and IPv6 traffic was routed by a dual-stack core router. WIDE Camp participants were able to connect to the environments trough a single SSID, *464exp*, handled by the Layer 2 Cisco WiFi Mesh.

Methodology. For operational capability the proposed metrics are: *configuration capability, troubleshooting capability* and *applications capability*. As measurement method for configuration capability, we are considering

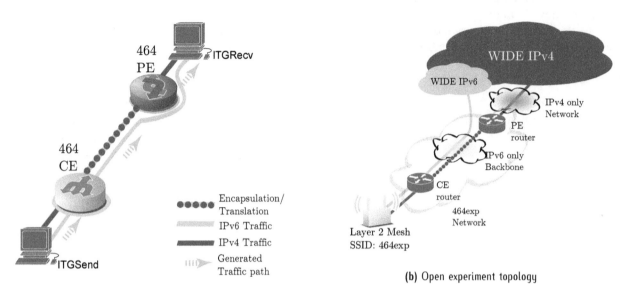

(a) Closed experiment topology

Figure 1. Experimental setup

Table 1. Workload *Framesize × Framerate*

No	Size	Rate 10 Mbps	Rate 100 Mbps	No	Size	Rate 10Mbps	Rate 100 Mbps
1	64	14880	148809	7	1518	812	8127
2	128	8445	84459	8	1522	810	8106
3	256	4528	45289	9	2048	604	6044
4	512	2349	23496	10	4096	303	3036
5	1024	1197	11973	11	8192	152	1523
6	1280	961	9615	12	9216	135	1353

a number of configuration tasks, which have been inspired by the abstracted guidelines presented in [27]. The tasks can be organized in three generic groups, *initial setup*, *reconfiguration* and *confirmation*. For ease of reference we have associated each task with a task code in accordance with the respective group association.

1. IinitialSetup1: Configure an encapsulation/translation virtual interface using a command line interface or a graphical user interface

2. IinitialSetup2: Save the current temporary configuration commands in a file which can be loaded at start-up

3. IinitialSetup3: Self configuration according to contextual configuration details

4. InitialSetup4: Display warnings in the case of misconfiguration and reject the misconfigured command

5. InitialSetup5: Display warnings in the case of missing command and reject saving the temporary configuration

6. InitialSetup6: Display contextual configuration commands help

7. Reconfiguration1: Convert current configuration settings to configuration commands

8. Reconfiguration2: Back-up and restore the current configuration

9. Confirmation1: Show the current configuration

10. Confirmation2: Show abstracted details for the 464 virtual interface

The configuration capability can be expressed as a ratio between the number of successfully completed configuration tasks and the total number of tasks. Similarly, for troubleshooting capability we are proposing a number of troubleshooting tasks. The tasks follow the fault isolation, fault determination and root cause analysis (RCA) guidelines presented in [27]. Consequently the tasks can be organized into the three generic categories: *fault isolation, fault determination* and root cause analysis RCA. For ease of reference, these tasks were associated as well with group codes:

1. FaultIsolation1: Capture and analyze IPv4 and IPv6 packets

2. FaultIsolation2: Send and receive contextual ICMP messages

3. FaultDetermination1: Identify a misconfigured contextual route

4. FaultDetermination2: Identify a misconfigured contextual line in the virtual 464 interface configuration

5. FaultDetermination3: Perform self-check troubleshooting sequence

6. RCA1: Log warning and error messages

7. RCA2: Display log

8. RCA3: Display in the user console the critical messages with contextual details

9. RCA4: Log statistical network interface information

10. RCA5: Display detailed statistical network interface information

The troubleshooting capability can also be expressed as a ratio of successful tasks over total number of troubleshooting tasks.

To measure applications capability, inspired by the efforts presented in [14], we have tested a non-exhaustive list of common user applications in relation with the 464 transition technologies. The measurement result can be presented as a ratio between the number of successfully-tested applications and the total number of applications.

4. Empirical results

4.1. Closed Experiment results

The network performance of the devices under testing (DUTs) was compared with a Direct Connection setup, in which the two test platform servers were connected directly. The results have been graphed as a function of frame size. The error bars present the margin of error for the mean, calculated at a 99% level of confidence, using the formula 1

$$moe = z_{\alpha/2} \frac{\sigma}{\sqrt{n}}$$
σ − standard deviation, n − sample size
$$z_{\alpha/2} = 2.575$$
(1)

The average of the results for the 10Mbps and 100Mbps workloads have been summarized in Table 2 and Table 3.

The latency results for the 10Mbps workload, composed of end-to-end delay (Fig. 2a, 2b) and jitter (Fig. 3a, 3b) indicate a better performance for 464XLAT, by comparison with the rest of the technologies. Also, in terms of average, translation-based technologies (MAPt, 464XLAT) had a better performance than encapsulation-based technologies (MAPe, DSLite).

The average throughput results, presented in Fig. 4, show a similar performance for the four technologies. The overall average shows a small lead for DSLite and encapsulation-based technologies in the case of the 10 Mbps workload.

In the case of the 100 Mbps workload results , presented in Fig. 2c, 2d for delay, 3c 3d for jitter, and 4c 4d for throughput, the high values of the Margin of Error do not allow us to draw any clear overall conclusion. However, the results help to point out some *unexpected behaviours*, which are consistent. One example of this is the decrease in throughput for the *1280 frame size*, presented in Fig. 4c and 4d. Another example is the lower throughput of the Direct Connection, which is counter-intuitive. The root causes of these behaviors need further analysis.

The loss rates, with the exception of some outliers for translation-based technologies over UDP (MAPt and 464XLAT), are very close to 0. For the outliers, the maximum loss-rate is approximately 0.003%, considered negligible in most cases.

Considering the overall average of these measurements, the best performance was achieved by MAPe, followed closely by DSLite, MAPt and 464XLAT.

4.2. Data collection and repeatability

For the closed experiment a full factorial design was employed, hence $12(frame\ sizes) \times 2(transport\ layer\ protocols) \times 2(workloads) \times 5(transition\ technologies) \times 1(implementation) = 240$ different experiments were conducted. Each experiment was repeated 20 times. The estimated time for each of the experiments was approximately 70 sec , resulting in a total data collection time of *5600 min*, or *93 h*. For post-processing the raw data we have spent an average of 20 sec for each experiment, bringing us to a total of *1600 min* or *26 h*.

The 100 Mbps workload experiment was replicated 17 times on 68 different StartBED nodes to check the repeatability of the experiments. The repeatability results for the Direct Connection have been plotted in Fig. 5.

Table 4 presents the average of the relative standard deviation calculated with the formula 2.

Table 2. 10 Mbps Results Averages

	RT Delay (ms)	+/-	Jitter (ms)	+/-	Throughput (Kbps)	+/-
DC	0.225	0.000	0.016	0.000	8039.0	0.4
MAPe	0.809	0.001	0.167	0.000	7951.8	1.4
MAPt	0.802	0.001	0.177	0.001	7934.6	1.7
DSLite	0.810	0.001	0.167	0.001	7953.5	1.4
464XLAT	0.787	0.001	0.167	0.000	7810.4	1.5

Table 3. 100 Mbps Results Averages

	RT Delay (ms)	+/-	Jitter (ms)	+/-	Throughput (Kbps)	+/-
DC	0.253	0.003	0.130	0.003	57196.1	333.4
MAPe	0.417	0.013	0.486	0.011	58575.2	380.9
MAPt	0.419	0.015	0.480	0.022	58309.4	490.8
DSLite	0.423	0.013	0.493	0.008	58089.2	361.7
464XLAT	0.422	0.013	0.487	0.008	58158.5	361.7

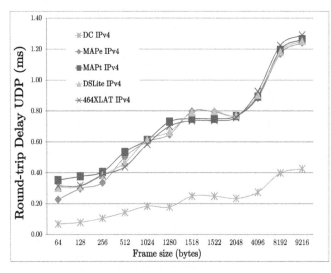

(a) UDP 10Mbps

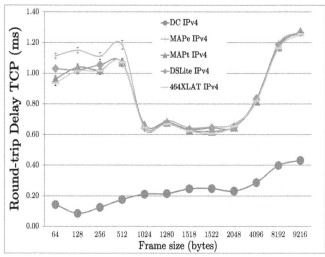

(b) TCP 10Mbps

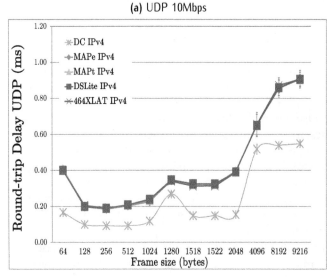

(c) UDP 100Mbps

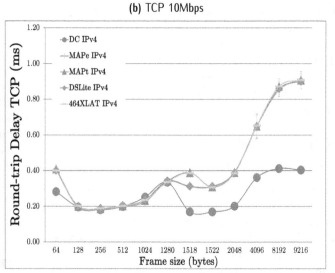

(d) TCP 100Mbps

Figure 2. Delay results

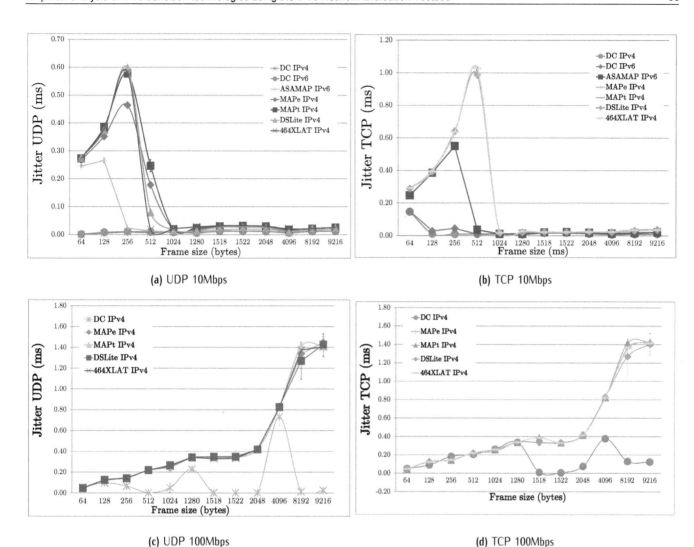

(a) UDP 10Mbps

(b) TCP 10Mbps

(c) UDP 100Mbps

(d) TCP 100Mbps

Figure 3. Jitter results

Table 4. Relative standard deviation average

	RT Delay (%)	Jitter (%)	Throughput (%)
DC	2.21	3.42	0.93
MAPe	5.10	3.71	1.04
MAPt	5.90	7.48	1.34
DSLite	4.85	2.60	0.99
464XLAT	5.67	5.41	0.93

$$\%rsd = \frac{\sigma}{\bar{x}} \times 100 \qquad (2)$$
$$\sigma - standard\ deviation, \bar{x} - mean$$

The low percentages indicate a low variability among datasets, and by extrapolation a high repeatability for the experiments.

4.3. Open Experiment results

During the four days of the WIDE Camp 1309 event, we had the chance to test the operational capability of the Asamap implementation. However the results are only limited to our experiences. The detailed tasks are included in Appendix A for configuration capability and Appendix B for troubleshooting capability. The results for configuration and troubleshooting capability have been summarized in table 5.

Regarding the configuration capability, most of the tasks have been completed successfully. However, a self-configuration setup sequence is not yet available for the Asamap implementation. Given the complexity of the transition technologies, a guided self-configuring setup

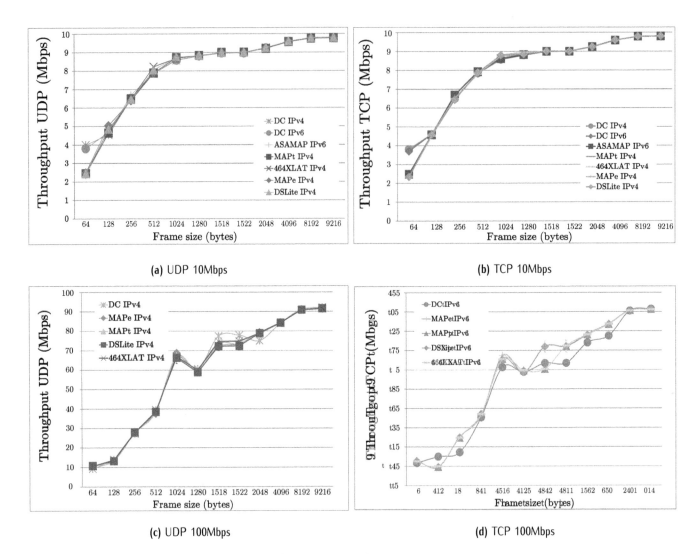

(a) UDP 10Mbps

(b) TCP 10Mbps

(c) UDP 100Mbps

(d) TCP 100Mbps

Figure 4. Throughput results

would be a beneficial feature. For the troubleshooting capability, most of the tasks have been completed successfully. Two of the troubleshooting tasks could not be completed: FaultDetermination3: Displaying critical messages with associated details and RCA3: self-check sequence. Regarding the first one, some critical messages were displayed in the user console. However these are hard to interpret and understand. We believe this feature needs improvement. As for the second one, a self-check sequence is not available yet. This would represent a substantial improvement of the troubleshooting capability.

In terms of applications capability, we tested a non-exhaustive list of common applications, in accordance with [14]. The full list of applications and the results are presented in table 6. To summarize we did not encounter any applications troubles for any of the four technologies.

5. Discussion

IPv6 transition scenarios and IPv6 transition technologies have already been known for some time to the Internet community. However the worldwide deployment rate of IPv6 is still very low. Given the complexity and the diversity of transition technologies, one of the biggest challenges is understanding which technology to use in a certain network scenario.

This article is proposing an answer to that challenge in the form of a network evaluation testbed, called IPv6NET. The contribution of this paper is the detailed testing methodology associated with IPv6NET and the empirical feasibility results, which to the best of our knowledge represent a first in current literature.

Analyzing the empirical results we found that one transition technology is *more feasible* than the rest,

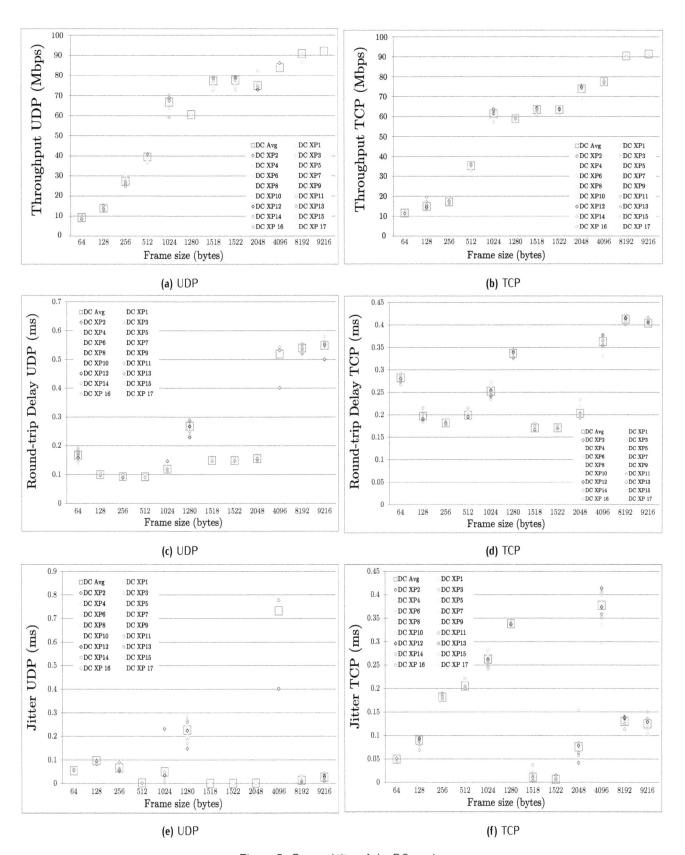

Figure 5. Repeatability of the DC results

Table 5. Operational capability results

Operational Capability		Asamap			
		MAPe	MAPt	464XLAT	DSLite
Configuration Capability	IinitialSetup1	Pass	Pass	Pass	Pass
	IinitialSetup2	Pass	Pass	Pass	Pass
	IinitialSetup3	Fail	Fail	Fail	Fail
	IinitialSetup4	Pass	Pass	Pass	Pass
	IinitialSetup5	Pass	Pass	Pass	Pass
	InitialSetup6	Pass	Pass	Pass	Pass
	Reconfiguration1	Pass	Pass	Pass	Pass
	Reconfiguration2	Pass	Pass	Pass	Pass
	Confirmation1	Pass	Pass	Pass	Pass
	Confirmation2	Pass	Pass	Pass	Pass
Configuration capability result		9/10 = 0.9	9/10 = 0.9	9/10 = 0.9	9/10 = 0.9
Troubleshooting Capability	FaultIsolation1	Pass	Pass	Pass	Pass
	FaultIsolation2	Pass	Pass	Pass	Pass
	FaultDetermination1	Pass	Pass	Pass	Pass
	FaultDetermination2	Pass	Pass	Pass	Pass
	FaultDetermination3	Fail	Fail	Fail	Fail
	RCA1	Pass	Pass	Pass	Pass
	RCA2	Pass	Pass	Pass	Pass
	RCA3	Fail	Fail	Fail	Fail
	RCA4	Pass	Pass	Pass	Pass
	RCA5	Pass	Pass	Pass	Pass
Troubleshooting capability result		8/10 = 0.8	8/10 = 0.8	8/10 = 0.8	8/10 = 0.8

Table 6. Applications capability results

Applications			Asamap			
			MAPe	MAPt	464XLAT	DSLite
Win 7 / Win 8 / Ubuntu 12.04 / Android 2.3	Browsing	Chrome	Pass	Pass	Pass	Pass
		Firefox	Pass	Pass	Pass	Pass
		Dolphin	Pass	Pass	Pass	Pass
	E-mail	Outlook	Pass	Pass	Pass	Pass
		Thunderbird	Pass	Pass	Pass	Pass
		Aquamail	Pass	Pass	Pass	Pass
	IM&VoIP	Skype	Pass	Pass	Pass	Pass
		Facebook	Pass	Pass	Pass	Pass
		Google+	Pass	Pass	Pass	Pass
		VoIP Buster	Pass	Pass	Pass	Pass
		Viber	Pass	Pass	Pass	Pass
		DigiOriunde	Pass	Pass	Pass	Pass
	VPN	OpenVPN	Pass	Pass	Pass	Pass
		Spotflux	Pass	Pass	Pass	Pass
	Cloud	Dropbox	Pass	Pass	Pass	Pass
		GDrive	Pass	Pass	Pass	Pass
	FTP	Filezilla	Pass	Pass	Pass	Pass
	Troubleshooting	puTTY	Pass	Pass	Pass	Pass
		WinSCP	Pass	Pass	Pass	Pass
		ConnectBot	Pass	Pass	Pass	Pass
Applications capability result			20/20 = 1	20/20 = 1	20/20 = 1	20/20 = 1

namely *MAPe*. We have also identified possible performance trends in IPv6 transition technologies benchmarking, for example, encapsulation-based technologies seem to have better throughput performance and translation-based technologies better latency performance. However, we must note that the empirical results are highly dependent on the quality of the implementation. In other words, the same transition technology can perform differently under different implementations. This is why we decided to test the IPv6 transition technologies on a per-implementation basis.

We were also able to point out some *unexpected behaviors*, which could have been overlooked if simulators or analytical tools are employed. This underlines the need for a testbed and gives us motivation for a further root cause analysis. The high repeatability results indicate that the methodology is also easy to replicate on systems with the same hardware and software characteristics.

A limitation of this method is represented by the lack of control data, given there is no similar alternative system to act as a comparison base for the empirical results. We are planning to solve this by comparing the current open-source-based measurement system with existing commercial network benchmarking tools.

The empirical results can serve as a direct guideline to enterprise network operators faced with a similar transition scenario. Many enterprise networks nowadays include industrial segments, which in many cases run over IP networks. The performance and operational aspects of the underlaying networks can have a critical impact on industrial applications. In this context, the guidelines and empirical data can serve as a rough impact analysis of the IPv6 transition on the industrial network segments.

Another limitation of this approach is represented by the diversity and complexity of existing production networks by comparison with the presented scenario. However by using the detailed methodology any interested party could potentially implement it and obtain customized feasibility data. The methodology can also serve as guideline for other researchers interested in joining this effort. Coping with a large number of technologies and their future developments may very well be solved by research collaboration, which can transform this project in an exhaustive IPv6 transition resource.

6. Conclusion

In this article we have introduced IPv6NET, a project aiming to empirically analyze the feasibility of IPv6 transition technologies in relation with specific network scenarios. From the methodology standpoint, IPv6NET combines two types of testing environments: closed environments for thorough network performance data, and open environments for operational data. By using the proposed IPv6NET and the associated methodology we were able to indicate MAPe as having the best network performance, followed closely by DSLite, MAPt and 464XLAT. We were also able to identify some performance general guidelines, e.g. for latency, the translation-based technologies (464XLAT, MAPt) had a better performance. For throughput, the results were in favor of encapsulation-based technologies (MAPe, DSLite). However, we must note that the empirical results are highly dependent on the quality of the used implementation. Consequently, this results should be interpreted in association with the Asamap implementation.

Some of the empirical results also pointed out *unexpected behaviors*, which further underline the need for a testbed. By replicating the experiments 17 times, on 68 different nodes, we have shown that the proposed methodology has a a high level of repeatability. In terms of operational capability, we have proposed a task-based methodology. However, the data we have so far is limited to our experiences. As a future plan, we would like to replicate the proposed system and the associated methodology, and organize a survey with people of different network operating skills. Also as future work, we intend to increase the scale of the network template, and propose an associated metric for scalability. Another future step is proposing a unique general feasibility indicator (GFI), associated with each transition technology, which would help to better centralize and compare the the results.

Acknowledgments

The authors would like to thank Mr. Masakazu Asama for providing the vyatta Asamap distribution, upon which the experimental networks were implemented. Special thanks should be given to the teams at NICT StarBED and WIDE Project for their continuous support.

Appendix A. Configuration capability tasks

For the Asamap vyatta implementation the tasks were:

1. IinitialSetup1: Please input the following commands in the console:

```
configure
set interfaces map map0 br-address
'2001:200:16a:2109::a/64'
set interfaces map map0 default-
forwarding-mode 'encapsulation'
set interfaces map map0 default-
forwarding-rule 'true'
set interfaces map map0 ipv6-fragment-
size '1500'
set interfaces map map0 ipv4-fragment-
inner false
set interfaces map map0 role 'br'
set interfaces map map0 rule 1 ea-length
'8'
set interfaces map map0 rule 1 ipv4-
prefix '163.221.135.16/28'
set interfaces map map0 rule 1 ipv6-
prefix '2001:200:16a:2100::/56'
commit
exit
```

These commands should create a new 464 virtual interface called map0. To check the existence of the map0 interface please input the following command:

```
show interfaces detail
```

The command should display details about all interfaces, including the map0 interface. Was the map0 interface created successfully ?

☐ Yes

☐ No

2. InitialSetup2: Please input the following commands in the console:

```
configure
save
```

The command should have saved the temporary configuration which should be loaded at start-up.

Reboot the machine by typing in the console the command:

```
sudo reboot
```

To check that the setup of the map0 interface was saved use again:

```
show interfaces
```

Was the configuration saved successfully ?

☐ Yes

☐ No

3. InitialSetup3: The non-existence of a self-configuration command can be verified by pressing the *Tab* key while using the console. It should display the existing commands. To check also the configuration mode we must enter it by typing:

```
configure
```

and pressing again the *Tab* key. Is there any self-configuration command available:

☐ Yes

☐ No

4. InitialSetup4: Please input the following command:

```
shw interfaces
```

The console should display a message warning the user that the command is invalid and should discard it. Was the warning displayed and the command discarded ?

☐ Yes

☐ No

5. InitialSetup5: Please input the following commands:

```
configure
set interfaces map map1 default-
forwarding-mode 'encapsulation' set
interfaces map map1 default-forwarding-
rule 'true'
```

The console should accept the commands, as they are formally correct. However after trying to commit the temporary configuration:

```
commit
```

the console should display a message warning that additional configuration details are needed and discarding the action. Was a warning message displayed and the commit action discarded ?

☐ Yes

☐ No

6. InitialSetup6: While typing the command:

```
set interfaces ethernet eth0 address
```

press the *Tab* key.

The console should display information about possible completions for the command or contextual help. Was the contextual help displayed in the console ?

☐ Yes

☐ No

7. Reconfiguration1: Input the following command:

```
show configuration commands
```

The console should display all commands needed to rebuild the current configuration. Was the set of commands displayed?

☐ Yes

☐ No

8. Reconfiguration2: Input the following commands:

```
configure
save backup.config
```

The console should display a message confirming the current was saved and showing the location of the back-up file. To restore the configuration type:

```
load backup.config
```

A message confirming the configuration file was loaded successfully should be displayed.

Were the back-up and restore actions successful ?

☐ Yes

☐ No

9. Confirmation1: Type the command:

```
show configuration
```

The console should display the detailed configuration. Was the detailed configuration displayed ?

☐ Yes

☐ No

10. Confirmation2: Type the command:

```
show interface map map0
```

The console should display the details of the previously configured map0 interface. Was the detailed configuration of the map0 interface displayed ?

☐ Yes

☐ No

Appendix B. Troubleshooting capability tasks

The troubleshooting capability test of the Asamap vyatta implementation contained the following tasks.

1. FaultIsolation1: Type the command:

```
sudo tcpdump -i map0
```

The console should display in a human readable form IPv4 and IPv6 packets captured on the map0 interface. Were there analyzed packets displayed ?

☐ Yes

☐ No

2. FaultIsolation2: Type the command:

```
ping 192.168.255.1
```

The console should display statistics about the round-trip ICMPv4 packet exchange with the host identified with the IPv4 address 192.168.255.1 .

Type the command:

```
ping 2001:200:16a:2101::2
```

The console should display statistics about the round-trip ICMPv6 packet exchange with the host identified with the IPv6 address 2001:200:16a:2101::2 .

☐ Yes

☐ No

3. FaultDetermination1: Type the command:

```
show ipv6 route
show ip route
```

The console should display the IPv4 and IPv6 routing details. This information should be able to help identify a misconfigured IPv4 or IPv6 route. Were the routing details displayed ?

☐ Yes

☐ No

4. FaultDetermination2: Input the command:

```
show interface map map0
show interface map map0 rule
```

The console should display detailed information about the map0 interface and the mapping rule it employs. The information should help identify a misconfigured line of the 464 virtual interface, map0. Was the information displayed ?

☐ Yes

☐ No

5. FaultDetermination3: The non-existence of a self-troubleshooting command can be verified by pressing the *Tab* key while using the console. It should display the existing commands. To check also the configuration mode we must enter it first by typing:

```
configure
```

and pressing again the *Tab* key. Is there any self-troubleshooting command available:

☐ Yes

☐ No

6. RCA1 and RCA2: Type the commands:

```
show log all | tail
show log all
```

The first command should confirm that error and warning messages are being logged. The second command should confirm all log information can be displayed. Were the log information displayed ?

☐ Yes

☐ No

7. RCA3: Create a critical event by intentionally failing to login on a parallel console. The critical events should be displayed in the current console with contextual details. Was any information displayed about these events ?

☐ Yes

☐ No

8. RCA4 and RCA5: Type the command:

```
show interfaces detail
```

The command should confirm that statistical network information are being logged and can be displayed. Were the network statistics displayed ?

☐ Yes

☐ No

References

[1] APNIC, "IPv6 measurements for The World," Apr. 2014.

[2] M. Lind, V. Ksinant, S. Park, A. Baudot, and P. Savola, "Scenarios and Analysis for Introducing IPv6 into ISP Networks." RFC 4029 (Informational), Mar. 2005.

[3] J. Bound, "IPv6 Enterprise Network Scenarios." RFC 4057 (Informational), June 2005.

[4] J. Wiljakka, "Analysis on IPv6 Transition in Third Generation Partnership Project (3GPP) Networks." RFC 4215 (Informational), Oct. 2005.

[5] C. Huitema, R. Austein, S. Satapati, and R. van der Pol, "Unmanaged Networks IPv6 Transition Scenarios." RFC 3750 (Informational), Apr. 2004.

[6] I. Raicu and S. Zeadally, "Evaluating ipv4 to ipv6 transition mechanisms," *IEEE International Conference on Telecommunications 2003*, 2003.

[7] S. Narayan, P. Shang, and N. Fan, "Network performance evaluation of internet protocols ipv4 and ipv6 on operating systems," in *Proceedings of the Sixth international conference on Wireless and Optical Communications Networks*, WOCN'09, (Piscataway, NJ, USA), pp. 242–246, IEEE Press, 2009.

[8] S. Sasanus and K. Kaemarungsi, "Differences in bandwidth requirements of various applications due to ipv6 migration," in *Proceedings of the The International Conference on Information Network 2012*, ICOIN '12, (Washington, DC, USA), pp. 462–467, IEEE Computer Society, 2012.

[9] P. Grayeli, S. Sarkani, and T. Mazzuchi, "Performance analysis of ipv6 transition mechanisms over mpls," *International Journal of Communication Networks and Information Security*, vol. 4, no. 2, 2012.

[10] G. Lencse and S. Repas, "Performance analysis and comparison of different dns64 implementations for linux, openbsd and freebsd," in *Proceedings of the 2013 IEEE 27th International Conference on Advanced Information Networking and Applications*, AINA '13, (Washington, DC, USA), pp. 877–884, IEEE Computer Society, 2013.

[11] P. Wu, Y. Cui, J. Wu, J. Liu, and C. Metz, "Transition from ipv4 to ipv6: A state-of-the-art survey," *IEEE Communications Surveys and Tutorials*, vol. 15, no. 3, pp. 1407–1424, 2013.

[12] R. Hiromi and H. Yoshifuji, "Problems on ipv4-ipv6 network transition," in *Proceedings of the International Symposium on Applications on Internet Workshops*, SAINT-W '06, (Washington, DC, USA), pp. 38–42, IEEE Computer Society, 2006.

[13] H. Babiker, I. Nikolova, and K. K. Chittimaneni, "Deploying ipv6 in the google enterprise network lessons learned," in *Proceedings of the 25th international conference on Large Installation System Administration*, LISA'11, (Berkeley, CA, USA), pp. 10–10, USENIX Association, 2011.

[14] J. Arkko and A. Keranen, "Experiences from an IPv6-Only Network." RFC 6586 (Informational), Apr. 2012.

[15] H. Hazeyama, R. Hiromi, T. Ishihara, and O. Nakamura, *Experiences from IPv6-Only Networks with Transition Technologies in the WIDE Camp Spring 2012*, Mar 2012. draft-hazeyama-widecamp-ipv6-only-experience-01.txt.

[16] O. Troan, W. Dec, X. Li, C. Bao, S. Matsushima, T. Murakami, and T. Taylor, "Mapping of Address and Port with Encapsulation (MAP)." draft-ietf-softwire-map-08, Aug. 2013.

[17] X. Li, C. Bao, W. Dec, O. Troan, S. Matsushima, and T. Murakami, "Mapping of Address and Port using Translation (MAP-T)." draft-ietf-softwire-map-t-04, Sept. 2013.

[18] A. Durand, R. Droms, J. Woodyatt, and Y. Lee, "Dual-Stack Lite Broadband Deployments Following IPv4 Exhaustion." RFC 6333 (Proposed Standard), Aug. 2011.

[19] M. Mawatari, M. Kawashima, and C. Byrne, "464XLAT: Combination of Stateful and Stateless Translation." RFC 6877, Apr. 2013.

[20] N. Matsuhira, " Stateless Automatic IPv4 over IPv6 Encapsulation / Decapsulation." draft-matsuhira-sa46t-spec-07, July 2013.

[21] M. Asama, "MAP supported Vyatta. Online available: http://enog.jp/ masakazu/vyatta/map/," Mar. 2014.

[22] T. Miyachi, K. Chinen, and Y. Shinoda, "Starbed and springos: large-scale general purpose network testbed and supporting software," in *Proceedings of the 1st international conference on Performance evaluation methodolgies and tools*, valuetools '06, (New York, NY, USA), ACM, 2006.

[23] A. Botta, A. Dainotti, and A. Pescapè, "A tool for the generation of realistic network workload for emerging networking scenarios," *Computer Networks*, vol. 56, no. 15, pp. 3531–3547, 2012.

[24] C. Popoviciu, A. Hamza, G. V. de Velde, and D. Dugatkin, "Ipv6 benchmarking methodology for network interconnect devices," 2008.

[25] S. Bradner and J. McQuaid, "Benchmarking methodology for network interconnect devices," 1999.

[26] M. Georgescu, H. Hazeyama, Y. Kadobayashi, S. Yamaguchi, "An empirical study of IPv6 transition in an open environment - experiences from WIDE camp's Life with IPv6 Workshop," in *The Fourteenth Workshop on Internet Technology*, June 2013.

[27] D. Harrington, "Guidelines for Considering Operations and Management of New Protocols and Protocol Extensions." RFC 5706 (Informational), Nov. 2009.

6

How to Make Business Processes "Socialize"?

Zakaria Maamar[1,*], Noura Faci[2], Ejub Kajan[3], Sherif Sakr[4], Mohamed Boukhebouze[5], and Ahmed Barnawi[6]

[1]Zayed University, Dubai, U.A.E
[2]Claude Bernard Lyon 1 University, Lyon, France
[3]State University of Novi Pazar, Novi Pazar, Serbia
[4]University of New South Wales, Sydney, Australia & King Saud bin Abdulaziz University for Health Sciences, Riyadh, Saudi Arabia
[5]CETIC, Charleroi, Belgium
[6]King Abdulaziz University, Jeddah, Saudi Arabia

Abstract

This paper presents an approach that builds upon social computing principles to make business processes "socialize". First the approach identifies the main components of a business process that are task, person, and machine. A task is a work unit that forms with other tasks a business process and that a person and/or machine execute. Afterwards the approach enriches a business process with details captured from the (execution and social) relations that connect tasks together, persons together, and machines together. While execution relations are widely reported in the literature, there is a growing interest in studying the role of social relations in business processes. The approach uses social relations to build configuration network of tasks, social network of persons, and support network of machines. These networks capture the ongoing interactions that arise when business processes are executed. A system illustrating how these networks are developed is also demonstrated in the paper.

Keywords: Business process; Machine; Network; Person; Social relation; Task.

1. Introduction

Social software, exemplified by Web 2.0 applications like social networks, Wikis, and blogs, has forced companies to review their ways of doing business. Many, if not all, companies have an online social presence so they can reach out to more customers, open up new communication channels with stakeholders, and also, showcase their embracement of the latest IT advances and gadgets [1]. Many companies recognize the need of rethinking their strategies and reevaluating their operation models as the world is getting more "social" [2].

Despite the Web 2.0 "fever", a recent study by Gartner reveals that "...many large companies are embracing internal social networks, but for the most part, they're not getting much from them" [3]. Social software does not work like an enterprise resource planning application where procedures are defined and employees are told to comply with these procedures. Employees' commitments (also participation in[1]) are critical to the success of social software, i.e., employees must opt-in rather than be forced [5]. On top of employees' commitments we argue that other elements contribute to this success, for instance (i) establishing guidelines and techniques to assist IT practitioners integrate social elements into business processes and (ii) demonstrating the social software's benefits through tangible results (e.g., number of new customers attracted because of a Facebook campaign).

---

*Corresponding author. Email: zakaria.maamar@zu.ac.ae

---

[1]Four factors drive user motivations to community contribution [4]: expectation of help in return, increase in positive reputation, sense of efficiency, and commitment to the community.

According to Gartner narrowing down the social-software view to social networks, only does not shed the light on other systems like business process management systems that exhibit some social aspects [2]. Various interactions take place during the execution of business processes, so we map some of these interactions onto specific social relations between these processes' components. We refer to these components as task, machine, and person. Indeed tasks are put together to form processes, persons collaborate together on complex tasks, and machines replace each other in the case of failure, are examples of social relations that business process management systems exhibit and hence, can be captured. While we acknowledge that tasks and machines cannot "socialize" (in the strict sense), combining tasks together and machines together presents some similarities with how people behave daily. Different initiatives already demonstrate the successful blend of social software with many disciplines such as learning [6], healthcare [7], and commerce [8]. Supporting our proposal of socializing tasks and machines, Tan et al. state that *"Currently, most social networks connect people or groups who expose similar interests or features. In the near future, we expect that such networks will connect **other entities, such as software components, Web-based services, data resources, and workflows**. More importantly, the interactions among people and nonhuman artifacts have significantly enhanced data scientists' productivity"* [9].

Our contributions in this paper include

1. Definition and specification of a set of social (execution as well) relations that permit to connect tasks together, persons together, and machines together in a business process;

2. Development of a set of networks built upon social relations; these networks are referred to as configuration for tasks, support for machines, and social for persons.

3. Demonstration through a proof-of-concept of configuration, support, and social networks development.

4. Brief discussion of the role of configuration, support, and social networks in addressing some issues that hinder business process execution.

The remainder of this paper is organized as follows. Section 2 is an overview of social software. A case study is presented in Section 3. Section 4 introduces the approach to manage social business processes. Prior to concluding in Section 6, a prototype system is discussed in Section 5.

2. Overview of social software

We report on what social software refers to and then, on some initiatives that blend social software with business processes. Dustdar and Bhattacharya stress out *"the huge gap between business process management technologies, usage patterns, and workflows on the one hand, and social computing as it is known today"* [10].

In the literature there is not a common definition of social software. Warr states that *"social software includes a large number of tools used for online communication, e.g., instant messaging, text chat, internet fora, weblogs, Wikis, social network services, social guides, social bookmarking, social citations, social libraries, and virtual worlds"* [11]. For Schmidt and Nurcan, social software supports productivity by raising the level and scope of interactions because of the use of computers and networks [12]. Erol et al. note that the roots of social software can be traced back to the 40s and add that *"impressive results are created without a central plan or organization. Instead, social software uses a self-organization and bottom-up approach where interaction is coordinated by the "collective intelligence" of the individuals; the latter does not necessarily know each other and are a priori not organized in a hierarchy. Furthermore, social software follows a rather egalitarian approach; decisions are not made by small elites but by combining a multitude of inputs from different users"* [13]. For Liptchinsky et al., social software *"fosters collaboration of individuals who work across time, space, cultural, and organizational boundaries"* [14]. People engage in conversations and transactions so that common deliverables are produced promptly and with minimum of conflicts. Finally, Bruno et al. identify the four characteristics of social software [15]: (*i*) weak ties are spontaneously established contacts creating new views on problems and allowing competency combination, (*ii*) social production breaks with the paradigm of centralized a-priori planning of production and promotes unforeseen and innovative contributors and contributions, (*iii*) egalitarianism abolishes hierarchical structures, merges the roles of contributors and consumers, and introduces a culture of trust, and (*iv*) mutual service provisioning changes the cooperation model from a client-server model to a model based on exchanging services.

The blend of social software with business processes is reported throughout the literature. In [16], Rito Silva et al. describe the AGILIPO project that embeds social features into business process tools. The AGILIPO modeling and execution environment includes three roles known as executor, modeler, and developer that stakeholders take over. Executor carries out business processes either by making use of specified activities or by creating generic activities whenever the specified activities are not sufficient. Modeler changes the business process model by specifying new non-automated activities. Finally developer may consider automating the non-automated activities. To foster collaboration between these stakeholders, social software features such as tagging, versioning, comments, and rating are adopted. In [17], Brambilla et al. propose a specific notation to design social business processes. Social networking helps organizations harness the value of information relations and weak ties without compromising the consolidated business practices that are found in conventional business process management solutions. Despite these benefits there is a lack of appropriate notations that can be used to reflect social aspects on business process models. Brambilla et al.'s notation includes event and task types like broadcast, posting, and invitation to activity. In [18], Koschmider et al. demonstrate how social networks help enhance trust between users. Two networks are built upon a set of business processes and recommendations. The first network provides an organizational view of business processes by suggesting for instance, the average distance between performers who participated in existing business processes and those who are now participating in developing business processes. The second network shows the relations among modelers who use the recommendation system to build the business process model. In [19], Grim-Yefsah et al. reveal the existence of informal networks that people at work rely on to conduct their business. These networks perfectly coexist with regular networks where formal relations like supervision are reported. Grim-Yefsah et al. discuss how the "official" executor of a task informally seeks other persons' help in the organization known as contributors. The help takes different forms like asking for advices or confirming technical details. The informal networks back the work of regular networks and do not compete with them.

The aforementioned initiatives on blending social software with business processes develop different solutions such as tagging business processes, using social networks to enhance trust, and mixing formal and informal networks. However what social relations connect a business process's components, how business processes are adjusted in response to these relations, and what benefits these relations offer to companies, are left unanswered. In this paper we address the first question by showing how to connect tasks together, machines together, and persons together using social relations.

3. Case study

Our case study refers to the electronic-patient-folder system at Anderson Hospital that handles approximately 6000 annual inpatient admissions[2]. We leverage this system to identify first, some business processes' components (i.e., tasks, persons and machines) and second, the execution nature of some tasks. When a patient shows up at the hospital, the necessary documentation is scanned into a system known as ImageNow. Upon completion the patient's MEDITECH record is updated automatically. An advantage of this update is that different stakeholders like billing staff, coders, and other authorized people have immediate, electronic access to the necessary information instead of waiting for the paper documentation to arrive. Prior to implementing the new system Anderson Hospital faced different challenges such as paper records limit access to one user at a time and paper and manual processes hamper compliance with some healthcare standards.

We use this case study to shed the light on the social dimension of business processes by establishing relations between tasks, between machines, and between persons. It is common that events "disturb" the normal completion of business processes due to call-in-sick doctors, last-minute changes in surgery dates, appointment system failure, etc. When dealing with these events we would like to assist the hospital's managers in considering doctors' recommendations when looking for substitutes, interchanging tasks to avoid policy violation, and identifying machines based on their coupling level. These are some of the benefits that networks build upon relations between tasks, between machines, and between persons will provide to these managers.

4. Our approach to social business processes

We recall that a business process is "a set of logically related tasks performed to achieve a defined business outcome" [20]. We also recall that the execution of some processes is strictly confined into the borders of single units (e.g., finance department), while the execution of others crosses several independent units raising security, privacy, heterogeneity, and monitoring concerns among IT practitioners and end-users as well [21].

4.1. Overview

Our approach fosters the intertwining of the three components of a business process that are task, person, and machine (Fig. 1). The success of this intertwining depends on (i) identifying execution and

[2]http://www.perceptivesoftware.com/pdfs/casestudies/psi_cs_anderson.pdf

social relations between tasks (*t*), between executors (i.e., persons (*p*) and machines (*m*)), and between tasks and executors; and (*ii*) developing categories of networks upon these relations as per the characteristics of each component. These two points are thoroughly discussed in Sections 4.2 and 4.3, respectively.

Fig. 1 illustrates an example of business process for Anderson Hospital case-study. It includes multiple tasks such as t_1: scan documentation, t_2: update records, and t_i: prepare bill. Tasks connect to each other through input and output dependencies, e.g., patient's data from t_1 are sent to t_2 so that patient records are updated. However these dependencies are primarily meant for data exchange and thus, do not help much in enriching a business process with any social element nor in shedding the light on the potential social relations between this process's components. Fig. 1 also shows the execution nature of tasks. Some tasks are completely manual (p_j: cashier executing t_i) while others are either completely automated (m_2: ImageNow executing t_2) or semi-automated/semi-manual (p_1/m_1: operator/scanner taking turns in executing t_1).

In preparation for exposing the social dimension of business processes, we associate task with *requirements* (e.g., t_2: update records must be done within one hour of scan receipt), person with *capacities* (e.g., p_1: operate scanner), and machine with *capacities* as well (e.g., m_1: produce high-resolution scan). Requirements impose restrictions on those who will execute tasks in terms of execution nature (e.g., manual), necessary expertise level for persons, reliability level for machines, simultaneous involvement of persons and machines, etc. In addition to requirements we label task as *self-contained* when its output does not require any additional processing by another task. Additional elements that make a task self-contained are discussed in [22]. Encrypt data is an example of not-self-contained task since decrypting data for proper use is required at a later stage. Unless stated a task is by default self-contained. Task assignment to executors depends on matching requirements to capacities. However the matching does not fall into this paper's scope.

4.2. Relation identification

We identify relations between tasks, between persons, and between machines from two perspectives: Execution ($\mathcal{E}$) and Social ($\mathcal{S}$). *As stated earlier making tasks and machines "socialize" is backed by first, the relations between tasks and between machines that map perfectly onto relations between persons and second, Roush's statement that computing means connecting* [23]. We exemplify the proposed social and execution relations by the case study. It is worth noting that some relations between persons are appropriate for machines and

vice-versa. This is primarily due to the semantics of these relations.

Relations between tasks. From an $\mathcal{E}$ perspective, execution relations (*aka* dependencies) between tasks are well defined in the literature [24] such as, *prerequisite* (e.g., t_1 and t_2), *parallel prerequisite* (e.g., t_2 and t_k: synchronize patient records), and *parallel* (e.g., t_i and t_j: check pending bills). To deal with not self-contained tasks, we propose *completion* as an additional execution relation between tasks (e.g., compress scan prior to archiving and then decompress scan upon request); t_i and t_j engage in a completion relation when t_i is not self-contained and needs t_j to process its output (e.g., compress and decompress).

From a $\mathcal{S}$ perspective, we propose two social relations:

- *Interchange*: t_i and t_j engage in an interchange relation when both produce similar output with respect to similar input received for processing and their requirements do not overlap (e.g., t_1 and t_1': enter patient details manually in the case the scanner is down). The non-overlap condition is necessary to avoid blockage when t_i's requirements (e.g., online data entry) cannot be met due to lack of executors and thus, t_i needs to be interchanged with t_j that has different requirements (e.g., offline data entry). In terms of benefits, interchange indicates how difficult a task's requirements are satisfied if the task is constantly replaced and what tasks are frequently used as replacements.

- *Coupling*: t_i and t_j engage in a coupling relation when they interact in the same business processes through one of the aforementioned execution relations (excluding completion). In terms of benefits, coupling indicates how strong or weak the connection between tasks is, which should help recommend tasks when putting business processes together at design time.

Relations between machines. In companies, machines (e.g., scanner and ImageNow) ensure the performance of automated and semi-automated tasks. Each machine (m_i) is overseen by a dedicated software component for management purposes, but this is outside this paper's scope. As stated earlier, matching capacities to requirements identifies the necessary machines that will execute tasks.

From an $\mathcal{E}$ perspective, we identify execution relations between m_i and m_j by analyzing Decker and Lesser's six coordination relations between tasks [25]. These relations are *enables, facilitates, cancels, constrains, inhibits,* and *causes,* and only two are considered as per our needs of connecting machines together to execute joint tasks: (*i*) *enablement* is established when m_i produces (internal) output that allows m_j to continue

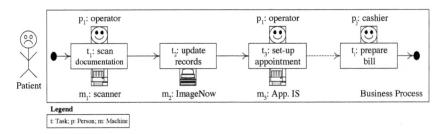

Figure 1. Business process's components

the execution of the task (e.g., t_x: do chest Xray requiring m_x: Xray machine to take Xrays and m_y: communication app. to send the doctor Xrays), and (*ii*) *inhibition* is established when m_j executes its part of the task after a certain time elapses since m_i completed the execution of its part (e.g., t_x: do blood test where the results are sent by email some time later after blood collection and analysis using specialized equipment). It is worth mentioning that defining execution relations between independent machines in charge of dependent tasks is not relevant for our work. The previous execution relations between tasks in the $\mathcal{E}$-perspective impose automatically an execution chronology on the machines.

From a $\mathcal{S}$ perspective, we consider three social relations:

- *Backup*: m_i (e.g., scanner in main reception) and m_j (e.g., 3-in-1 printer in nurse station) engage in a backup relation when both have similar capacities (subsumption relation between capacities can also be considered using ontology). In terms of benefits, backup indicates how reliable a machine is and what machines are frequently requested as backups.

- *Cooperation*: m_i and m_j engage in a cooperation relation when both are already engaged in a backup relation (because of similar capacities) and the simultaneous combination of their respective capacities is necessary to meet a task's requirements. In terms of benefits, cooperation indicates how often similar machines work together on executing tasks, which should help recommend machines when carrying out the matching. Though the machines are similar their collective performance might not correspond to the combination of their individual performances.

- *Partnership*: m_i and m_j engage in a partnership relation when their capacities are complementary and the simultaneous combination of their respective capacities is necessary to meet a task's requirements (e.g., t_x: analyze blood sample requiring different types of machines). In terms of

benefits, partnership indicates how often separate machines work together on tasks, which should help recommend machines when carrying out the matching. Since machines are different their collective performance needs to take into account the particularities of each in terms of individual performances and functional constraints, for example.

Relations between persons. In companies persons make decisions, trigger processes, exchange information, etc. As stated earlier, matching capacities to requirements identifies the necessary persons to execute tasks.

From an $\mathcal{E}$ perspective, we adopt the same execution relations for machines in order to connect p_i and p_j that are assigned joint tasks: (*i*) *enablement* is established when p_i performs other (internal) tasks whose completion allows p_j to continue the execution of the task (e.g., t_y: check patient requiring p_x: nurse to check patient's vitals and p_y: doctor to consult patient and provide medication), and (*ii*) *inhibition* is established when p_j executes her part of the task after a certain time elapses since p_i completed the execution of her part (e.g., t_y: perform surgery requiring p_x: anesthetist and p_y: surgeon who intervenes after the anesthetic becomes effective).

From a $\mathcal{S}$ perspective, we consider three social relations:

- *Substitution*: p_i (e.g., general practitioner in family medicine) and p_j (emergency physician in emergency department) engage in a substitution relation when both have similar capacities (subsumption relation between capacities can also be considered using ontology). In terms of benefits, substitution indicates how available a person is and what persons are frequent substitutes.

- *Delegation*: p_i and p_j engage in a delegation relation when both are already engaged in a substitution relation (in term of capacity assessment) and p_i decides to assign a task that she will execute or is now executing to p_j due to unexpected changes in her status, e.g., call-in-sick or situation of overload (e.g., emergency physician transfers patient to general practitioner due to the arrival of an urgent case). In terms of benefits, delegation indicates the transfer-of-work between persons, which could help identify the right persons next time unexpected events arise.

- *Peering*: p_i and p_j engage in a peering relation when both are in different organizational units and their respective similar (e.g., managerial) and complementary (e.g., expertise) capacities are necessary to a meet a task's requirements. In terms of benefits, peering fosters cross-organization activities and indicates how often persons work together on common tasks, which should help recommend persons when the matching of capacities to requirements occurs.

Table 1. Substitution *versus* delegation

Substitution(p_i,p_j)	Delegation(p_i,p_j)
p_i stops executing ongoing tasks; p_j executes these tasks	p_i continues executing other ongoing tasks; p_j executes tasks assigned by p_i
p_j reports to whom p_i reports upon task completion; otherwise p_j waits for p_i return	p_j reports to p_i upon task completion

Table 1 compares substitution to delegation in terms of who does what and who reports to whom. Table 2 summarizes the social relations between tasks, between machines, and between persons along with their respective pre-conditions, conditions, and post-conditions. Pre-condition defines the rationale of a social relation between a process's components. Condition indicates when a network built upon a social relation is used so that solutions to conflicts that prevent a business process completion are addressed. Finally post-condition indicates the successful resolution of these conflicts so that network use is stopped. In Table 2 the occurrence of multiple relations (e.g., backup and cooperation) between the components of the same process is not exclusive if these relations' pre-conditions are simultaneously satisfied.

4.3. Network categorization

The social relations presented earlier are used for developing specialized networks, i.e., one network per relation. We group these networks into three categories: configuration network of tasks, support network of machines, and social network of persons. In this part of the paper we analyze the nodes and edges per network category and evaluate the edges that connect nodes.

Configuration network of tasks. In a configuration network of tasks, node and edge correspond to task and relation between tasks, respectively. We analyze both task and relation from $\mathcal{E}$ and $\mathcal{S}$ perspectives. On the one hand the $\mathcal{E}$ perspective sets the stage for connecting tasks together in order to form business processes and assigning tasks to executors. On the other hand the $\mathcal{S}$ perspective sets the stage for building networks of tasks based on Table 2's relations (pre-condition satisfaction) as well as using these networks when necessary (condition satisfaction).

Task. In the $\mathcal{E}$ perspective, a task (t_i) is a concrete work unit (e.g., do blood test) that acts upon the environment. We define t_i as a 5-tuple $<\mathcal{E}\text{-}\mathrm{Req}_{t_i}$, $\mathcal{E}\text{-}\mathrm{Pre\text{-}Condition}_{t_i}$, $\mathcal{E}\text{-}\mathrm{Input/Output}_{t_i}$, $\mathcal{E}\text{-}\mathrm{Condition}_{t_i}$, $\mathcal{E}\text{-}\mathrm{Post\text{-}Condition}_{t_i}>$ where $\mathcal{E}\text{-}\mathrm{Req}_{t_i}$ is t_i's requirements, $\mathcal{E}\text{-}\mathrm{Pre\text{-}Condition}_{t_i}$ is a set of physical and logical elements to verify so that t_i is assigned to an executor (i.e., $\mathcal{E}\text{-}\mathrm{Req}_{t_i}$ is satisfied with respect to the executor's capacities), $\mathcal{E}\text{-}\mathrm{Input}_{t_i}$ and $\mathcal{E}\text{-}\mathrm{Output}_{t_i}$ identify, respectively, the data that t_i may need for execution and the data that t_i may produce after execution, $\mathcal{E}\text{-}\mathrm{Condition}_{t_i}$ is a set of physical and logical elements to verify so that t_i can be executed after successful assignment to an executor (e.g., all necessary inputs are available), and $\mathcal{E}\text{-}\mathrm{Post\text{-}Condition}_{t_i}$ is a set of physical and logical elements to verify so that the execution of t_i is declared either successful or failure. In the case of failure corrective actions are taken and vary from one case study to another.

In the $\mathcal{S}$ perspective, a task (t_i) is an abstract work unit (i.e., narrative description) that "signs up" in the interchange and/or coupling networks. We define t_i as a couple $1[<\mathcal{S}\text{-}\mathrm{Network}_{rel}$, $1[\mathcal{S}\text{-}\mathrm{Connect}_{rel}(t_j, w_j)]n>]2$ where $\mathcal{S}\text{-}\mathrm{Network}_{rel}$ is either interchange network or coupling network, $\mathcal{S}\text{-}\mathrm{Connect}_{rel}(t_j, w_j)$ lists all $t_{j=1\cdots n, j\neq i, t_j \in \mathcal{S}\text{-}\mathrm{Network}_{rel}}$ that are connected to t_i through rel, and w_j is the weight of the edge from t_i to t_j. Weight assessment is given a little bit later.

Relation. In the $\mathcal{E}$ perspective, a relation ($r_{(t_i,t_j)}$) establishes a concrete dependency between t_i and t_j at run time. A dependency can be either direct (i.e., t_j follows t_i) or indirect (i.e., because t_i is not self-contained, t_j is called whenever t_i's output needs to be processed). To handle task dependencies we decompose Input_t into either $\mathrm{initialInput}_t$ (i.e., submitted to t prior to execution) or $\mathrm{partialInput}_t$ (submitted to t during execution) and also decompose Output_t into either $\mathrm{partialOutput}_t$ (i.e., produced by t

Table 2. Summary of social relations

Between	Types	Pre-Conditions	Conditions	Post-Conditions
t_i, t_j	Coupling	t_i and t_i participated in joint business processes	review of business process design or concern over coupling level	business process design completion or coupling level satisfaction
	Interchange	t_i and t_j producing similar output in receipt of similar input	t_i lacking of executor who satisfies its requirements	executor found for t_j
m_i, m_j	Backup	m_i and m_j having similar capacities	m_i unexpected failure or concern over m_i reliability	backup/replacement machine found for m_i
	Cooperation	m_i and m_j having similar capacities	concern over machine collective performance	collective performance level satisfaction
	Partnership	m_i and m_j having complementary capacities	concern over machine collective performance	collective performance level satisfaction
p_i, p_j	Substitution[1]	p_i and p_j having similar capacities	p_i expected unavailability (e.g., annual leave and sick leave) or concern over p_i availability	substitute found for p_i
	Delegation	p_i and p_j having similar capacities	p_i unexpected unavailability (e.g., call-in-sick, urgent tasks to complete, and risk of overload)	delegate found for p_i
	Peering	p_i and p_j having similar or complementary capacities	concern over peering appropriateness	peer found for either p_i or p_j

[1] **Substitution example:** (t_1:scan documentation) and (t_1':enter patient details manually) are connected together in the substitution network since the interchange pre-condition is met, i.e., producing similar output (e.g., patient's healthcare provider) in receipt of similar input (e.g., patient's number). This network will be used when the interchange condition is met, which is scanner down so t_1 cannot be executed and replaced with t_1'. After identifying an executor for t_1' who is the agent at the reception, the use of this network is stopped since the interchange pre-condition is met.

during execution) or $finalOutput_t$ (i.e., produced by t at the end of execution). Unless stated Input and Output refer to initialInput and finalOutput, respectively. We define $r_{(t_i,t_j)}$ as a triple $<t_i$, t_j, $\mathcal{E}$-Type$>$ where $\mathcal{E}$-Type is either prerequisite dependency (i.e., t_i successful execution as per $\mathcal{E}$-Post-Condition$_{t_i}$ and $\mathcal{E}$-finalOutput$_{t_i}$ $\cap$ $\mathcal{E}$-initialInput$_{t_j}$ $\neq$ $\varnothing$), parallel-prerequisite dependency (i.e., $\mathcal{E}$-partialOutput$_{t_i}$ $\cap$ $\mathcal{E}$-initialInput$_{t_j}$ $\neq$ $\varnothing$), parallel dependency ($\mathcal{E}$-partialOutput$_{t_i}$ $\cap$ $\mathcal{E}$-partialInput$_{t_j}$ $\neq$ $\varnothing$, and $\mathcal{E}$-partialOutput$_{t_j}$ $\cap$ $\mathcal{E}$-partialInput$_{t_i}$ $\neq$ $\varnothing$), or completion relation ($\mathcal{E}$-Output$_{t_i}$ requires processing).

In the $\mathcal{S}$ perspective a relation ($r_{(t_i,t_j)}$) establishes a link between t_i and t_j both members of a network that is built upon this relation. We define $r_{(t_i,t_j)}$ as a 5-tuple $<t_i$, t_j, $\mathcal{S}$-Pre-Condition$_{(t_i,t_j)}$, $\mathcal{S}$-Condition$_{(t_i,t_j)}$, $\mathcal{S}$-Post-Condition$_{(t_i,t_j)}>$ where $\mathcal{S}$-Pre-Condition$_{(t_i,t_j)}$ is a set of physical and logical elements to verify so that t_i connects t_j (i.e., either ($\mathcal{E}$-Output$_{t_i}$ and $\mathcal{E}$-Output$_{t_j}$ are equivalent with respect to similar input received) or (t_i and t_j participate in joint business processes)), $\mathcal{S}$-Condition$_{(t_i,t_j)}$ is a set of physical and logical elements to verify so that the network associated with $r_{(t_i,t_j)}$ is used, and $\mathcal{S}$-Post-Condition$_{t_i,t_j}$ is a set of physical and logical elements to verify before the ongoing use of the network associated with $r_{(t_i,t_j)}$ is stopped (i.e., executor found for t_i, business process enrichment completion, or coupling level satisfaction).

Relation evaluation. Assessing the weight (w) of $r_{(t_i,t_j)}$ is restricted to the $\mathcal{S}$ perspective, only.

- *Interchange relation.* Equation 1 measures the weight of an interchange edge where $|interchange_{(t_i,t_j)}|$ is the number of times that t_i is interchanged successfully with t_j (i.e., an executor is found for t_j) and $|failure_{t_i}|$ is the number of times that t_i is not executed due to lack of executors. A higher combined interchange weight for a task (e.g., close to 1) indicates the excessive interchange of this task, which should be taken into account when implementing critical business processes.

$$w^{\mathcal{S}}_{interchange_{(t_i,t_j)}} = \frac{|interchange_{(t_i,t_j)}|}{|failure_{t_i}|} \quad (1)$$

- *Coupling relation.* Equation 2 measures the weight of a coupling edge where $|participateJointProcess_{(t_i,t_j)}|$ is the number of times that t_i is directly coupled with t_j in joint business processes and $|participateProcess_{t_i}|$ is the number of times that t_i participates in business processes. A higher coupling weight (e.g., close to 1) indicates the "smoothness" of exchanging data between tasks due to "limited" semantic mismatches.

$$w^{\mathcal{S}}_{coupling_{(t_i,t_j)}} = \frac{|participateJointProcess_{(t_i,t_j)}|}{|participateProcess_{t_i}|} \quad (2)$$

Support network of machines. In a support network of machines, node and edge correspond to machine and relation between machines, respectively. We analyze both from $\mathcal{E}$ and $\mathcal{S}$ perspectives. On the one hand the $\mathcal{E}$ perspective sets the stage for assisting machines schedule task execution and also initiating this execution. On the other hand the $\mathcal{S}$ perspective sets the stage for building networks of machines using the relations listed in Table 2 (pre-condition satisfaction) and also using these networks when needed (condition satisfaction).

Machine. In the $\mathcal{E}$ perspective, a machine (m_i) is a concrete processing unit (e.g., printer) that receives tasks (e.g., print out document) for execution after confirming that the machine's capacities meet these tasks' requirements, i.e., tasks' pre-conditions satisfied. Like with task we define m_i as a 5-tuple $<\mathcal{E}$-Cap$_{m_i}$, $\mathcal{E}$-Pre-Condition$_{m_i}$, $\mathcal{E}$-Input/Output$_{m_i}$, $\mathcal{E}$-Condition$_{m_i}$, $\mathcal{E}$-Post-Condition$_{m_i}>$ where $\mathcal{E}$-Cap$_{m_i}$ is m_i's capacities, $\mathcal{E}$-Pre-Condition$_{m_i}$ is a set of physical and logical elements to verify so that m_i schedules the execution of a task taking into account $\mathcal{E}$-Cap$_{m_i}$, $\mathcal{E}$-Input$_{m_i}$ and $\mathcal{E}$-Output$_{m_i}$ (optional) identify, respectively, the tasks that m_i receives for execution and the results (e.g., data and product) that m_i may produce after execution, $\mathcal{E}$-Condition$_{m_i}$ is a set of physical and logical elements to verify so that m_i begins executing a task (e.g., no pending tasks exist), and $\mathcal{E}$-Post-Condition$_{m_i}$ is a set of physical and logical elements to verify so that m_i detaches a task after execution and updates $\mathcal{E}$-Cap$_{m_i}$. The success or failure of this execution is dependent on the task's post-conditions.

In the $\mathcal{S}$ perspective, a machine (m_i) is an abstract processing unit (i.e., narrative description) that "signs up" in networks built upon the three possible social relations between machines. We define m_i as a couple $1[<S\text{-Network}_{rel}, 1[S\text{-Connect}_{rel}(m_j, w_j)]n>]3$ where $S\text{-Network}_{rel}$ is either backup network, cooperation network, or partnership network, $S\text{-Connect}_{rel}(m_j, w_j)$ lists all $m_{j=1\cdots n, j\neq i, m_j \in S\text{-Network}_{rel}}$ connected to m_i through rel, and w_j is the weight of the edge from m_i to m_j. Weight assessment is given a little bit later.

Relation. In the $\mathcal{E}$ perspective, a relation $(r_{(m_i,m_j)})$ establishes a link between two machines m_i and m_j both in charge of executing joint tasks. We define $r_{(m_i,m_j)}$ as a triple $<m_i, m_j, \mathcal{E}\text{-Type}>$ where $\mathcal{E}\text{-Type}$ is either enablement relation or inhibition relation.

In the S perspective, a relation $(r_{(m_i,m_j)})$ establishes a link between two machines m_i and m_j both members of a network built upon this relation. We define $r_{(m_i,m_j)}$ as a 5-tuple $<m_i, m_j, S\text{-Pre-Condition}_{m_i,m_j}, S\text{-Condition}_{m_i,m_j}, S\text{-Post-Condition}_{m_i,m_j}>$ where $S\text{-Pre-Condition}_{m_i,m_j}$ is a set of physical and logical elements to check so that m_i connects m_j (i.e., either ($\mathcal{E}\text{-Cap}_{m_i}$ and $\mathcal{E}\text{-Cap}_{m_j}$ are equivalent (m_i and m_j do the same job) or ($\mathcal{E}\text{-Cap}_{m_i}$ and $\mathcal{E}\text{-Cap}_{m_j}$ are simultaneously required)), $S\text{-Condition}_{(m_i,m_j)}$ is a set of physical and logical elements to verify so that the network associated with $r_{(m_i,m_j)}$ is used (i.e., either m_i fails unexpectedly, concern over m_i reliability, or concern over the collective performance of m_i and m_j), and $S\text{-Post-Condition}_{m_i,m_j}$ is a set of physical and logical elements to check before the ongoing use of the network associated with $r_{(m_i,m_j)}$ is stopped (i.e., backup/replacement machine found for m_i or satisfaction with collective performance of m_i and m_j).

Relation evaluation. Assessing the weight (w) of $r_{(m_i,m_j)}$ is restricted to the S perspective, only. In the following $\mathcal{T}_m$ is the set of all tasks assigned to m.

- *Backup relation.* Equation 3 measures the weight of a backup edge where $\mathcal{T}_{m_i}^{fail} \subseteq \mathcal{T}_{m_i}$ is the set of tasks that m_i failed to execute and $|replaceSuc_{\mathcal{T}_{m_i}^{fail},(m_i,m_j)}|$ is the number of failed tasks in $\mathcal{T}_{m_i}^{fail}$ that m_j completes successfully. A higher combined backup weight for a machine (e.g., close to 1) indicates its reliability, which should be taken into account prior to finalizing task assignments.

$$w_{backup(m_i,m_j)}^{S} = \frac{|replaceSuc_{\mathcal{T}_{m_i}^{fail},(m_i,m_j)}|}{|\mathcal{T}_{m_i}^{fail}|} \quad (3)$$

- *Cooperation relation.* Equation 4 measures the weight of a cooperation edge where $\mathcal{T}_{m_i}^{coop} \subseteq \mathcal{T}_{m_i}$ is the set of all tasks that m_i executes in cooperation with other machines and $|cooperateSuc_{(\mathcal{T}_{m_i}^{coop} \cap \mathcal{T}_{m_j}^{coop})(m_i,m_j)}|$ is the number of tasks in $\mathcal{T}_{m_i}^{coop} \cap \mathcal{T}_{m_j}^{coop}$ that m_i and m_j execute successfully together. A cooperation weight reveals the collective performance of similar machines executing joint tasks.

$$w_{cooperation(m_i,m_j)}^{S} = \frac{|cooperateSuc_{(\mathcal{T}_{m_i}^{coop} \cap \mathcal{T}_{m_j}^{coop})(m_i,m_j)}|}{|\mathcal{T}_{m_i}^{coop}|} \quad (4)$$

- *Partnership relation.* Equation 5 measures the weight of a partnership edge where $\mathcal{T}_{m_i}^{part} \subseteq \mathcal{T}_{m_i}$ is the set of all tasks that m_i executes in partnership with other machines and $|partnerSuc_{(\mathcal{T}_{m_i}^{part} \cap \mathcal{T}_{m_j}^{part}),(m_i,m_j)}|$ is the number of tasks in $\mathcal{T}_{m_i}^{part} \cap \mathcal{T}_{m_j}^{part}$ that m_i and m_j complete successfully together. A partnership weight reveals the collective performance of different machines executing joint tasks.

$$w_{partnership(m_i,m_j)}^{S} = \frac{|partnerSuc_{(\mathcal{T}_{m_i}^{part} \cap \mathcal{T}_{m_j}^{part}),(m_i,m_j)}|}{|\mathcal{T}_{m_i}^{part}|} \quad (5)$$

Social networks of persons. In a social network of persons, node and edge correspond to person and relation between persons, respectively. We analyze both from $\mathcal{E}$ and S perspectives. On the one hand the $\mathcal{E}$ perspective sets the stage for assisting persons plan task execution and also initiating this execution. On the other hand the S perspective sets the stage for building networks of persons using the relations listed in Table 2 (pre-condition satisfaction) and also using these networks when needed (condition satisfaction).

- **Person.** In the $\mathcal{E}$ perspective, a person (p_i) is a concrete "processing unit" (e.g., doctor) who receives tasks (e.g., check patient) for execution after confirming that the person's capacities meet these tasks' requirements, i.e., tasks' pre-conditions satisfied. Like with tasks and machines we define p_i as a 5-tuple $<\mathcal{E}\text{-Cap}_{p_i}, \mathcal{E}\text{-Pre-Condition}_{p_i}, \mathcal{E}\text{-Input/Output}_{p_i}, \mathcal{E}\text{-Condition}_{p_i}, \mathcal{E}\text{-Post-Condition}_{p_i}>$ where $\mathcal{E}\text{-Cap}_{p_i}$ is p_i's capacities, $\mathcal{E}\text{-Pre-Condition}_{p_i}$ is a set of physical and logical elements to verify so that p_i plans the execution of a task taking into account $\mathcal{E}\text{-Cap}_{p_i}$, $\mathcal{E}\text{-Input}_{p_i}$ and $\mathcal{E}\text{-Output}_{p_i}$ identify, respectively, the tasks that p_i receives for execution and the tasks/results that p_i might generate/produce after execution, $\mathcal{E}\text{-Condition}_{p_i}$ is a set of physical and logical elements to verify so that p_i begins executing a task (e.g., no-higher priority tasks exist), and $\mathcal{E}\text{-Post-Condition}_{p_i}$ is a set of physical and logical elements to verify so that p_i detaches a task after execution and updates $\mathcal{E}\text{-Cap}_{p_i}$. The success or failure of this execution is dependent on the task's post-conditions.

In the $\mathcal{S}$ perspective, a person (p_i) is an abstract "processing unit" (i.e., narrative description) who signs up in networks built upon the three possible relations between persons namely, substitution, delegation, or peering. We define p_i as a couple $1[<\mathcal{S}\text{-Network}_{rel}, 1[\mathcal{S}\text{-Connect}_{rel}(p_j, w_j)]n>]2$ where $\mathcal{S}\text{-Network}_{rel}$ is either substitution network, delegation network, or peering network, $\mathcal{S}\text{-Connect}_{rel}(p_j, w_j)$ lists all $p_{j=1 \cdots n, j \neq i, p_i \in \mathcal{S}\text{-Network}_{rel}}$ connected to p_i through rel, and w_j is the weight of the edge from p_i to p_j. Weight assessment is given a little bit later.

- **Relation.** In the $\mathcal{E}$ perspective, a relation $(r_{(p_i,p_j)})$ establishes a link between two persons p_i and p_j in charge of executing joint tasks. We define $r_{(p_i,p_j)}$ as a triple $<m_i, m_j, \mathcal{E}\text{-Type}>$ where $\mathcal{E}\text{-Type}$ is either enablement relation or inhibition relation.

In the $\mathcal{S}$ perspective, a relation $(r_{(p_i,p_j)})$ establishes a link between two persons p_i and p_j both members of a network built upon this relation. We define $r_{(p_i,p_j)}$ as a 5-tuple $<p_i, p_j, \mathcal{S}\text{-Pre-Condition}_{p_i,p_j}, \mathcal{S}\text{-Condition}_{p_i,p_j}, \mathcal{S}\text{-Post-Condition}_{p_i,p_j}>$ where $\mathcal{S}\text{-Pre-Condition}_{p_i,p_j}$ is a set of physical and logical elements to check so that p_i connects p_j (i.e., $\mathcal{E}\text{-Cap}_{p_i}$ and $\mathcal{E}\text{-Cap}_{p_j}$ are similar or complementary), $\mathcal{S}\text{-Condition}_{(p_i,p_j)}$ is a set of physical and logical elements to verify so that the network associated with $r_{(p_i,p_j)}$ is used (i.e., p_i is unavailable, concern over p_i or p_j availability, or concern over peering p_i and p_j together), and $\mathcal{S}\text{-Post-Condition}_{p_i,p_j}$ is a set of physical and logical elements to check before the ongoing use of the network associated with $r_{(p_i,p_j)}$ is stopped (i.e., substitute/delegate was identified for p_i or peer found for either p_i or p_j).

- **Relation evaluation.** Assessing the weight (w) of $r_{(p_i,p_j)}$ is restricted to the $\mathcal{S}$ perspective, only. In the following $\mathcal{T}_p$ is the set of tasks assigned to p.

- *Substitution relation.* Equation 6 measures the weight of a substitution edge where $\mathcal{T}_{p_i}^{sub} \subseteq \mathcal{T}_{p_i}$ is the set of all tasks assigned to p_i but then are assigned to a different person due to p_i expected unavailability and $|substituteSuc_{\mathcal{T}_{p_i}^{sub},(p_i,p_j)}|$ is the number of tasks in $\mathcal{T}_{p_i}^{sub}$ that p_j completes successfully. A higher combined substitution weight for a person (e.g., close to 1) indicates her availability, which should be taken into account prior to finalizing task assignment.

$$w^{\mathcal{S}}_{substitution_{(p_i,p_j)}} = \frac{|substituteSuc_{\mathcal{T}_{p_i}^{sub},(p_i,p_j)}|}{|\mathcal{T}_{p_i}^{sub}|} \quad (6)$$

- *Delegation relation.* Equation 7 measures the weight of a delegation edge where $\mathcal{T}_{p_i}^{del} \subseteq \mathcal{T}_{p_i}$ is the set of all tasks assigned to p_i but then are delegated to p_j due to her unexpected unavailability and $|delegateSuc_{\mathcal{T}_{p_i}^{del},(p_i,p_j)}|$ is the number of tasks in $\mathcal{T}_{p_i}^{del}$ that p_i delegates. A higher combined delegation weight for a person (e.g., close to 1) indicates her work-of-transfer level to other persons.

$$w^{\mathcal{S}}_{delegation_{(p_i,p_j)}} = \frac{|delegateSuc_{\mathcal{T}_{p_i}^{del},(p_i,p_j)}|}{|\mathcal{T}_{p_i}^{del}|} \quad (7)$$

- *Peering relation.* Equation 8 measures the weight of a peering edge where $\mathcal{T}_{p_i}^{peer} \subseteq \mathcal{T}_{p_i}$ is the set of all tasks that p_i executes with other peers and $|peeringSuc_{(\mathcal{T}_{p_i} \cap \mathcal{T}_{p_j}^{peer}),(p_i,p_j)}|$ is the number of tasks assigned to p_i and p_j that both complete successfully together in different business processes. A higher combined peering weight for a person (e.g., close to 1) reveals the appropriateness of having this person execute joint tasks with other persons.

$$w^{\mathcal{S}}_{peering_{(p_i,p_j)}} = \frac{|peerSuc_{(\mathcal{T}_{p_i} \cap \mathcal{T}_{p_j}^{peer}),(p_i,p_j)}|}{|\mathcal{T}_{p_i}^{peers}|} \quad (8)$$

4.4. Role of networks in addressing conflicts

In [26] we detail the role of the networks in addressing conflicts that hinder BP execution. This role refers to BP social coordination that includes four steps: categorize resources that tasks require for their execution, define how tasks/machines/persons of a BP bind to resources during this execution, categorize conflicts on resources that arise between tasks, between machines, and between persons, and finally analyze the appropriateness of certain networks of tasks/persons/machines for addressing these conflicts.

First we categorize resources into (i) logical, i.e., their use/consumption does not lead into a decrease in their reliability/availability level and (ii) physical, i.e., their use/consumption does lead into a decrease in their reliability/availability level. This decrease requires resource replacement[3]/replenishment at a certain stage. For the sake of illustration in this paper we restrict discussions to logical resources, only. Afterwards we define a set of properties that allow to describe a resource (Table 3). These properties are *unlimited* (ul, by default), *limited* (l - when a resource use/consumption is measured or a resource ceases to exist due to temporal constraints, for example), and *limited but renewable* (lr - when a resource use/consumption either hits a certain threshold or is subject to temporal constraints, for example; in either case renewal is possible). Additional properties could be considered if need be, such as *non-shareable* (ns - when a resource simultaneous use/consumption has to be scheduled) and *shareable* (s, by default).

Table 3. Examples of logical resources per property type

Resource		Examples
Category	Property	
Logical	Unlimited (ul)	Data (read mode), software (no cap on number of licences)
	Limited (l)	Thread
	Limited but renewable (lr)	File access right (valid for a certain time with possible extension), password (valid for a certain time with possible extension)

$\mathcal{T}$-Conflict$_1$ is an example of conflicts between tasks with emphasis on resource consumption and not data (inputs and outputs) and policy incompatibilities between these tasks. $\mathcal{T}$-Conflict$_1$ arises when (i) a pre-requisite relation between t_i and t_j exists, (ii) consume(t_i, r_i) $\rightarrow$ produce(t_i, $r_{i,j}$), and (iii) t_j needs $r_{i,j}$ (i.e., $t_j \nrightarrow r_j$, no r_j is made available for t_j). Potential conflicts on $r_{i,j}$ (and eventually $r_{\{i,k,\cdots\},j}$ and $r_{i,\{j,k,\cdots\}}$) because of the *limited* property of $r_{i,j}$, include:

- l: two cases result out of the prerequisite relation between $t_{\{k,\cdots\}}$ (e.g., complete necessary paperwork) and t_j (e.g., direct patient to appropriate department) on top of the same relation between t_i (e.g., check patient vitals) and t_j:

  a) $r_{i,j}$ (e.g., report on vital levels) ceases to exist (e.g., blood sample no longer valid) before the execution of t_j begins; t_j waits for $t_{\{k,\cdots\}}$ to produce $r_{\{k,\cdots\},j}$ (e.g., insurance provider approval); (at least one) $t_{\{k,\cdots\}}$ either is still under

execution (e.g., due to delay in receiving approval from insurance provider) or failed.

  b) Only one consumption cycle of $r_{i,j}$ is permitted (per type of property) but it turns out that several consumption cycles of $r_{i,j}$ are required to complete the execution of t_j and finish the consumption of $r_{\{k,\cdots\},j}$ that $t_{\{k,\cdots\}}$ produce.

After identifying the different task conflicts on resources, we suggest solutions for these conflicts based on the aforementioned networks. These solutions consider the fact that tasks are associated with transactional properties (e.g., pivot, retriable, and compensatable) that limit their re-execution in the case of failure [27]. The following examines briefly how the interchange and coupling networks of tasks are used to address $\mathcal{T}$-Conflict$_1$-Case a.

  a) $r_{i,j}$ ceases to exist before the execution of t_j begins; t_j waits for $t_{\{k,\cdots\}}$ to produce $r_{\{k,\cdots\},j}$; at least one t_k either is still under execution or failed. Current statuses of tasks and resources are: state(t_i): done; state($r_{i,j}$): withdrawn; state(t_j): not-activated; and state(t_k): either activated (still under execution) or failed with focus on the latter state below. Because t_i now takes on done state, pivot (canceling t_i) and retriable (re-executing t_i) transactional properties are excluded from the analysis of developing solutions to address resource conflicts. This analysis is given in Table 4. The objective is to re-produce $r_{i,j}$ (or produce $r_{i',j}$ with $t_{i'}$ being obtained through the interchange network of t_i). Because of t_k failure, $r_{k',j}$ is produced using $t_{k'}$ that is obtained through the interchange network of t_k.

5. Implementation

In this section we describe the architecture of the **S**ocial-based b**U**siness **P**rocess manag**E**ment f**R**amework (SUPER) that supports our research on the social enterprise (or enterprise 2.0) [28]. SUPER is a Business Process Management System (BPMS) that uses social computing principles (i.e., connecting entities together through relations, developing networks upon these relations, and analyzing these networks) to model and develop business processes. Fig. 2 illustrates the architecture of SUPER that is built upon multiple components discussed below.

At design time, process engineers (or designers) define new Business Processes (BP)s using the BP modeling component. This component is an extension of the Yaoqiang BPMN editor [29] with new operations that for instance, assign executors (persons and/or machines) to tasks and specify the requirements and capacities of tasks, persons, and machines accordingly. Fig. 3 shows

---

[3]Replacement can be the result of degradation.

Table 4. Possible coordination actions in the case of $\mathcal{T}$-Conflict$_1$/limited property/case a

Transactional property		Coordination actions	Network involved
t_i	t_k		
Null	Null	– re-execute t_i to re-produce $r_{i,j}$ – re-execute t_k to produce $t_{k,j}$	N/A
	Pivot	Deadlock	N/A
	Compensatable	Deadlock	N/A
	Retriable	– re-execute t_i to re-produce $r_{i,j}$ – replace t_k with $t_{k'}$, then execute $t_{k'}$ to produce $r_{k',j}$	Interchange($t_k, t_{k'}$)
Compensatable	Null	– compensate t_i; either re-execute t_i to re-produce $r_{i,j}$ or replace t_i with $t_{i'}$, then execute $t_{i'}$ to produce $r_{i',j}$ – either re-execute t_k to produce $r_{k,j}$ or replace t_k with $t_{k'}$, then execute $t_{k'}$ to produce $r_{k',j}$	Interchange($t_i, t_{i'}$) Interchange($t_k, t_{k'}$)
	Pivot	Deadlock	N/A
	Compensatable	– compensate t_i; either re-execute t_i to re-produce $r_{i,j}$ or replace t_i with $t_{i'}$, then execute $t_{i'}$ to produce $r_{i',j}$ – replace t_k with $t_{k'}$, then execute $t_{k'}$ to produce $r_{k',j}$	Interchange($t_i, t_{i'}$) Interchange($t_k, t_{k'}$)
	Retriable	– compensate t_i; either re-execute t_i to re-produce $r_{i,j}$ or replace t_i with $t_{i'}$, then execute $t_{i'}$ to produce $r_{i',j}$ – re-execute t_k to produce $r_{k,j}$	Interchange($t_i, t_{i'}$)

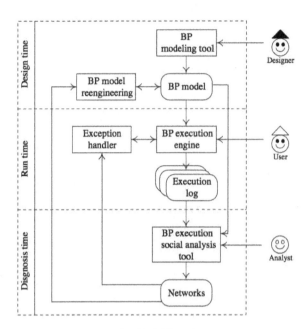

Figure 2. SUPER architecture

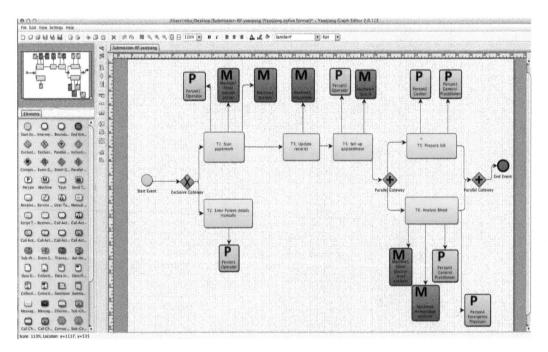

Figure 3. Screenshot of Yaoqiang BPMN editor

a screenshot of the Yaoqiang BPMN editor extension in which a part of the electronic-patient-folder system BP is modeled (Section 3).

At run time, BPs are executed using appropriate engines for instance, Jboss JBPM engine[4]. This engine interprets the specification of the BP model that is generated from the Jboss JBPM editor. The different execution traces accumulated during the execution of

BP instances are stored in a log file. These traces contain information about events referring to the execution of tasks in terms of execution time (timestamp) and executors. The traces are in e**X**tensible **E**vent **S**tream (XES) format[5] [30]. XES is the de facto standard for process execution log expression and adopted by

---

[4]www.jboss.org/jbpm

[5]http://www.xes-standard.org/

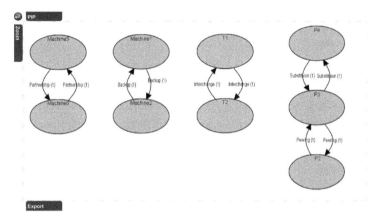

Figure 4. Screenshot of the BP execution social analysis component, a demo video is available at https://www.youtube.com/watch?v=Py5oGPQot64

several log analyzer tools such as the popular process mining framework, ProM[6].

At diagnosis time, a BP execution social analysis component discovers and builds the necessary category of networks (configuration, machine, and social) based on process execution logs as well as BP models. This component is developed as a plugin of the ProM framework and represents the discovered networks using a well-known XML-based format for representing graphs, GraphML[7]. This format is supported by several graph drawing and analyzing tools such as yED Graph Editor[8] and Eclipse Plugin Postfuse[9]. Therefore, such tools can also be used to visualize and analyze the discovered networks by the BP execution social analysis component.

Fig. 4 depicts examples of networks related to the electronic-patient-folder system that are generated using the BP execution social analysis component. For example, a network of machines is built to specify the backup relation between m_1 (scanner) and m_2 (three-function-printer) since both machines have the similar capacities (using subsumption). A configuration network of tasks is also constructed to express the interchange relation between t_1 (scan-documentation) and t_2 (enter-patient-details-manually). Both tasks produce similar output and their requirements do not overlap. Last and not least, a social network of persons is built to describe the peering relation between p_2 (cashier) and p_3 (financial-manager) since both persons have complementary capacities that are necessary to achieve t_5 (prepare-bill). This social network expresses also a substitution relation between p_3 (general-practitioner) and

p_4 (emergency-physician) since both have the same capacity.

6. Conclusion

This paper discussed business processes from a social perspective. Different relations with a "social flavor" have been proposed such as interchange, substitution, delegation, and peering. They permitted to connect the components of a business process that are task, person, and machine together. A case study illustrated these components as well as these relations. For instance, tasks can be substituted when their requirements are not met. Persons delegate their tasks when unexpected changes occur in their schedules. Last but not least machines act as backups when their peers fail. The role of all these networks in conflict resolution is detailed in [26]. In term of future work, we would like to conduct some acceptance tests by end-users and to extend the analysis component of SUPER to handle cases like load balancing and resource management.

References

[1] BADR, Y. and MAAMAR, Z. (October 2009) Can Enterprises Capitalize on Their Social Networks? *Cutter IT Journal* 22(10).

[2] CHANDLER, S. (November 2011), Social BPM: Gateway to Enhanced Process Efficiency. Http://www.virtusa.com/blog/2011/11/, visited September 2014.

[3] KANARACUS, C. (2013), Gartner: Social Business Efforts Largely Unsuccessful so Far. Http://www.computerworld.com/s/article/9236323/.

[4] KILLOCK, P. (1999) The Economies of Online Cooperation: Gifts and Public Goods in Cyberspace. In A., S.M. and KOLLOCK, P. [eds.] *Communities in Cyberspace* (Routledge, London), 259–262.

[5] FARZAN, R., DIMICCO, J.M., MILLEN, D.R., BROWNHOLTZ, B., GEYER, W. and DUGAN, C. (2008) Results from Deploying a Participation Incentive Mechanisms within

---

[6]www.promtools.org
[7]http://graphml.graphdrawing.org/
[8]www.yworks.com
[9]http://postfuse.macrolab.de

the Entrerprise. In *Proceedings of the 2008 Conference on Human Factors in Computing Systems (CHI'2008)* (Florence, Italy).

[6] CRESS, U., HELD, C. and KIMMERLE, J. (2013) The Collective Knowledge of Social Tags: Direct and Indirect Influences on Navigation, Learning, and Information Processing. *Computers & Education* 60(1).

[7] DOMINGO, M.C. (July 2010) Managing Healthcare Through Social Networks. *Computer* 43(7).

[8] MAAMAR, Z., FACI, N., KOUADRI MOSTÉFAOUI, S. and AKHTER, F. (2011) Towards a Framework for Weaving Social Networks Into Mobile Commerce. *International Journal of Systems and Service-Oriented Engineering* 2(3).

[9] TAN, W., BLAKE, M.B., SALEH, I. and DUSTDAR, S. (September/October 2013) Social-Network-Sourced Big Data Analytics. *IEEE Internet Computing* 17(5).

[10] DUSTDAR, S. and BHATTACHARYA, K. (May/June 2011) The Social Compute Unit. *IEEE Internet Computing* 15(3).

[11] WARR, W. (2008) Social Software: Fun and Games, or Business Tools? *Journal of Information Science* 34(4).

[12] SCHMIDT, R. and NURCAN, S. (2008), BPM and Social Software. Proceedings of the First Workshop on Business Process Management and Social Software (BPMS2'2008), Milan, Italy.

[13] EROL, S., GRANITZER, M., HAPP, S., JANTUNEN, S., JENNINGS, B., KOSCHMIDER, A., NURCAN, S. *et al.* (October-November 2010) Combining BPM and Social Software Contradiction or Chance. *Journal of Software Maintenance and Evolution: Research and Practice* 22(6-7).

[14] LIPTCHINSKY, V., KHAZANKIN, R., TRUONG, H.L. and DUSTDAR, S. (2012) A Novel Approach to Modeling Context-Aware and Social Collaboration Processes. In *Proceedings of the 24th International Conference on Advanced Information Systems Engineering (CAiSE'2012)* (Gdansk, Poland).

[15] BRUNO, G., DENGLER, F., JENNINGS, B., KHALAF, R., NURCAN, S., PRILLA, M., SARINI, M. *et al.* (2011) Key Challenges for Enabling Agile BPM with Social Software. *Journal of Software Maintenance and Evolution: Research and Practice* 23(10).

[16] RITO SILVA, A., MEZIANI, R., MAGALHÃES, R., MARTINHO, D., AGUIAR, A. and FLORES, N. (2010) AGILIPO: Embedding Social Software Features into Business Process Tools. In *Proceedings of the Third International Workshop on the Business Process Model and Notation (BPMN'2010)* (Ulm, Germany).

[17] BRAMBILLA, M., FRATERNALI, P. and VACA, C. (2011) A Notation for supporting Social Business Process Modeling. In *Proceedings of the Fourth Workshop on Business Process Management and Social Software (BPMS2'2011) held in conjunction with The Seventh International Conference*

on *Business Process Management (BPM'2011)* (Lucerne, Switzerland).

[18] KOSCHMIDER, A., SONG, M. and REIJERS, H. (2010) Social Software for Modeling Business Processes. *Journal of Information Technology* 25(3).

[19] GRIM-YEFSAH, M., ROSENTHAL-SABROUX, C. and THION, V. (2011) Using Information of an Informal Network to Evaluate Business Process Robustness. In *Proceedings of the International Conference on Knowledge Management and Information Sharing (KMIS'2011)* (Paris, France).

[20] DAVENPORT, T.H. and SHORT, J.E. (1990) The New Industrial Engineering: Information Technology and Business Process Redesign. *Sloan Management Review* .

[21] ALFARO SAIZ, J.J., RODRÍGUEZ-RODRÍGUEZ, R., VERDECHO, M.J. and ORTIZ, A. (2009) Business Process Interoperability and Collaborative Performance Measurement. *International Journal Computer Integrated Manufacturing* 22(9).

[22] CARSTENSEN, A., HOLMBERG, L., SANDKUHL, K. and STIRNA, J. (2008) Integrated Requirement and Solution Modelling: An Approach Based on Enterprise Models. In T., H., J., K. and E., P. [eds.] *Innovations in Information Systems Modeling: Methods and Best Practices* (IGI Global), 89–105.

[23] ROUSH, W. (August 2005) Social Machines - Computing means Connecting. *MIT Technology Review* .

[24] LIMTHANMAPHON, B. and ZHANG, Y. (2003) Web Service Composition with Case-Based Reasoning. In *Proceedings of the 14th Australasian Database Conference (ADC'2003)* (Adelaide, Australia).

[25] DECKER, K. and LESSER, V. (1992) Generalizing the Partial Global Planning Algorithm. *International Journal Cooperative Information Systems* 1(2).

[26] MAAMAR, Z., NOURA, F., KOUADRI MOSTÉFAOUI, S. and KAJAN, E. (2013) Network-based Conflict Resolution in Business Processes. In *Proceedings of the 10th IEEE International Conference on e-Business Engineering (ICEBE'2013)* (Coventry, UK).

[27] LITTLE, M. (2003) Transactions and Web Services. *Communications of the ACM* 46(10).

[28] FACI, N., MAAMAR, Z., KAJAN, E. and BENSLIMANE, D. (2014) Research Roadmap for the Enterprise 2.0 Ů Issues & Solutions. *Scientific Publications of the State University Of Novi Pazar Journal, Series A: Applied Mathematics, Informatics & Mechanics* 2(2).

[29] KAJAN, E., FACI, N., MAAMAR, Z., LOO, A., PLJASKOVIC, A. and SHENG, Q.Z. (March/April 2014) The Network-based Business Process. *IEEE Internet Computing* 18(2).

[30] VERBEEK, H., BUIJS, J., VAN DONGEN, B. and VAN DER AALST, W. (2011) XES, XESame, and ProM 6. *Information Systems Evolution* 72.

7

Wireless Broadband Opportunities through TVWS for Networking in Rural areas of Africa

Dramane Ouattara[1,*], Mohamed Aymen Chalouf[2], Francine Krief[1,3] and Omessaad Hamdi[1]

[1]Univ. Bordeaux, LaBRI, Talence, France
[2]Univ. Rennes 1, IRISA, Lannion, France
[3]IPB, Bordeaux, France

Abstract

In this paper, we propose a new approach based on Cognitive Radio technology to address the challenges for ensuring connectivity in remote areas of Africa. Indeed, the current network coverage is concentrated around the cities with high density of population. Through the deployment of Cognitive Radio, emergency services in rural areas will benefit from low cost access networks. Cognitive Radio will be used to manage the selection/switching across different frequency UHF/VHF bands or TV White Spaces (TVWS), while avoiding interference.

Keywords: Cognitive Radio, TV White Spaces, Rural areas, Remote zone connectivity, Emergency services

1. Introduction

The use of mobile technologies and networks in Africa is growing rapidly and services are increasingly diversified. The quality of the available networks differs from one geographical area to another. In many areas, the network deliver a poor connectivity, while some areas have no connectivity. These deficiencies are related to the operators policies and the economic benefits they should derive from their investment. However, Internet or network access could considerably improve the inhabitants social condition in remote areas. Providing low cost Internet access anywhere through Cognitive Radio Networks (CRNs) and using TV White Space (TVWS) is the main objective of this contribution. In this paper, we introduce the Cognitive Radio technology, with a detailed description of its main modules in section 2. The main advantages of this technology in African context are presented in section 3 through the services that it could offer. We give an overview on the related work, referring to some works addressing the use of cognitive radio in African context in section 4. The deployment plan that we propose is considered in section 5, an experimentation idea and

results are studied in 6. We open a discussion section (Section 7) before concluding this chapter in section 8.

2. Cognitive Radio networks

2.1. Definition and principle of cognitive radio networks

Cognitive Radio [1] is a paradigm for wireless networks where a node is able to automatically modify its transmitting parameters in order to communicate efficiently, while avoiding interferences with other users, the Primary Users (PU[1]). This self-configuration and self-adaptation of parameters is based on a set of modules and several factors in the internal or the external environment of the radio such as radio frequency, user behaviour and the network state.

2.2. Cognitive radio modules

Figure 1 summarizes the cognitive radio modules and details of its functions are given below.

---

*Dramane Ouattara. Email: dramane.ouattara@labri.fr

[1]Users that have the band-use license, the TV users.

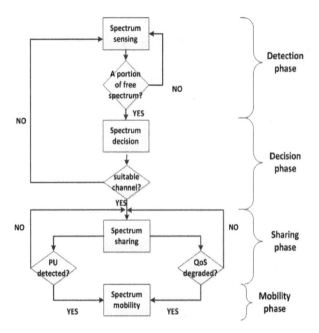

Figure 1. Operating diagram of a cognitive radio node

Channel	Spectrum	Bands
2, 3, 4	54-72 MHz	VHF Low bands
7-13	174-216 MHz	VHF High bands
5,6	76-88 MHz	VHF Low bands
14-51	470-698 MHz	UHF bands

Table 1. TVWS frequency bands [2]

Standards	Description
IEEE 802.22.1	Interferences avoidance, primary TV users protection
IEEE 802.22.2	Practice for the systems deployment and installation

Table 2. Network standards [2]

Spectrum sensing: The spectrum sensing is defined as the ability to measure, examine, learn and be aware of the parameters related to the characteristics of the radio channel. This module measures the availability of spectrum, the signal strength, the interferences and noise, scans operating environment of the radio, estimates the needs of users and applications, checks the availability of networks and nodes, learns about the local policies and other operators restrictions.

Spectrum decision: Decision-making is based on the appropriate communication channel choice, justifying the quality of service required for the data or the collected information transmission.

Spectrum sharing: Channel sharing has to comply with the requirement of synchronized access to the detected free-band portions. This scheduling is done between the secondary[2] users on the one hand, and between these users and the primary users on the other hand.

Spectrum mobility: Spectrum mobility reflects the fact that each transceiver, must be able to change frequency band if the initial band becomes busy. Moving to a new frequency band could happen also when the initial band fails to provide the desired quality of service to applications.

2.3. The standard for cognitive radio: IEEE 802.22

The Federal Communications Commission (FCC[3]) established the TV white spaces rules by which unlicensed devices, in our case, the cognitive radio devices, can make use of specific TV channels in the Very High Frequency (VHF) and Ultra High Frequency (UHF) bands. Table 1 summarises these frequency bands.

The use of cognitive radio approach in rural areas in Africa is based on this principle of TV white spaces (TVWS), even if the constraints and objectives are different from European and American continents. Indeed, the scarcity of spectrum resources in Europe and America led to the exploration of this new alternative. In Africa, it will provide technology services in regions with limited economic resources, often remote areas at a very insignificant cost or even free. The use of TV White Spaces in Africa to ensure a connection is a topic increasingly studied and therefore, has recently been the subject of the TV white spaces Africa Forum in Dakar (Senegal) with partners such as Google and Microsoft [3]. The 802.22 working group is developing standards for wireless regional network based on TV white spaces usage. Some specifications[4] of the standard on cognitive radio are given in table 2.

Table 2 shows the work in progress and all the interest in the use of TV bands to provide internet services.

---

[2]Cognitive radio users, who do not have any band-use license, such as emergency services users in our context.

[3] http://www.fcc.gov/
[4]IEEE 802.22-2011 Standard for Wireless Regional Area Networks, July 27th 2011.

3. Services that could be offered

Given the ability of the Cognitive Radio Networks to realize opportunistic communications, this technology could provide a set of services in rural zones, among these are:

3.1. Chronic disease patient monitoring : e.g diabetic patient

Chronic diseases such as diabetes are reaching an increasingly large proportion of the rural population. Patients in rural areas with appropriate monitoring, combine with timely hospital visits should save lives. In fact, diabetic patient fitted with glucose sensors connected to a smart-phone as a relay node to the internet allows to remotely inform the caregivers on abnormal high levels of sugar in the blood. This could avoid many painful movement of the patients from rural areas to the city (Hospital). The principle remains the same for other type of chronic conditions such as cardiovascular, cancer and respiratory diseases.

3.2. Hospital services automation : e.g for epidemic disease prevention

To accelerate treatment and diagnosis, health services in Africa should be automated. It begins with the electronic record of the patient's medical history and allows the anywhere medical records access even for people living in rural areas. The patients often helped by nurses could access, modify and control remotely their medical information or send a message on his health state to the doctors. The statistics from this automation could be helpful for early detection of health risks such as epidemics.

3.3. Emergency alerts : e.g Bushfire and accident alerts

Bushfire are often disastrous for people in rural areas and often, these people do not have the ability to call for help due to the lack of communication infrastructure. It is the same for accident occurring in very remote areas where the victims have no access networks to call the firemen. The emergency networks seem enough efficient for saving lives in similar situation with rescue arrival on time.

3.4. Internet for children

In addition to emergency centers that could benefit from Internet, the primary schools should be connected and the children in remote villages could very soon become familiar with computers and social networks. This gives them an opening to the world, an opportunity to interact with other children, thus contributing to the reduction of social and technological gap.

3.5. Improving government services : e.g births registration

Children births in villages are often not reported because of the distance to reach an administration office. This raises the problem of persons with no administrative paper for example in Côte d'Ivoire remote areas. The on-line registration of births through cognitive radio could significantly reduce the problem of undocumented persons. At the same time, several administrative services may be offered by the Internet access in villages.

4. Related Works

Researchers are increasingly interested in issues of connectivity in inaccessible areas. Projects are initiated and various technologies are considered. In this section, we first present the Loon project initiated by Google and based on the use of ISM bands before seeing the works dealing with the use of TV bands.

4.1. Example of experimental project for providing internet in rural areas: Loon project

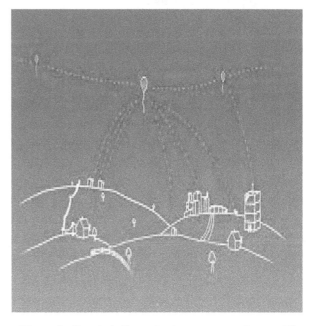

Figure 2. Google balloons for Internet in rural areas [4]

Project Loon is a network of balloons, initiated by Google company, traveling on the edge of space, designed to connect people in rural and remote areas, help fill coverage gaps, and bring people back online after disasters [4]. People are connecting to the balloon network using a special Internet antenna attached to their building. The signal bounces from balloon to balloon, then to the global Internet back on Earth as described on figure 2. This project is based on the use of 2.4 and 5.8 GHz ISM bands. However, various issues remain unanswered in this project, namely the life of the balloons in the air or in flying. This time is estimated to be ten days to the current time and this very short time could make the balloon management/redirection as a very complex process. Indeed, if the balloons can not stay long time in the air, the stability of the network will be affected and the process of change balloons or resettlement could remain very tedious for scalability needs. In addition, the principle of low cost connection is not guaranteed and this project to our knowledge does not provide mechanisms for inevitable interference management. Loon project initiated by Google, may not be of a social nature and its cost would be unbearable for impoverished populations as living in rural areas of Africa. We therefore propose the cognitive radio technology that implement interference management functions and will be based on the TV bands to provide connectivity at a lower cost in rural areas. Also, the use of the TVWS has the advantage of being long-range frequency-bands than the ISM bands used in Loon project.

4.2. Research on TVWS and Cognitive Radio for network coverage in remote areas

In developed countries, the growing number of wireless devices and the increased spectrum occupancy have resulted to the spectrum scarcity. In this context of scarce resources in traditional networks, the idea of exploring the TV bands is increasingly considered. Also, to ensure a better coexistence of technologies with efficient management of interference and better sharing of spectrum resources, Cognitive Radio technology is experienced. Cognitive Radio is considered in Europe and USA as the new wireless communication paradigm that could address the potential spectrum exhaustion problem and should be proposed for future wireless communication devices. In India, Cognitive Radio technology is seems as a real opportunity to provide wireless broadband for the applications like e-education, e-agriculture, e-animal husbandry and e-health as described by Dhope et al. [5]. Use cases for the exploitation of TV White Space for improving rural India services are discussed. Spectrum measurements of TV band in India to show the potential of frequency bands for Cognitive Radio operations have been performed by Patil et al. [6]. Geographically unused TV frequencies have been shown and this allows offering people in rural areas internet access opportunities. In the African context, this technology could mostly serve as knowledge sharing and social development tool. Cognitive Radio Networks are therefore a

promising field for social networks deployment in Africa and the domain has an increasingly interest for researchers. Thus, Moshe et al. [7] have studied the White space opportunity. They have performed measurements that indicate the existence of substantial TV White Spaces available in both rural and urban areas. This work is an interesting introduction and opens up practical deployment studies which remain unexplored. Implementation of OpenBTS in rural Zambia has been studied by Jacqueline et al. [8]. This work focused on providing telecommunication system such as mobile communications in rural villages. Even if this study addresses the low cost communication issue, the solution is obviously valid and valuable for the only villages with GSM networks infrastructure. However, the African countries reality proves that the majority of villages are not covered by the existing standard networks. In fact, the economic profitability in terms of return on investment is not guaranteed for telecommunications operators. The use of Cognitive Radio technology becomes therefore necessary with its bearable costs because of the existence of TV bands infrastructure in rural areas.

5. Cognitive Radio deployment process in remote areas

Depending on the isotropic radiated power, the cognitive radio base station could connect users terminals located as far as 100 km [9] as described in figure 3. A good base stations planning could provide a network to cover two distant areas (villages) of about 100 km and greatly reduce the cost of network infrastructure. The financing by governments and the acquisition of such infrastructure and its deployment will aim to improve public services in Africa remote rural areas.

5.1. Cognitive radio networks planning scenario

Figure 3 describes the deployment scenario with a set of cities (c), villages (v) with distances estimation and the corresponding coverage plan. The cognitive radio antennas at the city allow the switching between our cognitive radio network and the existing operators networks. Also, the cognitive radio antennas set near a city, due to their sensing capability will help avoiding interferences that may be generated by the broadcasting signal of our cognitive radio networks. Relay nodes (R1) are provided to repeat the signal when the distance between two access points or base stations is greater than 100 km. Thus, it can be seen that the fundamental interest of this proposal lies in its ability to cover a large area and long distance. It should be noted that the TV band could be used only in areas lacking the standard network coverage. A proper planning and deployment will achieve a very high scope for

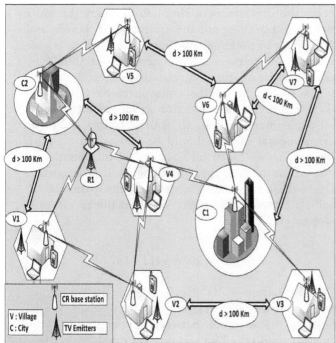

Figure 3. Planned Cognitive Radio Networks

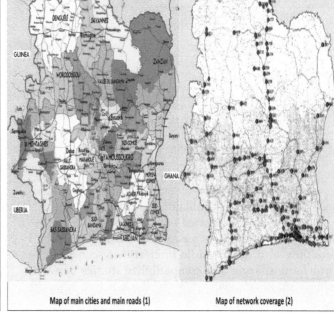

Figure 4. Network coverage map in Côte d'Ivoire [10]

possible internet access in the most remote locations. The cognitive radio is therefore an extension of network coverage anywhere and any-time even if its access must be controlled and limited to emergency services, public safety services or public services to avoid disorder in its usage. Based on a strong existing infrastructure such as TV bands (TV White Spaces), the solution we propose provides a stable network connection and facilitates its management and control. However, a number of challenges remain to make the effective deployment of this technology in rural areas in Africa.

5.2. Example of application to a geographical area

Under the National Rural Telephony Project (PNTR), the Ivorian Ministry[5] of Post and Information Technology and Communication began building a highspeed fiber optic network throughout the national territory. Thus, this country is a good example which clearly shows disparities in terms of network coverage from one area to another one and the impossibility to bring fiber everywhere and especially in more remote areas. Indeed, 6,700 km of optical fiber are considered for linking all prefectures and sub-prefectures. The first phase of the project planned will focus on the deployment of a fiber optic artery on San Pedro - Tabou and Man - Odienné - Korhogo - Ferkessédougou city-axis, along 1,400 km on one hand and on Abidjan Bondoukou - Bouna city-axis, along 549 km on the other

hand. The cost of this project is estimated to 163 million euros for 6700 km. Despite all these efforts and its significant financial cost, this project will not be enough to cover remote areas. The figure 4 confirms that the deployment policy focuses on the main arteries or main road connecting the large agglomerations, the densely populated areas. This map shows the deployment of BTS antennas from operator COMIUM in Côte d'Ivoire which is almost similar to all other operators. In this context, cognitive radio and TVWS usage will help ensure connectivity for emergency services with low cost in these remote areas. However, the deployment of cognitive radio technology must take into account radio-environmental constraints.

6. Contributions and main results

6.1. Constraints analysis

To provide network access in remote areas, it will be deployed the cognitive radio technology in rural areas but also find a link between this technology and traditional networks (i.e. Backbone). This link is the point of connection or switching between traditional networks and the newly deployed cognitive radio networks. Although the impact in terms of interference on the TV users is minimal in rural areas due to the very low number of TV, signals from cognitive radio transmitters could cause enormous interference around the connecting areas near cities and most populated zones. We therefore performed simulations to assess the importance of these disturbing noise

---

[5]http://www.telecom.gouv.ci/main.php

Parameters	Values/description
Reference frequency	VHF Low bands
Receiver bandwidth	1 Mhz
Sensitivity	-110
Antenna height	30 m
Emitter transmit power	35 dBm
Event generation(sample)	10000
Coverage radius	30 km
Density of TV users	$20/km^2$
Environment	Rural/outdoor

Table 3. Simulation parameters

through the network simulator SEAMCAT. SEAMCAT is a free of charge integrated software tool based on the Monte-Carlo simulation method. It permits statistical modelling of different radio interference scenarios for performing sharing and compatibility studies between radiocommunications systems in the same or adjacent frequency bands[6].

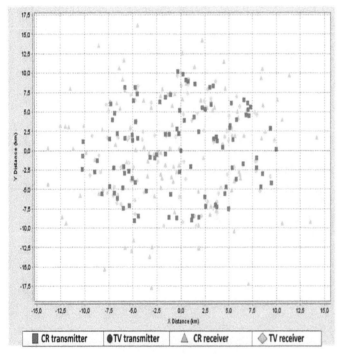

| CR transmitter | TV transmitter | CR receiver | TV receiver |

Figure 5. TV users and CR transmitter distribution scenario

Figure 5 shows the scenario of simulation and the description of the selected parameters are given in table 3.

Operating in the band of 54-72 MHz, our statistical Monte-Carlo simulation using SEAMCAT are based on uniform random distribution of TV users in the cognitive radio transmitter disk-coverage. Table 3

details the parameters of simulations where the more important variables are the transmission power and the number of potential TV users. The simulations are performed in a rural environment and it should be noted that the attenuation related to obstacles such as forests, mountains or the atmosphere have not been taken into account. In practice and in cognitive radio real deployment process, all of these factors and other environmental factors should be taken into account. The attenuation taken into account in this simulation is based on the free space model [11]. It is important to note that for free space model, the path loss in decibels between the transmitter and the receivers is given by [12]:

$$20log_{10}(d) + 20log_{10}(f) - 147.55 \qquad (1)$$

Where f represents the frequency in use and d the distance between transmitter and receiver. In this scenario, the distance between the cognitive radio transmitter and the TV users is in the range of $]0; 15km]$ and all nodes (TV users and CR transmitter) are assumed to be fixed. This characteristic looks realistic because TV users are not mobile. The execution of this simulation has generated a signal which in principle should create the communication link for cognitive radio terminals. This signal expected for providing connectivity between a cognitive radio node (e.g. node offering emergency services) is interference factor for TV users with the noises it generates as shown in figure 6.

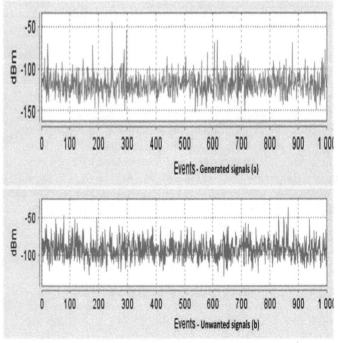

Figure 6. Unwanted signal and interference induced

[6]http://www.seamcat.org/

In figure 6, the generated signal for cognitive radio communications (Sub-figure a) is almost equivalent to the noise suffered by the TV users (Unwanted signals: Sub-figure b). The tests performed through these simulations have shown that at least 92.25% of TV users in the coverage of the CR transmitter and sharing the same frequency band are affected by the generated noise in a radius of 1 km. The distance and position of TV users are then appeared as very important factors because when the distance between the transmitter and TV users increases, the proportion of affected nodes decreases to 22% for a distance of 15 km as example. These probabilities of high interference provided by the simulation results seem unbearable in rural areas and these emissions from cognitive radio transmitters could be catastrophic for TV users around the cities and densely populated areas. This allows us to note that any deployment of cognitive radio technology to provide emergency services in rural areas, will inevitably take into account the positions of the TV users in cognitive radio base station's planning process.

6.2. Engineering and deployment

For better reduction of costs, a proper study should be conducted, that enables efficient deployment of network infrastructure. Thus, must be taken into account the best locations for cognitive radio base stations and relay nodes in order to minimize the infrastructure's cost while maximizing the network coverage area. This planning process could also take into account the transmission power of the emitter, based on the area population density. Indeed, the choice of the transmission power, the intensity and frequency sensing will differ from one zone to another. As an example, a control/management of interference by cognitive radio nodes nearby cities will be highly increased compared to less populated areas and the deployment process should take into account the transmission parameters (Transmission power) and their possible values for better planning of the emitters. Indeed, each cognitive radio node must implement functions and algorithms for interference avoidance.

6.3. Interference avoidance with TV users

The deployment of cognitive radio networks creates a new type of opportunistic users whose major constraint remains achieving transmissions or communications without interfering with the TV users as shown in section 6.1. Figure 7 shows the general principle used by the cognitive radio Medium Access Control (MAC) protocols for collisions mitigation. This figure illustrates the different steps performed by a cognitive radio node before the frequency band access. There is a sensing period (scan), a period of reconfiguration and synchronization before any transmissions on the

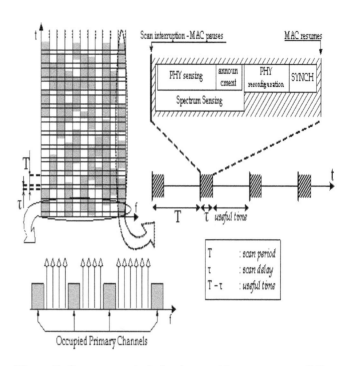

Figure 7. Spectrum analysis for the cognitive users access [12]

detected free channels (useful time). Occupied primary channels denote in this case, the occupation of the frequency band by TV users and useful time are periods that can be exploited by the cognitive radio users for their transmissions. To avoid, for example, interfering with the TV users, we define a set of actions that will be implemented on the cognitive radio base station (or cognitive radio relay antenna). In general, these functions allow antennas to react to various changes that can impact the radio environment such as changes in the air index (medium wave propagation) because of the rain for example, or following the arrival of TV users. Currently, we have defined two functions. The objective of the first function (decreaseTrPower) is to adjust the transmission power of the antenna. As for the second one (moveToBand), it allows antennas to change their transmission channel. Each of the defined two functions was expressed by the rules of logic programming which are then translated to one computer programming language. So, a function is composed of an action which is executed when a set of conditions are satisfied. We recall that 'Actions' are operations performed in order to change the state of a CR base station transmission parameters. To each 'Action', we associate a set of 'Preconditions' (REQUIRE) and another set of 'Postconditions' (ENSURE). Preconditions includes the conditions that must be satisfied for the action execution. The Postconditions describe the new state that some parameters must satisfy after the action execution. In this paper, we provide two examples of functions (actions implementation) aiming at changing the transmission power (Algorithm 1) and to change the transmission central frequency/bandwidth (Algorithm 2). Algorithm 1 enables the adaptation of the transmission power to meet the requirements concerning the interference limit and the air index. Algorithm 2 allows two base stations to execute a frequency hopping when the minimum transmission power (minPowerAccept) required for ensuring better transmissions is no longer guaranteed. Experimentation demonstrating the interest as well the good functioning of the frequency change algorithm will be described in section 6.4.

Algorithm 1 *Action :: DecreaseTrPower(P_i, W_i, F_c, P_j)*

$initFreq \leftarrow F_c$; $bandwidth \leftarrow W_i$;
$threshold \leftarrow \lambda_i$; $channelEnerg \leftarrow E_i$;
$minPowerAccept \leftarrow P_{min}$; $transmitPower \leftarrow P_i$;
$newTransmitPower \leftarrow P_j$.
while $channelEnerg(E_i) > threshold(\lambda_i)$ **do**
  if $(P_i) > (P_{min})$ **then**
Require: $(E_i \leq \lambda_i) \wedge P_j > P_{min}$
Ensure: $\neg(P_i) \wedge (W_i) \wedge (P_j)$
    else
      Action :: MoveToBand(W_j)
    end if
end while

Algorithm 1 describes the strategy which leads to an adaptation (*decrease*) of the transmission power to meet the requirements of the interference limit (*threshold*), compared to the detected energy on the channel (*channelEnerg*). It is important to note that the minimum acceptable power P_{min} must meet the needs of the transmissions quality. This value (P_{min}) must be chosen taking into account the constraints of the environment, vegetation (mountainous area, forest area, free space) and weather conditions (rain, air).

Algorithm 2 *Action :: moveToBand(F_i, W_i, F_j, W_j)*

$initFreq \leftarrow F_i$; $initBand \leftarrow W_i$; $newFreq \leftarrow F_j$
$threshold \leftarrow \lambda_i$; $channelEnerg \leftarrow E_i$;
$transmitPower \leftarrow P_j$; $numberOfDevice \leftarrow N$;
$newBandwidth \leftarrow W_j$; $tvDeviceSensitivity \leftarrow S_i$.
Require: $\forall_i \in N$, $notOverlap(F_j, W_j, P_j, S_i)$
  if $E_i \leq \lambda_i$ **then**
Ensure: $\neg(W_i \wedge F_i) \wedge W_j \wedge F_j$
  end if

Algorithm 2 shows the frequency hopping when the minimum transmission power (*minPowerAccept*) required for ensuring better transmissions is no longer guaranteed. Also, the function *notOverlap* ensures that the new frequency band chosen complies with the overlap constraints and therefore generates no

interference to TV users (*tvDeviceSensitivity*) in this area. Section 6.4 gives an idea of how these proposed algorithms could be implemented in practice.

6.4. The proposed algorithms experiment idea using the cognitive radio platform

We perform experiments of the frequency hopping scenario on cognitive radio platform acquired under the ANR[7]-LICORNE project.

(a) A CR node

(b) 3-nodes connected

Figure 8. Cognitive Radio platform

This platform is composed of five nodes and each node is composed of a USRP-1 box, two daughter-boards for transmission/reception (Tx/Rx) operating in GSM (RX/TX 900) and in WiFi (RX/TX 2400) accompanied with the corresponding antennas. A laptop with GNU software is interconnected to the USRP box as presented in figure 8a. This platform allowed us to do an experiment of transmission/reception on WiFi and GSM bands and to test the frequency hopping with the setup shown in figure 8b. This experiment demonstrates the functioning of the algorithm 2 implemented on a cognitive radio node. To test the frequency hopping, we generate a disruptive AWGN (Adds White Gaussian Noise) signal to create interferences on the transmission channel.The signal thus generated is seen as a transmission of a primary node. This then triggers the process of frequency hopping to avoid interferences as seen in figure 9. This experiment in GSM and WiFi bands remains valid for mitigating interferences to TV band users with cognitive radio networks deployed in rural areas. In addition, the transmission power adaptation model

---

[7]The French National Research Agency-ANR (Agence Nationale de la Recherche en France).

proposed by Ouattara et al. [13] and tested through the LICORNE platform, represents another strategy for mitigating interferences in cognitive radio networks and therefore for TV white spaces.

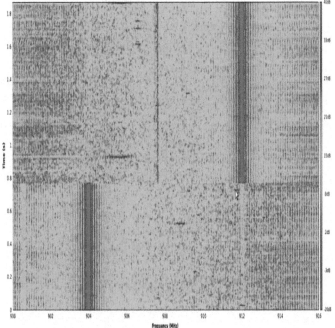

Figure 9. Frequency hopping for interferences avoidance

6.5. Other framework for test and experiments: The CREW project platform

The CREW platform [14] facilitates experimentally-driven research on spectrum sensing and sharing in licensed and unlicensed bands (TV bands). It offers test-bed capabilities to TV frequency bands experimenters. It combined indoor and outdoor installation deployed in the city of Logatec at Slovenia. The test-bed remote access portal[8] allows to show node status, choose particular cluster for performing an experiment remotely as shown in figure 10.

We worked on this platform during the CREW training days[9] and made tests remotely to validate the TV frequency bands potential in terms of data transmissions and interferences awareness as seen in figure 10. The transmitters radio coverage calculation and visualisation is expressed through the figure 10. The different colors (green, blue, red) and the characteristic of energy detected from one zone to another one, allows to confirm the presence or the absence of a transmission based on the measured power.

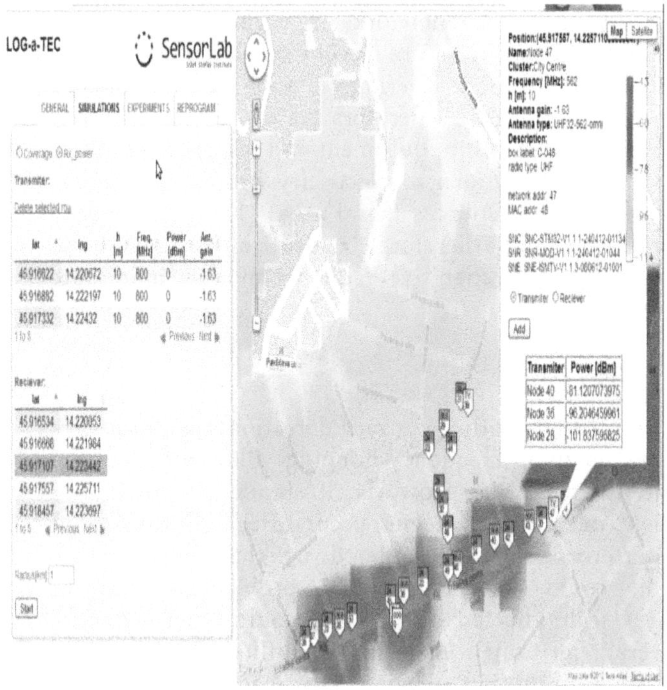

Figure 10. Platform for remote test on the TV bands

Also, this platform (CREW) allows for various tests such as the multi-hopping scenario that remains a very important aspect for transmissions reaching remote areas.

6.6. Other significant challenges

Network performance enhancement: A better network performance in terms of throughput and available bandwidth is an important interest in ensuring quality of service to users. Performance is thus linked to the availability of channels and the quality of these free bands. The work proposed by Ouattara et al. [15] on modelling the behaviour of primary users (TV users in this context) shows how to improve the process of detection of free bands and reduce latencies due to the frequency hopping induced by a primary user probable appearance. Umamaheswari et al. [16] works shown the capacity of cognitive radio technology to provide high throughput and good quality of service for users. In addition, Ouattara et al. [17] propose a best effort on-the-fly resource reservation, carrying the data flow end-to-end with a new scheduling plan that reduce latency and improve throughput with cognitive radio networks. This technology is therefore well suited for offering high quality of communication to emergency services in rural areas.

Energy for powering equipments and maintenance: The access to a source of energy to power the equipment to be installed is a real challenge for the deployment

---

[8]www.log-a-tec.eu
[9]CREW Training Days is the day which took place on February 2013 at Brussels

of cognitive radio networks in rural areas. In fact, rural areas in Africa are devoid of electric networks. However, there are alternatives such as solar energy increasingly used. Generators are also used as power source for electronic equipment and research continues to provide solutions to electricity problems in areas with limited resources (rural area) [18] . The energy problem can not therefore constitute an obstacle to the deployment of cognitive radio technology in remote areas.

7. Discussion

The sensing, with TV users detection and strategies experimented (frequency hopping) allow reducing the interference risks. However, it should be noted that these detection/strategies occur after a minimum of interference already suffered by the devices (TV). This could be an important problem in case of large-scale affected devices and could deteriorate the overall performance or the suitability of the general solution. Building a knowledge base that provides equipments geolocation information in accordance with the principle suggested by Thao et al. [19] is an appropriate solution to overcome this issue.

8. Conclusion

In this work, we have shown that cognitive radio is a real opportunity for network coverage in rural areas through the use of TV band. We have proposed a scenario for the deployment of this technology, noting its expansion capacity over long distances for ensuring network access in remote areas. The interference avoidance mechanism provided by cognitive radio makes this technology more suitable in this context (rural) with various constraints. The set of services (Section 3) that can be offered through the cognitive radio networks demonstrates its importance in African context. This next generation network is promising to improve life of many people living in remote and often inaccessible regions in Africa. In the future, we will propose a communication architecture based on cognitive radio networks to improve health services in rural areas. Health centers to be interconnected, medical applications to develop and install, patient to be remotely monitored are some challenges [20] for our future proposal in the context of rural areas in Africa. The platform of CREW project will be an additional framework for our experiments and testing considering the fact that the provided results will be based on a natural environment.

Acknowledgment

This work is partially supported by the LICoRNe project, funded in part by the National Agency for Research in France ANR (Agence Nationale de la Recherche).

References

[1] J. PALICOT. and DALY P.W. (2003) *Cognitive Radio: An Enabling Technology for the Green Radio Communications Concept*, Leipzig, Germany, June 21 - 24, 2009.

[2] FCC website: *http://www.fcc.gov/*; Accessed in February 2014.

[3] FORUM WEBSITE *https://sites.google.com/site/tvwsafrica2013/*; Accessed in February 2014.

[4] PROJECT WEBSITE *http://www.google.com/loon/* Accessed in February 2014.

[5] DHOPE, T.S. AND SIMUNIC, D.AND PRASAD, R. *TVWS opportunities and regulation: - Empowering rural India* Wireless Personal Multimedia Communications (WPMC), 2011 14th International Symposium, Oct. 2011.

[6] PATIL, KISHOR P. AND SKOUBY, KNUD ERIK AND PRASAD, RAMJEE *Cognitive Access to TVWS in India: TV Spectrum Occupancy and Wireless Broadband for Rural Areas* 16th International Symposium on Wireless Personal Multimedia Communications (WPMC) IEEE, 2013.

[7] MOSHE T. MASONTA AND DAVID J. AND MJUMO MZYECE *The White Space Opp. in Southern Africa : Measurement with Meraka C.R. Platform*; AFRICOMM 2011.

[8] JACQUELINE M. AND GERTJAN VAN S. *Open BTS, a GSM experiment in rural Zambia* 4th Int. Conf. ICST, AFRICOMM 2012.

[9] ALEXANDER M. WYGLINSKI AND AZIAR NEKOVEE AND THOMAS HOU *Cognitive Radio Communications and Networks* Principles and Practice,Academic Press, 13 nov. 2009.

[10] WEBSITE *www.koz.ci/couverture-reseau.php* Accessed in February 2014.

[11] HASIRCI, Z.; CAVDAR, I.H. *Propagation modeling dependent on frequency and distance for mobile communications via high altitude platforms (HAPs)* Telecommunications and Signal Processing (TSP), 2012 35th International Conference pp.287,291 July 2012.

[12] ATHANASSIOS V. AND ADAMIS AND PHILIP CONSTANTINOU *Intermittent DCF: a MAC protocol for Cognitive Radios in Overlay Networks* Cognitive Radio Systems; book edited by Wei Wang, november 2009.

[13] DRAMANE OUATTARA AND MINH T. QUACH AND FRANCINE KRIEF AND MOHAMED CHALOUF AND HICHAM KHALIFE *Mitigating the hospital area communication's interference using cognitive radio networks* IEEE Healthcom, International conference on E-health networking, application and services, October 2013.

[14] WEBSITE *http://www.crew-project.eu/*; Accessed in February 2014.

[15] DRAMANE OUATTARA AND FRANCINE KRIEF AND MOHAMED CHALOUF AND OMESSAAD HAMDI *Spectrum Sensing Improvement in Cognitive Radio Networks for Real-Time Patients Monitoring* Wireless Mobile Communication and Healthcare; Third International Conference, MOBIHEALTH 2012.

[16] UMAMAHESWARI, A. AND SUBASHINI, V. AND SUBHAPRIYA, P. *Survey on performance, reliability and future proposal of Cognitive Radio under wireless computing* Computing

Communication (ICCCNT): 2012 Third Int. Conf. July 2012.

[17] DRAMANE OUATTARA AND MOHAMED CHALOUF AND FRANCINE KRIEF AND OMESSAAD HAMDI *Multimedia content delivery for remote patient monitoring using Cognitive Radio Networks* Wireless Telecommunication Symposium, WTS 2014.

[18] GADO, ABLA AND EL-ZEFTAWY, ATEF *Design and economy of renewable energy sources to supply isolated loads at rural and remote areas of Egypt, Electricity Distribution* CIRED, 20th International Conference and Exhibition June 2009.

[19] MINH THAO QUACH; OUATTARA, D.; KRIEF, F.; KHALIFE, H.; CHALOUF, M.A, *Overlap regions and grey model-based approach for interference avoidance in cognitive radio networks* Ubiquitous and Future Networks (ICUFN), 2013 Fifth International Conference, pp.642,647, 2-5 July 2013.

[20] OMESSAAD HAMDIA, MOHAMED AYMEN CHALOUFB, DRAMANE OUATTARA AND FRANCINE KRIEF *eHealth: Survey on research projects, comparative study of telemonitoring architectures and main issues* Journal of Network and Computer Applications (JNCA), 9 August 2014, DOI: 10.1016/j.jnca.2014.07.026

8

On the Experimental Evaluation of Vehicular Networks: Issues, Requirements and Methodology Applied to a Real Use Case

Manabu Tsukada[1,2,*], José Santa[3,4], Satoshi Matsuura[5], Thierry Ernst[6], Kazutoshi Fujikawa[7]

[1]INRIA Paris - Rocquencourt, Domaine de Voluceau Rocquencourt - B.P. 105 78153 Le Chesnay Cedex, France
[2]The University of Tokyo, 1-1-1, Yayoi, Bunkyo-ku, Tokyo, 113-8656 Japan
[3]University Centre of Defence at the Spanish Air Force Academy, MDE-UPCT , Murcia, Spain
[4]University of Murcia, Campus de Espinardo, 30100 Murcia, Spain
[5]Tokyo Institute of Technology, 2-12-1, Ookayama, Meguro-ku, Tokyo, 152-8850, Japan
[6]Centre de Robotique, MINES ParisTech, Paris, France
[7]Nara Institute of Science and Technology, Nara, Japan

Abstract

One of the most challenging fields in vehicular communications has been the experimental assessment of protocols and novel technologies. Researchers usually tend to simulate vehicular scenarios and/or partially validate new contributions in the area by using constrained testbeds and carrying out minor tests. In this line, the present work reviews the issues that pioneers in the area of vehicular communications and, in general, in telematics, have to deal with if they want to perform a good evaluation campaign by real testing. The key needs for a good experimental evaluation is the use of proper software tools for gathering testing data, post-processing and generating relevant figures of merit and, finally, properly showing the most important results. For this reason, a key contribution of this paper is the presentation of an evaluation environment called AnaVANET, which covers the previous needs. By using this tool and presenting a reference case of study, a generic testing methodology is described and applied. This way, the usage of the IPv6 protocol over a vehicle-to-vehicle routing protocol, and supporting IETF-based network mobility, is tested at the same time the main features of the AnaVANET system are presented. This work contributes in laying the foundations for a proper experimental evaluation of vehicular networks and will be useful for many researchers in the area.

Keywords: Experimental Evaluation, Vehicular Ad-hoc Networks, Wireless Multihop Communication, Network Mobility, Cooperative ITS, Intelligent Transportation Systems

1. Introduction

Intelligent Transportation Systems (ITS) are systems deployed to optimize the road traffic and realize safe, efficient and comfortable human mobility. There are a number of research fields in ITS but cooperative ITS and vehicular communications have received an especial attention during the last years. Within this area various technologies are considered, such as wireless communications, network management, communication security, navigation, etc. In cooperative ITS, multiple entities share information and tasks to achieve common objectives. Thus, data exchange exists among vehicles, roadside infrastructure, traffic control centers, road users, road authorities and road operators, to support drivers, pedestrians, road authorities and

operators in different areas of safety, traffic efficiency and infotainment. The European Commission (EC), for instance, published the action plan [1] in Europe followed by ITS standardization mandate [2], to speed up the adoption of these systems in the European Union, but there are a number of initiatives worldwide to encourage the research and development in ITS, mainly from the US Department of Transport and the Japan Ministry of Land, Infrastructure, Transport and Tourism.

There are few barriers in the global road network among countries, and vehicles easily cross country borders, especially in Europe. Thus there is a huge necessity that cooperative ITS relies on the same architecture, protocols and technologies. As such, standardization organizations are developing cooperative ITS standards. The International Organization for Standardization (ISO) Technical Committee 204 Working Group

16 (TC204 WG16) (also known as Communications Architecture for Land Mobile (CALM)) is in charge of standardizing a communication architecture for cooperative ITS. TC204 WG16 is specially working on a communication architecture supporting all types of access media and applications. In Europe, the European Telecommunications Standards Institute (ETSI) TC ITS is working on building blocks of the same architecture in harmonization with ISO TC204 WG16. In 2010, both ISO TC204 WG16 and ETSI TC ITS defined the ITS Station reference architecture [3, 4].

In cooperative ITS and, in general, in vehicular networks, there are two main communication paradigms, vehicle to vehicle (V2V) and vehicle to infrastructure (V2I), depending on whether the communication is performed directly between vehicles or using nodes locally or remotely installed on the road infrastructure. When the V2V paradigm is considered, the research field is commonly called Vehicular Ad-hoc Networks, or VANET, as an especial case of Mobile Ad-hoc Networks (MANET) where nodes are vehicles. Although there are a lot of works related to VANET applications and basic research at physical, MAC and network layers, there is a significant lack of real evaluation analysis in this field, due to cost and effort implications. Many VANET solutions and protocols could be considered as non-practical designs if they were tested over real scenarios, as it has been proved in MANET [5]. Performance of VANET protocols based on a pure broadcast approach can be more or less expected in simple configurations, even if they are not experimentally tested; but the number of issues concerning the real performance of multi-hop designs is much more tricky. A similar problem can be found in V2I, which has received a great attention by the research community in the last years, due to the idea that V2I technologies and services will find a place in the market before V2V approaches. Nevertheless, a number of experimentation works and supporting tools should be improved in the short term, in order to give real evidences to car manufacturers and road operators of the benefits of vehicular communications.

Conventional network measurement tools (e.g. *iperf*, *ping* or *traceroute*) assume fixed networks and assess network performances in an end-to-end basis. However, under dynamic network conditions such as in the vehicular networks case, it is difficult to analyze in detail the operation of networks by using solely these tools, because vehicles are always changing their location and the performance of wireless channels fluctuates. In order to solve these issues, we have developed a packet analysis and visualization tool called AnaVANET[1], which considers the peculiarities of the vehicular environment for providing an exhaustive

evaluation software for outdoor scenarios (Figure 1 includes a preliminary screenshot of the visualization). Both V2V and V2I networks can be efficiently analyzed, thanks to the integrated features for collecting results, post-processing data, generate graphical figures of merit and, finally, publish the results in a dedicated web site (if desired). All tests and results are later available in the form of an animated webpage where both researchers and the general public can access the evaluations. AnaVANET has been successfully exploited for the moment in experimental evaluation campaigns in the GeoNet [6] and ITSSv6 [7] projects.

Figure 1. Screenshot of AnaVANET viewer

In this paper, apart from presenting our tool for assessing the performance of vehicular networks, we analyze in detail the problem of real testing in V2V and V2I, identifying the main issues, requirements, and proposing a general methodology useful for further works in the area. To sum up, the rest of the paper is organized as follows. Section 2 introduces the readers in network layer protocols for vehicular networks. Section 3 reviews related works in the area of testing vehicular networks. Then, the issues and requirements for evaluating vehicular networks are listed in Section 4. The evaluation methodology desired in this frame is described in Section 5 and, as a result of our analysis, the design and implementation of the AnaVANET evaluation tool is detailed in Section 6, together with a reference evaluation of a network testbed using the tool in Section 7. As a result of this evaluation, the functionalities provided by AnaVANET are analyzed in Section 8 according to the previously identified needs. Finally, Section 9 concludes the paper summarizing the main results and addressing future works.

---

[1] http://anavanet.net/

2. Network protocols in vehicular networks

Network protocols in vehicular networks can be classified in infrastructure-less scenarios, i.e. V2V, and infrastructure-based scenarios, i.e. V2I, as showed in Figure 2.

The infrastructure-less scenario is well-known in the research areas of VANET and MANET. These approaches are designed to enable wireless communications in dynamic topologies without any infrastructure. Routing protocols here are further classified as *topology-based* and *position-based* routing protocols. Upon the appearance of vehicular communications, a second class of infrastructure-less protocols added to the list: VANETs. Most of the VANET solutions are based on geographical routing, thus based on the node's position.

Topology-based protocols were divided into two main branches by the IETF MANET working group: *reactive*, where nodes periodically exchange messages to create routes, and *proactive*, in which control messages are exchanged on demand when it is necessary to reach a particular node. Generally, proactive protocols have the advantage of starting communication rapidly by making the routing table ahead, however, this makes battery life shorter due to frequent signaling. If the topology is highly dynamic and the data traffic is frequent, a proactive protocol could be better. Reactive protocols, on the contrary, keep the battery life longer by reducing signaling messages when there is no data to transmit. The *hybrid* protocols that take the advantage of both proactive and reactive protocols by maintaining routes to near neighbors regularly and searching the destination in long distance on demand.

Some routing protocols are specified by the IETF MANET working group [8]. Both IPv4 and IPv6 are supported in the working group. Ad hoc On-Demand Distance Vector Routing (AODV) [9] and Dynamic Source Routing Protocol (DSR) [10] are specified as reactive routing protocols. And Optimized Link State Routing (OLSR) [11] and Topology Dissemination Based on Reverse-Path Forwarding (TBRPF) [12] are specified as proactive routing protocols. As an example of a hybrid MANET protocol, Zone Routing Protocol (ZRP) [13] is proposed.

VANETs are a particular case of MANETs, and are not restricted by the battery of the communication nodes and are also characterized by the high speed of nodes, the availability of GPS information, and a regular distribution and foreseeable movements. First, vehicles have a larger battery than mobile terminals or sensor devices, which is also charged when the engine is running. Second, the speed of vehicles is also higher than common portable terminals, and relative speeds can reach 300 Km/h; hence, the duration of the routing entries is extremely short. Third, a GPS

device and digital map can be assumed in many cases, whose information improves the network performance in some proposals.

Unlike topology based routing, position based routing does not need to maintain part of the network structure in order to forward packets towards the destination node. When the routing is based on the position, nodes forward the packets with the aim of reaching the nodes within a geographical location. Thus, position based routing can eliminate the problem that appears in topology based protocols when routes become quickly unavailable in high mobility scenarios. In Greedy Perimeter Stateless Routing (GPSR) [14], for instance, intermediate nodes make a decision based on the destination position and neighbor positions. The Car-to-Car Communication Consortium (C2CC) also specified the C2CNet protocol, which was later enhanced by the GeoNet project to support IPv6. Within the ITS standardization domain, GeoNetworking [15] is being completed by ETSI at the moment, integrating several geo-aware strategies to better route packets in vehicular networks.

On the other side, infrastructure-based protocols have been focused on the global connectivity of nodes to the Internet. Mobile IPv6 [16] solved the mobility problem for mobile hosts and, later, Network Mobility Basic support (NEMO) [17] provided a solution for the mobility of a whole network (e.g. a vehicle or bus), which has been recommended by the ISO TC204 WG16 to achieve Internet mobility for vehicles. NEMO maintains a bi-directional tunnel between the router in the vehicle, known as the *mobile router (MR)*, and a server in the fixed infrastructure, known as the *home agent (HA)*, in order to provide a unchanged network prefix called *mobile network prefix (MNP)* to the in-vehicle network. All the in-vehicle nodes called *mobile network nodes (MNN)* maintain a permanent address derived from the MNP even when MR changes the point of attachment to the Internet during the movement (i.e. handover).

3. Experimental evaluation of VANET approaches in the literature

Because of equipment cost, logistic issues and, in general, the necessary effort, literature in experimental evaluation of vehicular network architectures is limited. However, these works are of key importance for the ITS community. Up to now, there are several works dealing with this issue, although most of them are still focused on studying the operation of WiFi, DSRC (Dedicated Short Range Communications) or IEEE 802.11p technologies in the vehicular field.

Communication between a vehicle and a static terminal is important for some ITS services. In [18] a communication scenario considering a static terminal

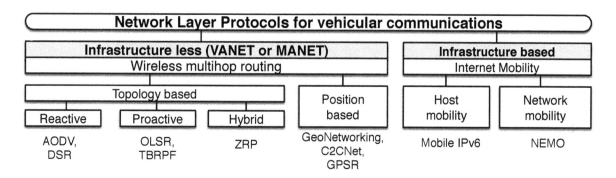

Figure 2. Network protocols in vehicular networks

and a moving vehicle is studied in detail. Among all metrics considered in this work, the transmission power is the more original one, determining the maximum communication range. The type of data traffic used to test the performance of the communication channel is also of interest. Most VANET designs use UDP packets, due to poor TCP performance over wireless channels [19, 20]. The evaluations performed in [21] with IEEE 802.11p reveal that the packet delivery ratio achieved by this technology is highly dependent on the distance between sender and receiver. These results are also confirmed in [22], where it is also concluded that the vehicle speed does not imply a noticeable performance degradation of the communication. A similar evaluation is performed in [23], but this time carrying out a great testing campaign in a city.

When V2V scenarios are considered, most of the previous works only consider two terminals in performance tests, what is not too representative when multi-hop schemes are evaluated. In [24], the applicability of 802.11b in V2V communications is evaluated over urban and highway scenarios, and it is demonstrated that a direct line of sight is one of the most important issues in the network performance. Two works evaluate a multi-hop VANET over real conditions, using three [25] and even six vehicles [26]. These papers offer a wide study about a real VANET set-up, and the last one includes an interesting analysis describing the impact of the number of hops on the final performance. Nonetheless, static routes are used in that work, presenting a non-realistic vehicular network. Our prior work [27], by contrast, considered a real and standardized ad-hoc routing protocol to dynamically modify communication paths. The hardware testbed presented is also suited for future ITS research, with a flexible in-vehicle and inter-vehicle IPv6 network based on mobile routers.

To the best of our knowledge, there exists a few works dealing with the evaluation of IPv6-based communications at network level in vehicular communications, and some of them are within our research line [28, 29]. However, our prior evaluations are only focused on IPv6 network mobility. In this work, the operation of NEMO over a V2V protocol is evaluated, using an implementation of GeoNetworking. This way, an integrated V2V and V2I approach is considered for providing an integral vehicular connectivity using IETF and ETSI standardized protocols. The novelty of this work is twofold, since not only this routing approach is experimentally analyzed, but also an evaluation tool especially designed for vehicular networks is used. As far as the authors know, no specific tools for assessing the performance of vehicular networks have been developed or used in previous research works.

4. VANET evaluation: issues and requirements

4.1. Issues

As said above, the experimental evaluations carried out in vehicular networks are mostly based on single-hop studies. In the case of multi-hop experiments, a static route configuration is often employed, but dynamic routing presents a more realistic view in vehicular communications.

Using multi-hop and dynamic routing strategies presents a challenge in the evaluation of vehicular networks. Common end-to-end evaluation tools such as *ping6* and *iperf* are useless to track the effect of route change, because they are unaware of the path taken during a communication test. An additional lack of these tools is the possibility to measure the performance of hop-by-hop links, since the study is carried out end-to-end. Also, geographical and external factors such as nodes position, distance between nodes or obstacles are not linked with network performance figures of merit. Therefore, the performance comparison of various dynamic routing protocols is essentially missing.

4.2. Requirements

With the aim of summarizing these main requirements when evaluating multi-hop vehicular networks, the next needs are found essential by the software tools used in experimental campaigns for evaluating both V2V and V2I:

Path detection. The topology and communication path of a vehicular network changes frequently with dynamic routing as vehicles move. Thus, the tool should take note of the communication path used in every moment.

Communication performance in links. The communication performance between ends is the sum of the links on the way between them. Once the communication path is tracked, the tool should measure the performance link by link as well as end-to-end.

Geographical awareness. The network performance in a link depends on various geographical factors. For example, the distance between the nodes affects the packet loss probability of the link; the movement speed and the direction are also important factors for the packet loss in the link; and the existence of obstacles between the nodes may screen the wireless radio propagation. Thus, the evaluation tool should take the above geographical factors into account.

Intuitive visualization. It is important to visualize the geographical factors such as node movement (speed, direction), distance and signal obstacles in order to analyze which of them affect the network performance. For intuitive visualization, performance figures of merit and environmental information should be shown together in a synchronized way. Moreover, the spatio-temporal data series should be available in post process to play them at different speeds, stop when desired, or replayed freely as he or she wants.

Independence from network protocols. As shown in Section 2, there are many network layer protocols in the literature for vehicular scenarios, both infrastructure-less and infrastructure based. The evaluation tool should be independent from the network protocols employed in the target vehicular network. This includes that the tool does not require changes to adapt to neither specific protocols nor special message or data transported.

Independent from devices. Depending on the experiment, the configuration of the used devices may differ in both vehicle and infrastructure sides. The devices include the antenna, wireless chipset, CPU, memory, GPS and so on. The tools should not rely on any of the specific devices functionalities. Most favorably, the same software and settings for an experimental test should work on multiple devices.

Adaptation to various scenarios. There are a number of possible networking scenarios in vehicular communications, such as using parked vehicles, slow speeds with surrounding buildings in a urban situation, vehicles moving at higher speeds in a highway, overtaking, vehicles crossing in a two-way road, different topological locations of the ends in a V2I setting, etc. The software evaluation tool should accommodate to all of these scenarios.

Easiness for data collection. In order to compare the network performance obtained when using different network protocols, a lot of experiments could be needed. This may require installing data collector software on many devices, depending on the scenario. Thus, the easiness of the installation of these software modules is very important. Of course, the most favorable case is to employ common software in all of them, such as *tcpdump* or *cat*.

Flexible experimental data format. The experimental data should be stored in a well-organized way. Therefore, the data format needs to be flexible for future extension. For example, the user of the system could require adding new attributes to the data format of evaluation results. We must consider flexible data formats in order not to impact the process of adding new attributes.

5. Evaluation methodology

As it is later described, the evaluation tool presented in this work (AnaVANET) copes with the previous requirements, but first it is important to identify a generic testing methodology that allow a researcher to success in a testing campaign with a vehicular network.

In general, the evaluation goals in computer networks are to analyze which *testing conditions* affect which *data flows or network protocols*. For achieving this end it is necessary to design a proper evaluation methodology. Within it, we should consider the tendency of results by repeating tests with the same settings or varying parameters under study, such as the network protocol, the mobility of nodes or the data volume. A proper evaluation tool, such as the later presented AnaVANET, should support the overall analysis. This section considers both the testing conditions and the possible routing protocols to consider in vehicular networks, as it is summarized in Figure 3, by introducing the concept and presenting our real use case for testing the performance of NEMO over IPv6 GeoNetworking.

5.1. Testing conditions

Testbed platform. The testbed used for the evaluation of network architecture should be carefully chosen to implement most relevant nodes in real software and hardware. In vehicular communications, this is

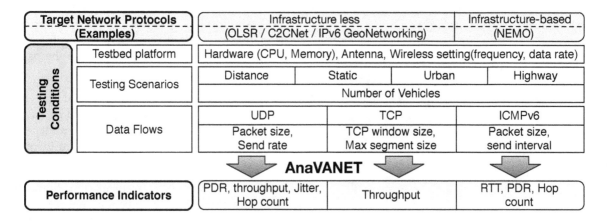

Target Network Protocols (Examples)	Infrastructure less (OLSR / C2CNet / IPv6 GeoNetworking)			Infrastructure-based (NEMO)
Testbed platform	Hardware (CPU, Memory), Antenna, Wireless setting(frequency, data rate)			
Testing Scenarios	Distance	Static	Urban	Highway
	Number of Vehicles			
Data Flows	UDP	TCP		ICMPv6
	Packet size, Send rate	TCP window size, Max segment size		Packet size, send interval
Performance Indicators	PDR, throughput, Jitter, Hop count	Throughput		RTT, PDR, Hop count

Figure 3. Evaluation methodology

extremely important, since a good deployment could be needed in case of testing V2V multi-hop networks.

In our particular case, the testbed comprises a set of four vehicles and two roadside stations, as illustrated in Figure 4. Each vehicle is equipped with a mobile router (MR), with at least two interfaces: an Ethernet link to connect mobile network nodes (MNNs) within the in-vehicle network, and a wireless adapter in ad-hoc mode used for both V2V and V2I communications. On the roadside, access routers (ARs) are fixed on the top of a building or any other elevated point near the road. Each one provides two interfaces: an Ethernet link for a wired Internet access, and a wireless adapter in ad-hoc mode to connect with vehicles in the surroundings. At a backend point on the Internet, a home agent (HA) is installed to support Internet mobility of MRs by using NEMO.

Among the various testbed conditions, the hardware specifications (CPU, memory, etc), antenna and wireless settings are important factors for the evaluation, since they will highly affect the results. In our case, MRs are Alix3d3 embedded boxes provided with a Linux 2.6.29.6 kernel. Each MR has a mini-pci wireless card Atheros AR5414 802.11 a/b/g Rev 0, and an antenna 2.4GHz 9dBi indoor OMNI RP-SMA6 is used. The frequency used has been 2.422Ghz and the data rate has been fixed to 6 Mbits/s.

Testing scenarios. Fixing the evaluation scenarios beforehand is essential in the planning of a testing campaign. In general, the main factors that determine the possible scenarios are:

Mobility Vehicle mobility is a key issue to cope with realistic vehicular network conditions. This way, we can consider not only static scenarios, to test the network operation in a controlled way, but also dynamic scenarios under common speed situations. Of course, field operational tests

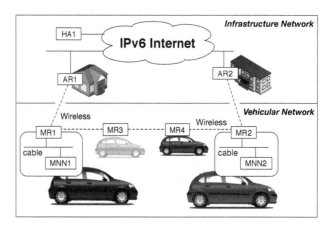

Figure 4. Reference network configuration

should be conducted to confirm the expected results, taking into account the proper handling of mobility, i.e. Doppler shifting, fast fading, etc.

Location Urban and interurban environments affect communication performance in a different way, because the signal propagation can be interfered by buildings (among other elements), and the line of sight between vehicles is not always possible. Two environments are considered in our tests: a semi-urban one located at INRIA-Rocquencourt, which contains a set of small buildings surrounded by streets, and a highway stretch, the A-12 one, near INRIA-Rocquencourt.

Number of vehicles The number of hops between the source and the destination vehicles affect the communication delay and the higher probability of packet looses, due to route changes or MAC transmission issues. Up to four conventional vehicles (Citroën C3) are considered in our case. This testing fleet is showed in Figure 5.

Figure 5. Testing vehicles

A set of possible testing scenarios when evaluating multi-hop vehicular networks is summarized in Figure 6. These have been divided into urban and highway. Mobility has been set to static, urban-like speed and high speed. In our particular evaluation, these scenarios have been considered with our fleet of vehicles, with the aim of covering a wide range of communication conditions. The obstacles have been in our case a set of building blocks located at the Paris - Rocquencourt premises. The chosen highway has been the French A13, near Versalles.

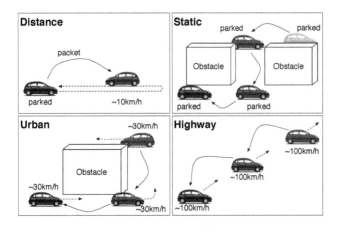

Figure 6. Proposal of movement scenarios

5.2. Data flows and performance indicators

A number or protocols and data flows can be set for evaluations, however, only the most representative and more used in the literature should be considered to study concrete performance indicators. For instance, in our case UDP, TCP and ICMPv6 are used to measure the network performance between two communication end-nodes (MNN to MNN) mounted within two vehicles:

UDP is a connection-less unidirectional transmission flow. The traffic is generated by *iperf* in our case. It is considered that with UDP the performance indicators under consideration can be the packet delivery ratio, throughput and jitter.

TCP is a connection-oriented bidirectional transmission flow. This traffic is also generated by *iperf* in our case. The performance indicator under consideration here has been the maximum throughput.

ICMPv6 is a bi-directional transmission flow. The traffic is generated by *ping6* in our case. The performance indicator under consideration can be the road trip delay time and packet deliveries.

The set of performance indicators most used in the literature are detailed next:

Round-Trip Time (RTT) can be measured using ICMPv6, as in our case. A host on the source vehicle, or located at an infrastructure point, sends ICMPv6 echo request to a host on the destination vehicle, or located at an infrastructure point. The destination host replies with an ICMPv6 echo reply. The period between the time that the request is sent and the time that the reply is received can be obtained by using ping6.

Throughput can be measured using UDP or TCP. It can be measured with a traffic generator tool, such as the *iperf* tool in our case. In UDP, iperf is executed in both the sender and the receiver nodes. The UDP packet transmission rate is set with a fixed rate and the sender is not able to see the result because the communication is unidirectional from the sender to the receiver. The throughput is shown on the receiver side. On the other hand, when using a TCP transmission, the sending rate is automatically adjusted with the TCP congestion control mechanism. The sending rate is adjusted depending on the acknowledgement messages received. The throughput appears in both the sender and receiver nodes.

Jitter is a measure of the variability over time of the packet latency across a network. A network with a constant latency has a null jitter. In general, the jitter is expressed as an average of the deviation from the network mean latency, and can be calculated using the RTT, as in our case.

Packet Delivery Ratio (PDR) is the percentage of packets received by the target node as compared with the number of packets sent by the source. iperf, for instance, shows this value at the receiver side when using TCP in an end-to-end manner, but AnaVANET is also able to calculate the PDR on each hop between the sender and destination nodes.

6. System design and implementation of AnaVANET

6.1. Overview of the software

AnaVANET (initially standing for Analyzer of VANET) is an evaluation tool implemented in Java to assess the performance of vehicular networks. It takes as input the logs generated by the *iperf*, *tcpdump* and/or *ping6*, together with navigation information in NMEA format, to compute the next performance metrics: network throughput, delay, jitter, hop count and list of intermediate nodes in the communication path, PDR end-to-end and hop-by-hop, speed, and instantaneous position.

In this part of the work AnaVANET is put in the context of the evaluation scenario described in the previous section in Figure 7, showing also the main inputs and outputs of the tool. The sender MNN (left most vehicle) is in charge of generating data traffic, and both the sender and the receiver (right most vehicle) MNNs record a high level log, according to the application used to generate network traffic (*iperf* and *ping6* for the moment). All MRs record information about forwarded data packets by means of the *tcpdump* tool, and log the vehicle position continuously. All this data is post-processed by the AnaVANET core software and then analyzed. The tool traces all the data packets transmitted from the sender node to detect packet losses and calculate statistics for each link and end-to-end, and then merge all these per-hop information with transport level statistics of the traffic generator. As a result, AnaVANET outputs a JSON file with statistics on a one-second basis (see Section 6.2 for details), and a packet trace file with the path followed by each data packet.

Once generated, performance metrics can be graphically showed through plots generated by *gnuplot* and a website where all tests are available. The screenshot of the website is shown on the left bottom corner of Figure 7 (which is also enlarged in the previous Figure 1). Accessing the website one can replay the tests on a map to see momentary figures of merit. Previous experiments can be chosen to monitor the main performance metrics at any time of the tests. Users can play and stop at any arbitrary point of the test with the control buttons on the upper left part of the window. The player speed, one step forward and one step backward are also implemented. On the map, the position and movement of the vehicle are depicted with the speed of each vehicle and the distance between them. The transferred data size, bandwidth, packet loss rate, RTT and jitter, for each link and end-to-end are displayed. The network performance is visualized by the width of links and the colors used to draw them.

6.2. Data format of experimental results

In this part, we describe the problems of the former AnaVANET data format [30], which was based on XML, and we detail the recent changes to improve the flexibility of the results using the JSON format [31].

There is a fundamental trade-off between flat data format and structured data format. Flat data format is more flexible than structured one, because if developers want to add a new attribute, they just put the attribute next to the other attributes. On the other hand, in a structured format, developers have to consider the layers and relationships to add a new attribute and they sometimes cannot add the new attribute because of its structure. However, when a flat data format is used, developers have to revise and adjust their applications, since the relationships among attributes can vary. In this line, a normalized way of calling the attributes is also important. If there is no rule of normalization, developers have to handle differences of an attribute name (e.g., temperature, Temperature, temp).

AnaVANET was initially developed to analyze the real operation of VANETs. The initial data format used as output of an evaluation had some problems regarding its flat format and the dynamic columns available per each data record. Hence it took several hours to check the results after carrying out new experiments. To solve these problems, we have designed a structured and normalized format, considering the features of vehicular networks. Our format is extensible and independent from concrete experimental environments and visualization tools. We have also adapted the initial visualization tool with an internal converter module within the web application, and an additional command line tool has been implemented to process the output logs of AnaVANET in a text-based basis. The new data format and tools enable us to check the results in several seconds after carrying out experiments, considering that users could require a fast evaluation to continue with new experiments.

The new structured and normalized data format of AnaVANET considers three layers, as it is shown in Figure 8. AnaVANET summarizes data on each time slot following the next scheme. The top layer is the "experiment" layer. This layer mainly manages static attributes (e.g. ID of experiment or the name of experiment). The second layer is the "data" layer. This layer manages results of an experiment on each time slot. This layer has time, total packet delivery ratio (PDR), total RTT and other attributes. The third layer is comprised by the "node" and "link" parts. The node part manages each node's statuses, whereas the link part

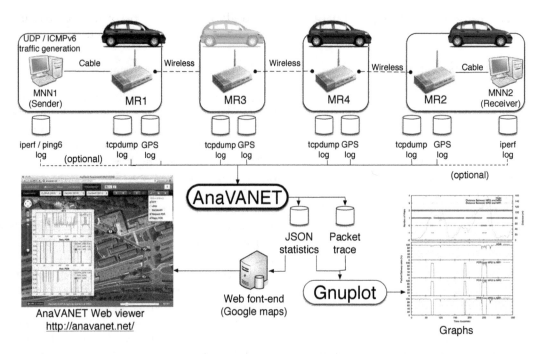

Figure 7. Overview of AnaVANET

manages each link's statuses. Link means a relationship between two nodes and especially represents wireless link statuses. An experiment has a series of data and each data has several nodes and links. We have also normalized the names of the attributes considered in each layer.

This data format based on time-series for saving node and link information is an abstracted representation that can be used to collect results from any kind of network. Moreover, by using this three-layer representation, the system can be easily adapted to future requirements.

7. Evaluation of NEMO over IPv6 GeoNetworking

Early versions of AnaVANET were designed for evaluating infrastructure less network protocols, as used in our previous works for analyzing OLSR in vehicular environments [32] and later tests of IPv6 over C2CNet [33] in the FP7 GeoNet project. The current version of AnaVANET can also analyze infrastructure-based network protocols such as NEMO.

In this section, we report a summary of the results collected in the evaluation of NEMO over IPv6 GeoNetworking when a vehicle connects with a node located in the Internet using two roadside units as access routers. The *umip.org*[2] implementation of NEMO is used, whereas the *cargeo6.org*[3] software is used for

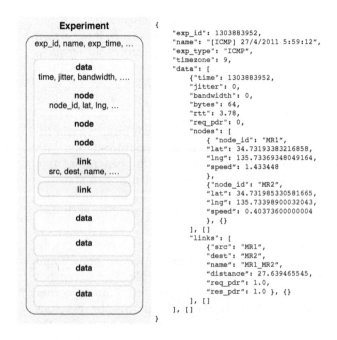

Figure 8. Three-layer model of the structured data format used by AnaVANET

IPv6 GeoNetworking. ICMPv6 and UDP evaluations in handover scenarios were performed at INRIA Paris-Rocquencourt campus with the two ARs previously presented in the testbed description. The speed of the

---

[2]*http://umip.org*
[3]*http://www.cargeo6.org*

vehicle was limited to less than 15 km/h, like in a low speed urban scenario.

The reader can directly click in from Figure 9 to Figure 12 to see the correspondent results in the AnaVANET web viewer, to further perceive the details of the gathered results.

7.1. ICMP evaluation in a handover scenario

ICMPv6 echo requests (64 bytes) are sent from the MNN to a common computer located in the wired network twice a second, which replies with ICMPv6 echo replies. The results collected in the ICMPv6 tests are plotted in Figure 9. The lower part shows the itinerary of the vehicle and the locations of AR1 and AR2 on the map, whereas the upper part shows the RTT, the packet loss and the result of the mobility signaling. The X-axis and the Y-axis of the upper part are the latitude/longitude of the vehicle, corresponding to the road stretch indicated in the lower part of the figure. When either the request or the reply is lost, the RTT is marked with a zero value and, at the same time, a packet loss is indicated. A binding registration success is plotted when the NEMO binding update (BU) and the corresponding binding acknowledgment (BA) are successfully processed. On the contrary, if either of them is lost, a binding registration fail is plotted at the position.

Figure 10 shows the same result of the test, but referred to the test time. The upper graph shows the RTT and the distance to the two ARs; the middle one shows the PDR obtained with the two ARs; and, finally, the lower plot shows the status of the NEMO signaling. A NEMO success means that the binding registration has been successfully performed, and a fail indicates that either the BU or the BA has been lost.

As can be seen in Figure 9 and Figure 10, the RTT is stable at the beginning of the test near AR2, with a value of around five milliseconds. AR2 is installed at about 100 meters away the road. It sends constant BU messages and, consequently, the MR successfully performs the binding registration every twelve seconds, without any packet loss. Soon, after the vehicle turns the first corner (north west of the square), packets start to be dropped until the second corner. This is because a near building screens the wireless radio. The binding signaling is dropped as well in the period. Then it recovers when the vehicle comes to the straight road on the south. The mobility signaling is successfully sent again with a regular interval.

The lower straight road of the stretch is less stable than the one on the north, because of two reasons. First, the location of the south straight road is 250 meters further to AR2 than the one on the north. Thus the signal strength is weaker now. Second, the trees at this location interfere the wireless radio, especially at the

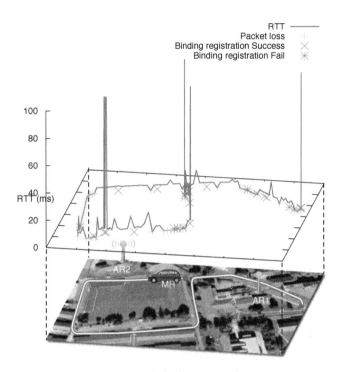

Figure 9. Map-based RTT, packet losses and mobility signaling in an ICMP evaluation under a handover scenario

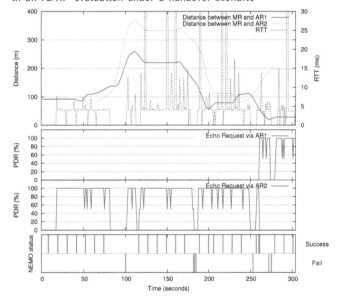

Figure 10. RTT, packet looses and mobility signaling in an ICMP evaluation under a handover scenario

end of this part of the circuit, as can be seen with the three consecutive binding registration fails. When the MR fails to receive a valid matching response within the selected initial retransmission interval, the MR should retransmit the message until a response is received. The retransmission by the MR must use an exponential back-off in which the timeout period is doubled upon each retransmission, until either the MR receives a response or the timeout period reaches the value of maximum timeout period as specified in [16]. In our particular case the mobility daemon tries to deliver the BU one second after the first failure of the binding. Then, when it fails, it increases the retransmission time in two, four, eight seconds, and so on.

The performance in the final part of the testing circuit is more stable, and no binding messages are lost. In this period the vehicle approaches AR2 and then leaves it turning right at the end of the test.

The MR starts receiving router advertisement (RA) messages from AR1 when the distance to AR1 is 50 meters, however, the RA messages from AR2 also reaches the zone. As the result, the vehicle triggers the movement detection, and sends the mobility signaling via the AR where it receives the RA. When the MR associates with AR2 some ICMP packets and mobility signaling messages are lost because of the distance and a near building. When the MR later switches to AR1, the packets are more stably transmitted.

7.2. UDP evaluation in a handover scenario

The results collected in the UDP tests are plotted in Figure 11. UDP packets are sent from the MNN to the wired node at a rate of 1 Mbps and a length of 1250 bytes. The lower part of the figure shows the itinerary of the vehicle, and the upper part corresponds to the PDR obtained with the ARs and the binding registration results, as in the previous case. The road stretch is the same one used above, but the vehicle moves on the contrary direction in this case.

Figure 12 shows the time-mapped results of the same UDP test. The upper graph shows the UDP throughput from the MNN to the wired node, the middle part shows the PDR to the two ARs, and the lower plot includes the status of the NEMO signaling.

The throughput of the UDP traffic is below 30% of the sending rate of 1Mbps (*i.e.* 300Kbps), however the PDR with the two ARs reaches 100%. This is because the throughput is measured between end nodes (MNN and a node in the Internet) by *iperf* and the PDR in the wireless links are calculated hop-by-hop by AnaVANET. In this case, it shows that more than 70% of the UDP packets are dropped outside the wireless links. In fact, the CarGeo6 software experimented a bottleneck in the processing of so many UDP packets at that time. This also explains the phenomenon where the binding registration messages are lost while none of the UDP packets are lost (this can be seen in the straight road in the south part of the circuit). In this case, the BUs are lost in the CarGeo6 software and are not transmitted from the wireless interface. We can detect where a packet is lost, especially the loss in a wireless link, thanks to the AnaVANET system (although the cause of the packet losses was not in the wireless links in the

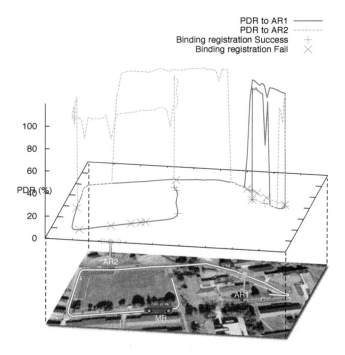

Figure 11. Map-based PDR of UDP evaluation using NEMO over IPv6 GeoNetworking

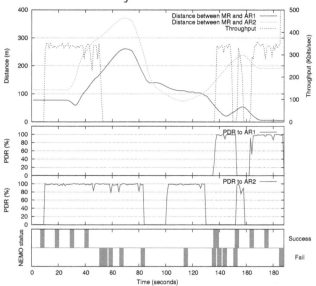

Figure 12. PDR of UDP evaluation using NEMO over IPv6 GeoNetworking

present case). This is because AnaVANET is capable of measuring both the hop-by-hop network performance and the end-to-end one.

As can be seen in Figure 11, AR2 is available most of the test period (especially, around the square) except for the end of the test. When the vehicle moves in the first straight road in the east, the PDR to AR2 is almost 100%. During this period, no binding message is dropped. The BUs are sent regularly at intervals of twelve seconds.

The packets start being dropped on the west of the square because the building on the north west corner of the square blocks the wireless radio. When the beacons exchanged between GeoNetworking nodes twice in a second are dropped, the correspondent entry of the location table expires in five seconds.

As can be seen in Figure 12, after the southwest corner, the end-to-end throughput drops to zero and the binding registration fails, while the hop-by-hop PDR to AR2 is still almost 100%. This shows that the mobility signaling packets are lost in CarGeo6 as explained earlier. Since the binding life time is configured as 24 seconds, the binding entry in the HA expires 24 seconds after the last successful binding registration. After the expiration of the binding, HA discards all the packet from the MR. During the period, the MR try to send the BUs in exponentially increased interval from 1 second to 32 seconds (1, 2, 4, 8, 16 and 32 seconds).

Then, at time 139 seconds, when the vehicle is 20 meters away from AR1, the first binding registration through AR1 successes. UDP packets are switched to AR1 from this moment. Then at time 155 seconds, the binding registration is successfully performed via AR2 again. During the handover from AR1 to AR2, from time 155 seconds to time 158 seconds, three seconds of disconnection are present in the iperf log. At time 166 seconds, the path to the Internet is switched to AR1 again. In this handover, UDP packets are lost during four seconds from time 166 seconds.

8. Qualitative evaluation of the system

As a result of the experience working with the recent version of AnaVANET, including the results presented above, we have revisited the requirements for an efficient testing environment in vehicular networks detailed in Section 4, with the aim of evaluating the advantages of the system. Table 1 summarizes the most important features, which demonstrate that AnaVANET fulfills the most important requirements and it is an efficient evaluation tool.

9. Conclusions and future work

The paper has presented the peculiarities of evaluating vehicular networks experimentally, through presenting the most used protocols and detailing the needs of the software tools to be used for this task. After that, the importance of the testing methodology is described, and a reference design of a vehicular network evaluation is used to exemplify it. The testbed design and implementation, testing scenarios, routing protocols and data flows, are found essential to be fixed beforehand to avoid improvisation during the testing campaign. The AnaVANET platform is then presented

Requirement	Proposal
Path detection	AnaVANET can track the nodes of the communication path for each transmission
Communication performance in links	The system can measure the PDR of each link as well as the end-to-end PDR
Geographical awareness	The system outputs the performance indicators in a geo-referenced way, which facilitates the analysis of results
Intuitive visualization	The movement of vehicles is showed using Google Maps in a Web application, together with the graphs of the desired performance metrics. It allows a step-by-step visual analysis of the results.
Independence from network protocols	The system adopts the MAC address for packet tracing. Therefore any kind of network layer protocol can be evaluated.
Independent from devices	The system does not require specific hardware.
Adaptation to various scenarios	The system can be used in a number of scenarios, including distance, static, urban and highway tests. Also it allows both V2V and V2I tests.
Easiness for data collection	The system does not require special software to gather experimental data. Packet dumps are taken with *tcpdump*, and GPS NMEA data is obtained directly from a serial interface, to finally generate results.
Flexible experimental data format	We have adopted a structured and normalized format defining a three-layer model in order to increase the flexibility for future extension.

Table 1. Qualitative evaluation of the system

as an efficient evaluation software to process the data gathered by common testing tools, and then generate lots of performance indicators of the trials. All of these performance parameters are put in the spatio-temporal context, through the collection and correlation of GPS information, and most important figures of merit can be exported in the form of graphics or showed interactively in a web front-end.

The capabilities of AnaVANET are exploited in a novel evaluation of NEMO over IPv6 GeoNetworking, using the tool to gather RTT, PDR and channel throughput information. The results reveal that mobile IPv6 connectivity can be maintained in a V2I case using

GeoNetworking over WiFi to pass NEMO IPv6 traffic between vehicles and infrastructure.

Our future work includes, first, a link layer extension of the system to analyze the channel quality (RSSI) and load ratio. This data will allow the development of coverage maps for the communication nodes. Second, it is considered the support for multicast data flows, since it is essential for the dissemination of events in vehicular networks. Third, we plan to evaluate a real application developed for cooperative ITS.

Acknowledgment

This work has been sponsored by the European 7th FP, through the ITSSv6 (contract 270519), FOTsis (contract 270447) and GEN6 (contract 297239) projects, and the Spanish Ministry of Science and Innovation, through the Walkie-Talkie project (TIN2011-27543-C03).

References

[1] Action plan for the deployment of Intelligent Transport Systems in Europe, December 2008. COM(2008) 886 final.

[2] Standardisation mandate addressed to CEN, CENELEC and ETSI in the field of information and communication technologies to support the interoperability of cooperative systems for intelligent transport in the european community, October 2009.

[3] ISO 21217:2010 Intelligent transport systems – Communications access for land mobiles (CALM) – Architecture, April 2010.

[4] Intelligent Transport Systems (ITS); Communications Architecture, September 2010. ETSI EN 302 665 V1.1.1 (2010-09).

[5] C. Tschudin, H. Lundgren, and E. Nordstrom. Embedding MANETs in the real world. *Lecture notes in computer science*, 2775(1):578–589, September 2003.

[6] T. Ernst, M. Goleva, I. Ben Jemaa, A. Kovacs, H. Menouar, C. Noguchi, S. Schulze, M. Tsukada, P. Zhang, and W. Zhang. GeoNet STREP No.216269 Deliverable 7.1 GeoNet Experimentation Results. 2010. GeoNet-D7.1-ExperimentationResults-v1.0.

[7] J. Santa, A. Kovacs, A. Varadi, A.F. Skarmeta, P.J. Fernandez, F. Bernal, M. Tsukada, B. Cama, F. Pereniguez, R. Marin, C. Schulze, A. Fitzner, O. Shagdar, and Y. Bouchaala. ITSSv6 STREP Grant Agreement 210519 Deliverable 4.2 Final Validation & Evaluation Results. March 2014. ITSSv6-D4.2-FinalValidation&EvaluationResults-v1.1.

[8] IETF: Mobile Ad-hoc Networks (MANET) Working Group, 1997. http://datatracker.ietf.org/wg/manet/charter/.

[9] C. Perkins, E. Belding-Royer, and S. Das. Ad hoc On-Demand Distance Vector (AODV) Routing. RFC 3561 (Experimental), July 2003.

[10] D. Johnson, Y. Hu, and D. Maltz. The Dynamic Source Routing Protocol (DSR) for Mobile Ad Hoc Networks for IPv4. RFC 4728 (Experimental), February 2007.

[11] T. Clausen and P. Jacquet. Optimized Link State Routing Protocol (OLSR). RFC 3626 (Experimental), October 2003.

[12] R. Ogier, F. Templin, and M. Lewis. Topology Dissemination Based on Reverse-Path Forwarding (TBRPF). RFC 3684 (Experimental), February 2004.

[13] Zygmunt J. Haas, Marc R. Pearlman, and Prince Samar. *The Zone Routing Protocol (ZRP) for Ad Hoc Networks*, July 2002. IETF work in progress, draft-ietf-manet-zone-zrp-04.

[14] Brad Karp and H. T. Kung. Gpsr: Greedy perimeter stateless routing for wireless networks. In *6th Annual International Conference on Mobile Computing and Networking, MobiCom 2000, August 6.-11., 2000, Boston, Massachusetts, USA*, pages 243–254. ACM / IEEE, August 2000.

[15] Intelligent Transport Systems (ITS); Vehicular Communications; Part 4: Geographical Addressing and Forwarding for Point-to-Point and Point-to-Multipoint Communications; Sub-part 1: Media-Independent Functionality, June 2011. ETSI TS 102 636-4-1 V1.1.1 (2011-06).

[16] C. Perkins, D. Johnson, and J. Arkko. Mobility Support in IPv6. RFC 6275 (Proposed Standard), July 2011.

[17] V. Devarapalli, R. Wakikawa, A. Petrescu, and P. Thubert. Network Mobility (NEMO) Basic Support Protocol. RFC 3963 (Proposed Standard), January 2005.

[18] C. Wewetzer, M. Caliskan, K. Meier, and A. Luebke. Experimental evaluation of umts and wireless lan for inter-vehicle communication. In *Proc. 7th International Conference on ITS Telecommunications ITST '07*, pages 1–6, 6–8 June 2007.

[19] F. Hui and P. Mohapatra. Experimental characterization of multi-hop communications in vehicular ad hoc network. In *ACM international workshop on Vehicular ad hoc networks*, pages 85–86, Cologne, Germany, September 2005.

[20] A. Festag, H. Fußler, H. Hartenstein, A. Sarma, and R. Schmitz. FLEETNET: BRINGING CAR-TO-CAR COMMUNICATION INTO THE REAL WORLD. *Computer*, 4(L15):16, 2004.

[21] Oyunchimeg Shagdar, Manabu Tsukada, Masatoshi Kakiuchi, Thouraya Toukabri, and Thierry Ernst. Experimentation Towards IPv6 over IEEE 802.11p with ITS Station Architecture. In *International Workshop on IPv6-based Vehicular Networks (colocated with IEEE Intelligent Vehicles Symposium)*, Alcala de Henares, Spain, June 2012.

[22] Jia-Chin Lin, Chi-Sheng Lin, Chih-Neng Liang, and Bo-Chiuan Chen. Wireless communication performance based on IEEE 802.11p R2V field trials. *IEEE Communications Magazine*, 50(5):184 –191, may 2012.

[23] J. Gozalvez, M. Sepulcre, and R. Bauza. IEEE 802.11p vehicle to infrastructure communications in urban environments. *IEEE Communications Magazine*, 50(5):176 –183, may 2012.

[24] Víctor González, Alberto Los Santos, Carolina Pinart, and Francisco Milagro. Experimental demonstration of the viability of ieee 802.11b based inter-vehicle communications. In *TridentCom 2008*, pages 1–7, ICST, Brussels, Belgium, Belgium, 2008. ICST (Institute for Computer Sciences, Social-Informatics and

Telecommunications Engineering).

[25] M. Jerbi, S. M. Senouci, and M. Al Haj. Extensive experimental characterization of communications in vehicular ad hoc networks within different environments. In *Proc. VTC2007-Spring Vehicular Technology Conference IEEE 65th*, pages 2590–2594, 2007.

[26] M. Jerbi and S. M. Senouci. Characterizing multi-hop communication in vehicular networks. In *Proc. IEEE Wireless Communications and Networking Conference WCNC 2008*, pages 3309–3313, 2008.

[27] Manabu Tsukada, José Santa, Olivier Mehani, Yacine Khaled, and Thierry Ernst. Design and Experimental Evaluation of a Vehicular Network Based on NEMO and MANET. In *The special issue for Vehicular Ad Hoc Networks, EURASIP Journal on Advances in Signal Processing*, 2010.

[28] Jose Santa, PedroJ. Fernandez, Fernando Pereniguez, Fernando Bernal, Antonio Moragon, and AntonioF. Skarmeta. Ipv6 communication stack for deploying cooperative vehicular services. *International Journal of Intelligent Transportation Systems Research*, 12(2):48–60, 2014.

[29] J. Santa, F. Pereniguez-Garcia, F. Bernal, P.J. Fernandez, R. Marin-Lopez, and A.F. Skarmeta. A framework for supporting network continuity in vehicular ipv6 communications. *Intelligent Transportation Systems Magazine, IEEE*, 6(1):17–34, Spring 2014.

[30] M. Tsukada, J. Santa, S. Matsuura, T. Ernst, and K. Fujikawa. Anavanet: an experiment and visualization tool for vehicular networks. In *9th International Conference on Testbeds and Research Infrastructures for the Development of Networks & Communities (TRIDENTCOM 2014)*, May 2014.

[31] T. Bray. The JavaScript Object Notation (JSON) Data Interchange Format. RFC 7159 (Proposed Standard), March 2014.

[32] Jose Santa, Manabu Tsukada, Thierry Ernst, Olivier Mehani, and A. F. Gomez-Skarmeta. Assessment of vanet multi-hop routing over an experimental platform. *Int. J. Internet Protoc. Technol.*, 4(3):158–172, September 2009.

[33] Manabu Tsukada, Ines Ben Jemaa, Hamid Menouar, Wenhui Zhang, Maria Goleva, and Thierry Ernst. Experimental evaluation for IPv6 over VANET geographic routing. In *IWCMC '10: Proceedings of the 6th International Wireless Communications and Mobile Computing Conference*, pages 736–741, New York, NY, USA, 2010. ACM.

9

An Investigation of Performance Analysis of Anomaly Detection Techniques for Big Data in SCADA Systems

Mohiuddin Ahmed[1], Adnan Anwar[1], Abdun Naser Mahmood[1], Zubair Shah and Michael J. Maher[1]

[1] School of Engineering and Information Technology, UNSW Canberra, ACT 2600, Australia

Abstract

Anomaly detection is an important aspect of data mining, where the main objective is to identify anomalous or unusual data from a given dataset. However, there is no formal categorization of application-specific anomaly detection techniques for big data and this ignites a confusion for the data miners. In this paper, we categorise anomaly detection techniques based on nearest neighbours, clustering and statistical approaches and investigate the performance analysis of these techniques in critical infrastructure applications such as SCADA systems. Extensive experimental analysis is conducted to compare representative algorithms from each of the categories using seven benchmark datasets (both real and simulated) in SCADA systems. The effectiveness of the representative algorithms is measured through a number of metrics. We highlighted the set of algorithms that are the best performing for SCADA systems.

Keywords: Anomaly detection, SCADA systems, big data.

1. Big Data Analysis in SCADA Systems

Supervisory Control and Data Acquisition (SCADA) systems are widely used for monitoring and control of Industrial Control System (ICS) of national critical infrastructures, including the emerging energy system, transportation system, gas and water systems, and so on. Generally, ICS is comprised of Programmable Logic Controllers (PLCs), Remote Terminal Units (RTUs) with Intelligent Electronic Devices (IEDs), a telemetry system, a Human Machine Interface (HMI) and a supervisory (computer) system. In a SCADA based ICS, communication infrastructures connect the supervisory (computer) systems and the RTUs. The operational process and requirements of SCADA systems, which are used for industrial networks, have characteristics distinct from enterprise networks. The primary objective of a SCADA system is to control real-life physical equipment and devices, e.g., an energy system SCADA may be used for monitoring and control of the generation plants. On the other hand, conventional information based traffic network is used for data processing and transfer [23]. As the primary objective of the SCADA is different from the conventional information network, the operational process and its requirements vary significantly. Since the SCADA is used to control critical infrastructures, the failure

severity is very high which requires a high level of reliability. Moreover, the data acquisition, processing, and transmission require real-time operation or atleast near real-time operation. Besides, the data transferred through the SCADA devices are both periodic and aperiodic [23]. For example, in a SCADA based energy transmission system, an RTU sends the information of the voltages and currents of a node every few seconds continually (which is periodic) and it also sends a warning when the current exceeds the maximum rating (which is aperiodic). It is also important to ensure that the transmitted data is received without losing any information within a specific time-frame. A conventional information traffic network can withstand even a high data loss but this is not the case for the SCADA devices as the real-time physical process is highly dependent on the data they receive. In Figure 1, a brief overview of SCADA architecture is given. Next, we briefly discuss the importance and significance of Big Data analysis in a SCADA based ICS.

Typically, big data has three dimensional properties (3V) that include volume, velocity and variety [28]. The term *'volume'* is related with the amount of data and its dimensionality. *'Velocity'* is the processing speed of the data. The last property of big data, *'variety'* refers

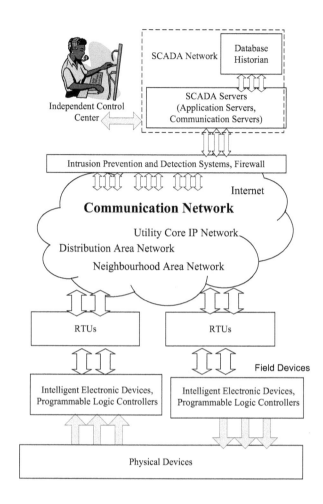

Figure 1. An overview of SCADA Architecture

to the mix of different types of data. Now, we discuss the essence of big data analysis in a SCADA network considering the *3V* properties of big data.

Generally, a SCADA system is dispersed across a large geographic area and is combined of multiple independent systems [23]. Hence, lots of sensor devices and actuators are used to monitor and control of this wide spread large networks. Therefore, the amount of data received in a SCADA is also huge which makes the data analysis a challenging issue. Moreover, the recent trend of using Ethernet and web standards combined with traditional SCADA standards has shifted the SCADA paradigm from event-driven to process-driven, enabling the control of SCADA devices under streaming information exchange. Besides, significant amount of monitoring devices are used to ensure the observability of the processes. All of these technological advancements have provided an improved control performance of the SCADA system; however, big data issue has been emerged with the increased volume of information used in a SCADA

network [28].

The second property of the Big data is the *'velocity'* at which the data is processed. In a SCADA system, this property is very crucial as the time requirement of SCADA data exchange is real-time or near real-time. Therefore, those applications which need faster processing, big data is a critical factor and needs significant attention. Even applications which are based on post-event analyses face noticeable challenge to handle the huge amount of data from a SCADA network. Therefore, improved and robust techniques, which are capable of handling big data within sufficient time frame, will add extra value to manage the SCADA network more efficiently and reliably.

In a SCADA system, field devices are responsible to collect different types of data for monitoring a physical system. Therefore, data received from *'variety'* of sources also make the processing very challenging. As a result, the big data issues need to be addressed as all 3V properties of big data is observed in the data received from the SCADA system.

Based on this scenario, performance analysis of anomaly detection techniques is a research requirement. Recently, a number of approaches have been proposed for big data analysis [4–10]. However, for SCADA systems, we are the pioneer to investigate the anomaly detection techniques in big data perspective. Our contribution in this paper are the following:

- We categorize the anomaly detection techniques based on nearest neighbour, clustering and statistics.

- Representative algorithms in each category are applied on benchmark SCADA systems datasets.

- We evaluate the performance of the algorithms using a number of metrics such as *accuracy, false positive rate, hit rate, F-measure* and *MCC*.

- Finally, we highlight the set of techniques that are efficient for big data analysis.

Rest of the papers are organized as follows. Section 2 provides fundamental aspects of anomaly detection and a taxonomy. Section 3 contains the discussion on the different categories of anomaly detection algorithms. Section 4 discusses the proposed criterion to benchmark anomaly detection algorithms and their merits/demerits. Section 5 provides the experimental results and detailed discussion on the performance comparison. We conclude our paper in section 6.

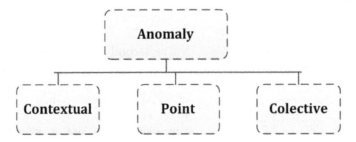

Figure 2. A simple taxonomy of anomaly

2. Anomaly Detection Fundamentals

Anomaly detection is an important data analysis task. The main objective of anomaly detection is to detect anomalous or abnormal data from a given dataset. This is an interesting area of data mining research as it involves discovering new and rare patterns from a dataset. Anomaly detection has been widely studied in statistics and machine learning. It is also known as outlier detection, novelty detection, deviation detection and exception mining [1]. Based on the characteristics of data instances, anomalies are grouped into three categories (Figure 2). These are discussed below:

- *Point Anomaly*: When a particular data instance deviates from the normal pattern of the dataset, it can be considered as a point anomaly. For a familiar example, we can consider expenditure on electricity bills. If the usual bill per month is about 100 dollars, and if for one month it is 500 dollars then obviously it is a point anomaly [3].

- *Contextual Anomaly*: When a data instance is anomalous in a particular context, but not in other times, then it is termed a contextual anomaly, or conditional anomaly. For example, the expenditure on credit card during a festive period, e.g., Christmas or New Year, is usually higher than the rest of the year. Although, the expenditure during a festive month can be high, it may not be anomalous due to the expenses being contextually normal in nature. On the other hand, an equally high expense during a non-festive month could be considered as a contextual anomaly.

- *Collective Anomaly*: Collective anomaly is a pattern in the data when a group of similar data instances behave anomalously with respect to the entire dataset. It might happen that the individual data instance is not an anomaly by itself, but due to its presence in a collection it is identified as an anomaly. For example, a denial of service attack can be considered as a group of network traffic instances affecting the network as well as collective anomaly [2, 24].

One important issue in anomaly detection is how the anomalies are represented as output. Generally there are two categories:

- **Scores:** Scoring based anomaly detection techniques assign a score to each of the data instances. Then the scores are ranked and analyst used to choose the anomalies or use a threshold to select.

- **Binary:** According to these techniques, outputs are considered in binary fashion, i.e. either anomaly or not. Techniques which provide binary labels are computationally efficient since each of the data instances do not have to provide scores.

3. Anomaly Detection Techniques

In this section, we discuss the anomaly detection techniques covered in the scope of this paper. There are various kinds of anomaly detection techniques based on different theories [1, 25]. In this paper, we classify the anomaly detection techniques in two major categories. These are the following:

- **Supervised Learning**: It is the machine learning task of inferring a function from labelled training data [39]. The training data consist of a set of training examples. In supervised learning, the training examples consist of an input object and a desired output value. A supervised learning algorithm learns from the training data and creates a knowledge base which can be used for mapping new and unseen data.

- **Unsupervised Learning**: It tries to find hidden structure in unlabelled data, which distinguishes unsupervised learning from supervised learning [44]. For example, clustering can be considered as unsupervised learning algorithms, where pre-labelled data is not necessary [48].

Supervised learning algorithms require pre-labelled data. Labelled data are rare and difficult to find. However, when pre-labelled data is available, the unseen data cannot be mapped which are not present in the labelled data, such as zero day attacks in the intrusion detection domain [24]. Inspired by this

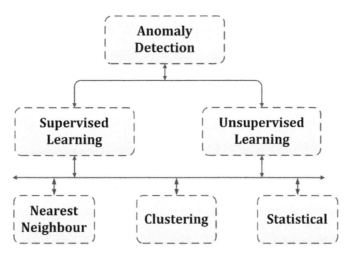

Figure 3. Taxonomy of Anomaly Detection Techniques

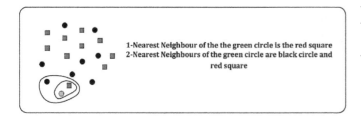

Figure 4. How *k-NN* works

fact, we emphasize unsupervised anomaly detection algorithms based on nearest neighbours, clustering and statistical approaches. Figure 3 shows a simple taxonomy for anomaly detection in the scope of this paper. The terms *anomaly* and *outlier* are used interchangeably throughout the paper.

3.1. Nearest Neighbor (NN) based Anomaly Detection and Related Works

The concept of nearest neighbor has been widely used in several anomaly detection techniques. The key assumption used in this scenario is *'Normal data instances stay in a dense neighborhoods and the anomalies stay far away from their neighbors'* [20]. Next, we present a couple of anomaly detection techniques [1] based on this idea. Figure 4 shows a simple example of *k-NN* method. The corresponding algorithm is shown in **Algorithm 1**.

Knorr et al [20] presented an algorithm to detect distance-based outliers. They consider a data point O in a dataset T a $DB(p;D)$-outlier if at least a fraction p of the data points in T lies greater than distance D from O. Their index-based algorithm executes a range search with radius D for each data point. If the number of data points in its D-*neighborhood* exceeds a threshold, the search stops and that data point is declared as

Algorithm 1: Basic *k-NN* Algorithm
Input: D = { (x_1,c_1),....,(x_N,c_N)} $x = (x_1,.....,x_N)$ *new instance to be classified.*

Begin
   for each labelled instance (x_i,c_i)
   Calculate $d(x_i,x)$, the distance from x_i to x
   Order $d(x_i,x)$ from lowest to highest, $(i=1,.....,N)$
   Let D_x^k be the k-nearest instances to x
   Label x by the most frequent label in D_x^k
   end
 End

a non-outlier, otherwise it is an outlier. This concept was further extended by Ramaswamy et al [11] where the anomaly score is based on the *k-nearest neighbor* implementation.

Ramaswamy et al [11] provided outlier definition based on the distance of a point from its kth *nearest neighbor*. They provided a ranking of top-n outliers by the measure of the outlierness of the points. According to them, *top-n* points with the maximum distance to their own k^{th} *nearest neighbor* are considered as outliers. They also exploited index-based and nested-loop algorithms to detect outliers. Furthermore, they proposed a partition-based algorithm to prune and process the partitioned groups to improve efficiency for outlier detection. Their algorithm reduces the cost of computation in large, multidimensional data sets.

Breunig et al [21] proposed to assign each object a degree of being outlier. This degree is called the Local Outlier Factor (LOF). LOF depends on how isolated the object is with respect to the surrounding neighbourhood. The local outlier factor of an object p is calculated using the equation (2), where *MinPts* defines the minimum number of points as a notion of density and *lrd* is the local reachability density (1). (For more details on the mathematical terms please see [21].

$$reach - dist_k(p, o) = \{k - distance(o), d(p, o)\} \quad (1)$$

$$LOF_{MinPts}(p) = \frac{\sum_{o \in N_{MinPts}(p)} \frac{lrd_{MinPts}(o)}{lrd_{MinPts}(p)}}{|N_{MinPts}(p)|} \quad (2)$$

This outlier factor of object p calculates the degree to which p can be called as outlier. The outlier factor is the average of the ratio of the local reachability density (*lrd*) of p and those of p's *MinPts-nearest neighbours*. The author also described mathematically the LOF for objects deep in a cluster along with general bounds (upper, lower, and tight). The **Theorem 1** depicts a general upper and lower bound on $LOF(p)$ for any data object p. For the theorem, following terms are necessary.

- $direct_{min}(p) = \min\{reach\text{-}dist(p,q)|r \in N_{MinPts}(p)\}$
- $direct_{max}(p) = \max\{reach\text{-}dist(p,q)|r \in N_{MinPts}(p)\}$
- $indirect_{min}(p) = \min\{reach\text{-}dist(q,o)|q \in N_{MinPts}(p)$ and $o \in N_{MinPts}(q)\}$
- $indirect_{max}(p) = \max\{reach\text{-}dist(q,o)|q \in N_{MinPts}(p)$ and $o \in N_{MinPts}(q)\}$

Theorem 1: When p is a data object from the dataset D and $1 \leq MinPts \leq |D|$. Then the $LOF(p)$ can be represented by equation (3) [21].

$$\frac{direct_{min}(p)}{indirect_{max}(p)} \leq LOF(p) \leq \frac{direct_{max}(p)}{indirect_{min}(p)} \quad (3)$$

Proof:

Left hand side: $\frac{direct_{min}(p)}{indirect_{max}(p)} \leq LOF(p)$. Following the terms defined above,

$$LOF(p) = \frac{\sum_{o \in N_{MinPts}(p)} \frac{lrd(o)}{lrd(p)}}{|N_{MinPts}(p)|} \geq \frac{\sum_{o \in N_{MinPts}(p)} \frac{\frac{1}{indirect_{max}(p)}}{\frac{1}{direct_{min}(p)}}}{|N_{MinPts}(p)|} = \frac{direct_{min}(p)}{indirect_{max}(p)} \quad (4)$$

Right hand side: $LOF(p) \leq \frac{direct_{max}(p)}{indirect_{min}(p)}$: analogously proved.

Jin et al [36] proposed an approach for mining only *top-n* local outliers because the LOF [21] values for every data object require a large number of *k-nearest neighbour* searches and can be very computationally expensive. They proposed an efficient microcluster-based local outlier mining algorithm to find the *top-n* local outliers in a large database. A microcluster MC (n, c, and r) is a summarized representation of a group of data $p_1, , p_n$, which are so close together that they are likely to belong to the same cluster. Here, $c = \frac{\sum_{i=1}^{n} p_i}{n}$, is the mean center while $r = max(d(p_i, c))$, $i = 1, ..., n$, is the radius. Data are compressed into small clusters, and small clusters are represented using

some statistical information as microclusters. Three different algorithms are combined to find *top-n* local outliers. First, *k-distance* bounds for each microcluster are computed. Then using these *k-distance* bounds, the LOF bounds are calculated. Finally, given an upper bound and a lower bound for the LOF of each microcluster, *top-n* local outliers are ranked.

He et al [26] introduced a new definition for outlier, the semantic outlier. A semantic outlier is a data point that behaves differently from the other data points in the same class. A measure for identifying the degree of each object being an outlier is presented, which is called the semantic outlier factor (SOF). To mine semantic outliers, an algorithm is also proposed. They used a *SQUEEZER* algorithm, which is used to produce good clusters for categorical datasets, and then used their algorithm to calculate the SOF value for each of the objects. Their proposed outlier definition works by identifying the similarity between a specific set and a record. Given a set of records R and a record t, the similarity between R and t is defined as follows:

$$Sim(t, R) = \frac{\sum_{i=1}^{|R|} similarity(t, t_i)}{|R|} \quad where \; \forall \; t_i \in R \quad (5)$$

The semantic outlier factor of a record t is defined as in equation (6).

$$SOF(t) = \frac{pr(cl_i|C_K) * Sim(t, R)}{pr(cl_i|D)} \quad (6)$$

Spiros et al [33] introduced local correlation integral (LOCI) for evaluating outlierness, which is very efficient in detecting outliers and groups of outliers. The main advantage of this approach is an automatic data-dictated cut-off to determine whether a point is an outlier. They introduced the multigranularity deviation factor (MDEF), which at radius r for a point p_i is the relative deviation of its local neighborhood density from the average local neighborhood density in its neighborhood.

Zhange et al [17] proposed a new outlier detection definition, local distance-based outlier factor (LDOF), which is sensitive to outliers in scattered datasets (Figure 5). LDOF uses the relative distances from an object to its neighborhood to measure how much objects deviate from their scattered neighborhood. The higher the violation degree an object has, the more likely the object is an outlier. The local distance-based outlier factor of p_i is defined in equation (7) where $\overline{d}_{p_i}$ the *k-nearest neighbors* are the distance of object p_i and $\overline{D}_{p_i}$ is the *k-nearest neighbor* inner distance of p_i.

$$LDOF_k(p_i) = \frac{\overline{d}_{p_i}}{\overline{D}_{p_i}} \quad (7)$$

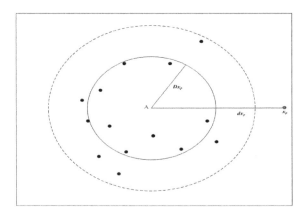

Figure 5. The explicit outlierness of object p_i with the help of LDOF definition. **A** is the center of the neighborhood system of p_i. The dashed circle includes all neighbors of p_i. The solid circle is reformed neighborhood region of p_i. Adapted from [1]

Kriegel et al [47] formulated a local density-based outlier detection method providing an outlier score in the range of [0,1] that is directly interpretable as a probability of a data object for being an outlier. The probabilistic local outlier factor (PLOF) of an object $o \in D$ w.r.t. a significance λ and a context set $S(o)$, can be defined as follows in equation (8). To achieve a normalization making the scaling of PLOF independent of the particular data distribution, the aggregate value nPLOF (9) is obtained during PLOF computation.

$$PLOF_{\lambda,S}(o) = \frac{pdist(\lambda, o, S(o))}{E_{s \in S(o)}[pdist(\lambda, s, S(s))]} \quad (8)$$

$$nPLOF = \lambda . \sqrt{E[(PLOF)^2]} \quad (9)$$

Finally, Local outlier probability (LoOP) (10), indicating the probability that a point $o \in D$ is an outlier. In equation (10) erf is the Gaussian error function.

$$LoOP_s(o) = max\left\{0, erf\left(\frac{PLOF_{\lambda,S}(o)}{nPLOF.\sqrt{2}}\right)\right\} \quad (10)$$

3.2. Clustering based Anomaly Detection and Related Works

As discussed earlier that anomaly deviates from the regular characteristics of the data. Consequently, the goal of clustering is to group together similar data and it is used to detect anomalous patterns in a dataset [40]. There are three key assumptions when using clustering to detect anomalies [24]:

1. **Assumption 1:** Once the clusters are created, any new data that do not fit well with existing clusters of normal data are considered as anomalous. For example, if we consider density based clustering algorithms [48] such as *DBSCAN*, we find that

it does not include noise inside the clusters. As a result, noise is considered anomalous. For example, in the Figure 6, *C1* and *C2* are clusters containing normal instances and *A1*, *A2* are anomalies.

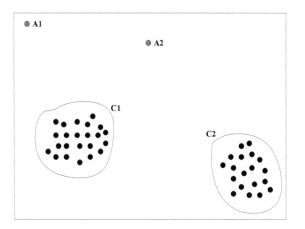

Figure 6. Example of anomaly based on assumption 1

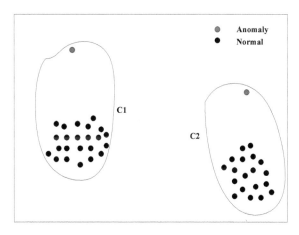

Figure 7. Example of anomaly based on assumption 2

2. **Assumption 2:** In some cases, a cluster contains both normal and anomalous data. It is expected that normal data lie close to the nearest cluster centroid and anomalies are far away from the centroids (Figure 7). Based on this assumption, anomalies are detected using a distance score.

In [40], the authors considered an outlier according to distance of a data instance from the centroid. If the distance is a fixed multiple of mean distances of all other data points from the centroid then it is considered as an outlier. Formally, *'an object in a set of data is an outlier if the distance between the object and the centroid of the dataset is greater than multi times the mean of the distances between centroid and other objects in the dataset'* [40]. They also showed that removing outliers from clusters can significantly improve clustering objective function.

Svetlona et al [41] presented an outlier removal clustering algorithm (ORC) that provides outlier detection and data clustering simultaneously. Their proposed algorithm has two stages. First, the *k-means* clustering is applied and then *outlyingness factor* o_i for each of the data points, p_i is calculated by taking the ratio of a point's distance to the centroid C and the maximum distance, d_{max} from the centroid to any other point, stated in equation (11). If outlying factor for any point is greater than a threshold T, it is considered as an outlier and removed from dataset. Their experimental data includes synthetic data and some map images. Mean Absolute Error (MAE) is used to evaluate their algorithm performance.

$$o_i = \frac{\|p_i - C\|}{d_{max}} \qquad (11)$$

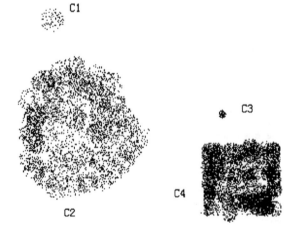

Figure 8. Anomalous clusters *C1,C3*; adapted from [22]

3. **Assumption 3:** In this scenario, it is assumed that in a dataset normal data objects are significantly high in volume than the anomalies. As a result, after clustering the dataset, smaller and sparser clusters are considered as anomalous and thicker clusters are normal. The instances belonging to clusters whose size and/or density is below a threshold are considered anomalous.

He et al [22] proposed a definition for cluster based local anomalies. According to their definition, all the data points in a certain cluster are considered as anomalies rather than a single point, as shown in Figure 8. The clusters *C1* and *C3* are considered as anomalous. They used some numeric parameters, i.e. α, β to identify Small Cluster (SC) and Large Cluster (LC). The clustering technique depends on these parameters but it is not clear

Algorithm 2: CBLOF Algorithm
Input: Dataset, D
The Parameters, α, β
Output: CBLOF score
Begin
Cluster the Dataset, D
Clusters: $C=\{C_1, C_2, .., C_k\}$ and $|C_1| \geq |C_2| \geq ... \geq |C_k|$
Calculate *LC* and *SC* with the α, β
Let C_i be the cluster containing t
if $C_i \in SC$ **do**
CBLOF $= |C_i|^* \min\{d(t, C_j)|C_j \in LC\}$
else
CBLOF $= |C_i| * d(t, C_i)$
End

how the values can be determined for various datasets. They used the *SQUEEZER* algorithm to cluster data, as it achieves both high quality of clustering and can handle high dimensional data. Then the *FindCBLOF* algorithm determines outlier factor of each individual record in dataset (shown in **Algorithm 2**). CBLOF(t) for each record t is calculated following equation (12):

$$CBLOF(t) = \begin{cases} |C_i| * min(d(t, C_j)) \text{ where } t \in C_i, C_i \in SC \\ \qquad and \ C_j \in LC \ for \ j = 1 \ to \ b \\ |C_i| * (d(t, C_i)) \text{ where } t \in C_i \\ \qquad and \ C_i \in LC \end{cases}$$
$$(12)$$

Amer et al [14] introduced Local Density Cluster-Based Outlier Factor (LDCOF) which can be considered as a variant of CBLOF [22]. The LDCOF score (16) is calculated as the distance to the nearest large cluster divided by the average distance to the cluster center of the elements in that large cluster. LDCOF score will be **A** when $p \in C_i \in SC$ where $C_j \in LC$ and **B** when $p \in C_i \in LC$.

$$distance_{avg}(C) = \frac{\sum_{i \in C} d(i, C)}{|C|} \qquad (13)$$

$$A = \frac{min(d(p, C_j))}{distance_{avg}(C_j)} \qquad (14)$$

$$B = \frac{d(p, C_i)}{distance_{avg}(C_i)} \qquad (15)$$

$$LDCOF(p) = A \ | \ B; \qquad (16)$$

Jiang et al [34] presented a two-phase clustering technique to detect outliers. First, they used a modified *k-means* algorithm to create clusters. If the points in the same cluster are not close enough, the cluster can be split into two smaller clusters and merged when a given threshold exceeds. In the second step, they construct a

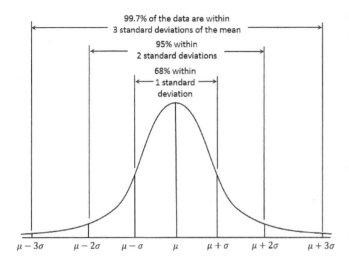

Figure 9. Concept of statistical anomaly detection, adapted from Internet

minimum spanning tree with the cluster centres and remove the longest edge. The smaller sub trees are considered outliers. Their technique considers an entire cluster as an outlier, which may not be applicable for many datasets and may increase *False Positive rate*.

Cluster Based Outlier Detection (*CBOD*) [37] is another technique which consists of two stages. In the first stage, it generates clusters from a given dataset and in the second stage it computes outlier factor as the weighted sum of distances between a particular cluster and rest of the clusters. The outlier factor of cluster C_i, OF(C_i) is defined as the *weighted sum* of distances between cluster C_i and the rest of the clusters. The outlier factor $OF(C_i)$ measures the outlier degree of cluster, the bigger the value is, the bigger the possibility of being an outlier cluster.

$$OF(C_i) = \Sigma_{j \neq i}(C_j) * d(C_i, C_j) \qquad (17)$$

Minimum b clusters which satisfy the criteria as follows are labelled as outlier clusters. They used detection rate and false alarm rate to measure performance.

3.3. Statistical based Anomaly Detection and Related Works

The statistical approaches discussed here are considered as the first generation techniques for anomaly detection. Figure 9 portrays the the most commonly used $\mu \pm 3\sigma$ rule for detecting anomalous data. A normally distributed data follows a bell curve and can be mathematically represented in equation (18). Here, μ stands for the mean or average, σ is the standard deviation and σ^2 is the variance. When

the $\mu=0$ and $\sigma = 1$, the distribution is called standard normal distribution. The data with values greater than $\mu + 3\sigma$ or less than $\mu - 3\sigma$ is considered anomalous.

$$f(x, \mu, \sigma) = \frac{1}{\sigma \sqrt{2\pi}} e^{-\frac{(x-\mu)^2}{2\sigma^2}} \qquad (18)$$

These techniques are also named as model-based techniques. Models are based on probability distribution of the data and anomalies are detected as how well the data fit into the model. Statistical based approaches are categorized into two groups depending on probability distribution as follows:

- **Parametric Approaches:** In these approaches the probability distribution of the data is known (supervised). Then, using the distribution parameters, anomalies are detected. A point is an anomaly if it deviates significantly from the data model. However in many situations prior knowledge of distribution is not possible to attain. As a result, supervised learning techniques are not preferred over the unsupervised learning techniques instead of having less accuracy.

  Wu et al [30] proposed two algorithms for outlying sensors and event boundary detection. The basic idea of outlying sensor detection is as such, each sensor first computes the difference between its reading and the median of the neighboring readings. Each sensor then collects all differences from its neighborhood and standardizes them. A sensor is an outlier if the absolute value of its standardized difference is sufficiently large. The algorithm for event boundary detection is based on the outlying sensor detection algorithm. For an event sensor, there often exist two regions, with each containing the sensor, such that the absolute value of the difference between the reading of the sensor and the median reading from all other sensors in one region is much larger than that in another region. These approaches are not effective because they do not consider the temporal correlation of sensor readings [1].

  Bettencourt et al [29] proposed an anomaly detection technique to identify anomalous events and errors in ecological applications of distributed sensor networks. This method uses spatio-temporal correlation of sensor data to distinguish erroneous measurements and events. A measurement is considered anomalous when its value in the statistical significance test is less than user specified threshold. The disadvantage of this approach is dependence on the user specified threshold [1].

  Jun et al [31] presents a statistical based approach,

which uses alpha-stable distribution. The proposed algorithm consists of collaborative time-series estimation, variogram application and principle component analysis (PCA). Each node detects any temporally abnormal data and transmits the verified data to a local cluster-head, which detects any survived spatial outlier and determines the faulty sensors accordingly. Their approach achieves 94% accuracy when the noise level is alpha = 0.9. Although alpha-stable distribution might be considered for real sensor data and cluster based structure may be susceptible to dynamic changes of network topology [1].

- **Non Parametric Approaches:** These approaches have no knowledge about the underlying data distribution like unsupervised learning methods. A distance measure is used to identify anomalies in this scenario. Anomalies are those points which are distant from their own neighborhood in a dataset. Various detection techniques are available with a wide range of parameters. They resemble anomaly detection using clustering based assumption 2. Parametric methods are not flexible enough like non-parametric methods but due to dimensionality and computational complexity the efficiency might deteriorate in some cases. There are two widely used approaches in this category are discussed as follows-

    - **Histogramming:** This model counts the frequency of occurrence of different data instances and compares the test instance with each of histogram categories to test whether it belongs to any of them [18].
      Sheng et al [32] proposed a histogram-based technique for anomaly detection to reduce communication cost for data collection applications of sensor networks. Rather than collecting all the data in one location for centralized processing, they propose collecting hints about the data distribution and using the hints to filter out unnecessary data and identify potential anomalies. Main drawbacks of this technique are communication overhead and one dimensional data [1].

    - **Kernel Function:** This function is used to estimate the probability distribution function (pdf) of the normal instances. Data instances which lie in the low probability area of pdf are declared as anomalies.
      Palapans et al [15] proposed a technique for online deviation detection in streaming data. They discussed how their technique can be operated efficiently in the distributed

environment of a sensor network. In the sensor data, a value is considered as an anomaly if the number of values being in its neighborhood is less than a user specified threshold. This technique can also be implemented for identification for of anomalies in a more global perspective [1].

4. Criteria for Benchmarking Anomaly Detection Algorithms

This section provides a discussion on the key aspects to evaluate anomaly detection algorithms in terms of big data. We propose the following points to be considered while selecting the benchmark anomaly detection techniques in SCADA systems:

- **Size of the Data (Volume):** Size is an important factor for anomaly detection algorithms. More importantly, in case of big data, it is a crucial parameter to measure the efficiency of the anomaly detection algorithm. Some anomaly detection technique might work well on small dataset but perform poorly on big data and vice-versa!

- **Dimensionality:** It is closely related with the computing efficiency of any data mining techniques. It is quite common that big data has high dimensionality and as the dimensionality increases the data become sparse. As a result similarity/dissimilarity calculation at this situation is challenging.

- **Type of Data:** Handling identical data type and mixed type is completely different. For example, handling only numerical data for anomaly detection is more computationally efficient than dataset with numerical, categorical and binary type of data. Also, in case of big data, it is an important issue to consider the efficiency of the anomaly detection.

- **Velocity:** This criterion deals with complexity of the anomaly detection algorithms.

- **Input Parameter:** Selecting the best possible parameters for any algorithm is a challenge. It is more challenging when input parameters required for big data. A non-optimal value of input parameter causes computational burden. Also more the number of input parameters more it gets complex. In unsupervised fashion, it is also a challenge to provide the best parameter values to the anomaly detection techniques. So, less is better in this case.

In Table 1, we showcase the characteristics of anomaly detection algorithms based on the criterion

Table 1. Characteristics of anomaly detection algorithms

Category	Size	Dimensionality	Variety	Velocity	Input Parameters
NN	Large	High	Yes	High	≥ 2
Clustering	Large	Low and High	Yes	Medium	≥ 2
Statistical	Large	High	Yes	High	≥ 1

discussed above. It is evident that each category has the ability to handle a large volume of data. However, clustering based techniques have greater computational complexity than the others. Also, statistical techniques are better in terms of selection of input parameters.

4.1. Strength and Weakness

We highlight the merits and demerits of the anomaly detection techniques discussed in Section 3.

Nearest Neighbour Techniques: The main advantage of nearest neighbour based techniques is their unsupervised characteristics. However, when anomalies have a large number of close neighbours, it is not possible to identify them correctly. Also, the distance computation requires significant computation and it becomes more complex when the data has mixed type of data such as numerical, categorical, binary etc.

Clustering Techniques: The techniques used to detect anomalies in binary fashion are computationally efficient irrespective of the clustering algorithm since each object in dataset is not required to assign an outlying factor like scoring based output. The *top-N* anomaly concept is absent in these techniques and hence are unsupervised. The main drawback of these techniques is inaccuracy of detecting all the rare class instances. Since not all the data objects are taken into consideration for being outlier, many of them might be missing and normal instances may be detected as anomalies. The scoring based techniques have the maximum effectiveness in detecting anomaly accurately since all the objects are under consideration as candidate anomalies. But the loophole of these techniques is computational cost. Since all the objects are taken under consideration to assign outlyingness factor. *Top-N* anomalies must have to be specified by data analyst and thus the approach becomes supervised.

Statistical Techniques: Statistical approaches come with strong mathematical background to detect anomalies. But parametric approaches are not feasible when the prior knowledge on the data distribution is not available and hence quite useless in many aspects. In comparison, non-parametric methods are quite useful since the

data distribution knowledge is not required. However, these methods might have high computational complexity for high dimensional datasets. Also user-defined parameters are not easy to set.

Table 2. Characteristics of the SCADA datasets

Dataset	Normal	Anomaly
Urban Waster Water Treatment Plant (WTP)	97.5%	2.5%
Single-hop Indoor (SI)	97.35%	2.65%
Single-hop Outdoor (SO)	99.37%	0.63%
Simulated-Data1 (Sim1)	99.02%	0.98%
Simulated-Data2 (Sim2)	99.05%	0.95%
Multi-hop Indoor (MI)	97.86%	2.14%
Multi-hop Outdoor (MO)	98.76%	1.24%

5. Experimental Evaluation on SCADA Systems Big Data

This section starts with a brief discussion on the datasets used. Then we discuss about the evaluation metrics used in the paper. Finally, we showcase the evaluation results showing in figures and tables.

5.1. SCADA Datasets used in this paper

Table 2 contains the description of the characteristics of some of the common SCADA datasets widely used [28]. Figure 10 displays a simple taxonomy of anomalous scenarios in SCADA systems. There are three major categories of anomalies based on the datasets used in this paper. The real anomalies are from water treatment plant. The simulated anomalies are designed by computer software. In real sensor nodes, the anomalies are injected by creating changes in temperature.

The real anomalies in the *WTP* dataset [35] are caused by the inclement weather. It contains data of the daily measures of sensors in a urban waste water treatment plant. Solid overload caused by stormy

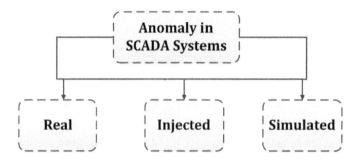

Figure 10. Taxonomy of anomaly in SCADA systems

weather are considered anomalous data in the system.

The simulated anomalies in the *Sim1* and *Sim2* contain man-in-the-middle attacks [38]. Here a water distribution system is simulated using the EPANET library [46]. Anomalies were created using the *man-in-the-middle* attacks. In this scenario, water pumps were turned off when the reserve in the tanks are low.

In the single-hop, multi-hop (indoor and outdoor) datasets, anomalies are injected [45]. For the single-hop scenario, two indoor and two outdoor sensor nodes are used to collect the temperature and humidity data for six hours. Anomalies are introduced by using a kettle of hot water at one of the sensors. The simultaneous raise in the temperature and humidity is considered anomalous in this scenario. In the multi-hop situation, multi-hop routing is used to create a larger sensor network. Like single-hop datasets, anomalies are introduced using the hot water at the temperature and humidity sensors.

5.2. Evaluation Measures

We measure the performance of the anomaly detection algorithms using the standard evaluation criteria [1]. These are briefly discussed here. All of them share some common concept of confusion matrix. The 2 × 2 matrix contains the number of True Positive (TP), False Positive (FP), True Negative (TN), False negative (FN). Table 3 displays the confusion matrix.

TP: No. of anomalies correctly identified as anomalous.

FP: No. of normal data incorrectly identified as anomalous.

TN: No. of normal data correctly identified as normal.

FN: No. of anomalies incorrectly identified as normal.

Listed below are the five evaluation measures based on confusion matrix.

- **Accuracy** - The accuracy is computed using equation (19).

Table 3. Standard confusion metrics for evaluation of anomaly detection algorithm

Label	Normal	Anomaly
Normal	TN	FP
Anomaly	FN	TP

$$Accuracy = \frac{TP + TN}{TP + TN + FP + FN} \quad (19)$$

- **FPR** - False Positive Rate also named as *FPR* is another metric which is the proportion of non-relevant data that are retrieved, out of all non-relevant data available. The lower the value is better the anomaly detection technique is. Equation (20) shows the way to calculate *FPR*.

$$FPR = \frac{FP}{FP + TN} \quad (20)$$

- **Recall** - Recall is the fraction of the data that are relevant to the query that are successfully retrieved. In the case of anomaly detection, *recall* is also known as *TPR*, *Hit Rate*, can be calculated using (21).

$$Recall = \frac{TP}{TP + FN} \quad (21)$$

- **F-1** - *F-1* score is the harmonic mean of precision (*TP/TP + FP*) and recall. Equation (22) shows the way to calculate *F-1*.

$$F\text{-}1 = \frac{2TP}{2TP + FP + FN} \quad (22)$$

- **MCC** - The Matthews correlation coefficient is a popular measure in machine learning to identify the quality of binary (two-class) classifications. It considers the true and false positives and negatives for calculating the measure. The *MCC* provides a value between -1 and +1. A *MCC* score of +1 represents a perfect anticipation and -1 indicates complete opposite scenario between observation and prediction (23).

$$MCC = \frac{(TP * TN) - (FP * FN)}{\sqrt{(TP + FP)(TP + FN)(TN + FP)(TN + FN)}} \quad (23)$$

Last but not least, we also consider the run time (in seconds) as an important evaluation criteria for anomaly detection algorithms.

5.3. Experimental Results

This section contains the performance analysis of anomaly detection techniques based on the evaluation measures discussed in the previous section. For simplicity, we scale all the metrics between 0 and ±100. The representative algorithms are the following and standard values are considered for the input parameters for all the techniques:

- **Nearest Neighbour:**

  - **k-NN:** Each data instance is given score for being anomalous based on the average distance to the nearest neighbours [11].

  - **LOF:** LOF provides anomaly score to the data instances based on the local density of the data points [21].

  - **COF:** The connectivity based outlier factor is a modification of the *LOF* approach which can handle outliers deviating from low density patterns [43]

  - **aLOCI:** Calculates the outlier score based on local correlation integral [33].

  - **LoOP:** The LoOP score represents the probability that the object is a local density outlier [47].

  - **INFLO:** Calculates the outlier score based on Influenced outlierness, proposed by Jin et al [19].

- **Clustering:**

  - **CBLOF:** CBLOF creates clusters from the given dataset and then it categorizes the clusters into small clusters and large clusters using the parameters α and β. The anomaly score is then calculated based on the size of the cluster the point belongs to as well as the distance to the nearest large cluster centroid [22].

  - **LDCOF:** This local density based anomaly detection algorithm sets the anomaly score based on the distance to the nearest large cluster divided by the average cluster distance of the large cluster [14].

- **CMGOS:** This method calculates the anomaly score based on a clustering result. The outlier score of an instance is dependent on the probability of how likely its distance to the cluster center is [14].

- **Statistical:**

  - **HBOS:** Calculates an outlier score by creating an histogram with a fixed or a dynamic binwidth [18].

  - **LIBSVM:** Computes the outlier score using one-class SVMs [42]. This operator extends the semi-supervised one-class SVM such that it can be used for unsupervised anomaly detection.

Table 4. Performance of Anomaly Detection Techniques on Real SCADA Dataset (WTP: Water Treatment Plant)

Technique	Recall	FPR	Accuracy	F-1	MCC	Run Time
k-NN	85.71	0.38	97.39	85.71	85.32	≤1
LOF	78.57	0.58	97.38	78.57	77.98	≤1
COF	57.14	1.16	97.35	57.14	55.97	≤1
aLOCI	85.71	0.38	97.39	85.71	85.32	≤69
LoOP	42.85	1.55	97.33	42.85	41.29	≤1
INFLO	57.14	1.16	97.35	57.14	55.97	≤1
CBLOF	92.85	0.19	97.40	92.85	92.66	≤1
LDCOF	85.71	0.38	97.39	85.71	85.32	≤1
CMGOS	57.14	1.16	97.35	57.14	55.97	≤1
HBOS	28.57	1.94	97.32	28.57	26.62	≤1
LIBSVM	85.71	0.38	97.39	85.71	85.32	≤1

Table 5. Performance of Anomaly Detection Techniques on Simulated SCADA Datasets

Results on Sim1 Dataset						
Technique	Recall	FPR	Accuracy	F-1	MCC	Run Time
k-NN	64.70	0.34	99.03	64.70	64.35	≤4
LOF	0	0.98	99.01	0	-0.98	≤4
COF	0	0.98	99.01	0	-0.98	≤5
aLOCI	0	0.98	99.01	0	-0.98	≤10
LoOP	0.98	0.97	99.01	0.98	0.009	≤4
INFLO	0	0.98	99.01	0	-0.98	≤3.5
CBLOF	0	0.98	99.01	0	-0.98	≤2
LDCOF	0	0.98	99.01	0	-0.98	≤2
CMGOS	18.62	0.79	99.02	18.62	17.82	≤2
HBOS	30.39	0.682757957	99.02	30.39	29.70	≤2
LIBSVM	74.50	0.25	99.03	74.50	74.25	≤322
Results on Sim2 Dataset						
Technique	Recall	FPR	Accuracy	F-1	MCC	Run Time
k-NN	63	0.35	99.05	63	62.64	≤3
LOF	0	0.96	99.03	0	-0.96	≤4
COF	2	0.94	99.03	2	1.05	≤3
aLOCI	0	0.96	99.03	0	-0.96	≤23
LoOP	0	0.96	99.03	0	-0.96	≤4
INFLO	0	0.96	99.03	0	-0.96	≤4
CBLOF	0	0.96	99.03	0	-0.96	≤2
LDCOF	0	0.96	99.03	0	-0.96	≤4
CMGOS	97	0.02	99.05	97	96.97	≤2
HBOS	27	0.70	99.04	6	7.31	≤1
LIBSVM	68	0.30	99.05	68	67.69	≤220

We categorize the performance of the anomaly detection algorithms based on the taxonomy of anomaly in SCADA systems (Figure 10). For the real

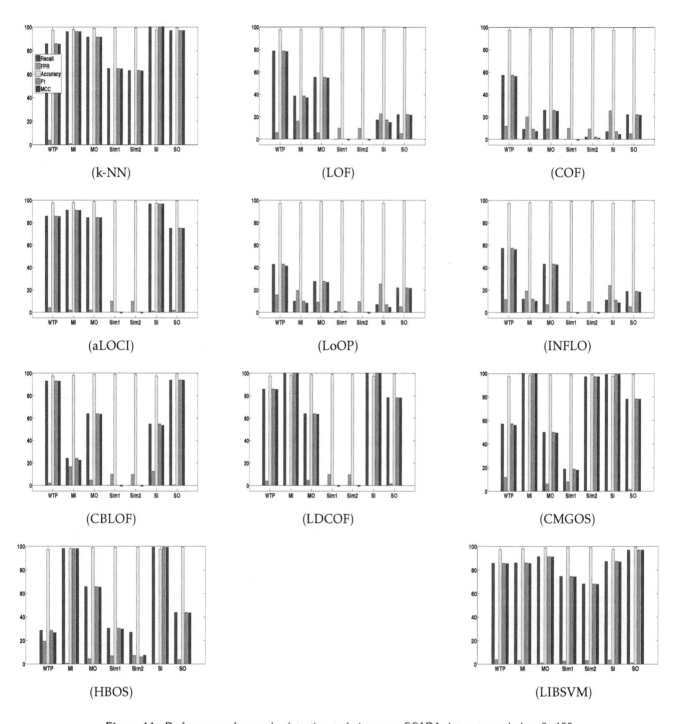

Figure 11. Performance of anomaly detection techniques on SCADA datasets, scaled to 0±100

SCADA dataset *WTP*, from Table 4 it is evident that the clustering based anomaly detection technique *CBLOF* performs best and second best performance is attained by the nearest neighbour based technique *k-NN*. Statistical based approach *HBOS* does not perform well here.

For the simulated datasets, it is surprising that semi-supervised anomaly detection technique *LIBSVM* has better *recall* than others, however suffers from unacceptable run time. On the other hand, nearest neighbour based method *k-NN* has very low run time complexity and acceptable *recall*. Clustering based approaches are not well suited for the simulated datasets here and statistical approach *HBOS* outperforms clustering techniques. Table 5 displays the results on simulated datasets.

Table 6. Performance of Anomaly Detection Techniques on Datasets with Injected Anomalies

Results on Multi-hop Indoor (MI) Dataset					
Technique	Recall	FPR	Accuracy	F-1	MCC	Run Time
k-NN	96	0.08	97.90	96	95.91	≤1
LOF	38.33	1.61	97.43	38.33	36.72	≤1
COF	9	1.98	97.82	9	7.01	≤1
aLOCI	91	0.19	97.90	91	90.80	≤11
LoOP	10	1.96	97.83	10	8.03	≤1
INFLO	12	1.91	97.83	12	10.08	≤1
CBLOF	24	1.65	97.84	24	22.34	≤1
LDCOF	100	0	97.91	100	100	≤1
CMGOS	100	0	97.91	100	100	≤1
HBOS	98	0.04	97.91	98	97.95	≤1
LIBSVM	86	0.30	97.90	86	85.69	≤39
Results on Multi-hop Outdoor (MO) Dataset					
Technique	Recall	FPR	Accuracy	F-1	MCC	Run Time
k-NN	91.37	0.10	98.77	91.37	91.27	≤1
LOF	55.17	0.56	98.76	55.17	54.61	≤1
COF	25.86	0.92	98.75	25.86	24.93	≤1
aLOCI	84.48	0.19	98.77	84.48	84.28	≤13
LoOP	27.58	0.90	98.75	27.58	26.67	≤1
INFLO	43.10	0.71	98.76	43.10	42.39	≤1
CBLOF	63.79	0.45	98.76	63.79	63.33	≤1
LDCOF	63.79	0.45	98.76	63.79	63.33	≤1
CMGOS	50	0.62	98.76	50	49.37	≤1
HBOS	65.51	0.43	98.76	65.51	65.08	≤1
LIBSVM	91.37	0.10	98.77	91.37	91.27	≤39

Table 7. Performance of Anomaly Detection Techniques on Datasets with Injected Anomalies (Single-Hop)

Results on Single-hop Indoor (SI) Dataset					
Technique	Recall	FPR	Accuracy	F-1	MCC	Run Time
k-NN	100	0	97.41	100	100	≤1
LOF	17.09	2.25	97.30	17.09	14.83	≤1
COF	6.83	2.53	97.28	6.83	4.30	≤1
aLOCI	96.58	0.09	97.41	96.58	96.48	≤114
LoOP	6.83	2.53	97.28	6.83	4.30	≤9
INFLO	11.11	2.41	97.29	11.11	8.69	≤14
CBLOF	54.70	1.23	97.35	54.70	53.46	≤1
LDCOF	100	0	97.41	100	100	≤1
CMGOS	99.14	0.02	97.41	99.14	99.12	≤1
HBOS	99.14	0.02	97.41	99.14	99.12	≤1
LIBSVM	87.17	0.34	97.40	87.17	86.83	≤22
Results on Single-hop Outdoor (SO) Dataset					
Technique	Recall	FPR	Accuracy	F-1	MCC	Run Time
k-NN	96.87	0.01	99.36	96.87	96.85	≤2
LOF	21.87	0.49	99.36	21.87	21.37	≤1
COF	21.87	0.49	99.36	21.87	21.37	≤1
aLOCI	75	0.15	99.36	75	74.84	≤16
LoOP	21.87	0.49	99.36	21.87	21.37	≤2
INFLO	18.75	0.51	99.36	18.75	18.23	≤2
CBLOF	93.75	0.03	99.36	93.75	93.71	≤1
LDCOF	78.12	0.13	99.36	78.12	77.98	≤1
CMGOS	78.12	0.13	99.36	78.12	77.98	≤1
HBOS	43.75	0.35	99.36	43.75	43.39	≤1
LIBSVM	96.87	0.01	99.36	96.87	96.85	≤16

For the datasets with injected anomalies in multi-hop senario, we found the performance (Table 6) of clustering based approaches is the best considering the evaluation measures. Nearest neighbour based approaches are the next best. Among the *HBOS* and *LIBSVM* approach, the latter has the better results in terms of anomaly detection but attains high computational burden (run time).

Finally, for the datasets in single-hop scenario, it is seen that, the clustering-based methods perform

consistently well, but the nearest neighbour methods are quite variable (Table 7). *LIBSVM* performs better than *HBOS* but still suffers from high run time complexity.

It is interesting to observe that, for all the anomaly detection techniques the *Recall* and *F-1* values are identical. Since, top N anomalies detected by the techniques are matched with the actual N number of anomalies in the dataset, the *Recall* and *F-1* scores will always yield exactly the same values. Finally, we

Table 8. Characteristics of anomaly detection algorithms

Category	Real	Simulated	Injected
NN	√	√	√
Clustering	√	×	√
Statistical	×	√	×

summarise the performance of each of the anomaly detection techniques in Figure 11. In Table 8 we also summarize the performance on different SCADA datasets. We suggest the usage of these techniques analysing the results discussed earlier. The sign (√) indicates the affirmative gesture to apply the techniques and the sign (×) discourages the usage.

6. Conclusion and Future Works

This paper gives a detailed discussion on the popular anomaly detection techniques on SCADA systems and analysed their performance. We come to a conclusion that *nearest neighbour* and *clustering* based approaches are more suitable for SCADA systems than statistical and semi-supervised support vector machine based approaches. In future we will investigate the following:

- How to find the most suitable input parameter values?

- How to incorporate the idea of contextual anomaly in big data perspective?

- How can incorporation of multi-view clustering [16], hierarchical clustering [12] and co-clustering [13] improve the efficiency of clustering-based anomaly detection techniques?

- How to reduce the run time complexity of semi-supervised support vector machine based anomaly detection?

References

[1] M. Ahmed, A. N. Mahmood, J. Hu, Outlier detection, in: The State of the Art in Intrusion Prevention and Detection, CRC Press, USA, 2014, pp. 3–23.

[2] M. Ahmed and A. N. Mahmood, "Network traffic pattern analysis using improved information-theoretic co-clustering based collective anomaly detection," in *Security and Privacy in Communication Networks*, ser. Lecture Notes of the Institute for Computer Sciences, Social Informatics and Telecommunications Engineering. Springer Berlin Heidelberg, 2014.

[3] M. Ahmed, A. N. Mahmood, and M. R. Islam, "A survey of anomaly detection techniques in financial domain," *Future Generation Computer Systems*, 2015.

[4] I. A. Karatepe and E. Zeydan, "Anomaly detection in cellular network data using big data analytics," in *European Wireless 2014; 20th European Wireless Conference; Proceedings of*, May 2014, pp. 1–5.

[5] X. Miao and D. Zhang, "The opportunity and challenge of big data's application in distribution grids," in *Electricity Distribution (CICED), 2014 China International Conference on*, Sept 2014, pp. 962–964.

[6] L. Wang, J. Zhan, C. Luo, Y. Zhu, Q. Yang, Y. He, W. Gao, Z. Jia, Y. Shi, S. Zhang, C. Zheng, G. Lu, K. Zhan, X. Li, and B. Qiu, "Bigdatabench: A big data benchmark suite from internet services," in *High Performance Computer Architecture (HPCA), 2014 IEEE 20th International Symposium on*, Feb 2014, pp. 488–499.

[7] S. Pandey and V. Tokekar, "Prominence of mapreduce in big data processing," in *Communication Systems and Network Technologies (CSNT), 2014 Fourth International Conference on*, April 2014, pp. 555–560.

[8] Z. Zheng, J. Zhu, and M. Lyu, "Service-generated big data and big data-as-a-service: An overview," in *Big Data (BigData Congress), 2013 IEEE International Congress on*, June 2013, pp. 403–410.

[9] H. Hu, Y. Wen, T.-S. Chua, and X. Li, "Toward scalable systems for big data analytics: A technology tutorial," *Access, IEEE*, vol. 2, pp. 652–687, 2014.

[10] C.-S. Leung, R. MacKinnon, and F. Jiang, "Reducing the search space for big data mining for interesting patterns from uncertain data," in *Big Data (BigData Congress), 2014 IEEE International Congress on*, June 2014, pp. 315–322.

[11] S. Ramaswamy, R. Rastogi, and K. Shim, "Efficient algorithms for mining outliers from large data sets," *SIGMOD Rec.*, vol. 29, no. 2, pp. 427–438, May 2000.

[12] A. N. Mahmood, C. Leckie, and P. Udaya, "An efficient clustering scheme to exploit hierarchical data in network traffic analysis," *IEEE Trans. on Knowl. and Data Eng.*, vol. 20, no. 6, pp. 752–767, Jun. 2008.

[13] I. S. Dhillon, S. Mallela, and D. S. Modha, "Information-theoretic co-clustering," in *Proceedings of the Ninth ACM SIGKDD International Conference on Knowledge Discovery and Data Mining*, ser. KDD '03, USA: ACM, 2003, pp. 89–98.

[14] M. G. Mennatallah Amer, Nearest-neighbor and clustering based anomaly detection algorithms for rapidminer, Shaker Verlag GmbH, Aachen, 2012, pp. 1–12.

[15] T. Palpanas, D. Papadopoulos, V. Kalogeraki, and D. Gunopulos, "Distributed deviation detection in sensor networks," *SIGMOD Rec.*, vol. 32, no. 4, pp. 77–82, Dec. 2003.

[16] X. H. Dang and J. Bailey, "A framework to uncover multiple alternative clusterings," *Machine Learning*, pp. 1–24, 2013.

[17] K. Zhang, M. Hutter, and H. Jin, "A new local distance-based outlier detection approach for scattered real-world data," in *Advances in Knowledge Discovery and Data Mining*, ser. Lecture Notes in Computer Science. Springer Berlin Heidelberg, 2009, vol. 5476, pp. 813–822.

[18] M. Hofmann and R. Klinkenberg, *RapidMiner: Data Mining Use Cases and Business Analytics Applications*. Chapman & Hall/CRC, 2013.

[19] W. Jin, A. K. H. Tung, J. Han, and W. Wang, "Ranking outliers using symmetric neighborhood relationship," in *Proceedings of the 10th Pacific-Asia Conference on Advances in Knowledge Discovery and Data Mining*, ser. PAKDD'06. Berlin, Heidelberg: Springer-Verlag, 2006, pp. 577–593.

[20] E. M. Knorr and R. T. Ng, "Algorithms for mining distance-based outliers in large datasets," in *Proceedings of the 24rd International Conference on Very Large Data Bases*. San Francisco, CA, USA: Morgan Kaufmann Publishers Inc., 1998, pp. 392–403.

[21] M. M. Breunig, H.-P. Kriegel, R. T. Ng, and J. Sander, "Lof: Identifying density-based local outliers," *SIGMOD Rec.*, vol. 29, no. 2, pp. 93–104, May 2000.

[22] Z. He, X. Xu, S. Deng, Discovering cluster based local outliers, Pattern Recognition Letters 2003 (2003) 9–10.

[23] B. Galloway and G. Hancke, "Introduction to industrial control networks," *Communications Surveys Tutorials, IEEE*, vol. 15, no. 2, pp. 860–880, Second 2013.

[24] M. Ahmed and A. Mahmood, "Network traffic analysis based on collective anomaly detection," in *Industrial Electronics and Applications (ICIEA), 2014 IEEE 9th Conference on*, June 2014, pp. 1141–1146.

[25] V. Chandola, A. Banerjee, V. Kumar, Anomaly detection: A survey, ACM Comput. Surv. 41 (3) (2009) 15:1–15:58.

[26] Z. He, S. Deng, and X. Xu, "Outlier detection integrating semantic knowledge," in *Proceedings of the Third International Conference on Advances in Web-Age Information Management*, ser. WAIM '02. London, UK, UK: Springer-Verlag, 2002, pp. 126–131.

[27] S. Suthaharan, M. Alzahrani, S. Rajasegarar, C. Leckie, and M. Palaniswami, "Labelled data collection for anomaly detection in wireless sensor networks," in *Intelligent Sensors, Sensor Networks and Information Processing (ISSNIP), 2010 Sixth International Conference on*, Dec 2010, pp. 269–274.

[28] A. Fahad, N. Alshatri, Z. Tari, A. Alamri, I. Khalil, A. Zomaya, S. Foufou, and A. Bouras, "A survey of clustering algorithms for big data: Taxonomy and empirical analysis," *Emerging Topics in Computing, IEEE Transactions on*, vol. 2, no. 3, pp. 267–279, Sept 2014.

[29] L. Bettencourt, A. Hagberg, and L. Larkey, "Separating the wheat from the chaff: Practical anomaly detection schemes in ecological applications of distributed sensor networks," in *Distributed Computing in Sensor Systems*, ser. Lecture Notes in Computer Science. Springer Berlin Heidelberg, 2007, vol. 4549, pp. 223–239.

[30] W. Wu, X. Cheng, M. Ding, K. Xing, F. Liu, and P. Deng, "Localized outlying and boundary data detection in sensor networks," *Knowledge and Data Engineering, IEEE Transactions on*, vol. 19, no. 8, pp. 1145–1157, Aug 2007.

[31] M. C. Jun, H. Jeong, and C.-C. J. Kuo, "Distributed spatio-temporal outlier detection in sensor networks," pp. 273–284, 2005.

[32] B. Sheng, Q. Li, W. Mao, and W. Jin, "Outlier detection in sensor networks," ser. MobiHoc '07, 2007, pp. 219–228.

[33] S. Papadimitriou, H. Kitagawa, P. Gibbons, and C. Faloutsos, "Loci: fast outlier detection using the local correlation integral," in *Data Engineering, 2003. Proceedings. 19th International Conference on*, March 2003, pp. 315–326.

[34] M. Jiang, S. Tseng, and C. Su, "Two-phase clustering process for outliers detection," *Pattern Recognition Letters*, vol. 22, no. 6âĂŞ7, pp. 691 – 700, 2001.

[35] M. Lichman, "UCI machine learning repository," 2013. [Online]. Available: http://archive.ics.uci.edu/ml

[36] W. Jin, A. K. H. Tung, and J. Han, "Mining top-n local outliers in large databases," in *Proceedings of the Seventh ACM SIGKDD International Conference on Knowledge Discovery and Data Mining*, ser. KDD '01. New York, NY, USA: ACM, 2001, pp. 293–298.

[37] S.-y. Jiang and Q.-b. An, "Clustering-based outlier detection method," in *Proceedings of the 2008 Fifth International Conference on Fuzzy Systems and Knowledge Discovery - Volume 02*, ser. FSKD '08. Washington, DC, USA: IEEE Computer Society, 2008, pp. 429–433.

[38] A. Almalawi, Z. Tari, I. Khalil, and A. Fahad, "Scadavt-a framework for scada security testbed based on virtualization technology," in *Local Computer Networks (LCN), 2013 IEEE 38th Conference on*, Oct 2013, pp. 639–646.

[39] M. Mohri, A. Rostamizadeh, A. Talwalkar, Foundations of machine learning, The MIT Press, 2012.

[40] M. Ahmed, A. N. Mahmood, A novel approach for outlier detection and clustering improvement, in: Industrial Electronics and Applications (ICIEA), 2013 8th IEEE Conference on, 2013, pp. 577–582.

[41] V. Hautamäki, S. Cherednichenko, I. Kärkkäinen, T. Kinnunen, P. Fränti, Improving k-means by outlier removal, in: Proc. 14th Scandinavian Conference on Image Analysis (SCIA'05), 2005, pp. 978–987.

[42] M. Amer, M. Goldstein, and S. Abdennadher, "Enhancing one-class support vector machines for unsupervised anomaly detection," in *Proceedings of the ACM SIGKDD Workshop on Outlier Detection and Description*, ser. ODD '13. New York, NY, USA: ACM, 2013, pp. 8–15.

[43] J. Tang, Z. Chen, A. W. Fu, and D. W. Cheung, "Capabilities of outlier detection schemes in large datasets, framework and methodologies," *Knowl. Inf. Syst.*, vol. 11, no. 1, pp. 45–84, Dec. 2006.

[44] C. M. Bishop, Neural networks for pattern recognition, Oxford University Press, Inc., New York, NY, USA, 1995.

[45] S. Suthaharan, M. Alzahrani, S. Rajasegarar, C. Leckie, and M. Palaniswami, "Labelled data collection for anomaly detection in wireless sensor networks," in *Intelligent Sensors, Sensor Networks and Information Processing (ISSNIP), 2010 Sixth International Conference on*, Dec 2010, pp. 269–274.

[46] Lewis A. Rossman, "The EPANET Programmer's Toolkit for Analysis of Water Distribution Systems," in *Proceedings of the 29th Annual Water Resources Planning and Management Conference, 1999*, June 1999, pp. 1–10.

[47] H.-P. Kriegel, P. Kröger, E. Schubert, and A. Zimek, "LoOP: Local outlier probabilities," in *Proceedings of the 18th ACM Conference on Information and Knowledge Management*, ser. CIKM '09. New York, NY, USA: ACM, 2009, pp. 1649–1652.

[48] A. K. Jain, M. N. Murty, P. J. Flynn, Data clustering: a review, ACM Comput. Surv. 31 (3) (1999) 264–323.

10

A Research on Mobile Cloud Computing and Future Trends

Fei Gu[1,*], Jianwei Niu[1], Zhenxue He[1]

[1]State Key Laboratory of Virtual Reality Technology and Systems, School of Computer Science and Engineering, Beihang University, Beijing 100191, China

Abstract

With an exploding growth of the mobile applications and emerging of cloud computing, mobile cloud computing (MCC) has become a potential technology for mobile services. MCC is the combination of cloud computing, mobile computing and wireless networks to bring rich computational resources to mobile users, network operators, as well as cloud computing providers. Despite increasing usage of mobile computing, exploiting its full potential is difficult due to its inherent problems such as resource scarcity, frequent disconnections and mobility. MCC can address these problems by executing mobile applications on the resource providers' side. In this paper, we give a definition of mobile cloud computing and provide an overview of state-of-the-art progress, in particular, models of mobile cloud applications. We also highlight research challenges in the area of mobile cloud computing. We conclude that mobile cloud computing can help building more powerful mobile applications.

Keywords: Mobile Cloud Computing (MCC), Offloading, Mobile Services

1. Introduction

The market of mobile devices has expanded rapidly. According to IDC[24], the premier global market intelligence firm, the worldwide Smartphone market grew 55.3% year over year in 2015. Mobile devices allow users to run powerful applications that take advantage of the growing availability of built-in sensing and better data exchange capabilities of mobile devices. In recent years, applications targeted at mobile devices have started becoming abundant with applications in various categories such as entertainment, health, games, business, social networking, travel and news. The popularity of these are evident by browsing through mobile app download centers such as Apple's iTunes or Google's Play. The reason for this is that mobile computing is able to provide a tool to the user when and where it is needed irrespective of user movement, hence supporting location independence.

However, the mobile devices are facing many challenges in their resources (e.g., battery life, storage, and bandwidth) and communications (e.g., mobility and security)[39]. The limited resources significantly impede the improvement of service qualities. Given the abundance of and easy access to public cloud computing resources, the natural question to ask is,

can cloud computing bridge the resource gap of mobile computing?

The answer is definitively yes. Recently, we have witnessed several cases which cloud computing is called in to solve mobile computing problems. Apple's iCloud stores customers' music, photos, apps, calendars, documents, etc, and wirelessly pushes them to all their devices automatically. Apple's iCloud stores are hosted in Amazon Elastic Compute Cloud (EC2) and Microsoft Azure. Amazon has released its new "cloud-accelerated" Web browser Silk. Silk a "split browser" whose software resides both on Kindle Fire and EC2. With each web page request, Silk dynamically determines a division of labor between the mobile hardware and Amazon EC2 (i.e. which browser sub-components run where) that takes into consideration factors like network conditions, page complexity and the location of any cached content. We refer to mobile applications that leverage the public cloud (e.g. Amazon EC2 and Windows Azure) as mobile cloud applications or mCloud apps for short. We refer to the research area of mobile computing that taps in cloud resources as mobile cloud computing or mCloud computing for short. The public cloud today are designed for enterprise applications without any explicit consideration of mobile applications. Mobile computing demand fundamental changes to the public

*Corresponding author. Email: gufei@buaa.edu.cn

cloud. We refer to a public cloud that supports mobile applications seamlessly as mCloud.

Cloud computing (CC) has been widely recognized as the next generation computing infrastructure. CC offers some advantages by allowing users to use infrastructure (e.g., servers, networks, and storages), platforms (e.g., middleware services and operating systems), and softwares (e.g., application programs) provided by cloud providers (e.g., Google, Amazon, and Salesforce) at low cost. In addition, CC enables users to elastically utilize resources in an on-demand fashion. As a result, mobile applications can be rapidly provisioned and released with the minimal management efforts or service provider's interactions. With the explosion of mobile applications and the support of CC for a variety of services for mobile users, MCC is introduced as an integration of CC into the mobile environment. MCC brings new types of services and facilities mobile users to take full advantages of CC.

This paper presents a comprehensive summary on MCC. A brief background of MCC can be shown in Section 2. Section 3 provides a brief overview of MCC including definition, architecture, and its advantages. Then, Section 4 presents several open research issues and Section 5 shows the basic mobile cloud computing services. Finally, the future research Trends and the conclusion are outlined in Section 6.

2. Background

As a development and extension of Cloud Computing and Mobile Computing, Mobile Cloud Computing, as a new phrase, has been devised since 2009. In order to help us grasping better understanding of Mobile Cloud Computing, let's start from the two previous techniques: Mobile Computing and Cloud Computing.

2.1. Mobile Computing

Mobility has become a very popular word and rapidly increasing part in today's computing area. An incredible growth has appeared in the development of mobile devices such as, smartphone, PDA, GPS Navigation and laptops with a variety of mobile computing, networking and security technologies. In addition, with the development of wireless technology like WiMax, Ad Hoc Network and WIFI, users may be surfing the Internet much easier but not limited by the cables as before. Thus, those mobile devices have been accepted by more and more people as their first choice of working and entertainment in their daily lives.

So, what is Mobile computing exactly? In Wikipedia, it is described as a form of human-computer interaction by which a computer is expected to be transported during normal usage[32]. Mobile computing is based on a collection of three major concepts: hardware, software and communication. The concepts of hardware can be considered as mobile devices, such as smartphone and laptop, or their mobile components. Software of mobile computing is the numerous mobile applications in the devices, such as the mobile browser, anti-virus software and games. The communication issue includes the infrastructure of mobile networks, protocols and data delivery in their use. They must be transparent to end users.

Compared with the traditional wired network, mobile computing network may face various problems and challenges in different aspects, such as signal disturbance, security, hand-off delay, limited power, low computing ability, and so on, due to the wireless environment and numerous mobile nodes. In addition, the Quality of Service (QoS) in mobile computing network is much easier to be affected by the landforms, weather and buildings.

2.2. Cloud Computing

In the era of PC, many users found that the PCs bought 2 years ago cannot keep pace with the development of software nowadays; they need a higher speed CPU, a larger capacity hard disk, and a higher performance Operation System (OS). That is the magic of "Moores Law" which urges user upgrading their PCs constantly, but never ever overtakes the development of techniques. Thus, a term called "Cloud Computing" burst upon our lives.

Cloud Computing has become a popular phrase since 2007. However, there is no consensual definition on what a Cloud Computing or Cloud Computing System is, due to dozens of developers and organizations described it from different perspectives. C. Hewitt[22] introduces that the major function of a cloud computing system is storing data on the cloud servers, and uses of cache memory technology in the client to fetch the data. Those clients can be PCs, laptops, smartphones and so on. R. Buyya[9] gives a definition from the perspective of marking that cloud computing is a parallel and distributed computing system, which is combined by a group of virtual machines with internal links. Such systems dynamically offer computing resources from service providers to customers according to their Service level Agreement (SLA). However, some authors mentioned that cloud computing was not a completely new concept. L. Youseff[45] from University of California, Santa Barbara (UCSB) declares that cloud computing is just combined by many existent and few new concepts in many research fields, such as distributed and grid computing, Service-Oriented Architectures (SOA) and in virtualization.

3. Overview of Mobile Cloud Computing

The term "mobile cloud computing" was introduced not long after the concept of "cloud computing". It has been attracting the attentions of entrepreneurs as a profitable business option that reduces the development and running cost of mobile applications, of mobile users as a new technology to achieve rich experience of a variety of mobile services at low cost, and of researchers as a promising solution for green IT[3]. This section provides an overview of MCC including definition, architecture, and advantages of MCC.

3.1. Definition

MCC is the combination of cloud computing, mobile computing and wireless networks to bring rich computational resources to mobile users, network operators, as well as cloud computing providers[1][29]. The ultimate goal of MCC is to enable execution of rich mobile applications on a plethora of mobile devices, with a rich user experience[2]. MCC provides business opportunities for mobile network operators as well as cloud providers[14]. Move comprehensively, MCC can be defined as a rich mobile computing technology that leverages unified elastic resources of varied clouds and network technologies toward unrestricted functionality, storage, and mobility to serve a multitude of mobile devices anywhere, anytime through the channel of Ethernet or Internet regardless of heterogeneous environments and platforms based on the pay-as-you-use principle[36].

3.2. Architectures

From the concept of MCC, the general architecture of MCC can be shown in Figure 1. In Figure 1, mobile devices are connected to the mobile networks via base stations (e.g., base transceiver station, access point, or satellite) that establish and control the connections (air links) and functional interfaces between the networks and mobile devices. Mobile users' requests and information (e.g., ID and location) are transmitted to the central processors that are connected to servers providing mobile network services. Here, mobile network operators can provide services to mobile users as authentication, authorization, and accounting based on the home agent and subscribers' data stored in databases. After that, the subscribers' requests are delivered to a cloud through the Internet. In the cloud, cloud controllers process the requests to provide mobile users with the corresponding cloud services. These services are developed with the concepts of utility computing, virtualization, and service-oriented architecture (e.g., web, application, and database servers).

The details of cloud architecture could be different in different contexts. For example, a four-layer architecture is explained in [18] to compare cloud computing with grid computing. Alternatively, a service-oriented architecture, called Aneka, is introduced to

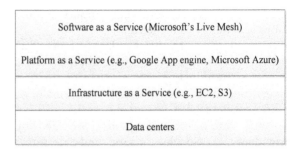

Figure 2. Service-oriented cloud computing architecture

enable developers to build. Microsoft .NET applications with the supports of application programming interfaces (APIs) and multiple programming models. [10] presents an architecture for creating market-oriented clouds and [23] proposes an architecture for web-delivered business services. In this paper, we focus on a layered architecture of cloud computing (CC) (Figure 2). This architecture is commonly used to demonstrate the effectiveness of the CC model in terms of meeting the user's requirements[43].

Generally, a CC is a large-scale distributed network system implemented based on a number of servers in data centers. The cloud services are generally classified based on a layer concept (Figure 2). In the upper layers of this paradigm, Infrastructure as a Service (IaaS), Platform as a Service (PaaS), and Software as a Service (SaaS) are stacked.

- **Data centers layer:** This layer provides the hardware facility and infrastructure for clouds. In data center layer, a number of servers are linked with high-speed networks to provide services for customers. Typically, data centers are built in less populated places, with a high power supply stability and a low risk of disaster.

- **IaaS:** Infrastructure as a Service is built on top of the data center layer. IaaS enables the provision of storage, hardware, servers, and networking components. The client typically pays on a per-use basis. Thus, clients can save cost as the payment is only based on how much resource they really use. Infrastructure can be expanded or shrunk dynamically as needed. The examples of IaaS are Amazon Elastic Cloud Computing and Simple Storage Service (S3).

- **PaaS:** Platform as a Service offers an advanced integrated environment for building, testing, and deploying custom applications. The examples of PaaS are Google App Engine, Microsoft Azure, and Amazon Map Reduce/Simple Storage Service.

- **SaaS:** Software as a Service supports a software distribution with specific requirements. In this

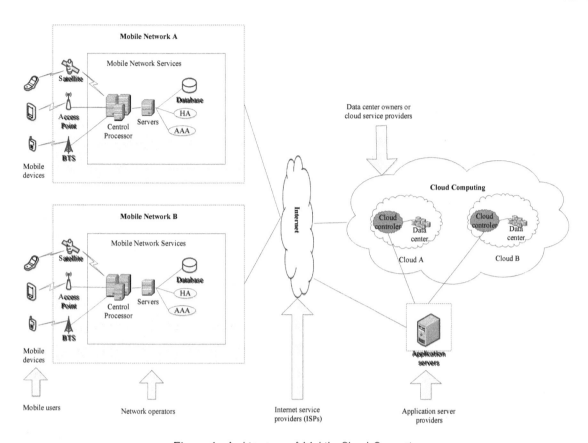

Figure 1. Architecture of Mobile Cloud Computing

layer, the users can access an application and information remotely via the Internet and pay only for that they use. Salesforce is one of the pioneers in providing this service model. Microsoft's Live Mesh also allows sharing files and folders across multiple devices simultaneously.

Although the CC architecture can be divided into four layers as shown in Figure 2, it does not mean that the top layer must be built on the layer directly below it. For example, the SaaS application can be deployed directly on IaaS, instead of PaaS. Also, some services can be considered as a part of more than one layer. For example, data storage service can be viewed as either in IaaS or PaaS. Given this architectural model, the users can use the services flexibly and efficiently.

3.3. Advantages

Cloud computing is known to be a promising solution for mobile computing (MC) because of many reasons (e.g., mobility, communication, and portability[17]). In the following, we describe how the cloud can be used to overcome obstacles in MC, thereby pointing out advantages of MCC.

- ***Extending battery lifetime.*** Battery is one of the main concerns for mobile devices. Several solutions have been proposed to enhance the CPU

performance[25][34] and to manage the disk and screen in an intelligent manner[13][30] to reduce power consumption. However, these solutions require changes in the structure of mobile devices, or they require a new hardware that results in an increase of cost and may not be feasible for all mobile devices. Computation offloading technique is proposed with the objective to migrate the large computations and complex processing from resource-limited devices (i.e., mobile devices) to resourceful machines (i.e., servers in clouds). This avoids taking a long application execution time on mobile devices which results in large amount of power consumption.

In [35] and [42], the effectiveness of offloading techniques were evaluated through several experiments. The results demonstrate that the remote application execution can save energy significantly. Especially, Rudenko[35] evaluates large-scale numerical computations and shows that up to 45% of energy consumption can be reduced for large matrix calculation. In addition, many mobile applications take advantages from task migration and remote processing. For example, offloading a compiler optimization for image processing[26] can reduce 41% for energy consumption of a mobile device. What's more, using memory arithmetic unit and interface (MAUI) to migrate mobile game components[12] to servers in the cloud can save 27% of energy consumption for computer games and 45% for the chess game.

- *Improving data storage capacity and processing power.* Storage capacity is also a constraint for mobile devices. MCC is developed to enable mobile users to store/access the large data on the cloud through wireless networks. First example is the Amazon Simple Storage Service[5] which supports file storage service. Another example is Image Exchange which utilizes the large storage space in clouds for mobile users[44]. This mobile photo sharing service enables mobile users to upload images to the clouds immediately after capturing. Users may access all images from any devices. With the cloud, the users can save considerable amount of energy and storage space on their mobile devices because all images are sent and processed on the clouds. Flickr[16] and ShoZu[41] are also the successful mobile photo sharing applications based on MCC. Facebook[15] is the most successful social network application today, and it is also a typical example of using cloud in sharing images.

Mobile cloud computing also helps in reducing the running cost for compute-intensive applications that take long time and large amount of energy when performed on the limited-resource devices. CC can efficiently support various tasks for data warehousing, managing and synchronizing multiple documents online. For example, clouds can be used for transcoding[19], playing chess[12][27], or broadcasting multimedia services[28] to mobile devices. In these cases, all the complex calculations for transcoding or offering an optimal chess move that take a long time when perform on mobile devices will be processed efficiently on the cloud. Mobile applications also are not constrained by storage capacity on the devices because their data now is stored on the cloud.

- *Improving reliability:* Storing data or running applications on clouds is an effective way to improve the reliability because the data and application are stored and backed up on a number of computers. This reduces the chance of data and application lost on the mobile devices. In addition, MCC can be designed as a comprehensive data security model for both service providers and users. For example, the cloud can be used to protect copyrighted digital contents (e.g., video, clip, and music) from

being abused and unauthorized distribution[46]. In addition, the cloud can remotely provide mobile users with security services such as virus scanning, malicious code detection, and authentication[33]. Such cloud-based security services also can make efficient use of the collected record from different users to improve the effectiveness of the services.

In addition, MCC also inherits some advantages of clouds for mobile services as follows:

- *Dynamic provisioning.* Dynamic on-demand provisioning of resources on a fine-grained, self-service basis is a flexible way for service providers and mobile users to run their applications without advanced reservation of resources.

- *Scalability.* The deployment of mobile applications can be performed and scaled to meet the unpredictable user demands due to flexible resource provisioning. Service providers can easily add and expand an application and service without or with little constraint on the resource usage.

- *Multitenancy.* Service providers (e.g., network operator and data center owner) can share the resources and costs to support a variety of applications and largenumber of users.

- *Ease of integration.* Multiple services from different service providers can be integrated easily through the cloud and Internet to meet the user demand.

4. Open Research Issues

4.1. Energy efficiency

Owing to the limited resources such as battery life, available network bandwidth, storage capacity and processor performance, on the mobile devices, researchers are always on the lookout for solutions that result in optimal utilization of available resources.

4.2. Security

The absence of standards poses a serious issue specifically with respect to security and privacy of data being delivered to and from the mobile devices to the cloud.

4.3. Better service

The original motivation behind MCC was to provide PC-like services to mobile devices. However, owing to the varied differences in features between fixed and mobile devices, transformation of services from one to the other may not be as direct.

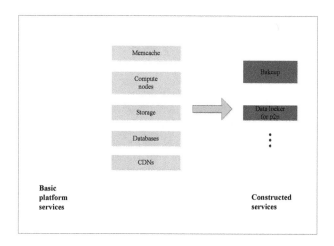

Figure 3. Platform services

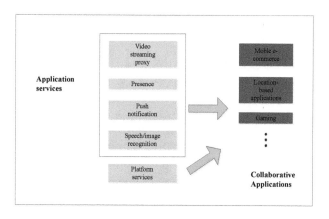

Figure 4. Application services

4.4. Task division

Researchers are always on the lookout for strategies and algorithms to offload computation tasks from mobile devices to cloud. However, due to differences in computational requirement of numerous applications available to the users and the variety of handsets available in the market, an optimal strategy is an area to be explored.

5. Basic Mobile Cloud Computing Services

We envision that cloud computing providers will provide a set of basic services for mobile computing. There are three types of services. The first one is what we refer as platform services, the second is application services, and the third is context-rich support services.

5.1. Platform Services

Platform services include computing, storage, database, memcache, content distribution as shown in Figure 3. Currently all EC2 services accessible from mobile devices are considered platform services. Some of these basic services can benefit from application sharing. Taking distributed memcache service for an example, we can see that many application may create same or access same data sets. With a shared memcache service, it will be more likely to have a cache hit due to the larger cache size. It will reduce computation demand to re-generate the cached results. Of course, sharing brings several issues, such as security, privacy as well as how much storage each application should have.

Out of the basic platform service, one can already build very useful applications. For example, with storage service, and computing service, one can build file backup service, and file syncing service (keep all registered devices in sync of the user content). One can also build a data locker service[4]. In essence, the

data locker protocol works with p2p protocols closely to service files on behalf of end hosts. It is particularly appealing in the mobile device context as it minimizes the usage of wireless access links.

5.2. Application Services

Public cloud provider can also offer a set of essential application services, which can be shown in Figure 4. For example, people may not trust each individual applications and thus, may not reveal their location information. This can hamper the development of location based services. If mobile devices are using the cloud services, then there is prior trusted relationship. For example, Apple iCloud users are comfortable that their private data will be protected from un-authorized use. So it is easier to trust the cloud provider for location privacy. Thus, a presence service can be an essential service so that any application that needs location information can talk to the presence service. The presence service will implement location privacy policies according to what are stipulated by the mobile subscribers. We recognize that different people have different levels of privacy requirements. It is conceivable that some people may not want to sign up with a presence service. However, the presence service will facilitate the development of location-based services. Presence service will save resources as it is not replicated for each location based application.

Given the popularity of video streaming applications, cloud providers can offer a video transcoding and streaming proxy. The reason is that mobile devices are limited by the availability of video codec as well as bandwidth variability. A proxy service alleviates this problem by performing transcoding. In addition, the proxy can take advantage of certain codec's inherent bandwidth adaptation capability, for example, H.264SVC can adapt in three dimensions with finer granularity of network bandwidths.

Many mobile applications need to send push notification to mobile devices. Because many mobile devices are behind NAT, in order to send push notification, a persistent TCP connection is needed. To maintain such a persistent TCP connection, periodic heartbeat messages have to be sent. Thus, it will be very inefficient if each application has to maintain a persistent TCP connection. To avoid such situation, Android offers a push notification service through an API so that one TCP connection is maintained between a mobile device and a Google server for the purpose of push notification.

Push notification services typically are used by servers to reach mobile clients. To allow mobile devices to communicate with each other, Microsoft Research Project Hawaii[21] has developed a relay service. The Hawaii Relay Service provides a relay point in the cloud that mobile applications can use to communicate. It provides an endpoint naming scheme and buffering for messages sent between endpoints. It also allows for messages to be multicast to multiple endpoints.

There are many applications that do speech and image recognition. It makes sense to provide a common service to implement the best algorithm while amortizing the cost. In fact, Google Android have a speech recognition API which enables developers to integrate speech input capabilities into their applications. Developers stream audio to Google's servers which then convert speech into text and feed it back to the applications. Project Hawaii[21] also provides a speech to text service.

5.3. Context-rich Services

We envision that many mobile applications will become more personalized, and more context aware, recognizing not only the location of the user and the time of day, but also a user's identity and their personal preferences. To support these mCloud services, we believe mCloud providers need to provide a set of context-rich support services. Application developers can use these context-rich support services as building blocks to build a large class of new mCloud services. We envision several context-rich support services such as context extraction service, recommendation service, and group privacy service. Context extraction service provides data mining analysis of mobile data combined with other forms of data, such as social networking data and sensor network data, in order to extract contextual clues relevant to the user. For example, recognizing the user's activity based on mobile accelerometer and audio data is one such contextual mining service that is currently being explored[31]. The context extraction service will be a common service that relieves each context-rich application from replicating context

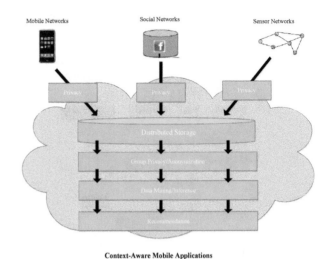

Context-Aware Mobile Applications

Figure 5. Privacy, Data Mining, and Recommendation Services in the Context-Aware Mobile Social Cloud.

extraction, thus saving energy and reduce computation costs of mobiles.

Based on these contextual clues, a layer of cloud recommendation services can be built that creates output that is tailored to an individual or set of individuals with those contextual characteristics. For example, some applications have begun to combine together mobile location with social networks to generate multimedia content, e.g. a song playlist or a recommended video[6], that is tailored to the individual or individuals who are nearby an audio jukebox or video screen that is aware of their presence.

Such contextual mobile applications would be composed as shown in Figure 5. This architecture fuses together multiple layers of cloud application services, as described in the SocialFusion architecture[8], wherein mobile, social, and sensor networks supply streams of data into a distributed storage service. Data mining/inference cloud services then operate on the assembled data to extract contextual clues. Finally, recommendation services in the cloud generate tailored multimedia output, either for the mobile device or for nearby multimedia devices such as LCD displays or loudspeakers.

We imagine that privacy protection services will emerge as a key component of context-aware mobile cloud services, as there is a fundamental tradeoff between supplying personal information to receive contextual services, and revealing too much private information for those services. Location privacy has already been discussed, but we think that new privacy services will have to be developed to protect user's data from data mining services that analyze mobile smartphone data, such as activity recognition services. New privacy services will also need to be devised to protect and anonymize information released from social networks[7] and sensor networks[20][37]. Moreover, we believe a new concept of "group privacy" or "collective privacy" will emerge, requiring privacy services that protect groups of individuals from collective inferences on their joint actions, tastes, and preferences.

6. Conclusion and Future Trends

Mobile Cloud Computing, as a development and extension of Cloud Computing and Mobile Computing, is the emerging and well accepted technology with fast growth. The combination of cloud computing, wireless communication infrastructure, portable computing devices, location-based services, mobile Web etc. has laid the foundation for the novel computing model.

We have given an extensive survey of current mobile cloud computing research in this paper. Highlighting the motivation for mobile cloud computing, we have also presented different definitions of mobile cloud computing in the literature. We have presented a taxonomy of issues found in this area, and the approaches in which these issues have been tackled, focusing on operational level, end user level, service and application level, security and context-awareness.

These are still early days in mobile cloud computing, with recent workshops in the area such as MobiSys[38], MCCTA[40], CMCVR[12], and MCNCS[11]. There are numerous new mobile applications that a mobile cloud framework can enable, when many more resources can be made available to the mobile device (via the mobile cloud facility). The future could also explore the potential of local mobile clouds formed from collections of computers in ubiquitous devices in shoes, clothing, watches, jewelry, furniture and other everyday objects, as indeed such embedded computers will become more powerful. And so, the infrastructure, platform or application available as services will be of new forms: the infrastructure could be a powerful massively distributed set of cameras on stationary and mobile devices formed ad hoc and metered to cover an event, or a collection of distributed computers formed to compute a job seamlessly from the user's mobile device while the user is shopping. A car can sell its computational resources and pay for its own parking, or the collection of computers on crowds of people in a busy area forms an "elastic" collective resource for ad hoc use. There is also potential to have context sources or sensors (and sensor networks) in the vicinity of a mobile user sold as services to the mobile user, to support context-aware applications. However, challenges are present in order to "elastically" on-demand form clouds of services and resources efficiently, seamlessly and in a robust manner.

References

[1] S. Abolfazli, Z. Sanaei, E. Ahmed, A. Gani, and R. Buyya. Cloud-based augmentation for mobile devices: motivation, taxonomies, and open challenges. *Communications Surveys & Tutorials, IEEE*, 16(1):337–368, 2014.

[2] S. Abolfazli, Z. Sanaei, A. Gani, F. Xia, and L. T. Yang. Rich mobile applications: genesis, taxonomy, and open issues. *Journal of Network and Computer Applications*, 40:345–362, 2014.

[3] M. Ali. Green cloud on the horizon. In *Cloud Computing*, pages 451–459. Springer, 2009.

[4] R. Alimi. Open content distribution using data lockers. Technical report, Technical Report TR1426, Feb. 2010.

[5] Amazon simple storage service. http://aws.amazon.com/s3/.

[6] A. Beach, M. Gartrell, S. Akkala, J. Elston, J. Kelley, K. Nishimoto, B. Ray, S. Razgulin, K. Sundaresan, B. Surendar, et al. Whozthat? evolving an ecosystem for context-aware mobile social networks. *Network, IEEE*, 22(4):50–55, 2008.

[7] A. Beach, M. Gartrell, and R. Han. q-anon: Rethinking anonymity for social networks. In *Social Computing (SocialCom), 2010 IEEE Second International Conference on*, pages 185–192. IEEE, 2010.

[8] A. Beach, M. Gartrell, X. Xing, R. Han, Q. Lv, S. Mishra, and K. Seada. Fusing mobile, sensor, and social data to fully enable context-aware computing. In *Proceedings of the Eleventh Workshop on Mobile Computing Systems & Applications*, pages 60–65. ACM, 2010.

[9] R. Buyya, C. S. Yeo, and S. Venugopal. Market-oriented cloud computing: Vision, hype, and reality for delivering it services as computing utilities. In *High Performance Computing and Communications, 2008. HPCC'08. 10th IEEE International Conference on*, pages 5–13. Ieee, 2008.

[10] R. Buyya, C. S. Yeo, S. Venugopal, J. Broberg, and I. Brandic. Cloud computing and emerging it platforms: Vision, hype, and reality for delivering computing as the 5th utility. *Future Generation computer systems*, 25(6):599–616, 2009.

[11] A. Coronato and G. De Pietro. Mipeg: A middleware infrastructure for pervasive grids. *Future Generation Computer Systems*, 24(1):17–29, 2008.

[12] E. Cuervo, A. Balasubramanian, D.-k. Cho, A. Wolman, S. Saroiu, R. Chandra, and P. Bahl. Maui: making smartphones last longer with code offload. In *Proceedings of the 8th international conference on Mobile systems, applications, and services*, pages 49–62. ACM, 2010.

[13] J. W. Davis. Power benchmark strategy for systems employing power management. In *Electronics and the Environment, 1993., Proceedings of the 1993 IEEE International Symposium on*, pages 117–119. IEEE, 1993.

[14] H. T. Dinh, C. Lee, D. Niyato, and P. Wang. A survey of mobile cloud computing: architecture, applications, and approaches. *Wireless communications and mobile computing*, 13(18):1587–1611, 2013.

[15] Facebook. http://www.facebook.com/.

[16] Flickr. http://www.flickr.com/.

[17] G. H. Forman and J. Zahorjan. The challenges of mobile computing. *Computer*, 27(4):38–47, 1994.

[18] I. Foster, Y. Zhao, I. Raicu, and S. Lu. Cloud computing and grid computing 360-degree compared. In *Grid Computing Environments Workshop, 2008. GCE'08*, pages 1–10. Ieee, 2008.

[19] A. Garcia and H. Kalva. Cloud transcoding for mobile video content delivery. In *Proceedings of the IEEE International Conference on Consumer Electronics (ICCE)*, volume 379, 2011.

[20] P. Gilbert, L. P. Cox, J. Jung, and D. Wetherall. Toward trustworthy mobile sensing. In *Proceedings of the Eleventh Workshop on Mobile Computing Systems & Applications*, pages 31–36. ACM, 2010.

[21] M. R. P. Hawaii. Hardware and software platforms for developing cloud-enabled applications for windows phone 7. http://research.microsoft.com/en-us/um/redmond/projects/hawaii/students/.

[22] C. Hewitt. Orgs for scalable, robust, privacy-friendly client cloud computing. *IEEE internet computing*, pages 96–99, 2008.

[23] Y. Huang, H. Su, W. Sun, J. M. Zhang, C. J. Guo, J. M. Xu, Z. B. Jiang, S. X. Yang, and J. Zhu. Framework for building a low-cost, scalable, and secured platform for web-delivered business services. *IBM Journal of Research and Development*, 54(6):4–1, 2010.

[24] International data corporation. http://www.idc.com/.

[25] R. Kakerow. Low power design methodologies for mobile communication. In *Computer Design: VLSI in Computers and Processors, 2002. Proceedings. 2002 IEEE International Conference on*, pages 8–13. IEEE, 2002.

[26] U. Kremer, J. Hicks, and J. Rehg. A compilation framework for power and energy management on mobile computers. In *Languages and Compilers for Parallel Computing*, pages 115–131. Springer, 2003.

[27] K. Kumar and Y.-H. Lu. Cloud computing for mobile users: Can offloading computation save energy? *Computer*, pages 51–56, 2010.

[28] L. Li, X. Li, S. Youxia, and L. Wen. Research on mobile multimedia broadcasting service integration based on cloud computing. In *Multimedia Technology (ICMT), 2010 International Conference on*, pages 1–4. IEEE, 2010.

[29] F. Liu, P. Shu, H. Jin, L. Ding, J. Yu, D. Niu, and B. Li. Gearing resource-poor mobile devices with powerful clouds: architectures, challenges, and applications. *Wireless Communications, IEEE*, 20(3):14–22, 2013.

[30] R. N. Mayo and P. Ranganathan. Energy consumption in mobile devices: why future systems need requirements–aware energy scale-down. In *Power-Aware Computer Systems*, pages 26–40. Springer, 2005.

[31] E. Miluzzo, N. D. Lane, K. Fodor, R. Peterson, H. Lu, M. Musolesi, S. B. Eisenman, X. Zheng, and A. T. Campbell. Sensing meets mobile social networks: the design, implementation and evaluation of the cenceme application. In *Proceedings of the 6th ACM conference on Embedded network sensor systems*, pages 337–350. ACM, 2008.

[32] Mobile cloud computing subscribers to total nearly one billion by 2014. http://www.abiresearch.com/press/1484/.

[33] J. Oberheide, K. Veeraraghavan, E. Cooke, J. Flinn, and F. Jahanian. Virtualized in-cloud security services for mobile devices. In *Proceedings of the First Workshop on Virtualization in Mobile Computing*, pages 31–35. ACM, 2008.

[34] L. D. Paulson. Low-power chips for high-powered handhelds. *Computer*, 36(1):21–23, 2003.

[35] A. Rudenko, P. Reiher, G. J. Popek, and G. H. Kuenning. Saving portable computer battery power through remote process execution. *ACM SIGMOBILE Mobile Computing and Communications Review*, 2(1):19–26, 1998.

[36] Z. Sanaei, S. Abolfazli, A. Gani, and R. Buyya. Heterogeneity in mobile cloud computing: taxonomy and open challenges. *Communications Surveys & Tutorials, IEEE*, 16(1):369–392, 2014.

[37] S. Saroiu and A. Wolman. I am a sensor, and i approve this message. In *Proceedings of the Eleventh Workshop on Mobile Computing Systems & Applications*, pages 37–42. ACM, 2010.

[38] Y. Sasaki and Y. Shibata. A disaster information sharing method by the mobile servers in challenged networks. In *Advanced Information Networking and Applications Workshops (WAINA), 2012 26th International Conference on*, pages 1048–1053. IEEE, 2012.

[39] M. Satyanarayanan. Fundamental challenges in mobile computing. In *Proceedings of the fifteenth annual ACM symposium on Principles of distributed computing*, pages 1–7. ACM, 1996.

[40] M. Satyanarayanan, P. Bahl, R. Caceres, and N. Davies. The case for vm-based cloudlets in mobile computing. *Pervasive Computing, IEEE*, 8(4):14–23, 2009.

[41] Shozu. http://www.shozu.com/portal/index.do/.

[42] A. Smailagic and M. Ettus. System design and power optimization for mobile computers. In *isvlsi*, page 0015. IEEE, 2002.

[43] W.-T. Tsai, X. Sun, and J. Balasooriya. Service-oriented cloud computing architecture. In *Information Technology: New Generations (ITNG), 2010 Seventh International Conference on*, pages 684–689. IEEE, 2010.

[44] E. Vartiainen and K. Väänänen-Vainio-Mattila. User experience of mobile photo sharing in the cloud. In *Proceedings of the 9th International Conference on Mobile and Ubiquitous Multimedia*, page 4. ACM, 2010.

[45] L. Youseff, M. Butrico, and D. Da Silva. Toward a unified ontology of cloud computing. In *Grid Computing Environments Workshop, 2008. GCE'08*, pages 1–10. IEEE, 2008.

[46] P. Zou, C. Wang, Z. Liu, and D. Bao. Phosphor: A cloud based drm scheme with sim card. In *Web Conference (APWEB), 2010 12th International Asia-Pacific*, pages 459–463. IEEE, 2010.

11

Scalable SOCP-based localization technique for wireless sensor network

Randa M. Abdelmoneem[1], Eman Shaaban[1,*]

[1]Department of Computer Systems, Faculty of Computer and Information Sciences, Ain-Shams University, Egypt

Abstract

Node localization is one of the essential requirements to most applications of wireless sensor networks. This paper presents a detailed implementation of a centralized localization technique for WSNs based on Second Order Cone Programming (SOCP). To allow scalability, it also proposes a clustered localization approach for WSNs based on that centralized SOCP technique. The cluster solves the SOCP problem as a global minimization problem to get positions of the cluster sensor nodes. To enhance localization accuracy, a cluster level refinement step is implemented using Gauss-Newton optimization. The initial position for the Gauss-Newton optimization is the position drawn from the preprocessor SOCP localization. The proposed approach scales well for large networks and provides a considerable reduction in computation time while yielding good localization accuracy.

Keywords: wireless sensor network, localization, second-order cone programming

1. Introduction

A wireless sensor network (WSN) is a group of a few to several hundreds or even thousands of sensor nodes deployed over a significant area. WSNs have a wide range of applications which include environmental monitoring, target tracking, home automation, military applications and others. To process sensor data in WSN, it is imperative to know where the data is coming from. So, knowledge of nodes locations is an essential requirement for many location-aware applications including aforementioned applications, location-based services (LBS) and location-based routing. Several surveys discussed localization strategies and attempted to classify different localization techniques like [1],[2],[3]. Localization techniques could be classified according to all calculations being performed on a single node or distributed on all the network sensor nodes to centralized localization technique (e.g. MDS-MAP [4] and Semi-Definite programming (SDP) [5]) and distributed localization technique (e.g. APIT [6]). Another new approach in this classification is called locally centralized or cluster-based localization techniques which are distributed techniques that achieve a global goal by communicating with nodes in some neighbourhood only. According to the process of estimating node-to-node distances or angles, the localization techniques are classified to range-based and range-free localization techniques. Range-based localization techniques are based on distances measurements between the nodes using Time of Arrival (TOA), time difference of arrival (TDOA) and received signal strength (RSS) (e.g. Trilateration) or based on angles between the nodes like angle of arrival (AOA) (e.g. Triangulation) [7]. Range-free localization techniques depend on network connectivity (e.g. DV-HOP) [6] to indirectly obtain the distances between the nodes. Also, localization techniques can be classified to anchor-based or anchor-free localization techniques. Anchor-based localization techniques usually provide absolute positions for the nodes whereas anchor-free localization techniques provide relative positions. Biswas and Ye who proposed a semi-definite programming (SDP) relaxation of the localization problem which has various nice properties [5]. SOCP-based localization technique was studied

* Corresponding author. Email: eman.shaaban@cis.asu.edu.eg

by Tseng [8] who provided a second order cone programming (SOCP) relaxation of localization problem, motivated by its simpler structure and its potential to be solved faster than SDP. This paper proposes a locally centralized technique for solving the sensor network localization problem. It is a Refined Clustered technique based on Second-Order Cone Programming (RC-SOCP). The proposed approach divides the large network into smaller sub networks. For each cluster, the cluster solves the SOCP problem as a global minimization problem to get initial positions of the cluster sensor nodes. To enhance localization accuracy, a cluster level refinement step is implemented using Gauss-Newton optimization. The initial position for the GaussNewton optimization is the position drawn from the preprocessor SOCP localization. Rest of the paper is organized as follows: Section 2 introduces the centralized SOCP localization technique. Proposed technique is presented in section 3. Simulation results and evaluations are presented in section 4 and we conclude in section 5.

2. Centralized SOCP localization technique

This section discuses a detailed description of SOCP problem formulation for Castalia wireless sensor networks simulator, providing the formulation algorithm and solver tools. It also investigates the results obtained.

2.1. Problem formulation

Second-order cone programming relaxation method for wireless sensor network localization was first studied by Tseng [8]. In this method $\mathbf{n}$ is the total number of nodes in R^d ($d \geq 1$), $\mathbf{m}$ are the nodes whose locations $x_i \in R^2$, $i = 1, \ldots, m$ are to be determined given $\mathbf{n-m}$ nodes called anchors with known locations and $\mathbf{d_{ij}}$ which is the euclidean distance between nodes i and j where $(i,j) \in \mathcal{A}$. $\mathcal{A}$ is the undirected neighbour set defined as $\mathcal{A} := \{(i,j) : \|x_i - x_j\| \leq RadioRange\}$. The problem is formulated as the non-convex minimization equation

$$v_{opt} = min \sum_{(i,j) \in \mathcal{A}} |y_{ij} - d_{ij}^2| \qquad (1)$$

$$s.t. \quad y_{ij} = \|x_i - x_j\|^2 \quad \forall (i,j) \in \mathcal{A}$$

Where $\| \cdot \|$ denotes the euclidean norm. Then in order to yield a convex-problem, the equality constraints are relaxed to non-equality constraints, the problem becomes

$$v_{opt} = min \sum_{(i,j) \in \mathcal{A}} |y_{ij} - d_{ij}^2| \qquad (2)$$

$$s.t. \quad y_{ij} \geq \|x_i - x_j\|^2 \quad \forall (i,j) \in \mathcal{A}$$

Equation (2) can be rewritten as

$$min \sum_{i,j \in \mathcal{A}} U_{ij} \qquad (3)$$

$$s.t. \qquad y_{ij} \geq \|x_i - x_j\|^2 \quad \forall (i,j) \in \mathcal{A}$$

$$u_{ij} \geq |y_{ij} - d_{ij}^2| \quad \forall (i,j) \in \mathcal{A}$$

$$u_{ij} \geq 0$$

2.2. Centralized SOCP localization implementation

Given a wireless sensor network with size n sensors, m are sensors with unknown locations, $n - m$ are sensors with known locations (anchors). To solve this localization problem, the centralized SOCP localization technique is performed in three phases. In the first phase, nodes estimate their distances with sensor and anchor neighbours which are within their communication ranges. The second phase involves wireless communication and routing between the nodes. In the third phase, the positions matrix and the lower triangle of the distances matrix are created with sizes 2×n, n×n respectively and filled with their relevant data received from the nodes.
Distances Matrix

$$\begin{pmatrix} 0 & 0 & 0 & .. & 0 \\ d_{10} & 0 & 0 & .. & 0 \\ d_{20} & d_{21} & 0 & .. & 0 \\ .. & .. & .. & .. & 0 \\ d_{n0} & d_{n1} & .. & .. & 0 \end{pmatrix}$$

where d_{ij} is the euclidean distance between nodes i,j.

Positions Matrix

$$\begin{pmatrix} x_0 & x_1 & x_2 & .. & x_n \\ y_0 & y_1 & y_2 & .. & y_n \end{pmatrix}$$

where x_i, y_i are the x,y co-ordinates of an anchor node or 0,0 if the sensor node is not an anchor. Algorithm 1 shows the pseudo-code of formulating the SOCP-localization problem according to equation (3). For a network of n total nodes and m non-positioned nodes, there are $\Omega(m)$ variables and $\Omega(m)$ inequality constraints using position and distance matrices [8].

2.3. Simulator and Solver Tools

Several surveys discussed various Simulators like [12, 14] that are used for simulation of ad-hoc networks specially wireless sensor networks. Castalia is an open-source simulator which is based on OMNet++ simulation environment and was developed at the National ICT Australia, It was developed for networks

Algorithm 1 : formulating the SOCP-localization problem

1: **procedure** CREATEMODEL(distanceMatrix, positionsMatrix)

2: Let model = model of the problem , vars = array of variables

3: **for all** d_{ij} in $distanceMatrix$ **do**

4:    #Read positions of nodes i,j from positions matrix

5:    $x1pos \leftarrow positionsMatrix[0][i]$

6:    $y1pos \leftarrow positionsMatrix[1][i]$

7:    $x2pos \leftarrow positionsMatrix[0][j]$

8:    $y2pos \leftarrow positionsMatrix[1][j]$

9:    **if** $x1pos! = 0$ or $y1pos! = 0$ **then** #Check node i being anchor

10:      $node \ i \ isAnchor$

11:    **else**

12:      # Search for variables in vars array and if not found create, add them

13:      **if** variables of i in $vars$ **then**

14:        $x_i \leftarrow vars[i].x$, $y_i \leftarrow vars[i].y$

15:      **else**

16:        $create \ vars \ x_i, y_i$

17:        $vars.add(x_i)$, $vars.add(y_i)$

18:      **end if**

19:    **end if**

20:    $Repeat \ steps \ 7\text{-}17 \ for \ the \ second \ node \ j$

21:    # If at least one of the nodes is not an anchor complete model formulation

22:    **if** $node \ i \ isAnchor{==}false \ Or \ node \ j \ isAnchor{==}false$ **then**

23:      $create \ variables \ u_{ij}, y_{ij}$

24:      $vars.add(u_{ij})$, $vars.add(y_{ij})$

25:      $objectiveExpression \leftarrow objectiveExpression + u_{ij}$

26:      $create \ constraint \ c$

27:      $c.expression \leftarrow y_{ij} - u_{ij}$

28:      $c.lowerbound \leftarrow 0$

29:      $c.upperbound \leftarrow d_{ij} * d_{ij}$

30:      $model.add(c)$

31:    **end if**

32:    # Create quadratic constraint. Substitue with position values for anchor node(s) if found

33:    **if** $node \ i \ isAnchor{==}false \ And \ node \ j \ isAnchor{==}false$ **then**

34:      $expr \leftarrow y - (x_i - x_j) * (x_i - x_j) - (y_i - y_j) * (y_i - y_j)$

35:    **else if** $node \ i \ isAnchor{==}true \ And \ node \ j \ isAnchor{==}false$ **then**

36:      $expr \leftarrow y - (x1pos - x_j) * (x1pos - x_j) - (y1pos - y_j) * (y1pos - x_j)$

37:    **else if** $node \ i \ isAnchor{==}false \ And \ node \ j \ isAnchor{==}true$ **then**

38:      $expr \leftarrow y - (x_i - x2pos) * (x_i - x2pos) - (y_i - y2pos) * (y_i - y2pos)$

39:    **end if**

Algorithm 1 Continue

40:    $create \ constraint \ q$

41:    $q.expression \leftarrow expr$

42:    $q.lowerbound \leftarrow 0$

43:    $q.upperbound \leftarrow \infty$

44:    $model.add(q)$

45: **end for**

46: $create \ objective \ obj$

47: $obj.fn \leftarrow minimization$

48: $obj.expression \leftarrow objExpression$

49: $model.add(obj)$

---

of low power embedded devices such as wireless sensor nodes [13]. Our simulation study is carried out using version 3.2 of Castalia which build upon version 4.1 of OMNet++.

The implementation of our SOCP-based localization technique uses IBM ILOG CPLEX. IBM LOG Concert Technology (modelling layer) C++ Interface Of OPL was used to integrate our problem model in Castalia with the CPLEX solver[15].

2.4. Performance Evaluation

We evaluate the performance of the centralized SOCP-based localization by measuring localization accuracy, computation time and problem size.

The mean error between the estimated and the true location of the non-anchor nodes in the network is adopted as the performance metric. It is defined as follows

$$LE = \frac{1}{N} \cdot \sum_{i=1}^{N} \|\hat{x}_i - x_i\|$$

Where LE denotes a localization error, N denotes the number of nodes in a network whose location is estimated, x_i is the true position of the node i in the network , $\hat{x}_i$ is estimated location of the node i (solution of the location system).

Computation time is defined as the time spent for formulating and solving the SOCP problem at the sink node and it is measured using C++ std.clock() function. The time needed for computing the relative distances at the nodes and communication or message exchanges time is excluded. Problem size corresponds to number of variables and constraints for the SOCP-localization problem formulated at the sink node.

We evaluate performance of the centralized SOCP-based localization technique by studying the effect of varying Network size (number of nodes), Anchors percentage, Communication radio range and Noise value added to distances measurements.

Anchors

Anchors are chosen to form a convex hull distribution around the sensor nodes in the network. This distribution was chosen to assure good localization accuracy when non-anchor nodes are in the convex hull of the anchors [11].

Radio range

Radio range is specified by replacing the path loss parameter $PL(d)$ of the log-normal shadowing model in equation (4)

$$PL(d) = PL(d_0) + 10.\eta.log(\frac{d}{d_0}) + X_\sigma \qquad (4)$$

with its equivalent

$$PL(d) = P_{Tx} - P_{Rx}$$

Equation(4) calculates the average path loss in the channel model in Castalia [13]. Setting the random variable X_σ to 0 for the case of no fading, thus simulating general environment conditions where stationary WSN is deployed in fairly static environments and fading is not very significant, thus it is ignored. η is substituted with 2.4 which is typical default value that will produce results similar to many outdoors (and sometimes indoors) environments. d is the path length allowing communications between two paired nodes, thus representing the radio range. So, the radio range can be specified by

$$RR = 10^{P_{Tx} - P_{Rx} - PL(d_0)/24} \qquad (5)$$

P_{Rx} is inferred from $ReceiverSensetivity$ value of the radio card chosen (radio model for CC2420 chip by Texas instrument) and is qual to -95 dBm. So the radio range is mainly controlled by the transmit power and the path loss at reference distance values specified according to

$$RR = 10^{P_{Tx} + 95 - PL(d_0)/24} \qquad (6)$$

The degree of connectivity is controlled by the radio range specified. It is calculated as the average connectivity of all the nodes which is equivalent to the average number of neighbours for all of the sensor nodes in the network for a specific radio range and environment area.

Noise to distance

We added normally distributed measurement noise to the true distance according to the equation

$$d_{ij} = \|x_i - x_j\|.max\{0, 1 + \epsilon_{ij}.nf_d\} \quad \forall(i,j) \in \mathcal{A}$$

Where ϵ_{ij} is a normal random variable N(0, 1) representing measurement noise and $nfd \in [0, 1]$ is the noise factor (standard deviation of the distance error in percentage) for the distance measurements [9].

2.5. Simulation Results

Simulations are conducted for a randomly generated 500 nodes uniformly distributed on the unit square area

$[-0.5, 0.5]^2$ with noise factor (nfd)=0.05, radio range (rr)=0.17 and Degree of Connectivity=38. Anchors are chosen to form a convex hull distribution around the sensor nodes in the network with percentage (p) of 15%. Simulations are averaged over 10 runs with confidence level of 95%. Simulations were carried out on a PC with 2.4 GHz Quad-Core processor and 4 GB RAM using Castalia simulator integrated with IBM CPLEX solver using C++ interface.

Fig.?? shows a snapshot of the true sensor positions and the estimated positions. True positions of the sensors are depicted in blue coloured points and the estimated node positions are depicted in red coloured points, solid lines indicate the error between the estimated and true sensor positions. A close match is observed between the estimated and true positions. The estimated positions become less accurate as we move towards the boundary. Fig.1b shows the Commulative distributive function (CDF) of localization errors. The

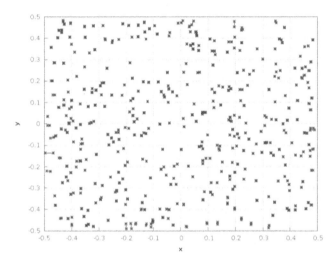

(a) Snapshot of the true vs estimated nodes locations

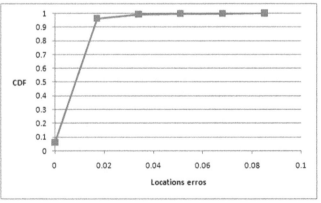

(b) CDF of localization errors

Figure 1. Centralized SOCP results for uniform topology: n = 500, $RadioRange$ =0.17, p =0.15 and nfd =0.05.

total mean localization error (LE) for the network in

Fig.1 is 0.02 with confidence interval (-0.002 , 0.04) and standard deviation 0.04 .

Effect of Varying Network Size. Fig.2 shows the CDF of localization errors (log scale) for different network sizes with the same radio range in the same area for a network with $nfd=0.05$, $rr=0.11$ and anchor percentage of 15%. Fig.2 shows that when the network size increases in the same area, the degree of connectivity is increased and this leads to larger communications between nodes. Consequently, more distances are obtained between nodes which directly improves the localization accuracy. On the other hand, it must be noted that increasing node density and hence communications between nodes increases network overhead and energy consumption.

The mean localization errors (LEs), and their

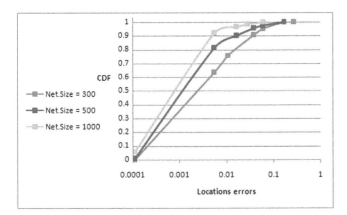

Figure 2. CDF of localization errors (log scale) for different network sizes

confidence intervals are listed in table 1 which shows a decrease in mean localization error when increasing the network size. Table 2 shows the number of variables, number of constraints, and the computation runtime spent for solving the networks in Fig.2. Computation runtime grows with increasing network size, thus limits the scalability of the technique for large networks.

Table 1. Mean localization errors for different network sizes

network size	mean error	standard deviation	confidence interval
300	0.01	0.022	(-0.001 , 0.025)
500	0.006	0.015	(-0.003 , 0.016)
1000	0.002	0.018	(-0.009 , 0.014)

Effect of Varying Anchors Percentage. Fig.3 shows the effect of changing anchor percentage on the localization accuracy for a network of 500 nodes, $rr=0.17$ and $nfd=0.05$. We changed number of anchor nodes while maintaining number of non-positioned nodes the

Table 2. Performance and computation runtime comparison of different network sizes.

network size	$|\mathcal{A}|$	# of variables	# of constraints	comp. run time (sec.)
300	1498	3472	1481	1.279
500	4388	9460	4305	5.936
1000	17051	35132	16716	152.044

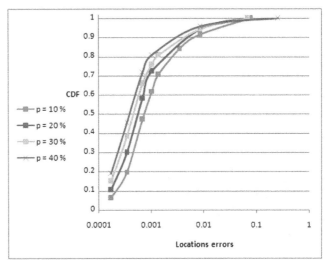

Figure 3. CDF of localization errors (log scale) for different percentage of anchors

same (500 non-positioned nodes). Fig.3 shows that increasing anchor percentage considerably increases the localization accuracy. For a network of 20% of anchors, 80% of the nodes have error less than 0.0017. For anchor percentage greater than 20%, slight improvement in localization accuracy is achieved. This means that the implemented technique requires a proper setting of percentage of anchors to achieve good localization accuracy. The mean localization errors (LEs) and their confidence intervals are listed in table 3. However, increasing anchors percentage increases the

Table 3. Mean localization errors for different anchor percentages

anchor percentage	mean error	standard deviation	confidence interval
10%	0.003	0.006	(-0.001 , 0.006)
20%	0.002	0.005	(-0.001 , 0.005)
30%	0.0018	0.0045	(-0.001 , 0.0048)
40%	0.0015	0.0046	(-0.001 , 0.0044)

total complexity of the computations. This is shown in table 4.

Effect of Varying Communication Radio Range. To study the effect of changing radio range on localization

Table 4. Performance and computation runtime comparison of different anchor percentages.

anchor percentage	$|\mathcal{A}|$	# of variables	# of constr-aints	comp. run time (sec.)
10%	12590	25970	12485	35.32
20%	15013	30370	14685	66.39
30%	17611	34566	16783	94.56
40%	20198	38306	18653	124.71

accuracy, we set rr to 0.08, 0.1 and 0.15. Fig.4

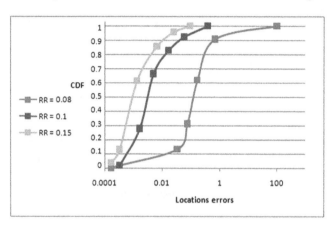

Figure 4. CDF of localization errors (log scale) for different radio ranges

shows that networks with lower radio range have higher localization error. This is due to less inter-node communications and hence distances information between nodes. It must be noted that for rr=0.08, 97% of total nodes are localized (413 node) whereas 100% of total nodes are localized for rr=0.1, 0.15. However, increasing radio range increases power consumption and adds more communication overhead to the network. The mean localization errors (LEs) and their confidence intervals are listed in table 5. Performance and computation runtime comparison is shown in table 6.

Table 5. Mean localization errors and computation time for different radio ranges

radio range	mean error	standard deviation	confidence interval
0.08	4.2	16.7	(-6.15 , 14.5)
0.1	0.015	0.034	(-0.006 , 0.036)
0.15	0.004	0.009	(-0.002 , 0.01)

Effect of Varying Noise Value Added to Distances Measurements. Fig.5 shows the effect of changing nfd on the localization accuracy. Fig.5 shows that there is no

Table 6. Performance and computation runtime comparison of different radio ranges.

radio range	$|\mathcal{A}|$	# of variables	# of constraints	comp. run time (sec.)
0.08	982	2750	965	0.62
0.1	3668	8052	3601	4.58
0.15	7819	16172	7661	29.82

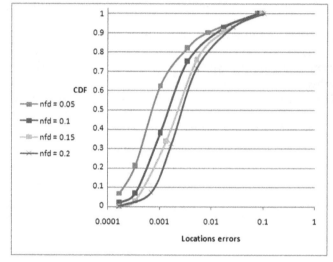

Figure 5. CDF of localization errors (log scale) for different nfd

significant improvement in localization accuracy when decreasing nfd. Thus, the implemented localization technique solves the localization problem with good localization accuracy in the presence of inaccuracies in distance measurements. The mean localization errors (LEs) and their confidence intervals for the networks in Fig.5 are listed in table 7.

Table 7. Mean localization errors for different nfd

nfd	mean error	standard deviation	confidence interval
0.05	0.003	0.007	(-0.001 , 0.007)
0.1	0.005	0.009	(-0.0008 , 0.01)
0.15	0.006	0.01	(-0.0005 , 0.012)
0.2	0.007	0.012	(-0.0001 , 0.014)

3. RC-SOCP: Proposed refined clustered SOCP localization approach

RC-SOCP is a refined clustered SOCP localization technique to allow scalability of the centralized SOCP-localization technique for large dense networks with thousands of nodes. This technique achieves better performance by reducing computation time, energy consumption, and communication overhead resulting from numerous communications overhead between the nodes in centralized localization approach. Its architecture is divided into three phases as shown in Fig.6: clustering phase, localization phase and refinement phase. In the first phase, Min-Max d clustering algorithm is used to divide the network and select the CH according to the IDs of the nodes. In the second phase, each cluster implements SOCP-based localization technique to localize the member nodes including the CH itself. In the third phase, each cluster implements Gauss Newton local algorithm to refine the estimated locations obtained.

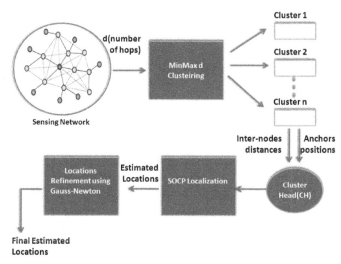

Figure 6. Refined Clustered SOCP Architecture

3.1. Clustering

Min-Max d clustering algorithm is used to divide the network and select the cluster head CH according to the IDs of the nodes. It was chosen because it is a simple, less computationally demanding and thus doesn't add extra complexity to the localization technique. This clustering algorithm runs asynchronously eliminating overhead of synchronizing the clocks of the nodes. Also, a low variance in cluster sizes leads to better load balancing among the cluster-heads [10].

3.2. Implementing SOCP on cluster–head

At the end of the clustering phase, the network is divided into multiple independent clusters. Each cluster of size CN sensors, CM sensors with unknown locations and $CN - CM$ sensors with known locations (anchors). Member nodes send their relevant distance information with their neighbours to their elected

CHs. Each CH constructs the positions matrix and the lower triangle of the distance matrix of sizes 2×CN, CN×CN respectively as in centralized technique then formulates SOCP localization problem for its cluster member nodes according to algorithm 1 and uses CPLEX optimization solver to estimate the positions of the nodes.

3.3. Refinement phase

To enhance localization accuracy of clustered SOCP (C-SOCP), a cluster level refinement step is implemented. Each cluster head solves the network localization problem using Gauss-Newton (iterative least-squares) algorithm [11]. The initial position guess for the Gauss-Newton optimization is the positions drawn from the preprocessor SOCP solver which is close to the global solution. Given m residual functions $r = (r_1, ..., r_m)$ of n variables $X = (X_1, ..., X_n)$, with $m \geq n$, a non-linear least square problem is an unconstrained optimization problem of the form

$$min \sum_{i=1}^{m} r_i(X)^2. \tag{7}$$

The Gauss-Newton algorithm iteratively finds the minimum of the sum of the squares in equation(7). For implementing the Gauss-Newton method as a refinement step, where X refers to the position coordinates of the sensor node (x,y), and hence n is set to 2. m is the number of residuals, and is equal to the number of anchor neighbours to that sensor node. The residual function r_i is defined as

$$r_i = \|X - a\|^2 - d^2 \tag{8}$$

Where a represents the positions of the anchor node (a_x, a_y) and d is the estimated distance between the sensor node and the non-positioned node. Starting with an initial guess $X^{(0)}$ for the minimum, the method proceeds by the iterations

$$X^{(s+1)} = X^{(s)} - \left(J_r^\top J_r\right)^{-1} J_r^\top r(X^{(s)}) \tag{9}$$

Where the symbol $^\top$ denotes the matrix transpose. If r and X are column vectors, the entries of the Jacobian matrix are

$$(J_r)_{ij} = \frac{\partial r_i(X^{(s)})}{\partial X_j} \tag{10}$$

The derivative of the residual function to the first variable x is:

$$\frac{\partial r_i(X^{(s)})}{\partial x} = \frac{(x - x0)}{r_i(X^{(s)})}$$

And the derivative of the residual function to the second variable y is:

$$\frac{\partial r_i(X^{(s)})}{\partial y} = \frac{(y - y0)}{r_i(X^{(s)})}$$

Algorithm 2 : Gauss-Newton Algorithm

1: **procedure** GAUSSNEWTON(distanceMatrix, positions-Matrix)

2: Let iters = number of iterations , neighbours = array of anchor neighbours

3: **for all** $node_i$ **do**

4:     $i_x \leftarrow$ initial guess of x coordinate for node i

5:     $i_y \leftarrow$ initial guess of y coordinate for node i

6:     $n \leftarrow$ number of neighbours of node i

7:     $neighbours \leftarrow$ getNeighboursOfNode(i)

8:     Let distanceEstimate = array of distances estimations with anchor neighbours of size $n \times 1$

9:     Let distanceNoise = array of distances noises between estimated distances and distances of initial guess $n \times 1$

10:     Let J = jaccobian matrix of size $n \times 2$

11:     Let J_T = transpose Jacobian matrix of size $2 \times n$

12:     Let delta = matrix of size 2×1 of values for updating x,y coordinates of node i

13:     **for** $j = 0$ to $iters$ **do**

14:         **for** $k = 0$ to n **do**

15:             $xdiff \leftarrow i_x - neighbours[k].x$

16:             $ydiff \leftarrow i_y - neighbours[k].y$

17:             $distance \leftarrow pow(xdiff, 2) + pow(ydiff, 2)$

18:             $distanceEstimate(k, 0) \leftarrow sqrt(distance)$

19:             $J(k, 0) \leftarrow xdiff/distanceEstimate(k, 0)$

20:             $J(k, 1) \leftarrow ydiff/distanceEstimate(k, 0)$

21:             $distance \leftarrow distanceMatrix[i, k]$

22:             $distanceEstimate(k,0) \leftarrow distanceNoise(k,0) - distance$

23:         **end for**

24:         $delta \leftarrow ((((J_T J)J_T).inverse())J_T) distanceNoise$

25:         $i_x \leftarrow i_x - delta(0, 0)$

26:         $i_y \leftarrow i_y - delta(1, 0)$

27:     **end for**

28: **end for**

Algorithm 2 shows the pseudo-code of the Gauss-Newton algorithm for refining the locations obtained from C-SOCP.

3.4. Performance evaluation of RC-SOCP

RC-SOCP performance is evaluated by measuring localization accuracy and computation time. The localization accuracy is calculated as defined in section 2.4. To calculate RC-SOCP computation time, we calculate C-SOCP runtime and Gauss-Newton refinement algorithm runtime on each CH. The computation time metric is measured as the maximum RC-SOCP computation time among CHs. C-SOCP runtime is the time spent for formulating and solving the SOCP problem on the CH using C++ std.clock() function. The time needed for computing the relative distances at the nodes and communication or message exchanges time is excluded. We evaluate

the performance of RC-SOCP localization technique by studying the effect of varying: cluster size , anchor percentage, communication radio range, noise value added to distances measurements.

4. Simulation results

Simulations are conducted for a randomly generated 500 nodes uniformly distributed on the unit square area $[-0.5, 0.5]^2$ with noise factor(nfd) = 0.05, radio range(rr) = 0.17, $d = 3$ and Degree of Connectivity = 37. Anchors are chosen to be uniformly distributed throughout the network with percentage(p) of 30%. Number of Gauss-Newton iterations is 25. Simulations are averaged over 10 runs with confidence level of 95%. Figs. (7a) and (7b) show a snapshot of the true sensor positions and the estimated positions of the C-SOCP and RC-SOCP respectively. True positions of the sensors are depicted in blue colored points and the estimated node positions are depicted in red colored points, solid lines indicate the error between the estimated and true sensor positions. An improvement in localization accuracy is observed for RC-SOCP compared to C-SOCP. It is also observed that the estimated positions become less accurate as we move towards the boundaries of the clusters in C-SOCP which is greatly refined in RC-SOCP. The mean localization error (LE) for the network in fig. 7 using C-SOCP is 0.02 and standard deviation 0.04, and LE is 0.01 and standard deviation 0.04 for RC-SOCP. This clarifies that the mean error is reduced by 50% using RC-SOCP. Fig.7c shows a comparison between the Commulative distributive function (CDF) of localization errors resulting from centralized-SOCP localization implemented in section 2, C-SOCP and RC-SOCP. The detailed CDF of localization errors for the results in fig. 7c are listed in table 8.

Fig.7c shows that RC-SOCP and centralized-SOCP lead to improved results for localization error compared to C-SOCP. Table 8 shows that, in RC-SOCP, a high percentage of nodes (90%) have a small localization error (<0.006), while the corresponding percentage of nodes is 59.9% in C-SOCP. However, due to the increase in the localization error of some of boundary nodes (outliers) of the network in RC-SOCP, the maximum localization error for both C-SOCP and RC-SOCP is the same(<0.35). It is worthy noting that RC-SOCP and centralized-SOCP has almost the same localization accuracy for most of nodes (>90%) which is (<0.006). For less than 10% of the nodes, there is a slight improvement in accuracy for centralized-SOCP. RC-SOCP provides a considerable reduction in computation time compared to centralized-SOCP due to clustering while still yielding good localization accuracy and scalability.

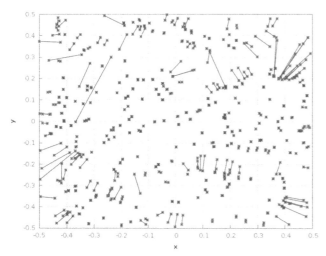

(a) Snapshot of real vs estimated nodes locations of C-SOCP localization

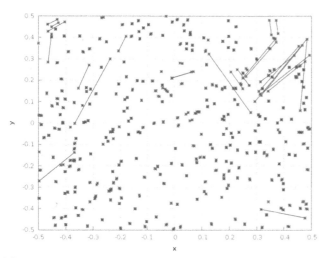

(b) Snapshot of real vs estimated nodes locations of RC-SOCP localization

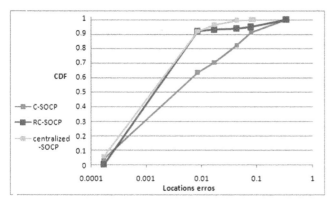

(c) CDF results of localization errors(log scale) of centralized SOCP, C-SOCP and RC-SOCP sizes

Figure 7. C-SOCP and RC-SOCP results for uniform topology: $n = 500, rr = 0.17, p = 0.15, d = 3$ and $nfd = 0.05$.

Table 8. CDF results of localization errors

Locali-zation error	technique	nodes perce-tage	mean error	stand. dev.
< 0.004	C-SOCP	55.5%	0.001	0.001
	RC-SOCP	70%	0.002	0.0009
	centralized-SOCP	87%	1.07e-1	0.0001
< 0.006	C-SOCP	59.9%	0.001	0.0016
	RC-SOCP	90%	0.0029	0.0013
	centralized-SOCP	90%	0.001	0.121
< 0.07	C-SOCP	91%	0.01	0.016
	RC-SOCP	95%	0.0039	0.005
	centralized-SOCP	99.5%	0.0025	0.118
< 0.2	C-SOCP	98%	0.019	0.03
	RC-SOCP	98%	0.0077	0.02
	centralized-SOCP	100%	0.0026	0.118
< 0.35	C-SOCP	100%	0.02	0.038
	RC-SOCP	100%	0.01	0.04
	centralized-SOCP	100%	0.0026	0.118

4.1. The effect of varying cluster Size

To study the effect of varying cluster size on localization error and computation time, we set the number of consecutive hops (d) to 1, 2, 3 and 4. Fig.8 shows CDF of localization errors (log scale) for C-SOCP and RC-SOCP with different d. Table 9 shows number of clusters, C-SOCP runtime, Gauss-Newton runtime and RC-SOCP runtime of networks. Fig.8 shows that the refinement phase of RC-SOCP enhances the result of the preprocessor C-SOCP. C-SOCP is highly dependent on cluster size compared to RC-SOCP. As the cluster size increases, the localization accuracy is improved since more nodes distances information is obtained at the CH. These distances information directly affect and enhance the formulation of the sub problems and hence improve the result of the SOCP problem solver. However, increasing cluster size increases the problem size and computation time and communication overhead of the cluster. For RC-SOCP, the localization accuracy is increased when d is increased from 1 to 2. For $d \geq 2$, there is not significant difference in localization accuracy for different cluster size (d), since refinement algorithm reaches the optimal solution for the estimate of locations of the nodes. So, adjusting cluster size using $d = 2$ which is approximated to number of clusters around 11 in this network size(500 nodes) as shown in table 9 yields good accepted localization accuracy. Table 9 shows that incrementing the cluster size d reduces the number of clusters approximately to the

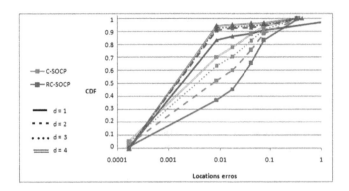

Figure 8. CDF reaults of localization errors (log scale) for different cluster sizes

half. As a result of increasing cluster sizes, C-SOCP and RC-SOCP run times are increased while Gauss-Newton runtime has no significant change. Table 10

Table 9. Performance and computation runtime comparison of different cluster sizes.

d	# of clusters	C-SOCP runtime (sec.)	Gauss-Newton runtime	RC-SOCP runtime (sec.)
1	24	2.117	0.014	2.128
2	11	6.468	0.011	6.475
3	7	14.761	0.019	14.791
4	5	20.554	0.016	20.57

Table 10. Mean localization errors for different cluster sizes for C-SOCP and RC-SOCP

d	technique	mean error	standard deviation	confidence interval
1	C-SOCP	0.03	0.04	(0.009 , 0.06)
	RC-SOCP	0.02	0.13	(-0.05 , 0.11)
2	C-SOCP	0.028	0.04	(0.002 , 0.05)
	RC-SOCP	0.015	0.05	(-0.016 , 0.047)
3	C-SOCP	0.02	0.038	(-0.002 , 0.045)
	RC-SOCP	0.013	0.04	(-0.01 , 0.04)
4	C-SOCP	0.016	0.033	(-0.004 , 0.037)
	RC-SOCP	0.01	0.036	(-0.01 , 0.03)

also shows that increasing the cluster size reduces LE in C-SOCP significantly for all d whereas it leads to slightly improved LE in RC-SOCP for $d \geq 2$.

4.2. The effect of varying anchors percentage

To investigate the effect of varying anchors percentage on localization error and computation time, we change number of anchor nodes to 10%, 20%, 30% and

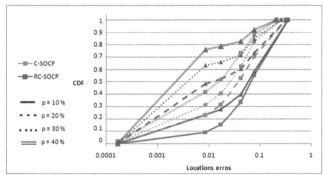

Figure 9. CDF results of localization errors(log scale) for different anchors percentage

40% of the number of non-positioned nodes while maintaining the number of non-positioned nodes the same (500 non-positioned nodes), $rr = 0.11$, $d = 2$ and $nfd = 0.05$ for C-SOCP and RC-SOCP. Fig.9 shows that increasing anchors percentage considerably increases the localization accuracy for both C-SOCP and RC-SOCP; and RC-SOCP has good localization accuracy compared to C-SOCP. Appropriate percentage of anchors ensures that each cluster has an acceptable number of anchors to perform the localization problem. However, increasing number of anchors often imposes additional costs. Table 11 shows that the number of clusters and computation runtime time are increased with increasing the number of anchors. This happens due to the increase of the total number of nodes in the network. Table 12 shows a reduction in LE when increasing anchors percentages in both C-SOCP and RC-SOCP.

Table 11. Performance and computation runtime comparison of different anchors percentages.

anchor percentage	# of clusters	C-SOCP runtime (sec.)	Gauss-Newton runtime (sec.)	RC-SOCP runtime (sec.)
10%	20	0.356	0.011	0.365
20%	24	0.393	0.016	0.405
30%	26	0.465	0.012	0.476
40%	27	1.693	0.022	1.71

4.3. The effect of varying communication radio range

To study the effect of changing radio range on localization accuracy, we set rr to 0.08, 0.1, 0.15 and 0.17. Fig.10 shows that for C-SOCP and RC-SOCP, higher radio range leads to higher degree of connectivity and hence results in higher localization accuracy. It is noticed in table 14 that for the network with rr =0.08, C-SOCP has a better localization accuracy for 50% of the nodes (LE =0.032) than in RC-SOCP (LE=0.038). This refers to low degree of connectivity for rr=0.08 and less distances information for C-SOCP resulting in bad initial guess

Table 12. Mean localization errors for different anchors percentages for C-SOCP and RC-SOCP

anchor percentage	technique	mean error	standard deviation	confidence interval
10%	C-SOCP	0.08	0.06	(0.042 , 0.118)
	RC-SOCP	0.083	0.07	(0.035 , 0.1)
20%	C-SOCP	0.05	0.048	(0.02 , 0.08)
	RC-SOCP	0.052	0.137	(-0.03 , 0.137)
30%	C-SOCP	0.03	0.04	(0.01 , 0.06)
	RC-SOCP	0.038	0.1	(-0.036 , 0.1)
40%	C-SOCP	0.02	0.03	(0.007 , 0.04)
	RC-SOCP	0.02	0.07	(-0.02 , 0.06)

Table 14. Mean localization errors for different radio ranges for C-SOCP and RC-SOCP

radio range	technique	mean error	stand-ard dev-iation	confidence interval
0.08	C-SOCP	0.032	0.02	(0.02 , 0.05)
	RC-SOCP	0.038	0.08	(-0.01 , 0.09)
0.1	C-SOCP	0.032	0.04	(0.017 , 0.07)
	RC-SOCP	0.025	0.13	(-0.04 , 0.12)
0.15	C-SOCP	0.032	0.04	(0.005 , 0.06)
	RC-SOCP	0.02	0.05	(-0.01 , 0.05)
0.17	C-SOCP	0.028	0.04	(0.002 , 0.05)
	RC-SOCP	0.015	0.05	(-0.02 , 0.05)

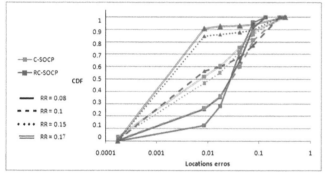

Figure 10. CDF results of localization errors (log scale) for different radio ranges

for Gauss-Newton iterations. Large radio ranges lead to higher localization accuracy. However, increasing radio range increases power consumption, and adds more communication overhead. Average degree of connectivity (doc), number of clusters and run-times of networks in fig. 10 are shown in table 13.

Table 13. Performance and computation runtime comparison of different radio ranges.

radio range	doc	# of clust-ers	SOCP runtime (sec.)	Gauss-Newton run time (sec.)	RC-SOCP runtime (sec.)
0.08	3	63	0.148	0.013	0.162
0.1	12	48	0.595	0.013	0.601
0.15	28	14	1.592	0.013	1.605
0.17	37	11	6.468	0.011	6.475

4.4. The effect of varying noise value added to distances measurements

Fig.11 shows that RC-SOCP is highly affected by nfd compared to C-SOCP while RC-SOCP has a good localization accuracy compared to C-SOCP for all nfds.

A slight improvement in localization accuracy for C-SOCP is noticed when decreasing nfd while significant improvement in localization accuracy is noticed when decreasing nfd in RC-SOCP. The localization accuracy of RC-SOCP for $nfd = 0.05$, $nfd = 0.1$ gives the same results. This means that Gauss-Newton was able to get the same localization accuracy when nfd is increased from 0.05 to 0.1, but was unable to do same for nfds greater that 0.1. The mean localization errors (LEs) for the network in fig. 11 are listed in table 15.

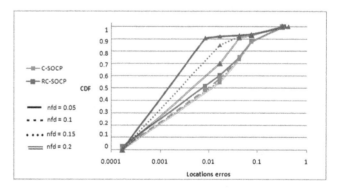

Figure 11. CDF results of localization errors (log scale) for different nfd

5. Conclusion

This paper presented an implementation of localization technique for WSNs based on Second Order Cone Programming (SOCP) to solve the localization problem in WSNs. We used our own experience trying to provide a detailed description of SOCP problem formulation for Castalia wireless sensor networks simulator. To allow scalability, it also proposed a refined clustered localization approach based on the centralized SOCP technique (RC-SOCP). An extensive simulation study of the approach under different

Table 15. Mean localization errors for different nfd for C-SOCP and RC-SOCP

nfd	technique	mean error	stand. dev.	confidence interval
0.05	C-SOCP	0.028	0.04	(0.002 , 0.05)
	RC-SOCP	0.015	0.05	(-0.016 , 0.047)
0.1	C-SOCP	0.029	0.04	(0.0037 , 0.052)
	RC-SOCP	0.0196	0.06	(-0.018 , 0.058)
0.15	C-SOCP	0.030	0.04	(0.0048 , 0.056)
	RC-SOCP	0.022	0.046	(-0.0068 , 0.051)
0.2	C-SOCP	0.032	0.04	(0.0052 , 0.059)
	RC-SOCP	0.026	0.047	(-0.003 , 0.051)

scenarios and with varying several networks parameters has been investigated. Simulation results show that RC-SOCP achieves good performance and acceptable localization accuracy with controlling cluster size (number of hops between the CH and gateway node), communication radio range of the sensor nodes and anchors percentage. Moreover, it shows that the proposed approach solves the localization problem with good localization accuracy in the presence of inaccuracies in distance measurements. The proposed refined clustered SOCP-based localization approach performs almost as well as the centralized-SOCP while providing a considerable reduction in computation time. However, it still yields good localization accuracy and scalability.

References

[1] KLOGO G.S. and GADZE J.D. (2013) *Energy constraints of localization techniques in wireless sensor networks (WSN): A survey. In IJCA* 75.

[2] EWA N.S. (2012) *Localization in wireless sensor networks: Classification and evaluation of techniques. In AMCS* 22 pp.281-297.

[3] HAN G. ET AL. (2012) *Localization in wireless sensor networks: Classification and evaluation of techniques. In AMCS* 22 pp.281-297.

[4] SHANG Y. ET AL. (2004) *Localization from connectivity in sensor networks. In IEEE Trans. TPDS* 15 pp.961-974.

[5] BISWAS P. ET AL. (2006) *Semidefinite programming approaches for sensor network localization with noisy distance measurements. In IEEE Trans. T-ASE* 3 pp.360-371.

[6] HE ET AL. (2003) *Range-free localization schemes for large scale sensor networks. In Proceedings of the 9th Annual International Conference on Mobile Computing and Networking ACM* pp.81-95.

[7] AKYILDIZ ET AL. (2010) *Wireless sensor networks. In John Wiley & Sons* 4.

[8] TSENG P. (2007) *Second-order cone programming relaxation of sensor network localization. In SIAM J OPTIMIZ* 18 pp.156-185.

[9] SRIRANGARAJAN S. ET AL. (2008) *Distributed sensor network localization using SOCP relaxation. In IEEE Trans. Wireless Commun.* 7 pp.4886-4895.

[10] AMIS A.D. ET AL. (2000) *Max-min d-cluster formation in wireless ad hoc networks. In INFOCOM 2000. Nineteenth Annual Joint Conference of the IEEE Computer and Communications Societies. Proceedings* pp.32-41.

[11] CALAFIORE G.C. ET AL. (2010) *Sensor Fusion for Position Estimation in Networked Systems. InNetworked Systems, Sensor Fusion and its Applications, Ciza Thomas (Ed.)* pp.251-276.

[12] STEHL K. and MARTIN (2011) *Comparison of Simulators for Wireless Sensor Networks.* Ph. D. dissertation, Masaryk University.

[13] ATHANASSIOS B. (2011) *Castalia A simulator for Wireless Sensor Networks and Body Area Networks User's Guide. Version 2.3 In NICTA.*

[14] SUNDANI ET AL. (2010) *Wireless Sensor Network Simulators A Survey and Comparisons. In International Journal Of Computer Networks (IJCN)* 2(5) pp.249-265.

[15] *IBM ILOG ODM Enterprise Developer Edition V3.4, Interface's User Manual [Online].* Available at:http://pic.dhe.ibm.com [Accessed:1st October 2013].

12

Linking Data According to Their Degree of Representativeness (DoR)

Frédéric Blanchard[1,*], Amine Aït-Younes[1], Michel Herbin[1]

[1]Université de Reims Champagne-Ardenne, CReSTIC, UFR Sciences Exactes et Naturelles, Moulin de la Housse, BP 1039, 51687 Reims CEDEX 2, FRANCE

Abstract

This contribution addresses the problem of extracting some representative data from complex datasets and connecting them in a directed graph. First we define a degree of representativeness (DoR) inspired of the Borda voting procedure. Secondly we present a method to connect pairwise data using neighborhoods and the DoR as an objective function. We then present case studies as illustrative purposes: unsupervised grouping of binary images, analysis of co-authorships in a research team and structuration of a medical patient-oriented database

Keywords: Mining complex data, Representativeness, Graph based data analysis

1. Introduction

The selection of a small subset from a dataset is a classical way for both reducing the cost of data processing and improving the efficiency of data analysis. In statistics, the process is called sampling. The selection of representative samples is generally based on a randomization process. Unfortunately this approach assumes implicitly or explicitly that data distributions are known. Then the statistical analysis often fails when exploring dataset with unknown distributions. In data mining, the goal is very different. The samples should define interesting patterns and structures to analyse the data set. Then each sample is selected taking into account its own *representativeness*. These samples are called *exemplars* [1]. The extraction of these representative elements presents a significant interest in designing recommendation systems [2], selecting leaders or specimens [3] for community detection [4] or for customer Relationship analysis [5]. In this context, this paper proposes a new approach for extracting exemplars (i.e. representative elements) from a dataset and for linking data to visualize the

structure of the dataset as a forest.

In the framework of data mining, the classical ways to determine representative elements refer to the task of clustering [6]. The representative elements are prototypes selected from a partition of the dataset into clusters. This approach assumes that the number of exemplars is equal to the number of clusters. Unfortunately when exploring a dataset, the number of clusters is unkown. If a cluster contains more than one sub-population, then only one prototype is extracted. But more than one exemplar is expected. Moreover the exemplars are real data extracted from the dataset. But the prototypes are often virtual elements that does not make sense. For instance the classical k−means algorithm (see [7] for a review of clustering methods including k−means algorithm) determines k mean-elements as prototypes that are not exemplars. There are multiple lacks of the approaches based on clustering. Firstly the partition into clusters is predate to the extraction of representative elements and the clusters have to be validated and interpreted to justify the prototypes. Secondly the choice of clustering algorithms depends on implicit assumptions about the shape of clusters and data distributions which are unkown. Then we assume that these methods based on clustering are not well suited for extracting exemplars

*Corresponding author. Email: frederic.blanchard@univ-reims.fr

from a dataset.

Most of the methods for extracting exemplars are iterative. That is the case when using the k-medoids algorithm [7] for determining k exemplars. First k exemplars are randomly selected from the dataset. Then the algorithm iteratively refines this set of exemplars. The afinity propagation method of Frey and Dueck [1] also proposes to extract exemplars by iterative process. Unfortunately the final elements proposed as exemplars are quite sensitive to the initial selection, they depend on input parameters and on the way to stop the iterative process. To circumvent this drawback, this paper proposes a one pass method to extract exemplars from a dataset without any assumption on the shape or the density of data distribution (unlike in [8]). The method we propose is only based on a relation that permits a pairwise comparison of data. Using this relation we define a *degree of representativeness* (DoR). The exemplars are finally chosen as local maxima of the DoR. Then we show how to build a directed graph to visualize the organization of dataset around the exemplars as trees. By fitting the locality parameter called *scale factor* we determine the exemplars at each scale that the user needs.

The new method we propose is deterministic. Thus each dataset leads to one specific set of exemplars. Some properties can indicate the ability of the method to reveal intrinsic structures of the dataset. Thus the paper study the stability and the robustness of our method to indicate this ability. When data is corrupted with noise or outliers, the selection of exemplars should be robust against such corruptions. When resampling the dataset, the stability of exemplars (i.e. the exemplars do not change when resampling) is another indication of the ability of the method to reveal dataset structures. Moreover our deterministic method gives one result at each scale. When the scale increase, we also study the variation of the set of exemplars and the forest we build on the dataset.

To sum up this paper proposes a new method for exemplar selection and it studies some of properties of the method. It is organized as follows. In the first section we introduce the context and expose our method. We present the formal definition of *degree of representativeness* (DoR) used to extract exemplars. The notion of *standard* is defined when only one exemplar is selected from the dataset. Then we show how to build a directed graph (more precisely a forest) to visualize the inherent structure of the dataset. For each definition we present some interesting and remarkable properties (robustness and stability).

The next section presents three case studies in very

different contexts. Firstly we apply our method on a set of binary images. We compute scores and exemplars and build the forest that emphases the structure of the set. The second application concerns the analysis of co-authorship in a research laboratory. We exhibit a co-authoring network (the forest of the co-authors) that permits to visualize how researchers are really clustered and how they work together.

Last section is a brief conclusion that outlines our main contributions and that expose our current and future works.

2. Method

Let Ω be a set of n elements in a multidimensional space. Let us describe the way we use to extract the exemplars from Ω for structuring this set as a forest. In this paper, the n elements are called objects. They consist of qualitative, quantitative or mixed data. We assume that Ω is only a relational dataset. We do not need for any assumption on underlying distribution of data. We only use the relation for comparisons between objects.

2.1. Pairwise Valued Relation

Let us specify the relation. Let R be a pairwise valued relation on Ω. R is defined by :

$$\begin{aligned} R: \quad \Omega \times \Omega \quad &\rightarrow \quad \mathbb{R}^+ \\ (x, y) \quad &\mapsto \quad R(x, y) \end{aligned}$$

The use of such a pairwise valued relation is very classical in data processing. For instance, the distance is a special case of this kind of relation. But a distance is frequently not available when processing qualitative data. Thus a relation is more widespread than a distance for pairwise comparisons of objects. In this paper, the value $R(x, y)$ is also called the *cost* from x to y, indicating the generality of the relation.

The relation must follow three trivial properties.

- The relation must be *total*. This means that each pair of objects of Ω is valued by R.

- The relation must be *positive*. The cost is a positive value for all pairs.

- The cost from x to x is null forall x (i.e. $\forall x \in \Omega, R(x, x) = 0$)

Unlike a distance, the relation does not necessarily respect the property of symmetry. $R(x, y)$ may be different from $R(y, x)$. For instance, if the cost from a point x to a point y is the time to go from x to y, then the cost from y to x could differ from the first one because of the slope, wind, flow, etc. Moreover, the relation does not respect the triangle inequality. A dissimilarity index gives a classical example of such a relation which does not respect the triangle inequality. x is dissimilar from y with $R(x, y)$ and y is dissimilar from z with $R(y, z)$ but x could be dissimilar from z with $R(x, z) > R(x, y) + R(y, z)$.

Such a relation can lead to a vote to designate exemplars within the dataset. Specifically, we can rank the objets of Ω taking into account the relation to set up votes between the objects themselves. The following subsection describes this procedure.

2.2. Degree of representativeness (DoR)

In this paper, we select an exemplar object from Ω according to the Borda voting method [9]. But firstly, we transform values of the relation into ranks [10][11][12]. Let us define these ranks. Let x be an object of Ω. All objects can be sorted by the ascending order of their costs relative to x. Let us note $Rk_x(y)$ the rank of y relative to x. Then the ranks are obtained when sorting the set $\{R(x, z)/z \in \Omega\}$. Using Borda method [9][13], the object x assigns a relative score to all objects of Ω. The score Sc_x relative to x is defined by:

$$\forall y \in \Omega, Sc_x(y) = n - Rk_x(y)$$

where n is the number of objects in Ω. Thereby the relative score is an integer and it lies between 0 and $n - 1$. The lower the cost from x to y, the higher the score of y relative to x.

Computing all relative scores, each object x receives n scores corresponding to the votes of all objects of Ω (i.e. the n values $Sc_y(x)$ with $y \in \Omega$). Then the relative scores are aggregated to define the *degree of representativeness* (DoR) of data. The DoR is finally used as an objective function to choose the winner of the voting procedure. The aggregate score is defined by:

$$\text{DoR}: \quad \Omega \quad \rightarrow \quad \mathbb{R}^+$$
$$x \quad \mapsto \quad \text{Aggreg}_{y \in \Omega}(Sc_y(x))$$

In this paper, the aggregation function is the *mean* function.

Let us observe the DoR in a simulated dataset. Figure 1 displays an example of a dataset with 120 two dimensional random samples (A). Euclidean distance is used as the pairwise valued relation between samples. The respective DoR (B) confirm that the score increases when the sample approaches the center of the dataset, i.e. in the midst of this one.

2.3. Standard

The object with highest DoR is called *standard*. The standard is usefull when only one exemplar is expected for resuming the dataset Ω.

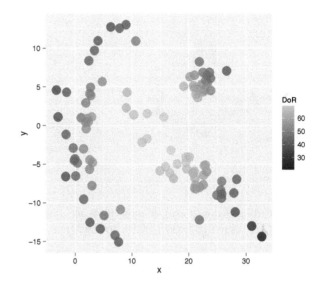

Figure 1. Example of a dataset with 120 random samples (A) and their respective DoR (B). The DoR increases in the midst of the dataset

Let us give three examples of *standard*. The figure 2 shows the graphical representations of three datasets A, B, and C. Each dataset is randomly generated and contains 100 data ($n = 100$) and two features x and y. The DoR is computed using Euclidean distance as pairwise valued relation. The maxima of the DoR are respectively 68.75, 70.55, and 68.77 for A, B and C. The red filled circles highlight the three respective standards (*i.e.* data with the highest DoR). The figure 2 confirms that each standard lies in the midst of its dataset.

Let us observe some properties of the *standard*. When resampling the dataset using the bootstrap technique [14], the standard could change. If it does not change, the extraction of this standard is robust against the resampling. We propose to quantify the robustness of the standard by bootstraping the extraction of the standard. We claim that the frequency of the extracted standards indicates the stability of the standard when resampling. This frequency characterizes the robustness of the standard. Our experiments using simulated data and real data show that the standard depends very weakly on the resampling. We have simulated three random datasets (let us call them *A B* and *C*) of 100 elements. We have computed the frequencies of the standards obtained with 200 bootstraps. The extracted standards remain in the center of the three datatsets. The frequencies of the most frequent standards when resampling the 100 initial samples are respectively equal to 40%, 32%, 36%. These frequencies assess the stability of the standard with respect to the samples. Respectively 90%, 88%, and 90% of the dataset elements are never extracted as

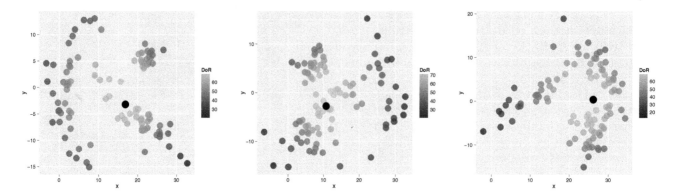

Figure 2. Standard examples (in red) for respectively the datasets (A), (B), and (C). The datasets have 100 random samples. The DoR of the standards are respectively 68.75, 70.55, and 68.77.

standards when resampling.

Thus we assume that a standard gives a clue on the center of the dataset. Because the standard is a real element, it avoids the nonsense that the classical averages could produce with a virtual out-of-scope element outside of the data distribution. Note that the stability of the standard (i.e. the frequency of the most frequent standard) increases when the number of objects increases.

Let us now examine the stability of the standard when outliers are feared. We simulate outliers that we append to an initial dataset. We consider that the standard extraction is robust against outliers when the extracted standard remains one of three most frequent standards of the initial dataset.

In this paper we describe the study of robustness (see [15] for more details about the concept of robustness) using the datasets A, B and C of Figure 2. The outliers are random elements out of the range of the initial data domain. In this section, the domain is defined by elements of coordinates (x, y) where $-10 \leq x \leq 40$ and $-15 \leq y \leq 15$. Outliers are simulated in a larger domain defined by $-10000 \leq x \leq 40000$ and $-15000 \leq y \leq 15000$ (the initial limits are multiplied by 1000) excluding the elements that are too close from the initial domain by keeping the elements (x, y) where $x \leq -1000$ or $4000 \leq x$ and $y \leq -1500$ or $1500 \leq y$ (the limits of initial domain are multiplied by 100). We add such random outliers to an initial dataset until the extracted standards changes (i.e. until the extracted standard from the new dataset with outliers will not be one of the three most frequent standards of the initial dataset). When outliers are randomly generated in a such very large domain, the percentage of outliers could be higher than 200% without changing the initial standard. Then the standard is robust when the outliers are spread in a large domain. But the standard remains also robust when outliers are concentrated into only one duplicate object. When only one outlier is randomly generated

in the very large domain, we could add up to 20% of out-of-range elements using this single outlier without changing the initial standard. Then we assume that the standard is particularly robust against outliers.

2.4. Exemplars and forest

The standard is the only exemplar extracted from a dataset. But the dataset may be complex and it could require more than one exemplar to represent the whole set. This section describes how the dataset can be structured to retrieve these exemplars from the set.

The first step consists in defining the neighborhood of each object within Ω. Let x be one of the n objects of Ω. Let k be a value between 0 and n. The k-nearest neighbors of x are defined using the ranks relative to x. Then the k–neighborhood of x in Ω is defined by:

$$\forall x \in \Omega, \quad \forall k \in \{1, ..., n\}, \quad N_k(x) = \{y \in \Omega / Rk_x(y) \leq k\}$$

Thus $N_k(x)$ is the set of k nearest objects of x.

In a second step, each object x is associated with the neighbor having the highest DoR. Thus we define a link from x to its preferred neighbor. Each object x is linked to an object y. The links are defined by:

$$\forall x \in \Omega, \quad x \mapsto y = \underset{z \in N_k(x)}{\operatorname{argmax}} \operatorname{DoR}(z)$$

In this definition, x is linked to y and y is generally different from x when $\operatorname{DoR}(y) > \operatorname{DoR}(x)$. If $Sc(x)$ is maximal inside $N_k(x)$, then $y = x$ and x is linked to x itself. These self-linked objects are simply called *exemplars* of Ω.

Using the links, the dataset becomes a forest where the nodes are the objects. The exemplars become the terminal nodes of this forest. The exemplars depend on the value of k which influences the forest configuration. In this paper, k is the size of the neighborhood we use. This parameter is called scale factor.

Figure 3 displays four forests obtained from the

simulated dataset of Figure 1 (A). The dataset has the 120 samples ($n = 120$). The four forests are configured using the scale factors 5, 10, 20, and 40. The exemplars are displayed with a filled circle, they are the terminal nodes of the forests. The numbers of extracted exemplars are respectively equal to 8, 4, 2 and 1. Distinctly the number of exemplars depends on the scale factor k. The following describes the influence of the scale factor.

2.5. Scale Factor

The higher the scale factor, the lower the number of exemplars. Moreover, when the scale factor increases from one to n, the number of exemplars decreases from n to one. Let us explain this property. When $k = 1$, $N_1(x)$ is the singleton equal to x. Therefore each object x is itself an exemplar of Ω (i.e. x is linked to x). Then the set of exemplars is Ω and the number of exemplars is equal to n. When $k = n$, $N_n(x)$ is equal to Ω. Each object x is linked to the standard which has the highest DoR within Ω. Then the number of exemplars is equal to 1 the forest becomes only one tree and the standard is its root. At the scale k, an exemplar x has the highest DoR within the neighborhood $N_k(x)$ (i.e. within the k nearest neighbors of x). If $k_1 \leq k_2$, then $N_{k_1}(x) \subseteq N_{k_2}(x)$. If x is an exemplar at the scale k_2, then it is an exemplar at the scale k_1. Therefore the number of exemplars necessarily decreases when the scale factor increases.

Increasing the scale factor, some exemplars could disappear among those who were extracted. But an object never appears as an exemplar if it was not extracted at lower scale factor. Figure 4 displays the duration of each exemplar when increasing the scale factor. The exemplars are extracted from Figure 1 dataset ($n = 100$). When the scale factor is equal to 1, all the objects are exemplars. When the scale factor increases, some exemplars disappear and their duration is shortened. Only the standard is kept from scale 1 to the scale n. It has the longest duration equal to n.

At the scale k, we assume that the numbers of exemplars is smaller than $n - (k - 1)$ where k is the scale factor and n is the number of objects of the dataset. At each scale k, we want to reduce the number of exemplars. When this number is equal to $n - k + 1$, we consider that the extraction of exemplars is suboptimal. This case is observed when $k = 1$ or $k = n$. In this paper, the scale factor becomes optimal when the difference between $n - k + 1$ and the number of extracted exemplars is maximum. Let $k_{optimum}$ be this optimal value of the scale factor we propose in this paper.

Figure 5 displays the numbers of exemplars according to the scale factor k. It uses the dataset of Figure 1 (A) ($n = 100$). The scale factor increases from 1 to 100 and the number of exemplars decreases from 100 to

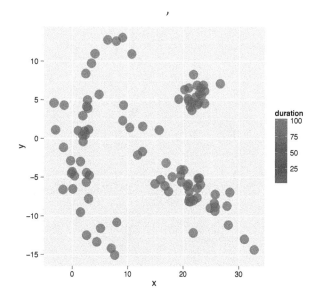

Figure 4. Duration of exemplars increasing the scale factor: The Figure 1 dataset has 100 objects ($n = 100$). The scale factor increases from 1 (black) to 100 (red). When the scale factor is equal to 1, all the objects are exemplars. When the scale factor increases, some exemplars disappear. Only the standard is always extracted when increasing scale factor. Then its duration is equal to 100.

1. The numbers of exemplars is smaller than $101k$. The difference between $121 - k$ and the number of exemplars is maximum when $k = 9$. The black filled circle shows this optimum value. Then four exemplars are extracted using $k = 9$.

3. Applications

This section presents applications of our method in two typical and very different contexts. The first application consists in extracting exemplars from a binary image database and building the graph of exemplars of this database. The second application present an analysis of the co-authoring in a research team by extracting exemplar authors and exhibiting the implicit structure.

3.1. Extraction of exemplars from a set of binary images

In this first application we consider a set of binary images contained in a database. The goal is to extract exemplar images from this database. The interest could be providing a set of resuming images or distinguishing subsets of images according to their content. In a first step we construct the matrix of the relation by using the Asymetric Haussdorff Distance. Classical methods of clustering have to work with *symmetric* distance. They are inapplicable when distance from an image A to image B is not equal to distance from image B to

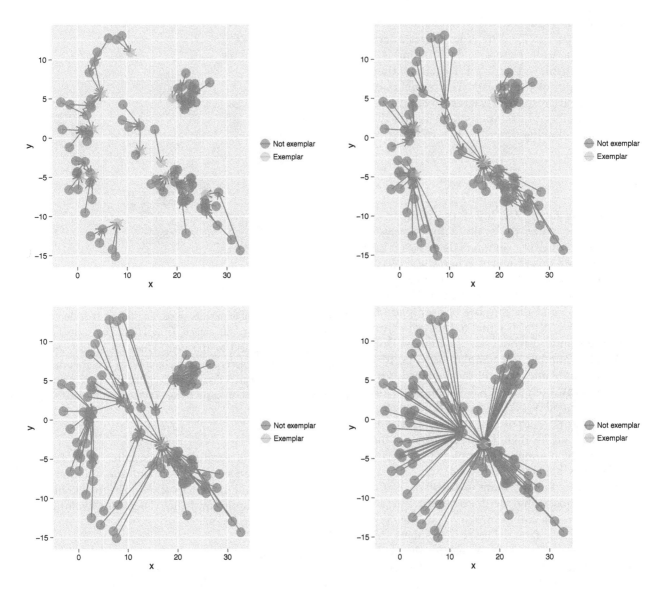

Figure 3. Networks obtained with scale factor $k = 5$, $k = 10$, $k = 20$, and $k = 40$ with dataset of Figure 1 (A). The exemplars are displayed with blue filled circles.

image A. As we wrote at the beginning of this paper, the symmetry property is not required in our method.

Firstly, we compute the score of each image of the database. In a second step we build the associated directed graph presented in Figure 6 and representing the exemplars network (with a scale factor of 4). This graph shows how the dataset is structured. We can observe that the connected components of this graph are grouping image according to the object they represent. The three images that have no successors in this network are the exemplars of this dataset and they provide a good summary of the whole dataset.

3.2. Exploration of co-authoring network

The second application of our concept deals with publication data inside a laboratory, a research team or any other group of researchers.

Co-authoring informations can be considered as relational data ([16], [17]). In this work, we consider that the value of the relation from a researcher named Alice to a researcher named Bob is computed as the sum for each common publication of the product of the number of coauthor on the publication and the number of publication of Alice. This relation is not symmetric. In fact, generally, Alice can be the "preferred" co-author of Bob, but Bob is not necessarily the "preferred" co-author of Alice. This valued relation characterizes the "quality" of links between the members and takes

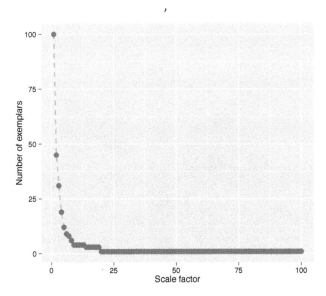

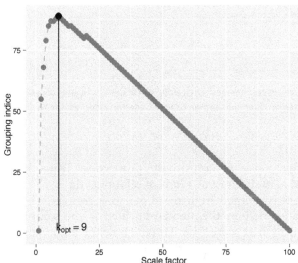

Figure 5. Number of Exemplars (top) from Figure 1 (A) dataset and Scale Factor : The number of exemplar is smaller than $100 - (k - 1)$ where k is the scale factor and 100 is the number of objects of the dataset. The grouping index (bottom) (the difference between $100 - (k - 1)$ (gray line) and the number of extracted exemplars (red points)) is maximal when the scale factor is equal to 9 (black circle).

account of their publication activity.

The dataset we used is the set of publications of the CReSTIC Laboratory (University of Reims, France) [18]. This information is extracted from the web site of the laboratory.

The graph of the Figure 7(Left) represents this dataset. Each node is a lab member and each edge between two members represents one common publication. Different colors are used to represents

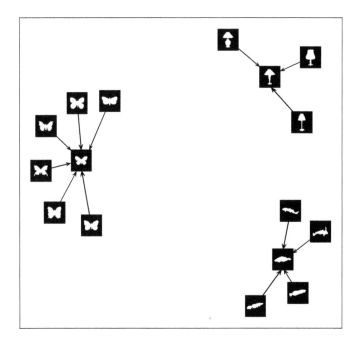

Figure 6. Network of the binary images where each image is connected to one exemplar. This directed graph exhibits three connected components forming three clusters coinciding with the content of images

the different teams that compose the laboratory (but this information is not used in the computation of the exemplars). Therefore the scale factor is not used in this application because the size of the neighborhood is implicitly fixed in the dataset (according to the number of co-author of each member of the team).

After computing the scores, we built the exemplars forest represented on the Figure 7(Right). The size of the node is proportional to its score. This graph is displayed using the same position for the nodes.

The graphs presented in the Figure 7 show several interests of our method. The first interests is the simplification of the graph of the Figure 7 (Left). When the numbers of vertices and edges are growing the graph becomes more unreadable. For big data, resuming and simplifying is a necessary task.

The second interest is to exhibit such a sub-structure of the team (this task is called community detection in a network [19]). The Figure 7 (Right) shows how groups are connected, and which members are the most representative. The exemplars members are connecting the others and can be viewed as natural leaders (or natural mentors) according to their publications and their co-authors. It emphasizes the important (critical) position of some members in a research team.

Incidentally, we can observe that the resulting clustering obtained by partitioning the graph in connected

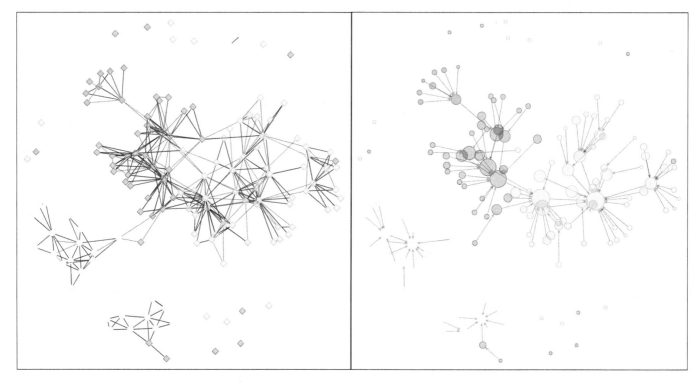

Figure 7. Left : Forest of the co-authoring in a laboratory. Each vertex is one researcher and each edge corresponds to one common publication. Right : Representative Network. The higher is the score of one researcher, the higher is the diameter of its vertex in the graph. In this graph, each edge is the link of one researcher to its exemplar.

components is a little bit different of the real partitioning in sub-groups (represented by the different colors)

3.3. Structuration of a medical database

In this case study, we consider a dataset of 71 diabetic patients described by 10 variables. This dataset was constitued by the endocrinology service of the University Hospital Center (CHU) of Reims. Our goal is to exhibit how the medical cases could be linked. After computing the distance matrix between patients with the Chebyshev distance [20], we obtain the forest shown in the figure 8 according to the DoR of patients.

The resulting forest structures the raw database as a network of medical cases. We can see this graph as a knowledge representation extracted from data and could be view as a first step for building a medical case based reasoning system.

4. Conclusion

In the framework of data mining, this paper describes a new way for extracting exemplars from a relational dataset. The method we propose is based on a pairwise comparison assuming a coarse relation on the dataset. This approach is particularly adapted when no distance is available or meaningful in the data domain. Moreover the coarse relation between data does not

need symmetry or transitivity properties. Thus the method is useful for any kinds of relational data.

The DoR is defined from these pairwise comparisons. The paper defines the standard which is the sample with the highest score. Simulations show the robustness of the standard against outliers and the stability of the standard when resampling dataset. Thus these results confirm the standard as a robust location estimator. Moreover the DoR is used to extract exemplars which are real objects. Then our approach of location estimator avoids the drawbacks of average objects which are meaningless when processing qualitative data.

Using a score based on the pairwise comparison, we define the k nearest neighbors of each datum. This approach permits us to extract exemplars depending on this k value. We state that the number of local exemplars decreases from n to 1 (n is the number of data samples) when k value increases from 1 to n. Thus k is considered as a scale factor. The method we propose allows us to explore the dataset through different scales. We can adjust the k value for extracting a reduced number of exemplars. An automated approach is proposed to determine an optimal number of exemplars.

On top of the extraction of exemplars, the method proposes to design a forest. The paper shows that the forest is reconfigured when the scale factor changes.

Figure 8. Forest obtained on a medical dataset. Data are diabetic (type 2) patients described by 10 features including age, sex, HBA1C, prescribed insulin, body mass index etc. Each vertex is a patient and the circle diameter is proportional to the DoR of the patient. The scale factor k is determined by the method proposed in the section 2.5

The forest eases the explanation of the exemplar roles in the dataset. When the scale factor increases, some exemplars could disappear keeping the most important ones (i.e. the exemplars which are important nodes for connecting some data).

In future works we propose to use the fuzzy set theory as in [21] to generalize our framework in the case of fuzzy relation, when ranking data is not easy.
The major way we would to explore is the area of Social Network Analysis. We are convinced that our concept of *exemplar* could be a significant tool for extracting leaders or mentors in social network and improve recommendation systems. Our concept of degree of representativeness should be compared to the different definitions of *centrality* in a network [22].

References

[1] FREY, B. and DUECK, D. (2007) Clustering by passing messages between data points. *Science* 315(5814): 972.

[2] PAZZANI, M. and BILLSUS, D. (2007) Content-Based Recommendation Systems The Adaptive Web. In BRUSILOVSKY, P., KOBSA, A. and NEJDL, W. [eds.] *The Adaptive Web* (Berlin, Heidelberg: Springer Berlin / Heidelberg), *Lecture Notes in Computer Science* 4321, chap. 10, 325–341. doi:10.1007/978-3-540-72079-9_10.

[3] BRUN, A., HAMAD, A., BUFFET, O. and BOYER, A. (2010) Towards preference relations in recommender systems. In *ECML/PKDD Workshop on Preference Learning (PL-10)*.

[4] NEWMAN, M.E.J. and GIRVAN, M. (2004) Finding and evaluating community structure in networks. *Phys. Rev. E* 69: 026113. doi:10.1103/PhysRevE.69.026113.

[5] TUZHILIN, A. (2012) Customer relationship management and web mining: the next frontier. *Data Mining and Knowledge Discovery* : 1–29.

[6] ALFRED, R. (2010) Summarizing relational data using semi-supervised genetic algorithm-based clustering techniques. *Journal of Computer Science* 6(7): 775–784.

[7] JAIN, A.K., MURTY, M.N. and FLYNN, P.J. (1999) Data clustering: a review. *ACM Computing Surveys* 31(3): 264–323.

[8] LÜHR, S. and LAZARESCU, M. (2008) Connectivity based stream clustering using localised density exemplars. In *Proceedings of the 12th Pacific-Asia conference on Advances in knowledge discovery and data mining*, PAKDD'08 (Berlin, Heidelberg: Springer-Verlag): 662–672.

[9] DE BORDA, J.C. (1781) Mémoire sur les élections au scrutin. *Mémoires de l'Académie Royale des Sciences* : 657–664.

[10] BARNETT, V. (1976) The ordering of multivariate data. *Journal of the Royal Statistical Society, Series A (General)* 139(3): 318–355.

[11] CONOVER, W.J. and IMAN, R.L. (1981) Rank transformations as a bridge between parametric and nonparametric statistics. *The American Statistician* 35(3): 124–129.

[12] DAVID, H.A. and NAGARAJA, H.N. (2003) *Order Statistics* (Wiley), 3rd ed.

[13] VAN ERP, M. and SCHOMAKER, L. (2000) Variants Of The Borda Count Method For Combining Ranked Classifier Hypotheses. In *Seventh International Workshop on Frontiers in Handwriting Recognition*: 443–452.

[14] THOMAS, G.E. (2000) Use of the bootstrap in robust estimation of location. *The Statictician* 49(1): 63–77.

[15] ROUSSEEUW, P.J. and LEROY, A.M. (2003) *Robust Regression and Outlier Detection* (Wiley).

[16] MCGOVERN, A., FRIEDL, L., HAY, M., GALLAGHER, B., FAST, A., NEVILLE, J. and JENSEN, D. (2003) Exploiting relational structure to understand publication patterns in high-energy physics. *SIGKDD Explorations* 5: 2003.

[17] NEVILLE, J., ADLER, M. and JENSEN, D. (2003) Clustering relational data using attribute and link information. In *Proceedings of the Text Mining and Link Analysis Workshop, 18th International Joint Conference on Artificial Intelligence*: 9–15.

[18] BENASSAROU, A. and CUTRONA, J. (2010), Crestic publication database. URL http://crestic.univ-reims.fr/.

[19] PAPADOPOULOS, A., LYRITSIS, A. and MANOLOPOULOS, Y. (2008) SkyGraph: an algorithm for important subgraph discovery in relational graphs. *Data Mining and Knowledge Discovery* 17(1): 57–76. doi:10.1007/s10618-008-0109-y.

[20] ABELLO, J., PARDALOS, P.M. and RESENDE, M.G.C. [eds.] (2002) *Handbook of Massive Data Sets* (Norwell, MA, USA: Kluwer Academic Publishers).

[21] BLANCHARD, F., VAUTROT, P., AKDAG, H. and HERBIN, M. (2010) Data representativeness based on fuzzy set theory. *Journal of Uncertain Systems* 4(3): 216–228.

[22] PFEIFFER, J.J. and NEVILLE, J. (2010) Probabilistic paths and centrality in time. In *In Proceedings of the 4th SNA-KDD Workshop, KDD.*

13

A Proposal for a Multi-Agent based Synchronization Method for Distributed Generators in Micro-Grid Systems

Paolo Giammatteo[1,*], Concettina Buccella[1], Carlo Cecati[1]

[1]Department of Information Engineering, Computer Science and Mathematics, University of L'Aquila, Via Vetoio, 67100, L'Aquila, Italy

Abstract

A synchronization technique based on the Multi-Agent Systems approach, is proposed for a group of Distributed Generators belonging to a Micro-Grid. The Average Time Synchronization consensus algorithm is used. A detailed description of system's hardware architecture is given and several simulations of the dynamic are performed. Since the synchronization take place on a dedicated layer, different from the power grid one, the proposed technique does not require voltage and current measurements. This gives scalable, flexible and resilient characteristics to the system by construction.

Keywords: Consensus Algorithm, Distributed Power Generation, Electric Grid, Multi-Agent System, Power Systems, Synchronization

1. Introduction

Until the advent of distributed generation, electric power grids were conceived as hierarchical systems, with few large electrical power plants (hundreds MVA), the large majority of which are electro-mechanical generators driven by heat-engines fueled by chemical combustion or nuclear fission, transmission and distribution lines and, at bottom level, a huge number of passive loads [1]. With such a philosophy, the energy flow is unidirectional, the control of the whole grid is centralized and the whole system including power plants, transmission lines, substations and distribution lines is coordinated by a Supervisory Control and Data Acquisition (SCADA) system [2, 3]. The potential difficulties and the limits imposed by such configuration, could lead to face catastrophic situations in case of large scale power blackouts [4, 5].

Distributed generation is based on a different approach: a huge amount of power plants, ranging from few kW up to MW and scattered on the territory, are directly connected with distribution lines, thus producing energy close to customers. In some circumstances, customers themselves produce energy, which is injected in the grid and sold to other customers through Distribution System Operators (DSO) [6, 7]. The high number and the different power level of Distributed Generators (DGs), lead to face several power grid interface problems. The huge number and the different power level of the available generators and energy fluctuations caused by, for example, intrinsic nature of renewable energy sources, lead to face several power grid interface problems. Voltage and currents produced by power plants must primarily satisfy strict requirements in terms of amplitude, frequency, phase and quality of waveform, which is expected to be pure sinusoidal. Total Harmonic Distortion (THD) and more in general Power Quality (PQ) requirements must be strictly ensured. This result can only be achieved using power converters, i.e. electronic interfaces inserted between distributed generators and power grid with the purpose of making the produced energy as much as possible similar to the one already available in the grid [8].

However, power electronics alone is not sufficient for full and efficient integration of DGs within the grid and a complex Information and Communication Technology (ICT) infrastructure is required, leading to the concept of Smart Grid (SG) [9]. In SGs, the power grid layer necessary to sustain energy flows, is now parallelized with an information and communication layer, necessary for exchanging real time processing

---

*Corresponding author. Email: paolo.giammatteo@graduate.univaq.it

data among generators, distribution chain nodes and customers [10, 11]. A decentralized architecture can be then obtained consisting of a number of interconnected Micro-Grids (MGs) [12, 13], including generators, loads and storage systems (SSs). Power and real-time informations flow across two separate layers in both ahead and astern, without any fixed direction. The resulting two networks (power grid and information network) could be distinct from a virtual level point of view, but they may insist either on the same physical infrastructure, as in the case of Power Line Communications (PLCs) [14], or on two different and dedicated physical media.

Many contributions to the decentralization of the power grid and its control, were presented, and different software architectures and paradigms were proposed, in order to define specific standards for the SG, necessary for avoiding proliferation of abnormal situations too difficult to be managed. The Multi-Agent Systems (MASs) approach, already exploited in industrial and scientific domain, is an example of these paradigms. An agent is an autonomous entity which observes through sensors and acts upon an environment using actuators and a MAS is a system composed of multiple interacting intelligent agents within an environment [15]. The MAS potential for the power grid is well documented in several simulation studies and projects [16, 17] and papers [18] and [19] give specifically a vision of how the MASs approach could be used into the power grid. The main benefit of this approach is that the SG can be seen as a very complex system, consisting of many distinct nodes (generators, loads, transformers, etc...) interconnected among each other, with different tasks to be accomplished [20]. MASs approach enhance and fits several functionalities typical of SG, such as distributed and real-time control, diagnosis, negotiation/consensus and self-maintenance. Furthermore, is surely useful for the large-scale integration and coordination of DGs and SSs.

Within the most important MAS applications, it is possible to find the control strategies for parameters optimization such as voltage level [18, 21] and the field of intelligent grid operations such as grid restoration and power distribution management [22, 23]. As mentioned above, the quality of power signals is fundamental for the functionality of a group of DGs inside a MG. While for the signal amplitude and THD, the generator's converter is capable to control and regulate them according to power grid specifications, injection of the generator signal or better signal synchronization inside the grid, depends on the presence of the other generators. Traditional synchronization methods used for large power plants appear too expensive and complex to be used in distributed generation. MASs paradigm, with the use of

a consensus algorithm [24], could be a viable alternative not only to these approaches, but also to the classical and known techniques of power grid synchronization for DGs.

This paper intends to focus its attention on the topic of the synchronization of a group of DGs inside a MG, by using the MAS approach. The paper is organized as follows. In Section 2 a review of synchronization techniques for distributed systems is given. In Section 3 definitions and mathematical model are described. In Section 4 the implementation of system's hardware architecture and simulations are discussed. Finally, Section 5 presents the conclusions of the paper.

2. Synchronization methods for distributed systems

The aim of this Section is to review the most important synchronization techniques and protocols already used in the electric system and more in general for distributed systems.

2.1. Synchronization methods used for distributed generators in power grids

There are two main categories of methods used for the synchronization of DGs. They are respectively the open-loop and the closed-loop methods [25].

Open-loop methods. Among the open-loop methods there are the Zero-Crossing (ZC) and the Filtering of the Grid Voltage (FGV). The ZC method is the most simple methodology to detect the phase information of a sinusoidal signal [26] and is also used for AC-DC converters with triacs or thyristors to calculate the firing angle for distributed gating pulses [27]. The phase is calculated through the use of a timer, which is always restarted when the input signal crosses the zero value. This specific method is very vulnerable when large loads are switched on, because harmonics can arise, providing an input signal no longer perfectly sinusoidal, but soiled by other frequencies, usually very high respect to the fundamental, and so causing multiple zero-crossing at high frequency, making the method totally unreliable.

FGV methods include Space-Vector-Filter (SVF)-based procedure and the Extended Kalman Filter (EKF) procedure [28]. The SVF is used specifically for three-phase applications and consists nothing more of a low-pass filter. The methodology is focused on the on the mutual dependence of the transformed $\alpha\beta$-components of the grid voltage. A SVF-based method can be tuned to provide highly distortion-free estimation [29]. On the other hand, the EKF algorithm consists of two steps: estimation and correction executed in loop. The first step define a prediction of the state estimation and of its covariance matrix, while the second step corrects both the prediction of the state estimation and its covariance matrix with a feedback mechanism with the help of the power grid measured quantities. The use of the EKF as a power grid synchronization method is not so diffused. Anyway, its use as a synchronization method to the power grid is technically feasible, but it requires a high computational resources, when implemented on a Digital Signal Processor (DSP).

Unfortunately, also these two methods are considered high sensitivity to the frequency deviations, voltage distortions and imbalance [26]. Infact, for example, SVF methods are not satisfactory in providing the desired performance and many difficulty and limitations are found in presence of noise and harmonics. So sensitivity to the input frequency variations and imbalance are the most important problems identified.

Closed-loop methods. Differently from the previous case, closed-loop methods insert in the process of synchronization, the acquisition of useful informations related to the grid to which the DGs want to synchronize. Infact, due to these acquired informations, such as the voltage and current values, a feedback loop triggers for the calculation of the necessary parameters. This loop helps the synchronization method to be more accurate, precise and, most important, reliable respect to the open one, giving the right parameter values in order to have a synchronized generator with the power grid. They are much more diffused than the open loop methods, thanks to their greater reliability, and so more attention is given to them.

A. Phased Locked Loop method. Typical examples of closed-loop methods include the PLL, which is a feedback frequency control system, whose functioning is based on the sensitive detection of phase difference between the input and output signals of a reference oscillator. In a nutshell, it consists of a system that allows to synthesize a signal, whose phase has a fixed relationship with that one of a reference signal. The PLL method is the most commonly used method of producing high frequency oscillations in nowadays communications instrumentation. The most, or maybe, the totality of the radio amateur or commercial receiver of any kind nowadays, employ at least one, if not several, PLL systems, to generate stable high frequency oscillations. The first PLL circuits were originally realized by Appleton in 1923 and Bellescize in 1932, and, as mentioned above, was mainly used for synchronous reception of radio signals [30]. Subsequently, PLL technique was used in various industrial fields such as communication systems. Infact, the first large-scale utilization of the PLL occurred in analog receivers for television devices, where a circuit with similar functionality was used for over three decades [30]. Then, other PLL applications were developed in the field of motor control systems [31] and in the induction heating power supplies

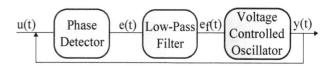

Figure 1. Basic topology of PLL.

[32]. However, the great popularity of this method started with the development of integrated circuits, which allow to realize, at low cost on a single integrated circuit, an entire PLL system. An example is the CD4046CMOS Micropower PLL, which became a popular integrated circuit. Many of the advanced technologies of recent years, including mobile phones, wireless communications, GPS and satellite and digital terrestrial television make an intensive use of the PLL circuit.

Recently, the PLL technique has been used for synchronization between grid-interfaced converters and the power grid, and nowadays covers the majority of the controllers of the grid-connected applications. In this case, the reference signal is the measured electric signal on the power grid to which the DG is connected. The PLL robustness and accuracy are basic to the operation of the controllers which are in charge to establish a synchronization with the power-grid. In general, the PLL classical configuration is shown in Figure (1). This mechanism can be implemented as either analog or digital circuits. Both implementations use the same basic structure. Both analog and digital PLL circuits include the four basic elements described in Figure (1), namely:

- Phase detector

- Loop filter

- Voltage-controlled oscillator

- Feedback path.

This is the easiest manner to describe a basic PLL thorough the block diagram formalism. Several PLL techniques has been proposed over the past years and many variations have been developed, depending on the kind of the specific application request. One of the most widely used technique is the Synchronously Rotating Reference Frame PLL (SRF PLL), which is diffused for the three-phase inverters [33], but also for single-phase applications [34]. The block diagram is shown in Figure (2). SRF PLL is really fast and good in tracking the power grid signal frequency and phase, diminishing the steady state error at very low values. Anyway, it is extremely sensitive to harmonics and imbalance in the voltage signal and more complex control techniques are

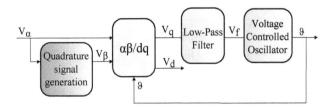

Figure 2. SRF-PLL for single-phase signals.

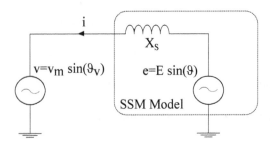

Figure 3. Model of an SSM connected to the grid.

necessary to compensate this aspect [35], so a trade-off is necessary between the two characteristic of fast tracking as well as good filtering.

Other declinations of the PLL method exist, such as the Second Order Generalized Integrator PLL (SOGI PLL) and the Sinusoidal Tracking Algorithm (STA), also known as the Enhanced PLL (EPLL) [36], which gained a lot of importance in recent years. Good comparative analysis and results on different PLL techniques are reported in paper [25] for single-phase PV systems and in paper [37] for advanced inverters used to connect electric vehicles to the grid. Furthermore, it is worthy mentioning that there are several other sophisticated techniques like Decoupled Double Synchronously Rotating Reference Frame PLL (DDSRF PLL) [38], the Delayed Signal Cancellation PLL [39], the Fixed-Reference-Frame PLL (FRF PLL) [35] and the Dual SOGI PLL (DSOGI PLL) [40].

A new and recent PLL technique, which could be a suitable solution for the exploitation of interconnected renewable energy systems with a fault ride through capability, is presented in paper [41]. It consists in the hybridization of three PLL techniques, respectively the SRF PLL, the FRF PLL and the DDSRF PLL. The result of this hybrid operation is called the Decoupled Stationary Reference Frame PLL ($D\alpha\beta$ PLL). The advantages of this technique derive from the aforementioned PLL ones, operating accurately under balanced and unbalanced conditions and reducing the errors on the estimation of the phase angle and frequency, which is the main disadvantage of the DDSRF PLL. This leads to a faster time response, making the $D\alpha\beta$ PLL useful for interconnected renewable energy systems, with particular attention in the design of a fault ride through control. Improvements of the $D\alpha\beta$ PLL have been developed in papers [42, 43], in particular its performances have been studied under grid faults, proposing an adaptive behavior.

However, all these method declinations show that the PLL is a control architecture which may be subject to the origin and/or to the propagation of interference and errors that normally travel through the reference signal of the grid, with consequent difficulties in the synchronization part of the generator. The $D\alpha\beta$ PLL

method goes in this direction and propose a fast and accurate synchronization under harmonic distorted voltage and low-voltage grid faults. Anyway, the PLL technique always require the presence of a reference signal within the electrical power grid on which insists the generator that has to be synchronized.

B. The Sinusoid Locked Loop method. Another closed-loop technique, different from the conventional PLL synchronization methods discussed above, is presented in papers [44, 45] and in book [46]. It is known as the Sinusoid Locked Loop (SLL) and it is based on the idea of mimicking a grid-connected synchronous machine, which does not exchange power with the grid. This because the generated signal is synthesized with the same instantaneous voltage as the grid voltage. So a generic distributed voltage source, which need to be synchronized to an existing power grid, which possess a prevalent signal, is seen as a Single-phase Synchronous Machine (SSM), with the aim that the active power P and the reactive power Q, flowing out of this generator, have to be leaded to the zero value. Their formulas are shown as follows [45, 46]:

$$P = \frac{v_m E}{2X_s} sin\left(\theta - \theta_v\right) \qquad (1)$$

$$Q = \frac{v_m}{2X_s}\left[E cos\left(\theta - \theta_v\right) - v_m\right] \qquad (2)$$

where all the parameters are defined in Figure (3). In order to fulfill the method, the values of Equations (1) and (2) must be equal to zero, and so that the conditions:

$$\begin{aligned} E &= v_m \\ \theta &= \theta_v \end{aligned} \qquad (3)$$

are verified. A frequency droop control is present in order to determine the correct phase which eliminate the active power flow, but the voltage droop control is not needed for the SLL because the generated voltage is expected to be the same as the voltage v, so $E = v_m$. Droop control is a control strategy commonly applied to generators for primary frequency control (and occasionally voltage control) to allow parallel generator operation, so that loads are shared among generators themselves in proportion to their power rating [47]. As shown in [45, 46], the SLL method is capable to provide fast times of response in synchronization, given that a small machine response (the DG) is surely faster than a big one response (the power grid).

2.2. Overview of the synchronization methodologies in distributed systems

Distributed systems, in general, are defined as a set of spatially separated, independently running processes, each equipped with a local time clock. The synchronization of these processes is fundamental for the whole system of which they belong [48–50]. Distributed systems can be implemented in different manners. An example is a network consisting of spatially wide distributed computers, which have to be coordinated because they share and work on the same task. Another example is the interaction of different block functions on a chip. The power grid itself, consisting of many devices spread on a wide area and connected through an infrastructure, is a distributed system. So it is straightforward, that the capability to synchronize devices with high precision and align their local clocks is of primary relevance in several contexts [51, 52]. The alignment of device local clocks to a single system-wide time is generally achieved through the exchange of messages over the network according to a clock synchronization algorithm or protocol. The aim of this protocol is to keep the local time clock of a group of networked devices aligned to each other to the same system time. How the exact system time is provided to the running processes of any single device, competes to the operating system. All clock synchronization protocols work basically in the same way, and must pass necessarily at least through these following points, preferably in this order:

1. estimation of the local clocks deviations respect to the system time with the utilization of time-stamp messages

2. computation of the correct compensation values through the acquired measurements

3. correction of the local time clock for each node.

These points could be slightly different or could be not so clearly separated in the process. The related operations, including the measurement of times and the exchange of informations, depends on a suitable choice of the time-stamp messages and the technique used to interchange these messages between the nodes of the network.

Mainly the estimation of the clock deviations are obtained through the time-stamps, taken by several network nodes. In this case, it is really important the way how the time-stamps are produced and taken. The three most important methods are:

- *Master-Slaves method*: a special node (the master) is in charge to keep the correct time and cyclically gives its time to the others (the slaves) who synchronize themselves to the value received

- *Server-Clients method*: a node (the server) is in charge to keep the correct time and the others (the clients) ask explicitly for synchronization sending a message to the first one when they need

- *Distributed method*: each node sends synchronization messages through the network, which are received by all the other reachable nodes, then a distributed procedure is taken, which enables them to reach a common average reference time value after some iterations of communication.

The clock compensation can be accomplished with two different steps:

1. *clock rate correction*: due to parameters like temperature, or other intrinsic features, oscillators may suffer of rate deviations so they must be monitored and adjusted accordingly

2. *clock offset correction*: even in the case of ideal clock with exactly the same frequency or rate, deviations may still occur on the offset value, because devices could be started at different time clock values.

Another aspect that must be considered is the transmission latency. The exchange of information among nodes is based on the communication services offered by the used network. Consequently, for every message exchanged, there is the propagation delay over the communication media (which depends on the physical distance between nodes and its material) and the pass-through delay of the network equipment, which is related to the used technology, the process running as well as the algorithms performed. For small networks, transmission latency of messages could be considered little and generally deterministic, while for large geographic networks, it could grow considerably and may suffer of stochastic noise. Propagation delays can be determined by the beginning in the design phase, considering suitable network topology and efficient algorithm procedures.

Synchronization protocols. Nowadays, several protocols are available for achieving accurate time clock synchronization in distributed systems. The current measurement techniques and distributed control used within the communication networks are mainly based on the use of special industrial bus, for the communication between different devices, or nodes. Time traceability of the activities carried out in the real-time networks of communication requires to ensure adequate synchronization between the nodes.

In general, the industrial bus does not allow to reach, in an autonomous way, the synchronization requests for measurement and control. Other procedures are based on systems of satellite type, by which is possible to obtain best performance in terms of synchronization at the expense of installation costs.

A. Network Time Protocol. One of the earliest, most widespread and advanced algorithm in the field of synchronization protocols, is the Network Time Protocol (NTP), proposed by Mills [53]. NTP was designed to meet large networks with topology quite static, such as the Internet, so it falls in the category of the industrial procedure type. In NTP, the network nodes are synchronized to a reference signal, which is injected into the network through a sub-group of master nodes, called *stratum-1 server*. These master nodes are directly synchronized to an external source of time such as a GPS device, which in turn form the *stratum-0*. The entire network consists of a series of hierarchical levels, where the leaf nodes are called clients, while internal nodes are called *stratum-L servers*, where L is the level of the node in the hierarchy. Each node must specify, in a configuration file, which are its parent nodes. These nodes frequently share synchronization messages with their fathers and use the informations obtained to regularly update its own clock. The synchronization is less accurate the further one moves away from the first layer. Going from the layers of higher level to those of lower level increases the transmission time of the signal through the network, therefore, in order to make the system more reliable, it is necessary to connect the computer to several servers of the upper layer. From the comparison between the different signals, is determined the more reliably server.

This method allows to maintain synchronization between the nodes in a fully automatic, continuous and transparent manner to the users, resulting at the same time suitable to the synchronization of a single device or an entire network. Since it has a unique format for messages, NTP is easily implemented and used by a large number of operating systems and network environments, guaranteeing the requirements of accuracy in the synchronization of the order of milliseconds. A different declension of this method is the Simple Network Time Protocol (SNTP).

B. Precise Time Protocol. IEEE 1588 standard, or more commonly known as Precision Time Protocol (PTP), is an industrial type and it was released in November 2002 and based on the work done by John Eidson at Agilent Labs [54]. IEEE 1588 specify hardware and software in order to allow networked devices (slaves) to synchronize their clocks to a master clock. The standard was originally developed for the environment of industrial automation where previously it was not possible a precise control using a Local Area Network (LAN), in particular it was developed to exploit Ethernet systems as a means to achieve the synchronization. After, this method was considered interesting in telecommunication, energy and military fields. The standard is applicable to LAN that support multicast communications, including and not limited to Ethernet. IEEE 1588 consists in a Master/Slaves protocol, which is based on the exchange of a series of packets between a master clock and several slave clocks. IEEE 1588 is able to synchronize heterogeneous systems, with clocks that vary in accuracy, resolution and stability, and superior accuracy to within microseconds. In order to reach such precision, it requires that the shipping/incoming time-stamp of the messages is generated by a specific hardware or a component as close as possible to the physical medium, in contrast to the NTP that acts only at the software level and does not require any particular hardware. An attempts to extend the PTP protocol to Wireless Local Area Network is presented in [55].

C. Real Time Networks. During the recent years, the Ethernet technology has taken over, becoming really popular and widely used [56] in the field of industrial applications, offering cost advantages, high-speed interconnections and the possibility of achieving an integration of different components into a network with several applications. Among the most popular synchronization protocols that exploit this technology, may be mentioned the distributed clock mechanism of EtherCAT, the synchronization technique of Ethernet Power-Link (EPL), and FlexRay (FR). These three protocols are generally known as special-purpose protocols, conceived explicitly for real-time control systems like industrial, embedded and automotive systems. In particular it is possible to highlight EtherCAT, which is mainly used in factory automation, and the synchronization protocol FR, which is intended for the automotive domain.

It is worth noting that the PTP is related with some other implementations in commercial industrial networks, such as EtherNet/IP and PROFINET [51, 57]. Another important example is the Time-Triggered Ethernet (TTEthernet), where the specification [58] gives detailed information about the architecture, the synchronization protocol, and the data flow.

D. Satellite protocols. Satellite systems posses nowadays a key role in several fields of science and technology. During the last years, there were incessant developments and increased adoptions of applications used in the life of every day, based on the use of satellite systems. The satellite systems, intended more generally as apparatus for positioning, navigation and timing, allow any user, equipped with adequate receiving devices, the use of the signals emitted by the satellite network, with the purpose of determining important informations, such as the geographic position, the altitude with respect to sea level and the signal of time synchronization reported to UTC, with a good degree of accuracy.

The principle of operation of any satellite system is based on the measure of the travel time of the signal between the satellites and the terrestrial reception apparatus. The receivers are equipped with an internal clock and are therefore capable of measuring the time interval that elapses between the instant of transmission of the signal and the instant of reception. Through the knowledge of this information, it is possible to obtain, at first approximation, the distance value between the satellite and the receiver.

Among the most important cases of satellite systems, is possible to list the Navigation System Time And Ranging Global Position System (NAVSTAR GPS) [59], the Global Navigation Satellite System (GLONASS) [60] and the GALILEO system [61]. The first two were designed for military applications, but just the GPS system evolved to other fields considering a multitude of civil applications giving a global and continuous coverage. The third case is the European answer to the American GPS, but its birth is due only for civilian purposes and its entry into service is scheduled for the end of the 2019.

3. System description

This Section gives a description of the MG architecture through the MAS paradigm and the theory of consensus [62]. The considered MG consists of n DGs feeding the local loads inside an isolated or peninsula network. These DGs could be Renewable Energy Sources (RESs) or SSs. In this structure there is not a real predominant generator, but a myriad of independent DGs; for this reason a new approach and the development of a synchronization method exploiting the information layer to synchronize several energy sources (PV panels, wind turbines, batteries, etc...) could be a valid purpose.

3.1. The Micro-Grid

A Microgrid can be represented as a set of nodes N_i $i = 1, \dots n$ as in Figure (4). Each node is twofold connected to its neighbors, thus forming a two layer network: the first layer provides to power exchange and the second one for information data flow.

Within the information layer, each node can exchange data only with its neighbors, which depends on how the information network topology has been realized, spreading messages and data packets about its state

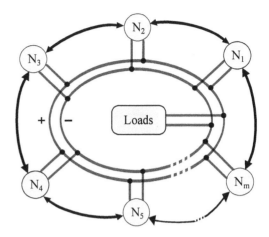

Figure 4. Microgrid: grey lines represent Power Grid, black arrows represent Information Network, circles represent nodes.

and updating it according to the received informations. Every node includes the energy source, the power converter and the Agent Control Unit (ACU), as shown in Figure (5). A synchronization process is required in order to obtain a common phase for all signals in order to get a good operation of the MG.

3.2. The agent

A typical ACU is featured by the following properties:

1. it is resident in a specific node

2. it is capable to send/receive data informations about its internal/external state and to act locally through a control scheme

3. it can interact only with a certain number of adjacent agents, according to the MG information network topology

4. it is modeled by a first-order dynamic system, whose initial state is determined by local data detected by the agent itself. Each single dynamic is mutually coupled with the nearby dynamics by a proper local coupling law, or better, by a consensus algorithm.

The whole MG system is capable to reach globally a consensus on local variables under certain conditions [63]. A consensus means that, after a time interval in the system dynamic, all the agents share the same value of certain parameters proper to their state, such as the signal phase and frequency. So, through this dynamic, the agents can solve global and complex problems, such as the synchronization, by only processing local informations. This ability allows each agent to estimate the most important variables that characterize the global MG, without the need to utilize central facilities and reference signals. Therefore, the MG functions

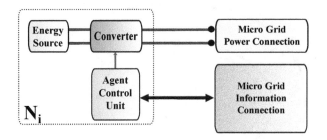

Figure 5. The generic node N_i and its subsystems: the energy source, the power converter and the ACU.

(i.e., monitoring, control and time synchronization) can be performed according to a decentralized and self-organized computing framework.

3.3. Mathematical model: the Consensus Algorithm

In the proposed model, each agent is equipped with its own clock and the consensus algorithm resides on the agent itself, i.e. the ACU shown in Figure (5). The clock evolution $\xi_i(t)$ provides the dynamic of a single agent; a synchronization among different agents is reached when all of them perform the same dynamics. Neglecting second order terms and stochastic effects, $\xi_i(t)$ is given by [64]:

$$\xi_i(t) = \alpha_i + \beta_i t \quad i = 1, \dots n \quad (4)$$

where α_i and β_i are the skew and the offset coefficients, respectively, t is the absolute time and n is the number of agents. In order to estimate these coefficients, the Average Time Synchronization (ATS) algorithm [64] is used. The goal of this algorithm is to obtain informations regarding the clock coefficients of the ith agent dynamic, processing the time offsets with its neighbors and synchronizing the agents dynamics to a virtual reference clock $\xi_v(t)$ to which each agent has to converge:

$$\xi_v(t) = \alpha_v + \beta_v t \quad (5)$$

The exact values of the two coefficients α_v and β_v are not important and depends on the initial conditions, so they may change according to them. During the consensus process, each agent has a local estimate of the virtual reference clock $\hat{\xi}_{v,i}(t)$:

$$\hat{\xi}_{v,i}(t) = \hat{o}_i + \hat{s}_i \xi_i(t) \quad i = 1, \dots n \quad (6)$$

In [64], it is demonstrated that the convergence is reached when:

$$\lim_{t \to +\infty} \hat{\xi}_{v,i}(t) = \xi_v(t) \quad i = 1, \dots n \quad (7)$$

where $\hat{s}_i$ and $\hat{o}_i$ are the local parameter estimations of the skew and offset, respectively, relatively to the time

$\xi_i(t)$. These parameters must be given to the ith local clock $\xi_i(t)$ in order to compensate its difference with the virtual reference clock $\hat{\xi}_{v,i}(t)$.

Substituting Equation (4) in Equation (6), the following non linear equation is obtained:

$$\hat{\xi}_{v,i}(t) = \hat{o}_i + \hat{s}_i \alpha_i + \hat{s}_i \beta_i t \quad i = 1, \dots n \quad (8)$$

ATS consensus algorithm estimates the relative speed $\beta_{ij} = \frac{\beta_j}{\beta_i}$ of the ith clock respect its jth neighbor. Denoting t_k the time when the ith agent receives a time-stamp $\xi_j(t_k)$ from the jth agent, the pair $\left[\xi_i(t_k), \xi_j(t_k)\right]$ is recorded by the ith agent in its own memory. When a second information packet arrives and a second pair $\left[\xi_i(t_{k+1}), \xi_j(t_{k+1})\right]$ is recorded, the following parameter is evaluated by the ith agent:

$$\mu_{ij}(t_{k+1}) = \lambda_\mu \mu_{ij}(t_k) + \left(1 - \lambda_\mu\right) \frac{\xi_j(t_{k+1}) - \xi_j(t_k)}{\xi_i(t_{k+1}) - \xi_i(t_k)} \quad (9)$$

where $\mu_{ij}(t_k)$ represents the estimation of the relative clock speed between the ith and j^{th} clock at the time t_k. The initial condition $\mu_{ij}(0) = \mu_0$ is given and $\lambda_\mu \in (0, 1)$ is a tunable parameter. It is shown in [64] that:

$$\lim_{k \to +\infty} \mu_{ij}(t_k) = \beta_{ij} \quad i, j = 1, \dots n \quad (10)$$

In order to estimate $\hat{s}_i$ and $\hat{o}_i$, useful to the Equation (6), the following relations are used:

$$\hat{s}_i(t_{k+1}) = \lambda_\omega \hat{s}_i(t_k) + \\ + (1 - \lambda_\omega) \mu_{ij}(t_k) \hat{s}_j(t_k) \quad i, j = 1, \dots n \quad (11)$$

$$\hat{o}_i(t_{k+1}) = \hat{o}_i(t_k) + (1 - \lambda_0)\left(\hat{s}_j(t_k) \xi_j(t_k) + \hat{o}_j(t_k) - \\ - \hat{s}_i(t_k) \xi_i(t_k) - \hat{o}_i(t_k)\right) \quad i, j = 1, \dots n \quad (12)$$

where $\lambda_\omega \in (0, 1)$ and $\lambda_0 \in (0, 1)$ are tunable parameters.

In [64] is proved that:

$$\lim_{t \to +\infty} \hat{s}_i(t) \beta_i = \beta_v \quad i = 1, \dots n \quad (13)$$

$$\lim_{t \to +\infty} \left(\hat{o}_i(t) + \frac{\beta_v}{\beta_i} \alpha_i\right) = \alpha_v \quad i = 1, \dots n \quad (14)$$

where it is possible to define the auxiliary parameters:

$$\begin{cases} \hat{s}_i(t)\beta_i = \Omega_i \\ \hat{o}_i(t) + \frac{\beta_v}{\beta_i}\alpha_i = \Theta_i \end{cases} \quad i = 1, \dots n \quad (15)$$

used in the Figures shown in next section. So, the information packet of the ith agent is given by the local parameters ξ_i, $\hat{s}_i$ and $\hat{o}_i$.

When each agent has got, for its own clock, the same reference virtual clock dynamic, the virtual time ξ_v is common to all agents and, consequently, a synchronization is reached. When all clock dynamics $\xi_i(t)$ $i = 1, \ldots n$ have been synchronized with ξ_v, all generic functions depending on ξ_v are, consequently, synchronized [65].

Pulse Width Modulation (PWM) is a typical modulation technique for low/medium power converters[66]. In this paper, the main duty of ACU is feed PWM unit toward synchronization. Carrier waveform η performing modulation, represents the function to be synchronized. A triangular carrier waveform (TCW) with period $2a$ and amplitude from A to $-A$, can be expressed as:

$$\eta\left(\xi_v\right) = A \cdot \frac{2}{a}\left(\xi_v - \left\lfloor \frac{\xi_v}{a} + \frac{1}{2}\right\rfloor a\right)(-1)^{\left\lfloor \frac{\xi_v}{a} - \frac{1}{2}\right\rfloor} \quad (16)$$

where the operator $\lfloor f \rfloor$ is the *floor function* of f.

Since each agent acts as a header emitting its own status information packets to the neighboring agents, the consensus, or better the synchronization, is obtained without the need of any cluster header or centralized supervisory structure.

4. System implementation

This section shows system implementation. Three distinct configurations have been considered for system's simulation with Matlab/Simulink®.

4.1. Two node case

Two distinct generators, i.e. nodes, have been considered, each one consisting of 5-level cascaded multilevel H-bridge converter (see Figure (6)). At this level of abstraction, the influence of the electric loads can be neglected and the attention can be focused on the information layer only. Moreover, the delay in communication network $tdel$ can be assumed symmetrical, thus the information propagation time between nodes N_1 and N_2 can be assumed equal in both directions (N_1-N_2) and (N_2-N_1).

As shown in Figure (6a), each node DG includes two DC power sources V_{dc}. The ACU block is represented in Figure (7), where it is possible to identify eight PWM signals IN_x^y, $x = 1, 2, 3, 4$ and $y = 1, 2$ produced by the ACU and used as shown in Figure (6b).

Converter output is the result of the application of modulation patterns generated by ACU, the latter could be realized using a very large scale integration component (VSLI), for instance a Field Programmable Gate Array (FPGA) or one or multiple micro-controllers [67]. In the considered case, ACU includes

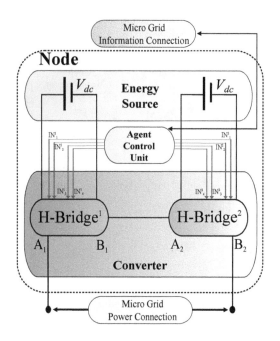

(a) Cascaded H-bridge 5-level converter.

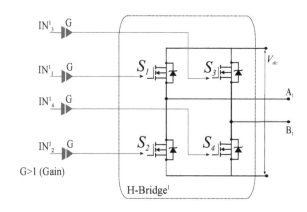

(b) Detail of H-Bridge^1.

Figure 6. Cascaded H-bridge multilevel converter description.

two microprocessors executing two concurrent tasks: converter control and synchronization. It is worth notice that there are some twin-core microcontrollers available on the market [68] each with several internal peripherals including a Shared Memory Unit (SMU) between the two microprocessors and the PWM Unit (PWMU). The ACU functions are summarized in the following steps:

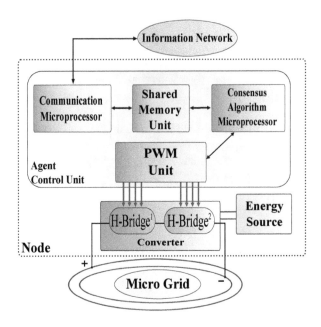

Figure 7. The ACU detail.

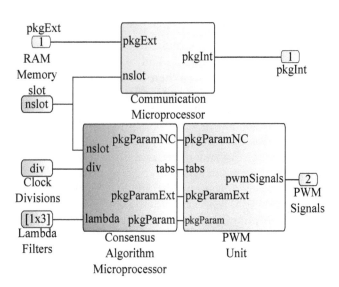

Figure 8. The single Agent developed in Matlab/Simulink®.

- data packets arrive from the Agent Network (AN) to the Communication Microprocessor (CM), bringing information from that particular agent who sent the package

- CM places informations inside the SMU, available for the Consensus Algorithm Microprocessor (CAM)

- CAM picks the external network informations from the SMU and executes the consensus algorithm also with its status informations

- the output of the consensus algorithm is used in order to give the right parameters to the PWMU, to synthesize properly the PWM signal to drive the converter

- the result of the consensus algorithm is also placed inside the SMU, available for the CM

- finally, the CM picks the new status informations of the agent from the SMU and sends them to the AN, so that another agent will perform the same steps.

At this stage, agents have been developed by using Matlab/Simulink® and implementing the blocks CM, CAM and PWMU, as shown in Figure (8).

1. *CM block*: this block receives data packets *pkgExt* from the AN, stores these informations inside the SMU, and then sends the internal data packet *pkgInt* to the AN. Packets *pkgExt* and *pkgInt* are vectors with three parameters $[\xi_h, \hat{s}_h, \hat{o}_h]$ supplied to the external ($h = j$) and internal ($h = i$)

agent, respectively. Furthermore, there is a third parameter *RAM Memory Slot (nslot)* representing the number of information packets stored inside the SMU, both in Input or Output direction, i.e. a buffer memory.

2. *CAM block*: this block takes *pkgExt* parameters from SMU, executes the consensus algorithm with internal and external clock informations, places results inside the SMU through *pkgInt* and then gives directives through the parameters *pkgParamNC*, *tabs*, *pkgParamExt* and *pkgParam* to the PWMU. The input parameters of this block are: *nslot*, *Clock Divisions (div)* and *Lambda Filters* $\left[\lambda_\mu, \lambda_\omega, \lambda_0\right]$. The *Clock Divisions* parameter controls the frequency of time-stamps extraction from the clock dynamic, the Equation (4). The *Lambda Filters* represent three λ parameters defined in Equations (9), (11) and (12), respectively, which control the convergence of the consensus algorithm.

3. *PWMU block*: this block generates output PWM signals. It receives directives from the CAM block through the input parameters *pkgParamNC*, *tabs*, *pkgParamExt* and *pkgParam*, then returns the vector *pwmSignlas*, which consists of the eight components IN_x^y, $x = 1, 2, 3, 4$ and $y = 1, 2$.

Table (1) shows two distinct parameter configurations used during simulations. These values are considered the same for both agents.

Figures (9), (10), (11) and (12) report the behaviors of the main system parameters. In particular Figures (9) and (10) show the convergence of the two clock parameters, skew and offset, to the common virtual reference clock value. For both considered parameters

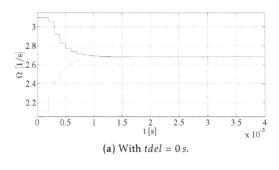

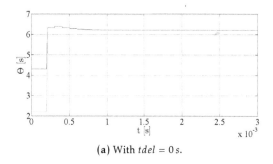

(a) With $tdel = 0\,s$.

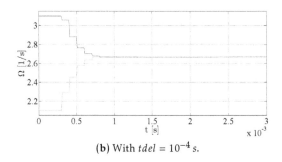

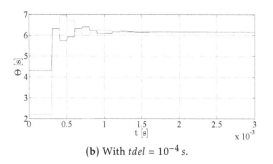

(b) With $tdel = 10^{-4}\,s$.

Figure 9. Clock skew convergence behaviors of the two nodes.

Figure 10. Clock offset convergence behaviors of the two nodes.

configurations, the system convergence is reached in less than 2 ms.

In this test PWM is implemented by using a TCW operating at $f_1 = 310\,kHz$ and at $f_2 = 210\,kHz$, respectively, for the two agents, in both delay times $tdel$. After clocks convergence, the TCW frequency is the same for both the agents, in particular $f_v = 265\,kHz$ for $tdel = 0\,s$ and $f_v = 280\,kHz$ for $tdel = 10^{-4}\,s$. As modulating signal, a fixed value comparator $comp = 0.8$ has been used. Figures (11) and (12) show the TCW and a pulse pattern, respectively, for the two agents, at different delay times. In particular in Figure (12) a single PWM signal is reported, among the eight available. It is imposed that the clocks compensation happens at 6 ms and consequently the two TCW are overlapped. The compensation time value is arbitrarily chosen, but in any case, it is longer than the time required for the mathematical convergence shown in Figures (9) and (10). In these figures it can be seen that after the compensation time, i.e. after agents' synchronization, the TCW and the PWM signal of the nodes are overlapped. The consequence is that the electric signal produced by the two converters are synchronized inside the MG, because the PWM

Table 1. System parameters configurations.

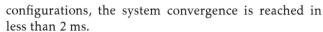

Mode	nsolt	div	λ_μ	λ_ω	λ_0	tdel (s)
Config 1	5	10	0.1	0.8	0.5	0
Config 2	5	10	0.1	0.8	0.5	0.0001

signals of each node drive their associated H-bridges semiconductor devices, synchronously respect to the other node.

4.2. Three node case

In this case, the considered MG consists of three DGs, therefore the system includes three nodes N_1, N_2 and N_3. For each node the 5-level converter has been adopted, as described in section 4.1.

As in the previous paragraph, power issues are neglected and the attention is focused just on the information layer. The network communication delay time $tdel$ is assumed symmetric also here, which means that the information propagation time between the three nodes N_1, N_2 and N_3 is equal in every directions. The information topology network is realized linking node N_1 to node N_2 and vice versa, and node N_1 to node N_3 and vice versa. No direct information connections are realized between nodes N_2 and N_3. This means that the influence of N_2 on N_3 passes only through the N_1 informations. This is the base of the principle *think locally, act globally*. All the system configuration set considered in the previous section is replicated in this case, both for hardware, software, parameters and algorithm point of view. Below are shown just some of the simulated characteristic trends.

Figures (13) and (14) report the behaviors of the main system parameters in this configuration, with a delay information propagation time $tdel = 10^{-4}\,s$. In Figure (13a) is possible to see the skew convergence of the three nodes. Compared to the two node network, the presence

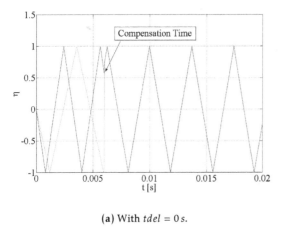

(a) With $tdel = 0\,s$.

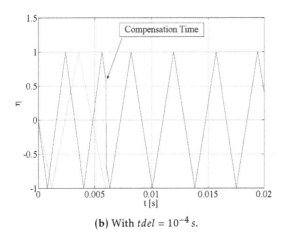

(b) With $tdel = 10^{-4}\,s$.

Figure 11. The PWM modulation waveform convergence behaviors of the two nodes.

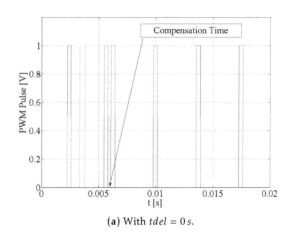

(a) With $tdel = 0\,s$.

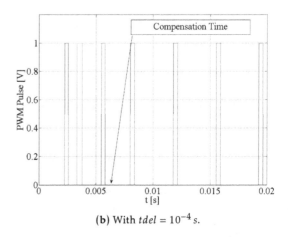

(b) With $tdel = 10^{-4}\,s$.

Figure 12. The PWM signal convergence behaviors of the two nodes.

of a third node increases the convergence time of system dynamics. In Figure (13b) is shown the dynamic of each single clock. It is evident the convergence behavior of the three clocks to a common linear trend.

In Figure (14) is reported the TCW convergence, used for the PWM. In this case clock compensation occur at 80 ms, resulting three overlapped TCW. As in the paragraph before, the compensation time value is arbitrarily chosen, but in any case, it is greater than the time required for the mathematical convergence shown in Figures (13a) and (13b). Similar conclusions to the previous paragraph can be deduced from the three clocks synchronization behaviors. The overlap of the three TCW after the compensation time imply the synchronization of the three converter electric signal inside the MG.

4.3. Six node case

Here six DGs are considered in the MG, therefore the system includes six nodes N_1, N_2, N_3, N_4, N_5 and N_6. Also here, for each node the 5-level converter has been adopted, as described in sections 4.1 and 4.2. The attention is always focused on the information layer and the network communication delay time $tdel$ is assumed symmetric. In this case, two information network topology are considered. In Figure (15) are reported the two information network. Figure (15a) shows a sort of centralized topology where every node has a bi-directional connection only with the node N_1, which behaves as a information hub. Figure (15b), on the other hand, shows a decentralized network with two cluster of three nodes, connected only by a bi-directional connection between the two nodes N_1 and N_2.

Figures (16), (17), (18) and (19) report the behaviors of the main system parameters for the six node case for both topology configurations, with a delay information

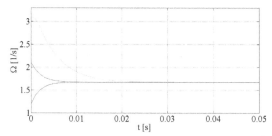

(a) The three clocks skew convergence, with $tdel = 10^{-4}\,s$

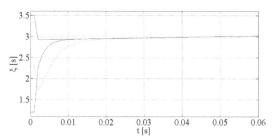

(b) The three clocks convergence dynamics, with $tdel = 10^{-4}\,s$.

Figure 13. The clocks behavior of the three nodes.

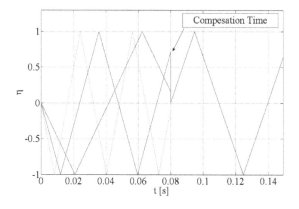

Figure 14. The PWM modulation waveform signals of the three nodes, with $tdel = 10^{-4}\,s$

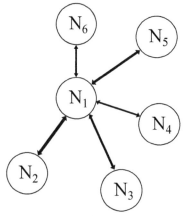

(a) The centralized network topology.

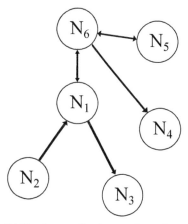

(b) The decentralized network topology.

Figure 15. The two topology considered for the six node case.

propagation time $tdel = 10^{-4}\,s$. In Figures (16a) and (18a) is possible to see the skew convergence of the six nodes respectively for the centralized and decentralized topology. Also here, the presence of more nodes increases the convergence time of system dynamics. In Figures (16b) and (18b) are shown the dynamic of each single clock respectively for the centralized and decentralized topology. Again, is evident the convergence behavior of the six clocks to a common linear trend in both cases.

The analysis in six node configuration opens to broader considerations and issues for a $N_i \ i = 1, \dots n$ nodes system. The most important and evident consequence,

is that the convergence time lengthens, because a higher number of agents must be mediated. This problem could be further investigated tuning the *div* and *Lambda Filters* $\left[\lambda_\mu \ \lambda_\omega, \ \lambda_0\right]$ agents parameters, searching the optimal configuration set which minimize the convergence time. The information network topology is also another aspect to consider. Both these observations depends according to the number of agents inside the network. Being connected to particular nodes could accelerate the convergence. These nodes are known as *hubs*, or better the nodes which collect the largest number of connections with other nodes. In scientific literature this behavior is know as the *preferential attachment* logic [69]. Furthermore a cluster synchronization could be also considered, thinking the system formed of cluster of nodes, which firstly reach the synchronization inside each cluster, and then all the clusters start to synchronize together between them.

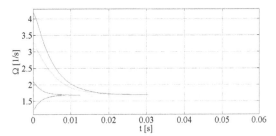

(a) The six clocks skew convergence, with $tdel = 10^{-4}\,s$

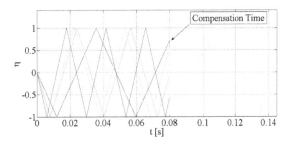

(b) The six clocks convergence dynamics, with $tdel = 10^{-4}\,s$.

Figure 16. The clocks behavior of the six nodes with centralized topology.

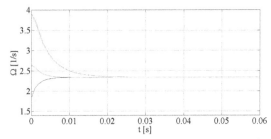

(a) The six clocks skew convergence, with $tdel = 10^{-4}\,s$

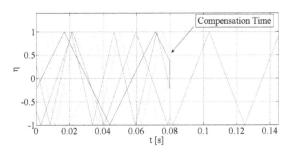

(b) The six clocks convergence dynamics, with $tdel = 10^{-4}\,s$.

Figure 18. The clocks behavior of the six nodes with decentralized topology.

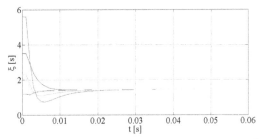

Figure 17. The PWM modulation waveform signals of the six node with centralized topology, with $tdel = 10^{-4}\,s$

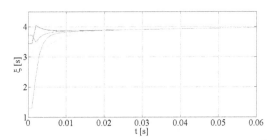

Figure 19. The PWM modulation waveform signals of the six node with decentralized topology, with $tdel = 10^{-4}\,s$

4.4. Communication specifications

An implementation of the system described in section 3 is possible nowadays, thanks to the improvements of the ICT, and several communication protocols have been developed. The attention must be focused on one aspect in particular, the communication protocol, through which the agent's informations flow. The choice, made in this paper, falls on the communication protocol Field-bus. The reason is because this is a particular industrial computer network protocol realized for real-time distributed control, standardized as IEC 61158 [70]. This protocol possesses advantages that well fit the system modeled, including flexible and scalable architecture; therefore, addition of new modules or integration of new functions is always possible without affecting existing wiring. The implementation of a network based on the proposed

technology corresponds to realization of a Local Area Network (LAN) resulting low impact, because of the well-known and inexpensive technology.

Following the Open Systems Interconnection (OSI) model ISO/IEC 7498-1 [71], the Field-bus functional model for communication is made of three levels, as show in Figure (20). In the Application layer resides those informations exchanged between the agents, organized in packets. This means that each agent's CM must be equipped with a peripheral able to generate informations packets, which satisfy the Field-bus protocol.

Among the existing examples of Field-bus, can be found AFDX, EtherCAT, EtherNet/IP, PROFINET IO, PROFINET IRT, TTEthernet and VARAN [51, 52]. All of them exploit in particular the Ethernet technology as Data Link layer, which is the protocol layer in charge to

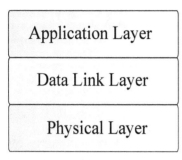

Figure 20. Field-bus functional layers.

transfers data between adjacent network nodes. Other Field-bus protocols are possible on different Data Link layer such as Token and SDLC.

5. Conclusions

In this paper a synchronization technique, based on the MAS approach, for a group of DGs inside a MG, has been proposed. A review of synchronization methods both for DGs in power grid and distributed systems is reported. Then, a description on how the system hardware architecture is given and system simulation results are shown primarily for a simple configuration of two agents, secondly for three agents and then for six agents. The ATS consensus algorithm has been applied and simulation results have been obtained.

The advantages of the proposed methodology are:

- it does not require voltage and current measurements, since the synchronization data travel on a different layer dedicated to the information exchanges, see Figure (4)

- it does not require a reference power signal inside the MG, so it is suitable for isolated MG without a connection to the main national power grid

- it is scalable, flexible and resilient, in fact it is automatically reconfigured if some DGs are excluded or added into the MG

- it represents a new synchronization technique which requires a new standard.

Ideally, this new technique creates an open-loop method, because all the measurements of the voltages and currents, required by the traditional synchronization methods such as the PLL [43, 46], are eliminated. Anyway, the open-loop hypothesis is certainly ideal and must be proved. It is evident that the quality of the information network is an important parameter, which must ensure the synchronization task with precision and speed.

Future work will focus its attention on the effect of *i)* the topology of the DGs information network *ii)* the effect of loads inside the MG. A more detailed study on the influence of delay time propagation could be performed, in order to find the parameters which help to optimize the convergence. Finally the proposed algorithm could be implemented on a real MG, with two or more control boards on which develop the code, in order to synthesize the synchronized PWM signals.

References

[1] Yu, X., Cecati, C., Dillon T. and M. G. Simoes (2011) The new Frontier of Smart Grids. *IEEE Ind. Electron. Mag.* **5**(3): 49-63.

[2] Rogers, K. M. et al. (2010) An Authenticated Control Framework for Distributed Voltage Support on the Smart Grid. *IEEE Trans. Smart Grid* **1**(1): 40-47.

[3] Aquino-Lugo, A.A., Klump, R. and Overbye, T.J. (2011) A Control Framework for the Smart Grid for Voltage Support Using Agent-Based Technologies. *IEEE Trans. Smart Grid* **2**(1): 173-180.

[4] Meliopoulos, A.P.S. et al. (2011) Smart Grid Technologies of Autonomous Operation and Control. *IEEE Ind. Electron. Mag.* **2**(1): 1-10.

[5] Arnold, G.W. (2011) Challenges and Opportunities in Smart Grid: A Position Article. *Proc. IEEE.* **99**(6): 922-927.

[6] Cossent, R., Gómez, T. and Frías, P. (2009) Towards a future with large penetration of distributed generation: Is the current regulation of electricity distribution ready? regulatory recommendations under a European perspective. *Energy Policy* **37**(3): 1145-1155.

[7] Joskow, P.L. (2008) Lessons learned from electricity market liberalization. *Energy Journal* **29**: 9.

[8] Carrasco, J.M. et al. (2006) Power-Electronics Systems for the Grid Integration of Renewable Energy Sources: A Survey. *IEEE Trans. Ind. Electron.* **53**(4): 1002-1015.

[9] Strasser, T. et al. (2014) A Review of Architectures and Concepts for Intelligence in Future Electric Energy Systems. *IEEE Trans. Ind. Electron.* **62**(4): 2424-2438.

[10] Güngör, V.C. et al. (2011) Smart Grid Technologies: Communication Technologies and Standards. *IEEE Trans. Ind. Informat.* **7**(4): 529-539.

[11] Sauter, T. and Lobashov M. (2011) End-to-End Communication Architecture for Smart Grid. *IEEE Trans. Ind. Electron.* **58**(4): 1218-1228.

[12] Lasseter, R.H. (2002) Microgrids *IEEE Power Engineering Society Winter Meeting* **1**: 305-308.

[13] Khodaei, A. (2014) Provisional Microgrids. *IEEE Trans. Smart Grid* **PP**(99): 1-9.

[14] Galli, S., Scaglione, A. and Zhifang, W. (2011) For the Grid and Through the Grid: The Role of

Power Line Communications in the Smart Grid. *Proc. IEEE* **99**(6): 998-1027.

[15] Luck, M., Marik, V., Štrpánková, O. and Trappl, R. (2001) *Multi-Agent Systems and Applications* (Berlin Springer-Verlag).

[16] Cao, Y., Yu, W., Ren, W. and Chen, G. (2013) An overview of recent progress in the study of distributed multi-agent coordination. *IEEE Trans. Ind. Informat.* **9**(1): 427-438.

[17] Leitão, P., Mařík, V. and Vrba, P. (2013) Past, present, and future of industrial agent applications. *IEEE Trans. Ind. Informat.* **9**(4): 2360-2372.

[18] Loia, V., Vaccaro, A. and Vaisakh, K. (2013) A self-organizing architecture based on cooperative fuzzy agents for smart grid voltage control. *IEEE Trans. Ind. Informat.* **9**(3): 1415-1422.

[19] Islam, S.R., Muttaqi, K.M. and Sutanto, D. (2014) Multi-agent receding horizon control with neighbour-to-neighbour communication for prevention of voltage collapse in a multi-area power system. *Generation, Transmission and Distribution, IET* **8**(9): 1604-1615.

[20] Vrba, P. et al. (2014) A Review of Agents and Service-Oriented Concepts Applied to Intelligent Energy Systems. *IEEE Trans. Ind. Informat.* **10**(3): 1890-1903.

[21] Aquino-Lugo, A.A., Klump, R. and Overbye, T.J. (2011) A Control Framework for the Smart Grid for Voltage Support Using Agent-Based Technologies Angel. *IEEE Trans. Smart Grid* **2**(1): 173-180.

[22] Nagata, T. and Okamoto, K. (2014) A decentralized distribution power system restoration by using multi-agent Approach. In *Proceedings of the International Electrical Engineering Congress* (Chonburi, Thailand, iEECON), 1-4.

[23] Fenghui, R., Minjie, Z. and Sutanto, D. (2013) A Multi-Agent Solution to Distribution System Management by Considering Distributed Generators. *IEEE Transactions on Power Systems* **28**(2): 1442-1451.

[24] Yao, C., Jinhu, L., Xinghuo, Y. and Hill, D.J. (2013) Multi-Agent Systems with Dynamical Topologies: Consensus and Applications. *IEEE Circuits and Systems Magazine* **13**(3): 21-34.

[25] Nagliero, A., Mastromauro, R.A., Liserre, M. and Dell'Aquila, A. (2010 Monitoring and Synchronization Technniques for Single-Phase PV Systems. In *Proceedings of the International Symposium on Power Electronics Electrical Drives Automation and Motion* (Pisa, Italy, SPEEDAM), 1404-1409.

[26] Timbus, A., Liserre, M., Teodorescu, R. and Blaabjerg, F. (2005) Synchronization methods for three phase distributed power generation systems - An overview and evaluation. In *Proceedings of the IEEE Power Electronics Specialists Conference* (Recife, Brazil, PESC), 2474-2481.

[27] Valiviita, S. (1999) Zero-crossing detection of distorted line voltages using 1-b measurements.

[28] Svensson, J. (2001) Synchronization methods for grid-connected voltage source converters. *IEEE Proceedings-Generation, Transmission and Distribution* **148**(3): 229-235.

[29] Karimi-Ghartemani, M. and Iravani, M.R. (2004) A method for synchronization of power electronic converters in polluted and variable-frequency environments. *IEEE Transactions on Power Systems* **19**(3): 1263-1270.

[30] Lee, T.H. (2003) *The Design of CMOS Radio-Frequency Integrated Circuits* (Cambridge University Press).

[31] Pan, C.T. and Fang, E. (2008) A phase-locked-loop-assisted internal model adjustable speed controller for BLDC motors. *IEEE Trans. Ind. Electron.* **55**(9): 3415-3425.

[32] Chen, M.P. et al. (2001) Surge analysis of induction heating power supply with PLL. *IEEE Trans. Power Electron.* **16**(5): 702-709.

[33] Kesler, M. and Ozdemir, E. (2011) Synchronous-Reference-Frame-Based Control Method for UPQC Under Unbalanced and Distorted Load Conditions. *IEEE Trans. Ind. Electron.* **58**(9): 3967-3975.

[34] Ciobotaru, M., Teodorescu, R. and Blaabjerg, F. (2006) A New Single-Phase PLL Structure Based on Second Order Generalized Integrator. In *Proceedings of the IEEE Power Electronics Specialists Conference* (Jeju, South Korea, PESC), 1-6.

[35] Escobar, G. et al. (2011) Fixed-reference-frame phase-locked loop for grid synchronization under unbalanced operation. *IEEE Trans. Ind. Electron.* **58**(5): 1943-1951.

[36] Ziariani, A.K. and Konrad, A. (2004) A method of extraction of non-stationary sinusoid. *Signal Processing* **84**(8): 1323-1346.

[37] Ferreira, R.J., Araújo, R.E. and Peças Lopes, J.A. (2011) A Comparative Analysis and Implementation of Various PLL Techniques Applied to Single-phase Grids. In *Proceedings of the 3rd International Youth Conference on Energetics* (Budapest, Hungary, IYCE), 1-8.

[38] Rodriguez, P. et al. (2007) Decoupled Double Synchronous Reference Frame PLL for Power Converters Control. *IEEE Trans. Power Electron.* **22**(2): 584-592.

[39] Wang, Y. and Li, Y. (2011) Grid synchronization PLL based on cascaded delayed signal cancellation. *IEEE Trans. Power Electron.* **26**(7): 1987-1997.

[40] Rodriguez, P. et al. (2006) Advanced grid synchronization system for power converters under unbalanced and distorted operating conditions. In *Proceedings of the IEEE Annual Conference on Industrial Electronics* (Paris, France, IECON), 5173-5178.

[41] Hadjidemetriou, L., Kyriakides, E. and Blaabjerg, F. (2013) A New Hybrid PLL for Interconnecting Renewable Energy Systems to the Grid.

[28] *IEEE Trans. Ind. Electron.* **46**(5) : 917-922.

IEEE Trans. Ind. Appl. **49**(6): 2709-2719.

[42] Hadjidemetriou, L., Kyriakides, E. and Blaabjerg, F. (2014) An Adaptive Tuning Mechanism for Phase-Locked Loop Algorithms for Faster Time Performance of Interconnected Renewable Energy Sources. *IEEE Trans. Ind. Appl.* **51**(2): 1792-1804.

[43] Hadjidemetriou, L., Kyriakides, E. and Blaabjerg, F. (2015) A Robust Synchronization to Enhance the Power Quality of Renewable Energy Systems. *IEEE Trans. Ind. Electron.* **62**(8): 4858-4868.

[44] Zhong, Q.C. and Weiss, G. (2011) Synchronverters: Inverters That Mimic Synchronous Generators. *IEEE Trans. Ind. Electron.* **58**(4): 1259-1267.

[45] Zhong, Q.C. and Nguyen, P.L. (2012) Sinusoidlocked loops based on the principles of synchronous machines. In *Proceedings of the Chinese Control and Decision Conference* (Taiyuan, China, CCDC), 1518-1523.

[46] Zhong, Q.C. and Hornik, T. (2013) *Control of Power Inverters in Renewable Energy and Smart Grid Integration* (Academic Press).

[47] Chandorkar, M.C (1993) Control of parallel connected inverters in standalone AC supply systems. *IEEE Trans. Ind. App.* **29**(1): 136-143.

[48] Li, L., Benliang, L. and Houjun, W. (2010) Clock Synchronization of Wireless Distributed System Based on IEEE 1588. In *Proceedings of the Cyber-Enabled Distributed Computing and Knowledge Discovery* (Huangshan, China, CyberC), 205-209.

[49] Cheng-I, C. (2013) A Phasor Estimator for Synchronization Between Power Grid and Distributed Generation System. *IEEE Trans. Ind. Electron.* **60**(8): 3248-3255.

[50] Yang, T., Huijun, G., Wei, Z. and Kurths, J. (2013) Distributed Synchronization in Networks of Agent Systems With Non-linearities and Random Switchings. *IEEE Trans. Cyber.*, **43**(1): 358-370.

[51] Cena, G. et al. (2013) Synchronize your watches: Part 1. *IEEE Ind. Electron. Mag.* **7**(1): 18-29.

[52] Cena, G. et al. (2013) Synchronize your watches: Part 2. *IEEE Ind. Electron. Mag.* **7**(2): 27-39.

[53] Mills, D.L. (1991) Internet time synchronization: the network time protocol. *IEEE Trans. Comm.* **39**(10): 1482-1493.

[54] National Institute of Standards and Technology, IEEE 1588 Web Site. `http://www.nist.gov/el/isd/ieee/ieee1588.cfm` (accessed on 30 November 2015).

[55] Lee, S. and Hong, C. (2012) An Accuracy Enhanced IEEE 1588 Synchronization Protocol for Dynamically Changing and Asymmetric Wireless Links. *IEEE Communications Letters* **16**(2): 190-192.

[56] Holler, R., Sauter, T. and Kero, N. (2003) Embedded SynUTC and IEEE 1588 clock synchronization for industrial Ethernet. In *Proceedings of the IEEE Conference Emerging Technologies and Factory Automation* (Lisbon, Portugal, ETFA): 422-426.

[57] Fan, L., Chen Z. and Zhao, C. (2011) The analysis of Clock Synchronization Protocol on Ethernet. In *Proceedings of the International Conference Remote Sensing, Environment and Transportation Engineering* (Nanjing, China, RSETE), 826-829.

[58] Steiner, W. (2008) *TTEthernet Specication* TTTech Computertechnik AG, SchÄŭnbrunner Strasse 7, 1040 Vienna, Austria, 0.9.1 edition.

[59] GPS Web Site. `http://www.gps.gov` (accessed on 30 November 2015).

[60] GLONASS Web Site. `http://www.glonass-ianc.rsa.ru` (accessed on 30 November 2015).

[61] GALILEO Web Site. `http://ec.europa.eu/growth/sectors/space/galileo/index_en.htm` (accessed on 30 November 2015).

[62] Olifati-Saber, R., Fax, J.A. and Murray, R.M. (2007) Consensus and Cooperation in Networked Multi-Agent Systems. *Proc. IEEE* **95**(1): 215-233.

[63] Barbarossa, S. and Scutari, G. (2007) Decentralized maximum likelihood estimation for sensor networks composed of non-linearly coupled dynamical systems. *IEEE Trans. Signal Process* **55**(7): 3456-3470.

[64] Schenato, L. and Fiorentin, F. (2011) Average TimeSynch: A consensus based protocol for clock synchronization in wireless sensor networks. *Automatica* **47**: 1878-1886.

[65] Vaccaro, A. et al. (2015) A Self-Organizing Architecture for Decentralized Smart Microgrids Synchronization. *IEEE Trans. Ind. Informat.* **11**(1): 289-298.

[66] Rashid, M.H. (2013) *Control of Power Inverters in Renewable Energy and Smart Grid Integration* (J. Wiley& Sons Ltd Publication IEEE Press).

[67] Buccella, C., Cecati, C. and Latafat H. (2012) Digital Control of Power Converters-A Survey. *IEEE Trans. Ind. Informat.* **8**(3): 437-447.

[68] Texas Instruments. `http://www.ti.com/lsds/ti/microcontrollers_16-bit_32-bit/c2000_performance/control_automation/f28m3x/overview.page` (accessed on 28 November 2015).

[69] Giammatteo, P., Donato, D., Zlatić, V. and Caldarelli, G. (2010) A PageRank-based preferential attachment model for the evolution of the World Wide Web. *Euro Physics Letters* **91**(1): 18004.

[70] International Electrotechnical Commission. IEC WebStore. `https://webstore.iec.ch/home` (accessed on 25 August 2015).

[71] International Organization for Standardization. OSI Model ISO/IEC 7498-1. `http://standards.iso.org/ittf/licence.html` (accessed on 25 August 2015).

14

A Particle Swarm Optimization with Adaptive Multi-Swarm Strategy for Capacitated Vehicle Routing Problem[*]

Kui-Ting Chen[1,*], Ke Fan[2], Yijun Dai[2] and Takaaki Baba[2]

[1]Research Center and [2]Graduate School of Information, Production and Systems, Waseda University, 2-7 Hibikino, Kitakyushu, Fukuoka, Japan

Abstract

Capacitated vehicle routing problem with pickups and deliveries (CVRPPD) is one of the most challenging combinatorial optimization problems which include goods delivery/pickup optimization, vehicle number optimization, routing path optimization and transportation cost minimization. The conventional particle swarm optimization (PSO) is difficult to find an optimal solution of the CVRPPD due to its simple search strategy. A PSO with adaptive multi-swarm strategy (AMSPSO) is proposed to solve the CVRPPD in this paper. The proposed AMSPSO employs multiple PSO algorithms and an adaptive algorithm with punishment mechanism to search the optimal solution, which can deal with large-scale optimization problems. The simulation results prove that the proposed AMSPSO can solve the CVRPPD with the least number of vehicles and less transportation cost, simultaneously.

Keywords: multi-swarm, particle swarm optimization, vehicle routing problem, adaptive algorithm

1. Introduction

Particle swarm optimization (PSO) is a powerful algorithm for finding an optimal solution in nonlinear search space. The PSO algorithm has been widely used in many applications. The main advantages of PSO algorithm are that it can produce excellent results with a reasonable resource cost and easy to be implemented in software [1]. However, the conventional PSO algorithm is difficult to be employed into combinatorial optimization problems such as capacitated vehicle routing problem with pickups and deliveries (CVRPPD) [2]. It includes several optimization subjects which are goods delivery/pickup optimization, vehicle number optimization, routing path optimization and transportation cost minimization. It is quite difficult for conventional PSO algorithm to find an optimal solution to simultaneously meet the requirements of different optimization subjects due to its simple search strategy.

Capacitated vehicle routing problem (CVRP) is one of the most challenging combinatorial optimization problems, which was introduced by G. B. Dantzig and J. H. Ramser in 1959 [3]. It concerns the problem of the goods distribution between depot and customers, which aims to simultaneously minimize the transportation cost and the number of vehicles. The CVRPPD is an extension version of the classical CVRP, where customers may both receive and send goods with a fixed capacity of vehicles. In the CVRPPD, the combination of a possible solution set is much more than the CVRP, since the pickup derive has a huge impact on the routing optimization. For example, if the quantity of both the pickup and delivery is required 20, the maximum capacity of each vehicle is 100. As shown in Figure 1, a purple routing path is a classic solution for CVRP, in which the vehicle can deliver the goods to customers without exceeding the maximum capacity. In contrast, a red routing path is an impossible route for the CVRP, since the total quantity (120) of required

[*]This is the extended version of the paper published in INISCom 2015

*Corresponding author. Email: nore@aoni.waseda.jp

goods is over the capacity (100) of the vehicle for six customers. However, if a pickup service is required in the red routing path, it will become a possible solution even if there are seven customers. The pickup service drastically increases the number of the possible solutions. It becomes much more difficult to find the optimal solution in the CVRPPD.

In order to overcome the above difficulty, a PSO algorithm with adaptive multi-swarm strategy (AMSPSO) is proposed. It can provide an adaptive search behavior for dealing with large-scale optimization problems. The proposed approach divides a particle swarm into various small groups which cooperate with an adaptive algorithm. The each group of swarm employs different PSO algorithms which can provide different search abilities such as global search ability, local search ability and so on. The proposed approach exploits the adaptive algorithm to regulate the number of the swarm groups according to the current convergence status of the whole particle swarm, which can immediately optimize search strategy for PSO algorithm.

The rest of this paper is organized as follows. In section 2, the concept of PSO algorithm and CVRPPD are briefly introduced. In section 3, the details of the proposed multi-swarm strategy of PSO algorithm is presented. In section 4, the simulation results of the proposed and conventional approach are provided. In section 5, the contributions of the AMSPSO for existing industrial applications are discussed. Finally, section 6 comprises a summary and the conclusions of this research.

2. Related Works

2.1. Vehicle routing problem

In the definition of CVRPPD [2], every vehicle (k) has a fixed cost of f, variable cost per distance unit g, capacity Q, and service duration limit D. Each customer (i) has a non-negative pickup quantity p_i, delivery quantity q_i, and a service time s_i. The optimal solution of the CVRPPD is a set of m routes, which must meet the requirement as follows

  (i) Each route starts and ends at the depot.

  (iii) Each customer (i) is visited once by one vehicle (k).

  (iii) The total load of vehicles does not exceed the capacity (Q) during the deliver and pickup.

  (iv) The total transportation time of each vehicle does not exceed a service duration limit D.

  (vi) The total cost (Z) is minimized.

The formulation of CVRPPD is given by [2]:

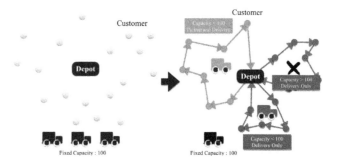

Figure 1. Concept of CVRPPD

$$\text{Minimize } Z = f \sum_{k=1}^{m} \sum_{j=1}^{n} x_{0jk} + g \sum_{i=0}^{n} \sum_{j=1}^{n+1} \sum_{k=1}^{m} d_{ji} x_{ijk} \quad (1)$$

Subject to

$$\sum_{i=0}^{n} \sum_{k=1}^{m} x_{ijk} = 1 \text{ for } 1 \le j \le n \quad (2)$$

$$\sum_{j=0}^{n} x_{ijk} = \sum_{j=1}^{m} x_{ijk} \text{ for } 1 \le j \le n, 1 \le k \le m \quad (3)$$

$$\sum_{j=1}^{n} x_{0jk} \le 1 \text{ for } 1 \le k \le m \quad (4)$$

$$\delta_{ik} + s_i + t_{i}j - \delta_{jk} \le (1 - x_{ijk})M$$
$$\text{for } 0 \le i \le n, 1 \le j \le n+1, 1 \le k \le m \quad (5)$$

$$\delta_{n+1,k} - \delta_{0k} \le D \text{ for } 1 \le k \le m \quad (6)$$

$$y_{ijk} \le x_{ijk} \text{ for } 0 \le i \le n, 1 \le j \le n+1, 1 \le k \le m \quad (7)$$

$$\sum_{y=1}^{n} y_{0jk} = \sum_{j=1}^{n} q_j \sum_{i=0}^{n} x_{ijk} \text{ for } 1 \le k \le m \quad (8)$$

$$\sum_{i=0}^{n} y_{ijk} + (p_j - q_j) \sum_{i=0}^{n} x_{ijk} = \sum_{i=1}^{n+1} y_{ijk} \quad (9)$$

$$\text{for } 1 \le j \le n, 1 \le k \le m$$

$$x \in \{0, 1\} \text{ for } 0 \le i \le n, 1 \le j \le n+1, 1 \le k \le m \quad (10)$$

$$y_{ijk} \ge 0 \text{ for } 0 \le i \le n, 1 \le j \le n+1, 1 \le k \le m \quad (11)$$

$$\delta_{ik} \ge 0 \text{ for } 1 \le j \le n+1, 1 \le k \le m \quad (12)$$

where n is the total number of the customers. m is the number of the total routing paths. x_{ijk} represents that a binary variable indicating status of each path (i, j) is traversed by vehicle k. y_{ijk} is load capability of vehicle k while traversing path (i, j). $_{ik}$ is starting service time of customer i by vehicle k. d_{ij} and t_{ij} are a distance matrix and a travel time matrix, respectively. Equation (1) minimizes routing cost, which consists of transportation fixed cost and variable cost. Equations (2) and (3) ensure that every customer is visited by one vehicle exactly. Equations (5) and (6) define the relationship between service time (s_i) and travel time (t_{ij}). The total transpiration time of vehicle cannot exceed the duration limit D. Vehicle load constraints are explained in (7), (8) and (9). Each vehicle cannot over load the goods during the pickup and deliver. Equations (10), (11) and (12) state the domain of decision variables: all x_{ijk} are binary variables, y_{ijk} and $_{ik}$ are positive real variables [2].

2.2. PSO algorithm for vehicle routing problem

PSO is a stochastic optimization algorithm based on swarm intelligence, which was introduced by J. Kennedy and R. Eberhart in 1995 [4]. The basic operation of PSO algorithm is updating the position and velocity of particle to find an optimal solution. Each particle l has current velocity v_l and a personal best position p_{ld} which represents a possible solution of optimization space. Considering an d-dimensional evaluation function, the position and velocity of the particle l in $(t+1)^{th}$ iteration are updated by the following equations:

$$
\begin{aligned}
v_{ld}^{t+1} &= \omega * v_{ld}^t + c_1 * r_1(p_{ld} - x_{ld}^t) \\
&+ c_2 * r_2(p_{gd} - x_{ld}^t)
\end{aligned} \tag{13}
$$

$$
x_{ld}^{t+1} = v_{ld}^{t+1} + x_{ld}^t \tag{14}
$$

where r_1 and r_2 are uniformly random numbers in the range $[0,1]$, p_{gd} is the location of the particle when the best fitness value is obtained for the whole population, c_1 and c_2 are two acceleration constants, ω is called the inertia weight factor, and d is the number of dimensions in the search space.

In the conventional PSO algorithm, the position and velocity of particle are defined in (13) and (14), respectively. The values of position and velocity are represented by real number. However, most variables of the CVRPPD are represented by binary number as mentioned in previous section. In order to employ PSO algorithm into CVRPPD, the real number needs to encode/decode for representing the binary variables. Some encoding/decoding approaches are introduced in [5, 6].

T. J. Ai and V. Kachitvichyanukul proposed two different encoding/decoding approaches that are named SR-1 and SR-2 [5]. These two approaches transform the position and velocity of particle from real number to binary number. In the SR-1, they increased the dimension number of particle to represent n customers and m vehicles. The dimension number of particles is defined by $(n + 2m)$. In the SR-2, they transform a particle into the vehicle orientation points and the vehicle coverage radius. The dimension number of particles is defined

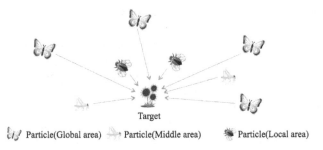

Target
Particle(Global area)   Particle(Middle area)   Particle(Local area)

Figure 2. Concept of the proposed PSO with multi-swarm

by $(3m)$. Their simulation results proved that SR-2 can produce better result than SR-1, since SR-1 leads to a larger number of particle's dimension than SR-2. In the comparison of calculation speed, the calculation speed of the SR-1 is much faster than SR-2. In addition, SR-1 is more suitable for dealing with CVRPPD, since SR-2 is difficult to take the requirements of customers into encoding/decoding procedure. However, it is difficult for the conventional PSO algorithm to find the optimal solution under $(n + 2m)$ dimension search space. In order to overcome this difficulty, the AMSPSO is proposed. The SR-1 is also employed in the proposed AMSPSO.

3. PSO with Adaptive Multi-Swarm Strategy

The proposed MSPSO divides particles into several groups, as illustrated in Figure 2. Each group employs the different PSO algorithms, which can maintain global search ability and local search ability. In addition, the search behavior of proposed algorithm is more similar to human society.

3.1. Multi-swarm strategy with mixed PSO

As shown in the Figure 2, the particles are divided into three groups as an example. One group is expert in the searching optimization solution on a global area, which employs quantum-behaved PSO (QPSO). Li et al. proved that QPSO is powerful on searching the optimal solution even if it is applied into a high dimensional search space [7]. The second group employs a PSO with random time-varying inertia weight and acceleration coefficients (PSO-RTVIWAC) which has a powerful searching ability on a local area [8]. The third one is PSO with passive congregation (PSOPC) which can help individuals to avoid misjudging information and becoming trapped by poor local optimal solution [9]. By employing the above PSO algorithms into different groups, the proposed approach cannot only prevent particles from converging on a local optimal solution, but also achieve powerful search ability on global and local area.

In this paper, different PSO algorithms are combined into generic equations based on the method which is

Table 1. The examples of particle motion coefficient for changing type of PSO

Type of PSO algorithm	Particle Motion Coefficients												
	sel_1	sel_2	sel_3	sel_4	sel_5	sel_6	sel_7	sel_8	sel_9	sel_{10}	sel_{11}	sel_{12}	sel_{13}
Original PSO [4]	1	0	1	1	0	0	0	0	0	1	2	2	0
PSO-RTVIWAC [8]	1	0	1	*	0	0	0	1	0	0	0	0	0
QPSO [7]	0	0	0	0	rand	$1-sel_5$	1	0	0	0	0	0	0
PSOPC [9]	1	1	1	1	0	0	0	1	0	0	0.5	0.5	*
Standard PSO [10]	cst.	0	1	1	0	0	0	0	0	0	0	0	0
PSO-TVIW [11]	1	0	1	1	0	0	0	1	0	0.4	2	2	0
PSO-TVAC [12]	1	0	1	1	0	0	0	0	0	0.9	c_{1min}	c_{2max}	0
PSO-RANDIW [13]	1	0	1	1	0	0	0	0	1	0.5	1.49	1.49	0
Gaussian PSO [14]	1	0	1	1	0	0	0	0	0	cst.	cst.	cst.	0

*:The value of the particle motion coefficient changes dynamically.
rand :A uniform random number [0,1].
cst. :A constant value.

introduced in [1]. The generic equations are given by

$$v_{ld}^{t+1} = sel_1 * [\omega * v_{ld}^t + c_1 * r_1(p_{ld} - x_{ld}^t)$$
$$+ c_2 * r_2(p_{gd} - x_{ld}^t)$$
$$+ sel_2 * c_3 * r_3(R_{gd}^t - x_{ld}^t)] \quad (15)$$

$$x_{ld}^{t+1} = sel_3 * x_{ld}^t + sel_4 * v_{ld}^{t+1} + sel_5 * p_{ld}$$
$$+ sel_6 * p_{gd}$$
$$\pm sel_7 * \beta * |mbest - x_{ld}^t| * \ln\left(\frac{1}{r_4}\right) \quad (16)$$

$$mbest = \sum_{i=1}^{N} \frac{P_{id}}{N} \quad (17)$$

where sel_1, sel_2, sel_3, sel_4, sel_5, sel_6 and sel_7 are the particle motion coefficients, other parameters have been defined in [1]. N is the population size of the particle swarm and $mbest$ is mean of the personal best position of all particles. The type of PSO algorithm can be changed by setting the values of particle motion coefficients, as presented in Table 1. The generic equation did not define the parameters (ω, β, c_1, c_2 and c_3) of PSO algorithm. In order to provide the better search performance of PSO algorithm, new calculation equation of ω, β, c_1, c_2 and c_3 are given by:

$$\omega = sel_8 * r_5 * (\omega_{max} - t * (\omega_{max} - \omega_{min})/T)$$
$$+ sel_9 * \frac{r_6}{2} + sel_{10} \quad (18)$$

$$c_1 = r_7 * (c_{1max} - \frac{t * (c_{1max} - c_{1min})}{T}) + sel_{11} \quad (19)$$

$$c_2 = r_8 * (c_{2max} - \frac{t * (c_{2max} - c_{2min})}{T}) + sel_{12} \quad (20)$$

$$c_3 = r_9 * (c_{3max} - \frac{t * (c_{3max} - c_{3min})}{T}) + sel_{13} \quad (21)$$

where t is the current iteration times, T is the maximal iteration times. The examples of particle motion coefficient for changing type of PSO algorithm are shown in Table 1.

3.2. Adaptive multi-swarm strategy

In the proposed approach, the particle swarm is divided into three groups to maintain the global search and local search ability. However, the particle number of each group cannot be a fixed value, since the global search ability has a huge impact on the early stage of the iterations. In contrast, the local search ability plays an important role during the later stage. Therefore, an appropriate regulation of the particle number can drastically improve the performance of the proposed approach.

Punishment mechanism. In order to figure out the appropriate regulation, an adaptive algorithm with punishment mechanism is proposed in this section. The adaptive algorithm aims to find the best combination of the particle numbers for each group. It exploits the punishment mechanism to arbitrate all the swarm groups for the current convergence status. Meanwhile, the punishment mechanism increases/decreases particle number of the swarm groups. The punishment mechanism makes swarm groups compete with each other, which is like resource plunder in human society. The winner can plunder most resources in the whole society. It means that the particle number of each swarm group is going to be increased or decreased which is based on its search performance. The search performance of all swarm groups has to be evaluated until all iterations is finished. In the beginning of the iterations, the punishment mechanism assigns the same particle number to each swarm group with a same credibility which is used for evaluating its search performance. The higher credibility can win more number of particles from other groups to assign into its swarm group.

Search performance evolution with credibility. The credibility of each swarm group is a counting value when global best(p_{gd}) is updated by the own particles. The equation of credibility ($Credi$) is given by

$$Credi_\varphi^{t+1} = Credi_\varphi^t + t * reward + 1 \qquad (22)$$

where φ is the number of swarm group. t is the current iteration times. $reward$ is an additional reward for updating the global best during the iteration. The additional reward is used to encourage the swarm group when it can produce better global best during searching procedure. Considering the global best is very easy to be updated during the early iterations, the additional reward is proportional to the number of iterations.

The punishment mechanism ranks the credibility of each swarm group with a fixed iteration cycle named punishment cycles. For example, the punishment mechanism calculates the credibility of each swarm groups at each 25 iteration times. The total particle number of whole groups is 50. The ranking credibility at first place (Group 1) can assign 2 particles into its group. The particle number of the second place (Group 2) is not changed. The particle number of the third group (Group 3) is deceased 2 particles. To prevent number of the swarm groups decrease to zero, the particle number of each group must to keep a fixed minimum value (P_{min}). Once the particle number of third group reaches P_{min}, Group 1 can get 2 particles from the Group 2. After the particle number of each swarm groups is reassigned, the credibility of each swarm group is reassessed by punishment mechanism to avoid that one group possess a great number of particles.

Credibility reassessing. In the (22), the additional reward is proportional to the number of iterations. However, it still cannot stop the Group A to rapidly accumulate the credibility in the early iterations. It leads to Group C never win the first place of the ranking credibility. In the punishment cycles, the value of the credibility is reassessed by

$$Credi_\varphi^{t+1} = Credi_\varphi^t * \left(1 - \frac{P_\varphi}{P_{total}}\right) \qquad (23)$$

where P_φ is assigned particle number of its swarm group. P_{total} is the population size of whole swarm groups. Equation (23) can drastically decrease the credibility of the winner group when its search performance is not good enough. The proposed AMSPSO employs the punishment mechanism which can regulate the search strategy with considering the convergence status of all particles. The above proposed approaches are evaluated in CVRPPD.

4. Simulation Results

The proposed AMSPSO algorithm is implemented by C# language with using Microsoft Visual Studio 2013

Table 2. Summary of simulation parameters

Parameters	Values
Number of particle	50
Number of iteration	500
Punishment cycles	25 iterations
Type of PSO algorithm	QPSO, PSO-RTVIWAC, PSOPC
PSO paramenters	$\omega = 0.4$ to 0.9, $\beta = 0.4$ to 0.9, $c_{min} = 0.5$, $c_{max} = 2.5$, $reward = 0.004$, $P_{min} = 10$
Particle motion coefficient (sel_4)	0.171 to 1.0 (PSO-RTVIWAC)

Table 3. Parameters of CMT instances

Instances (T, Q, H)	Capacity of Vehicle (Q)	Service Time Limit (D)	Service Time (s_i)
CMT1	160	∞	0
CMT2	140	∞	0
CMT3	200	∞	0
CMT4	200	∞	0
CMT5	200	∞	0
CMT6	160	200	10
CMT7	140	160	10
CMT8	200	230	10
CMT9	200	200	10
CMT10	200	200	10
CMT11	200	∞	0
CMT12	200	∞	0
CMT13	200	720	50
CMT14	200	1040	90

(.Net Framework 4.5) on a PC with Intel Core i7 3.6 GHz and 32 GB RAM. Three sets of benchmark instance data (CMT1 to CMT14) which are named CMTnT, CMTnQ and CMTnH [15]. The pickup ratio of the three sets is referred to 10% (CMTnT), 25% (CMTnQ) and 50% (CMTnH). In our previous research [16, 17], a performance analysis has been carried out by using CMTnT. In this paper, some parameters are changed to further evaluate the performance of the proposed AMSPSO. The required parameters of the simulation are shown in Table 2. The parameters of each benchmark instance are shown in Table 3.

In the CMT1 to CMT5 and CMT11 to CMT12, the vehicle can deliver/pickup the goods to customers without considering the service time limitation during the transportation, since the transportation time of the

Table 4. Simulation results of CMTnT

Benchmark Instances	Customer Numbers	Best Solution of Conventional PSO [2]		Best Solution of AMSPSO		Improve Ratio (%)
		No. of Vehicles	Total Cost (Z)	No. of Vehicles	Total Cost (Z^*)	
CMT1T	50	5	520	5	520	0.00%
CMT2T	75	9	810	9	794	1.98%
CMT3T	100	7	827	7	807	2.54%
CMT4T	150	11	1014	11	1014	0.00%
CMT5T	199	15	1297	15	1296	0.08%
CMT6T	50	6	555	6	555	0.00%
CMT7T	75	12	942	11	914	2.97%
CMT8T	100	9	904	9	876	3.10%
CMT9T	150	14	1206	14	1201	0.41%
CMT10T	199	18	1502	18	1470	2.13%
CMT11T	120	7	1026	7	1027	-0.10%
CMT12T	100	9	792	9	788	0.51%
CMT13T	120	11	1548	11	1556	-0.52%
CMT14T	100	10	846	10	848	-0.24%
Average Improve Ratio						**0.92%**

Table 5. Simulation results of CMTnQ

Benchmark Instances	Customer Numbers	Best Solution of Conventional PSO [2]		Best Solution of AMSPSO		Improve Ratio (%)
		No. of Vehicles	Total Cost (Z)	No. of Vehicles	Total Cost (Z^*)	
CMT1Q	50	4	490	4	489	0.20%
CMT2Q	75	8	739	8	734	0.68%
CMT3Q	100	6	768	6	753	1.95%
CMT4Q	150	9	938	9	921	1.81%
CMT5Q	199	13	1174	13	1162	1.02%
CMT6Q	50	6	557	6	555	0.36%
CMT7Q	75	12	933	11	904	3.11%
CMT8Q	100	9	890	9	869	2.36%
CMT9Q	150	14	1214	14	1191	1.89%
CMT10Q	199	18	1509	18	1444	4.31%
CMT11Q	120	6	964	6	972	-0.83%
CMT12Q	100	7	733	7	730	0.41%
CMT13Q	120	11	1570	11	1556	0.89%
CMT14Q	100	10	825	10	821	0.48%
Average Improve Ratio						**1.33%**

vehicle is infinite. In the CMT6 to CMT10 and CMT13 to CMT14, the transportation time of the vehicle is limited. The vehicles have to finish the deliver/pickup and return to the depot within the service duration limit (D), as shown in Table 3. In addition, each vehicle will spent 10 (CMT6 to CMT10), 50 (CMT13) or 90 (CMT14) limitation time to service a customer. Both of the fixed cost (f) and cost per distance unit (g) is set as 0 and 1, respectively. Each benchmark instance is executed 10 runs with 50 particles and 500 iteration times. The particle number of QPSO, PSO-RTVIWAC and PSOPC

is set by 17, 17 and 16, respectively. The AMSPSO is evaluated by the above benchmark instances and compared with the conventional PSO algorithm [2]. The all of the simulation environments are set same with [2]. The improve ratio (IR) is defined by

$$IR(\%) = \frac{Z^* - Z}{Z} * 100\% \qquad (24)$$

where Z^* is the total cost of AMSPSO. Z is the total cost of the conventional PSO algorithm. The simulation results are shown in Table 4, 5 and 6.

Table 6. Simulation results of CMTnH

Benchmark Instances	Customer Numbers	Best Solution of Conventional PSO [2]		Best Solution of AMSPSO		Improve Ratio (%)
		No. of Vehicles	*Total Cost* (Z)	*No. of Vehicles*	*Total Cost* (Z^*)	
CMT1H	50	3	464	3	461	0.65%
CMT2H	75	6	668	6	661	1.05%
CMT3H	100	4	701	4	697	0.57%
CMT4H	150	6	883	6	826	6.46%
CMT5H	199	9	1044	9	997	4.50%
CMT6H	50	6	557	6	556	0.18%
CMT7H	75	11	943	11	901	4.45%
CMT8H	100	9	899	9	869	3.34%
CMT9H	150	14	1207	14	1186	1.74%
CMT10H	199	19	1499	18	1441	3.87%
CMT11H	120	4	830	4	824	0.72%
CMT12H	100	5	635	5	628	1.10%
CMT13H	120	11	1565	11	1556	0.58%
CMT14H	100	10	824	10	821	0.36%
			Average Improve Ratio			2.11%

In most of the benchmark instances (CMTnT), the performance of the AMSPSO can produce a better results compared with the conventional PSO algorithm, even if the customer size is increased from 50 to 199. In the instance of CMT2T and CMT3T, the AMSPSO can respectively reduce the total cost by 1.98% and 2.54% within 500 iteration times which is 50% of the conventional approach. The average improve ratio of the CMTnT is about 0.92%. The simulation results prove that the proposed AMSPSO can realize the less cost than conventional PSO algorithm [2]. In addition, the AMSPSO can further reduce one vehicle usage for CMT7T. The conventional PSO algorithm needs 1,000 iteration times to achieve the same level results. In the other two instance sets (CMTnQ and CMTnH), the proposed AMSPSO can achieve better performance than the conventional PSO algorithm, even if pickup ratios are increased to 25% and 50%, as shown in Table 5 and 6. The average improve ratio can reach 1.33% and 2.11%, respectively. The vehicle usage of CMT7Q and CMT10H is also reduced by AMSPSO. The maximum improve ratio is 4.31% and 6.46% for CMTnQ and CMTnH, respectively. A simulation result of the particle number changes is illustrated on Figure 3. The QPSO (*GroupC*) is taken about the half of the total particle numbers, which means the search performance is much better than PSOPC (*GroupB*) and PSO-RTVIWAC (*GroupA*). However, the particle number of QPSO is decreased after 250 iteration times. It proved that proposed punishment mechanism successfully avoid the QPSO to accumulate its credibility for taking more particles into its own group. In the end of the iteration times, PSOPC and

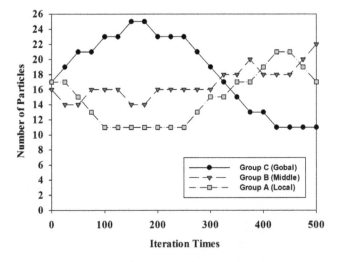

Figure 3. The simulation result of particle number changes

PSO-RTVIWAC performs well for searching a better solution on middle area and local area. This simulation result proves that the proposed adaptive multi-swarm strategy can let the multi-swarm group to compete with each other for producing a better performance.

The above simulation results prove that proposed AMSPSO can solve the VRPPD with less cost than conventional PSO algorithm. In addition, some new best known solutions of the benchmark instances are also found by the proposed AMSPSO.

5. Contributions to Existing Industrial Applications

The PSO algorithm is widely employed to deal with the optimization problem for industrial applications such as wireless sensor network [18], power system optimization [19], motor control [20], production scheduling [21] and so on. In the above, the PSO algorithm can produce a better performance than other conventional algorithms even if the problem space with high dimension. As a trade-off, the PSO algorithm is still time-consuming, since the PSO algorithm requires over several hundred iterative process to produce the better performance. The all of the above researches mentioned that once applying the PSO algorithm into real-time applications or real applications, the hardware implementation is highly required. However, it is very difficult to develop a generic PSO hardware to support various PSO applications, since the applications require different PSO algorithms to maintain its performance. Furthermore, the above mentioned applications require high adaptive capability for dynamic environment.

The proposed AMSPSO owns two features to meet the above requirements. The first feature is that the AMSPSO integrated nine different PSO into (15) to (21). The type of the PSO algorithm can be regulated by the particle motion coefficients. Compared with the conventional PSO algorithms, the hardware implement of AMSPSO can provide higher flexibility for various applications [22, 23]. In the [22, 23], the hardware implementation of AMSPSO can achieve twice processing speed compared with the hardware implementation of the conventional PSO algorithms. Another feature is the adaptive multi-swarm strategy which leads AMSPSO to provide very high adaptability for large-scale problem space or dynamic environment. AMSPSO exploits different PSO algorithms to cooperate with each others for preventing the particle swam from premature convergence as shown in section of simulation. The AMSPSO is expected to produce better performance for existing industrial applications based on the above two features.

6. Conclusions and Future Works

In this paper, a particle swarm optimization with adaptive multi-swarm strategy (AMSPSO) is proposed to solve a capacitated vehicle routing problem with pickups and deliveries (CVRPPD). The proposed AMSPSO employs the multiple PSO algorithms and an adaptive algorithm with punishment mechanism. The multiple PSO algorithms can simultaneously maintain the global and local search ability. The adaptive algorithm with punishment mechanism can drastically improve the performance of the multi-swarm strategy to reduce the iteration times. The proposed approaches can dynamically regulate the search strategy for dealing with large-scale optimization applications. The simulation results prove that the proposed AMSPSO can reduce 50% iteration times of the conventional

approach. The maximum improve ratios are 2.54%, 4.31% and 6.46% when the pickup ratios are 10%, 25% and 50%. In addition, the proposed adaptive multi-swarm strategy can let the multi-swarm groups to compete with each other for producing a better search performance. The AMSPSO can solve the CVRPPD with the less transportation cost. Furthermore, some new best known solutions of the benchmark problems are also found by the proposed AMSPSO. As the future work, the AMSPSO will compare with others similar approaches to further evaluate the performance under different kinds of VRP instances and real industrial applications. The parameter optimization of the AMSPSO will be carried out by different kinds of VRP instances.

Acknowledgement. This work was supported by Japan Society for the Promotion of Science (JSPS) Grant-in-Aid for Scientific Research (No. 26280017) and Grant-in-Aid for Young Scientists (No. 15K21435). The authors thank Yang Zeng, Ying Deng, Qi Liang, and Yu Zhang for their efforts to do the paper work in a very restricted time frame during the paper preparation.

References

[1] CHEN, K.-T., JIA, M., ZHANG, J. and BABA, T. (2012) A flexible hardware architecture for particle swarm optimization. *J. of Signal Process.* 16(6): 519-526. doi:10.2299/jsp.16.519

[2] AI, T.J. and KACHITVICHYANUKUL, V. (2009) A particle swarm optimization for the vehicle routing problem with simultaneous pickup and delivery. *Computers & Operations Research* 36(5): 1693-1702. doi:10.1016/j.cor.2008.04.003

[3] DANTZIG, G.B. and RAMSER, J.H. (1959) The truck dispatching problem. *Management science* 6(1): 80-91. doi:10.1287/mnsc.6.1.80

[4] KENNEDY, J. and EBERHART, R. (1995) Particle swarm optimization. In *Proceedings of IEEE Int. Conf. on Neural Networks* (Perth: IEEE), 1942-1948. doi:10.1109/ICNN.1995.488968

[5] AI, T.J. and KACHITVICHYANUKUL, V. (2009) Particle swarm optimization and two solution representations for solving the capacitated vehicle routing problem *Computers & Industrial Engineering* 56(1): 380-387. doi:10.1016/j.cie.2008.06.012

[6] WU, B., WANG, W., ZHAO, Y., XU, X. and YANG, F. (2006) A novel real number encoding method of particle swarm optimization for vehicle routing problem. In *Proceedings of the Sixth World Congress on Intelligent Control and Automation* (Dalian: IEEE), 3271-3275. doi:10.1109/WCICA.2006.1712972

[7] LIU, J., SUN, J. and XU, W. (2006) Improving quantum-behaved particle swarm optimization by simulated annealing. In *Proceedings of Int. Conf. on Intelligent Computing* (Kunming: Springer), 130-136. doi:10.1007/11816102_14

[8] ZHU, H., TANABE, Y. and BABA, T. (2008) A Random time-varying particle swarm optimization for

the real time location systems. *IEEJ Trans. on Electronics, Information and Systems* 128-C(12): 1747-1760. doi:10.1541/ieejeiss.128.1747

[9] HE, S., WU, Q.H., WEN, J.Y., SAUNDERS, J.R. and PATON, R.C. (2004). A particle swarm optimizer with passive congregation. *Biosystems* 78(1): 135-147. doi:10.1016/j.biosystems.2004.08.003

[10] BRATTON, D. and KENNEDY, J. (2007) Defining a standard for particle swarm optimization. In *Proceedings of Swarm Intelligence Symposium* (Honolulu: IEEE), 120-127. doi:10.1109/SIS.2007.368035

[11] SHI, Y. and EBERHART, R.C. (1999) Empirical study of particle swarm optimization. In *Proceedings of the 1999 Congress on Evolutionary Computation* (Washington: IEEE), 1945-1950. doi:10.1109/CEC.1999.785511

[12] RATNAWEERA, A., HALGAMUGE, S. and WATSON, H.C. (2004) Self-organizing hierarchical particle swarm optimizer with time-varying acceleration coefficients. *IEEE Trans. on Evolutionary Computation* 8(3): 240-255. doi:10.1109/TEVC.2004.826071

[13] EBERHART, R.C. and SHI, Y. (2001) Tracking and optimizing dynamic systems with particle swarms. In *Proceedings of the 2001 Congress on Evolutionary Computation* (Seoul: IEEE), 94-100. doi:10.1109/CEC.2001.934376

[14] KROHLING, R.A. (2004) Gaussian swarm: a novel particle swarm optimization algorithm. In *Proceedings of IEEE Conference on Cybernetics and Intelligent Systems* (Singapore: IEEE), 372-376. doi:10.1109/ICCIS.2004.1460443

[15] SALHI, S. and NAGY, G. (1999) A cluster insertion heuristic for single and multiple depot vehicle routing problems with backhauling. *J. of the Operational Research Society* 50(10): 1034-1042.

[16] CHEN, K.-T., DAI, Y., FAN, K. and BABA, T. (2015) Performance Analysis of AMSPSO on Capacitated Vehicle Routing Problem with Time Window. In *Proceedings of RISP Int. Workshop on Nonlinear Circuits and Signal Processing* (Kuala Lumpur:RISP), 334-337.

[17] CHEN, K.-T., DAI, Y., FAN, K. and BABA, T. (2015) A Particle Swarm Optimization with Adaptive Multi-Swarm Strategy for Capacitated Vehicle Routing Problem. In *Proceedings of the first Int. Conf. on Industrial Networks and Intelligent Systems* (Tokyo:EAI), (pp. to be appear).

[18] KULKARNI, R.V. and VENAYAGAMOORTHY, G.K. (2011) Particle Swarm Optimization in Wireless-Sensor Networks: A Brief Survey. *IEEE Trans. on Systems, Man, and Cybernetics, Part C: Applications and Reviews* 41(2): 262-267. doi:10.1109/TSMCC.2010.2054080

[19] DEL VALLE, Y., VENAYAGAMOORTHY, G.K., MOHAGHEGHI, S., HERNANDEZ, J.-C. and HARLEY, R.G. (2008) Particle Swarm Optimization: Basic Concepts, Variants and Applications in Power Systems. *IEEE Trans. on Evolutionary Computation* 12(2): 171-195. doi:10.1109/TEVC.2007.896686

[20] MU, S., TANAKA, K. and NAKASHIMA, S. (2013) Intelligent Control of Ultrasonic Motor Using PSO Type Neural Network. In *Proceeding of 14th ACIS Int. Conf. on Software Engineering, Artificial Intelligence, Networking and Parallel/Distributed Computing* (Honolulu: IEEE), 605-610. doi:10.1109/SNPD.2013.66

[21] TANG, L. and WANG, X. (2010) An Improved Particle Swarm Optimization Algorithm for the Hybrid Flowshop Scheduling to Minimize Total Weighted Completion Time in Process Industry. *IEEE Trans. on Control Systems Technology* 18(6): 1303-1314. doi:10.1109/TCST.2009.2036718

[22] FAN, K., CHEN, K.-T, WANG, P. and BABA, T. (2015) Two-level Pipeline Structure of Particle Swarm Optimization. In *Proceedings of RISP Int. Workshop on Nonlinear Circuits and Signal Processing* (Kuala Lumpur:RISP), 178-181.

[23] WANG, P., CHEN, K.-T., FAN, K. and BABA, T. (2015) A Hardware Implementation of Particle Swarm Optimization with Adaptive Multi-Swarm Strategy. In *Proceedings of RISP Int. Workshop on Nonlinear Circuits and Signal Processing* (Kuala Lumpur:RISP), 182-185.

15

GRAPP&S, a Peer-to-Peer Middleware for Interlinking and Sharing Educational Resources

Thierno Ahmadou Diallo[1,2,*], Olivier Flauzac[2], Luiz-Angelo Steffenel[2], Samba N'Diaye[1]

[1]Département d'Informatique, LMI, Université Cheikh Anta Diop, 5005 Dakar-Fann, Sénégal
[2]CReSTIC Laboratory - SYSCOM team, University of Reims Champagne-Ardenne, Reims, France

Abstract

This article presents GRAPP&S (Grid APPlication & Services), a specification of an E-learning architecture for the decentralized sharing of educational resources. By dealing with different resources such as files, data streams (video, audio, VoIP), queries on databases but also access to remote services (web services on a server, on a cloud, etc.), GRAPP&S groups the resources of each institution in the form of a community and allows sharing among different communities. Educational resources are managed on a transparent manner through proxies specific to each type of resources. The transparency provided by proxies concerns the location of sources of educational data, the processing of queries, the composition of the results and the management of educational data consistency. Furthermore, the architecture of GRAPP&S has been designed to allow security policies for data protection, both within a community and between different communities.

Keywords: E-learning, Peer-to-Peer, Prefix routing, Data proxies

1. Introduction

The pedagogical integration of information and communication technologies (ICTs) to all education degrees is promising way to improve the quality of African education systems. Online learning (E-learning) and mobile learning (M-learning) help not only to strength the planning and the management of a democratic and transparent education, but also to extend the access to learning, to improve quality and ensure inclusion.

Thanks to the opportunities they offer in terms of use or adaptation, in particular in environments where there are insufficient resources, free access educational resources constitute an excellent opportunity to achieve the goal of a education of quality for everyone. This is the first motivation of the project GRAPP&S. The objective of this project is to construct an E-learning architecture for sharing and decentralized management of all educational resources formats like files, streams (video, audio, VoIP) and resources from web services, cloud and distributed computing services. These resources are transparently presented to the user (student, teacher) thanks to the use of proxies adapters tailored for each educational resources.

Nowadays, it is very easy to share and learn using Internet. The Internet has contributed greatly to the education system by introducing the concept of E-learning. The latter is now accepted in the various educational institutions to improve the learning process for students and teachers or administrators. An important characteristic of E-learning systems is the sharing and use of educational resources.

Although most of E-learning repositories give free access to their repositories of educational resources, the integration process is still costly [5] as most learning repositories [6, 19] rely on different standards to access the resources [4]. Furthermore, several systems rely nowadays on storage facilities on the cloud, which poses a problem to remote localities due to the access speed.

Therefore, an intuitive approach is to regroup different local learning repositories from each institutes (schools, universities, repositories of research laboratories, etc.) in a "Community", which can foster the aims of reusing and sharing educational resources without costly duplicating them into local learning repositories. Through the use of communities, we can promote the goals of reuse and sharing educational resources. By extending the coverage to different educational resources (files, videos, data in a database, even a video stream for example when subscribing to TV channel for learning languages), we can integrate all tools to improve education in a single infrastructure, with a smaller cost. Following this approach, two major research challenges must be considered to ensure interoperability across the Web:

1. Compatibility between systems: if today most APIs (Dropbox, Google Drive, etc.) allow to handle simple files, it is less clear how to integrate complex data such as queries on a database, data streams or web services.

2. Decentralized data management: most platforms are migrating to the cloud, but at the expense of losing its proximity to the consumers, as well as poor access speed and privacy threats.

From these elements, we present GRAPP&S, an architecture designed to connect institutes interested on sharing educational data sources through the network. GRAPP&S brings therefore:

- a decentralized solution for sharing all types of educational resources, not only files (text/xml) but also databases, streams (video, audio), and resources from remote services such as web services and distributed computing, all integrated through the use of data proxies;

- a simpler way to connect a large number of institutes interested into resource sharing. This is obtained through the aggregation of resources from each educational institute in the form of a "community". This will allow quick access to resources due to the proximity to consumers, unlike most of the E-learning solutions based on cloud storage when consumers are penalized because of the slow access speed;

- an access to resources GRAPP&S independent from direct interconnection between nodes. In GRAPP&S, it is always possible to route data transfer by the inverse of the path used during the search.

- the possibility to define security policies for the protection of educational resources within a community, and access policies between different communities through the establishment of *Service-Level Agreements (SLAs)*;

The remaining sections of the paper cover: Section 2 discusses the related work. Section 3 presents an overview of GRAPP&S architecture and describes the elements of this architecture, while Section 4 describes the lookup algorithm used to locate resources inside GRAPP&S. Finally, Section 5 concludes this paper.

2. Related Work

2.1. E-learning Systems

Because GRAPP&S aims at the decentralized management of resources, it seems natural to identify peer-to-peer (P2P) works in this area. Indeed, an architecture for sharing educational resources among different learning institutions is proposed in [4]. This architecture, called LOP2P, aims at helping different educational institutions to create course material by using shared educational resource repositories. Nonetheless, resources of different formats cannot be easily integrated in this platform. Similarly, [9] develops a P2P based E-learning system that uses the video for learning. This system divides multimedia data into fragments managed by assigned agents, and this system allows the sharing of multimedia data, but it cannot deal with other data types.

Several E-learning systems based on cloud are being proposed, like [12] or [2]. In [12], an E-learning ecosystem based on cloud computing and Web 2.0 technologies is presented, and the article analyses the services provided by public cloud computing environments such as Google App Engine, Amazon Elastic Compute Cloud (EC2) or Windows Azure. It also highlights the advantages of deploying E-Learning 2.0 applications for such an infrastructures, and identify the benefits of cloud-based E-Learning 2.0 applications (scalability, feasibility, or availability) and underlined the enhancements regarding the cost and risk management. In addition, [2] is used to run web 2.0 applications, such as video teleconferencing, voice over IP, and remote management, over handheld devices and terminals. As it is targeted towards military usage, the work from [2] has a multi-level security and the network infrastructure is encrypted.

It is quite evident that the cloud-based system would help the educational institutes or universities to share and disseminate knowledge among students, teachers and researchers, but the use of Cloud Computing in the educational system presents many risks and limitations: not all applications run in cloud, there are risks related to data protection, security and accounts management. Also, the access speed to cloud infrastructures may be a critical factor, amplified by the lack of a stable Internet connection that may affect the work methods in some isolated areas.

2.2. Routing in Peer to Peer Systems

Resources in a P2P system are distributed among all peers. These resources must first be searched and located in order to access it. These resources are identified by a key and depending on how a P2P system searches for resources using these keys, and by the relationship between the key and the peer, the type of P2P system is defined differently.

In unstructured P2P Gnutella [8] example uses a method of flood routing queries rather than to a specific node. To return a response to a search query, Gnutella allows direct response back to the requesting node if possible (firewall could prevent such an item). Otherwise, the answer may come back along the path traversed by the query. However, because of the flood search algorithm is limited to the scale. Systems like KaZaA [15], Gnutella [11] have implemented a partial unstructured P2P, where supernodes concentrate metadata about the surrounding nodes and therefore can be asked before a flooding research, minimize the impact on the network.

Structured P2P networks Chord [16], Pastry [14] are based on DHT (*Distributed Hash Table*). Resource lookup works with a a peer p sending a request for a key k, p to one of its neighbors with the ID closest to k. Each peer receiving the request to repeat the same operation until the peer responsible for k is reached by the query.

All structured P2P network and unstructured are all horizontal design without hierarchical routing. All peers are identical in the sense that all peers use the same rules to determine the routing of a query. This approach is very different from that of the Internet, where the hierarchical routing is used. Hence, Kleinrock *et al.* [10] and *Peng et al.* [13] proposed the hierarchical routing to reduce the routing information in large scale networks. This technique consists on each node keepin a complete routing information for a set of closest nodes.

Bakker *et al.* [1] introduced the routing prefixes to minimize the routing information in dynamic networks. The idea of routing prefix is to assign each node n a label $\alpha(n)$, which is a word over an alphabet Σ containing at least two symbols. Each link is also labeled with a word Σ^* is a prefix of some labels of nodes. A message to then node n is transmitted on the link whose label is the longest prefix $\alpha(n)$. These authors demonstrated that any network admits a routing prefix and propose a method of constructing functions routing prefixes.

3. The GRAPP&S Architecture

The GRAPP&S framework is an E-learning solution for the decentralized sharing all types of resources. As stated before, our main objective is to propose a resource sharing middleware to support E-learning tools and applications that allies both flexibility, security and performance on remote locations. We observe indeed that current sharing tools tend to externalize data (on a dedicated server or in the cloud), but this solution is not adapted to remote locations whose computational resources are limited and the access speeds are reduced. To circumvent these limitations we to propose an alternative architecture inspired on the grid environments, where individual resources are gathered and shared among the grid members.

By relying on the GRAPP&S framework, we allow pooling of data from each institution in the form of community, and allow different communities to share resources based on predefined access rules. For this reason, GRAPP&S can also be extended to other areas of the school, by creating a community in the administrative part, separated from the education part, with safety rules and resource protection. GRAPP&S also allows a flexible deployment of its components, adapting therefore to the capacity of the computing nodes. Finally, the data proxy abstraction that composes the framework leafs (see the Data Manager component below) allow the integration of different data sources, making therefore GRAPP&S an unified resource sharing platform.

In the following sections, we present the different elements of our framework GRAPP&S for the decentralized sharing of educational resources.

3.1. Model

We consider a model of communication represented by an undirected and connected graph $G = (V, E)$, where V denotes the set of nodes in the system and E denotes the set of communication links between nodes [3]. Two nodes u and v are said to be adjacent or neighbors if and only if u, v is a communication link of G. $u_i, v_j \in E$ is a bidirectional channel connected to port i for u and to port j for v. Thus nodes u and v can mutually send and receive messages. Nodes communicate by using asynchronous messages.

A message m in transit is denoted $m(id(u), m', id(v))$ where $id(u)$ is the identifier of the node that sends the message, $id(v)$ is the identifier of the receiving node and, m' the message content. Each node u of the system has a unique id and has two primitives: **send(message)** and **receive(message)**.

3.2. Nodes of GRAPP&S

In order to present our architecture, we introduce some notations first. A community (C_i) is an autonomous entity, which includes educative resources sharing some properties: same location (resources institute, university, research laboratory), same administration authority, or same application domain (administrative resources vs teaching resources). A community contains one communicator process noted (c) and at least one *Resource Manager* process noted RM and one process *Data Manager* noted DM and these processes are hierarchically organized in the Community.

Communicator(c). nodes play an essential role that is related to information transmission and interconnection between different communities, such as when passing messages through firewalls. A Communicator is the community entry point and assures its security towards the outside, through establishment of *Service-Level Agreements (SLAs)* with other communities. The communicator also defines the security rules (access) for the protection of educational resources inside the community (for example the administration community can see the data on the educational system, but not the reverse, thanks to this access rules defined by the communicator).

Resource Manager(*RM*). processes ensure indexing and organization of educational resources in the community. The RM_i processes are involved in the search and indexing of data in the community c_i, and by receiving queries from its neighbors communities. Given the important role of *RM* processes in research and indexing of resources, we choose a *RM* among ordinary nodes that have good performance levels in both CPU, memory size and communication speed.

Data Manager(*DM*). processes interact with sources of educational data such as databases, file, email servers, WebDAV servers, FTP servers, disks, or cloud services. A DM node is a service that has the following components (see Figure 1):

- a proxy interface adapted to the various formats of educational data,

- a query manager that allows to express queries on local or global educational resources, and

- a communications manager that allows the DM node to communicate with the RM node to which it is connected.

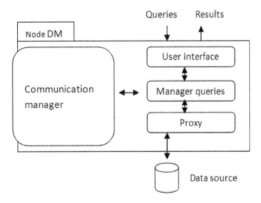

Figure 1. DM node architecture

3.3. Management of the Community

GRAPP&S can be deployed in several ways, depending on the placement of the nodes. For example, we can find the following deployment topologies;

1. nodes can be grouped into a single physical machine (see Figure 2a). This is an example of a machine of a teacher who wants to host a resource server and set different access rights to the users. With this organization, users from

other communities (see Figure 4) depend on inter-community SLAs to access the server data. An example of inter-community lookup and transfer is presented later in the next sections.

2. the nodes are organized in a server farm such as a cluster, which is characteristic of an HPC network or a classroom (Figure 2b). In this case, different nodes belong to the community and present different behaviors. Some of the nodes may act as data servers, while others act as clients. As in the previous item, inter-community SLAs can be defined to give access to nodes from other communities.

3. nodes can be distributed over different machines, which corresponds to a grouping of educational resources in a university or a school with remote sites. These resources share the same administration entity (see Figure 2c). This allows a better scaling of the resources and integration of several data sources, as well as clients.

These scenarios correspond to typical environments found on educational organizations. The nodes arrangement will depend on several factors such as storage capacity and computing power of the devices, as well as the security policies that must be implemented. While special access rights can always be implemented in a per-DataManager basis, we consider that nodes inside a community are considered to have full access to its resources, and that inter-community SLAs implement the access policies.

3.4. Hierarchical Addressing Nodes on GRAPP&S

In order to correctly identify each resource inside a GRAPP&S community (and between different communities), each node on GRAPP&S needs its own unique identifier (ID). The IP or the MAC addresses are not sufficiently accurate because they do not identify uniquely different nodes that can reside on a same machine (eg RM and DM). Thus, we rely on the identification method proposed by JXTA [18], which uses a string of 128 bits. Each node has a unique string $ID - local$, in the form $"urn : name - community : uuid : string - of - bit"$. As GRAPP&S is hierarchically structured, the expression of hierarchical addressing is done by concatenating the IDs as a prefix, i.e., ID c_i node is equivalent to its $ID - local$, the node ID is formed by RM_i ID-c_i/ID-RM_i, and DM_i node ID has the form ID-c_i/ID-RM_i/ID-DM_i.

An advantage of using an addressing model specific to GRAPP&S is that it is independent of the overlay network addressing model that is implemented. Indeed, Figure 3 presents an illustration of GRAPP&S implemented over the Pastry P2P middleware. Thus,

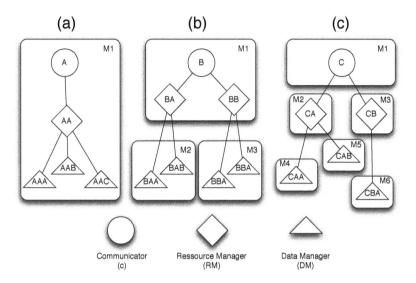

Figure 2. Organization of the nodes in a machine (a), in a cluster (b) and in a network (c)

two communities GRAPP&S implemented on different middleware can still be compatible, once the connection is established between their communicators.

The other advantage of hierarchical addressing scheme is to allow easy up structure GRAPP&S, defining the pathways by which transit requests. This will prevent flooding the network links.

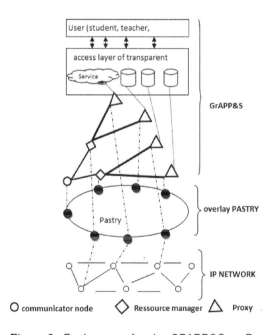

Figure 3. Deployment of nodes GRAPP&S on Pastry

4. Accessing the Resources

A GRAPP&S community is an hierarchical network with an addressing system independent from the underlying network. This addressing scheme is used to help data lookup and also to help route data during transfers. This hierarchical addressing also simplifies the integration to another network community. In the following paragraphs, we will propose a routing algorithm and a method of data lookup in our system.

4.1. Routing Algorithm

Let T be the tree of a community GRAPP&S. Thanks to the results of Fraigniaud *et al.* [7]; Thorup *et al.* [17] we can construct a routing scheme in the tree T.

Let T be a tree and a numbering of the vertices of T following a DFS [7] in the tree. For each vertex X identifier Id_X address of X consists of the binary string representing Id_X concatenated by the binary strings of parent vertices of X in T. The address of each vertex X is represented by a binary string $PATH\_X$ more than 3 bytes and an integer $Lpath\_X$ is the length of the chain.

For any vertex X of T:

Let $mask\_F$ the mask constituted by a binary string $Lpath_X+8$ bits including $Lpath\_X$ first bits are all 0 and the last 8 bits are 1 (e.g.: for a vertex X as $Lpath\_X= 16$, the mask will $mask\_X= 00000000. 00000000. 11111111$).

If Y is a descendant of X in T, then $PATH\_X$ is a substring of $PATH\_Y$ and applying a logical AND between $mask\_X = 00000000. 00000000. 11111111$ and $PATH\_Y$ was number Y.

If Y is not a descendant of X in T, then it must go through the father of X to go to Y.

Let $is\_parent(X, Y)$ the function for any pair of vertex returns TRUE or FALSE depending on whether X is the parent of Y in the tree T or not.

The shipping method in our hierarchical system is modeled after [1]. The basic routing algorithm (see Algorithm 1) allows the transmission of messages between two vertices knowing the identifier of the source node and the destination node.

```
m : message sent from a source node to the destination node;
source : source node;
destination : destination node;
add : address of a node;
Procedure Route(m,source, destination)
    If (areNeighbors(source, destination)) then
        add ← getAdd(destination);
        send(m, add);
    else
        If (is_Parent(source, destination)) then
            add ←getAdd(mask_source AND destination);
            send (m, add);
        else
            add ← getAdd(father(source));
            send(m, Add);
            source ← add;
            Route (m, source, destination);
        end If
    end If
End
```

Algorithm 1: Basic forwarding method

4.2. Research Data in GRAPP&S

Among main functionalities on GRAPP&S there exists research and data access. This section describes our data search algorithm in a community GRAPP&S. The nodes that intervenes in this research has a few primitives:

- *Route_request* allows a source node to send a request to a destination node. *Route_request* uses the function *Route()* (cf. Algorithm 1) to send the message m so its signature is *Route_request(m, source, destination)*.

- *Route_reply* allows to send a reply to m that follows the reverse path to the initiating node Message *Route_request*. The method *Route_reply* has almost the same structure as the *Route_request* function except that it does not use the same message in *Route_request*. The structure of the method *Route_reply* is *Route_reply(m', source, destination)*.

- *Route_RequestDirect*, enables a source node to send a message directly to the recipient, if the communication mechanism allows it.

- *Save()* allows a node receiving a message *Route_reply* to store it on a non-volatile support(for example a file on the hard-drive, on Dropbox, on Gmail etc.).

When a customer searches any data on GRAPP&S, it contacts a DM_i proxy that sends a request Y containing the characteristics of the data. This research is conducted in steps so as to respect the hierarchical organization of the network, as follows:

- $DM_i \in C_i$ sends its request Y to node $RM_i \in C_i$ through *Route_request()* (cf. Algorithm 1);

- RM_i uses the method *Verif_of_RM_i()* (cf. Algorithm 2) to check on its index if among his neighbors there is at least a DM that contains the requested information, thanks to the *Local_Search()* function (cf. Algorithm 3).

  - If yes, then the node RM_i returns to node DM_i a list of nodes DM that contain the requested information. An example is shown in Figure 4 where the node RM_i identifies id(RM_i)=AA and returns a list of nodes DM to the node Id(DM_i)=AAA.

  - Otherwise, the RM_i node forwards the request to the node $c_i \in C_i$ for broadcasting to all other nodes $RM_k \in C_i$ such that $RM_k \neq RM_i$ (cf. Algorithm 4). Figure 4 illustrates this distribution, where the node RM_i identifier $id(AA)$ forwards the request to its c_i identifier $id(A)$ for a broadcast to other nodes RM_k ($id(AB)$, $id(BA)$ and $id(BB)$).

- When a node $RM_k \in C_i$ finds a match for the searched information, it sends back an answere to sender node DM_i following the reverse path through *Route_reply()* function (cf. Algorithm 1). This is illustrated in Figure 4 where RM_k node identifier $id(BB)$ responds to the node DM_i identifier $id(AAA)$ taking the opposite route.

- If the requested data is not available in the community C_i, then c_i node may forward the request to other communities C_j. This is illustrated in Figure 4 where c_i node identifier $id(A)$ forwards the search request to the community C_j of node c_j with the specified $id(c_j)$ B.

4.3. Data Transfer in GRAPP&S

If successful in the search, the customer gets the node identifier DM_x responsible for the data. In this case, there are two possibilities for contacting DM_x and retrieve the data: using a direct connection or using a routed connection.

In the case of direct connections, the customer sends the request directly to DM_x by a simple *Send()* call (cf. Algorithm 6) in order to access the data. The customer can view or store the data with the *save()* function. In case this direct connection is not possible, then the data transfer is done by hierarchical routing in GRAPP&S,

based on the prefixes of identifiers of nodes to back up the hierarchy.

The steps in this routing prefix are as follows:

1. the customer sends a request Y $(m, id (DM_i), id(DM_x))$ to its RM_i, which forwards the request to the node communicator c_i;

2. using prefixed routing, node c_i sends the request Y to the RM node that has indexed the data. Using the same prefixed routing, the RM forwards the request to the node DM_x responsible for the data;

3. once the data is found on DM_x, it is sent back with the function $Route\_reply(m', id(DM_x), id(DM_i))$, returning the correct answer to DM_i through the prefixed tree.

```
Index_of_RM[0...n] : index node RM;
X ←{} : list of nodes DM;
TypeMime : mime type information;
TypeMimeRec : search term;
Function Verif_of_RM(TypeMimeRec) : X ←{}
    For (i from 0 to n) do
        [ If (Index_of_RM[i].TypeMime=TypeMimeRec ) then
            X₁ ← DMᵢ;

        end If
        ]
    end For
    return X;
End
```

Algorithm 2: Checking indexes RM

```
Procedure Local_Search()
    If (RM.Verif_of_RM()≠ empty) then
        Route(m', source, destination);

    end If

End
```

Algorithm 3: Local Search

```
For (each neighbor RMₖ of cᵢ such as RMₖ ≠ RMᵢ) do
    [ Route_request(m, source, destination) ]
end For

For (each neighbor RMₖ of cᵢ such as RMₖ ≠ RMᵢ) do
    [ If ( RMₖ.Verif_of_RM() ≠ empty ) then
        Route_reply(m', source, destination);

    end If
    ]
end For
```

Algorithm 4: Broadcasting message to nodes RMs

```
Function CanReach(source, destination) : boolean
    If (connect_direct(source, destination) is possible) then
        return True;

    else
        return False;
    end If
End
```

Algorithm 5: Method CanReach()

```
m : message sent from a source node to the destination node;
source : source node;
destination : destination node;
Procedure Get()
    If (CanReach(source, destination)=True) then
        send_RequestDirect(m, source, destination);
        send_reply(m', source, destination);
        source.save();
    else
        send message through route();
        Route_request(m, source, destination);
        resend message through route();
        Route_reply(m', source, destination);

    end If
    source.save();
End
```

Algorithm 6: Getting data in GRAPP&S

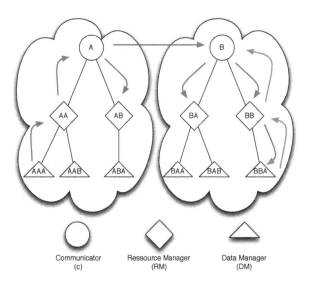

Figure 4. Resource lookup in a routing GRAPP&S

5. Conclusions

In this article we present an E-learning architecture specification named GRAPP&S, which is a decentralized solution for managing and sharing educational resources. GRAPP&S has been constructed as an hierarchical network to allows a pooling resources of each institute under the concept of "community", and to take advantage of the proximity of data and the users (students, teachers, administrative, etc.). One can even extend the use of a community of GRAPP&S to other sectors of an institute such as a community just for the administrative departments, separated from the educational users. In addition, GRAPP&S uses security rules to protect the resources of each community, and defines access policies between different community. The use of proxies for each specific type of data allows sharing a transparent manner not only files but also databases, streams (video, audio, VoIP), resources from the web services, cloud services, distributed computing.

The next step towards the validation of this specification is its use under real situations. We are starting to develop a prototype of GRAPP&S that will be used for testing and deployment on educational institutions. This prototype uses P2P Pastry underlying network to distribute the nodes of a community (local network institution) of GRAPP&S as illustrated in Figure 3. The choice of Pastry allows a community GRAPP&S a P2P network, which will allow a community institute include a large number of nodes and to perform scaling tests.

References

[1] BAKKER, E.M., VAN LEEUWEN, J. and TAN, R.B. (1993) Prefix routing schemes in dynamic networks. *Computer Networks and ISDN Systems* **26**(4): 403–421.

[2] CAYIRCI, E., RONG, C., HUISKAMP, W. and VERKOELEN, C. (2009) Snow leopard cloud: a multi-national education training and experimentation cloud and its security challenges. In *Cloud Computing* (Springer), 57–68.

[3] CHALOPIN, J., GODARD, E., MÉTIVIER, Y. and OSSAMY, R. (2006) Mobile agent algorithms versus message passing algorithms. In *Principle of distributed systems* (France: Springer), **4305**: 185–199.

[4] DE SANTIAGO, R. and RAABE, A. (2010) Architecture for learning objects sharing among learning institution-sâĂĪlop2p. *Learning Technologies, IEEE Transactions on* **3**(2): 91–95.

[5] DIETZE, S., YU, H.Q., GIORDANO, D., KALDOUDI, E., DOVROLIS, N. and TAIBI, D. (2012) Linked education: interlinking educational resources and the web of data. In *Proceedings of the 27th Annual ACM Symposium on Applied Computing* (ACM): 366–371.

[6] FARDOUN, H.M., LOPEZ, S.R., ALGHAZZAWI, D.M. and CASTILLO, J.R. (2012) Education system in the cloud to improve student communication in the institutes of: C-learnixml++. *Procedia-Social and Behavioral Sciences* **47**: 1762–1769.

[7] FRAIGNIAUD, P. and GAVOILLE, C. (2001) Routing in trees. In *Automata, Languages and Programming* (Springer), 757–772.

[8] FRANKEL, J. and PEPPER, T. (2003) The gnutella protocol specification v0. 4.

[9] HAYAKAWA, T., HIGASHINO, M., TAKAHASHI, K., KAWAMURA, T. and SUGAHARA, K. (2012) Management of multimedia data for streaming on a distributed e-learning system (IEEE): 1282–1285.

[10] KLEINROCK, L. and KAMOUN, F. (1977) Hierarchical routing for large networks. *Computer Networks* **1**: 155–174.

[11] KLINGBERG, T. and MANFREDI, R. (2002) The gnutella protocol specification v0. 6. *Technical specification of the Protocol* .

[12] OUF, S., NASR, M. and HELMY, Y. (2010) An enhanced e-learning ecosystem based on an integration between cloud computing and web2. 0. In *Signal Processing and Information Technology (ISSPIT), 2010 IEEE International Symposium on* (IEEE): 48–55.

[13] PENG, Z., DUAN, Z., QI, J.J., CAO, Y. and LV, E. (2007) Hp2p: A hybrid hierarchical p2p network. In *Digital Society, 2007. ICDS'07. First International Conference on the* (IEEE): 18–18.

[14] ROWSTRON, A. and DRUSCHEL, P. (2001) Pastry: Scalable, decentralized object location, and routing for large-scale peer-to-peer systems. In *Middleware 2001* (Springer): 329–350.

[15] SHIN, S., JUNG, J. and BALAKRISHNAN, H. (2006) Malware prevalence in the kazaa file-sharing network. In *Proceedings of the 6th ACM SIGCOMM conference on Internet measurement* (ACM): 333–338.

[16] STOICA, I., MORRIS, R., KARGER, D., KAASHOEK, M.F. and BALAKRISHNAN, H. (2001) Chord: A scalable peer-to-peer lookup service for internet applications. In *ACM SIGCOMM Computer Communication Review* (ACM), **31**: 149–160.

[17] THORUP, M. and ZWICK, U. (2001) Compact routing schemes. In *Proceedings of the thirteenth annual ACM symposium on Parallel algorithms and architectures* (ACM): 1–10.

[18] TRAVERSAT, B., ARORA, A., ABDELAZIZ, M., DUIGOU, M., HAYWOOD, C., HUGLY, J.C., POUYOUL, E. *et al.* (2003) Project jxta 2.0 super-peer virtual network. *Sun Microsystem White Paper. Available at www. jxta. org/project/www/docs* **92**.

[19] XU, C.Z., RAO, J. and BU, X. (2012) Url: A unified reinforcement learning approach for autonomic cloud management. *Journal of Parallel and Distributed Computing* **72**(2): 95–105.

16

Ant Colony Optimization Based Model Checking Extended by Smell-like Pheromone

Tsutomu Kumazawa[1,*], Chihiro Yokoyama[2], Munehiro Takimoto[2], Yasushi Kambayashi[3]

[1]Software Research Associates, Inc, 2-32-8 Minami-Ikebukuro, Toshima-ku, Tokyo 171-8513, Japan
[2]Tokyo University of Science, 2641 Yamazaki, Noda-shi, Chiba 278-8510, Japan
[3]Nippon Institute of Technology, 4-1 Gakuendai, Miyashiro-machi, Minamisaitama-gun, Saitama 345-8501, Japan

Abstract

Model Checking is a technique for automatically checking the model representing software or hardware about whether they satisfy the corresponding specifications. Traditionally, the model checking uses deterministic algorithms, but the deterministic algorithms have a fatal problem. They are consuming too many computer resources. In order to mitigate the problem, an approach based on the Ant Colony Optimization (ACO) was proposed. Instead of performing exhaustive checks on the entire model, the ACO based approach statistically checks a part of the model through movements of ants (ant-like software agents). Thus the ACO based approach not only suppresses resource consumption, but also guides the ants to reach the goals efficiently. The ACO based approach is known to generate shorter counter examples too. This article presents an improvement of the ACO based approach. We employ a technique that further suppresses futile movements of ants while suppressing the resource consumption by introducing a smell-like pheromone. While ACO detects the semi-shortest path to food by putting pheromones on the trails of ants, the smell-like pheromone diffuses differently from the traditional pheromone. In our approach, the smell-like pheromone diffuses from food, and guides ants to the food. Thus our approach not only makes the ants reach the goals farther and more efficiently but also generates much shorter counter examples than those of the traditional approaches. In order to demonstrate the effectiveness of our approach, we have implemented our approach on a practical model checker, and conducted numerical experiments. The experimental results show that our approach is effective for improving execution efficiency and the length of counter examples.

Keywords: Ant Colony Optimization, Model Checking, State Explosion

1. Introduction

Model Checking is a technique that checks whether the design of a software or hardware described as a state transition model satisfies the property specified by the user, which is called a specification [1]. Tools that automatically perform the model checking are called model checkers. General model checkers use a deterministic algorithm for the checking, which often consumes too much machine resources because they exhaustively check their search spaces. In order to mitigate this problem, techniques based on Ant Colony Optimization (ACO) [2] have been proposed [3–6]. They are nondeterministic algorithms. ACO is a swarm intelligence-based method inspired by the behaviors of ants' collecting food, and a multi-agent system that exploits artificial stigmergy (artificial pheromone) for the solution of combinatorial optimization problems. In other words, ACO is a kind of statistic algorithms that is categorized into meta-heuristics [7]. Since ACO only searches a part of entire search space based on the property in which pheromone attracts ants, the ACO based model checking can suppress the use of the computational resources.

One of the major features of the model checker is to present an error trace to its users (called a counter example), which helps the users understand why the model violates the property [8]. Thus, the shorter the presented counter example is, the more comprehensible it is for the users. As an optimization method, ACO based model checking enables model checkers to generate shorter counter examples.

We propose a new ACO-based model checking that consumes less computational resources than the traditional ACO approaches do. Most model checking techniques deal with properties roughly categorized into safety and liveness [9, 10]. Safety properties state that undesirable things never hold, while liveness properties assert that the desirable things finally hold. Our approach handles the safety and focuses on the fact that finding the violation of the safety is reduced to the reachability problem on directed graphs. In other words, the model checking for the safety just searches final (i.e. error) states starting with a specific start state. For safety checking, a path from the start state to a final state is a counter example.

In the ACO based model checking, ants move in the directed graph to look for a final state. Ants probabilistically choose the move direction according to the amounts of pheromone trails on the graph deposited by preceding ants. This behavior of ants helps ants to find relatively short paths to the final states, because the paths that have much pheromone tend be selected by many ants. Thus pheromone trails represent the quality of paths to the final state in terms of path length. In order to further assist ants to search final states, we introduce another special pheromone that attracts ants to the final states. The attraction of the pheromone efficiently guides ants, and localizes the search space, so that our approach can achieve the less consumption of the resources. We can summarize the contributions of our approach to the traditional ACO based approaches as follows:

1. Suppressing memory consumption,

2. Decreasing the time for completing checking, and

3. Shortening obtained counter examples.

The structure of the balance of this article is organized as follows. The next section presents preliminaries of our approach. In the third section, we give a brief explanation of a traditional ACO based approach for safety. After that, in the fourth section, we introduce the smell-like pheromone and the details of our ACO approach that takes advantages of the smell-like pheromone. In the fifth section, we demonstrate the feasibility of our approach, and conclude our discussion in the sixth section.

2. Model Checking

In this section, we give an overview of model checking, and explain the problems that we address.

2.1. Overview

Formal verification is one of the techniques that verify properties of software or hardware. The formal verification techniques can be categorized into two kinds in terms of their approaches. One is logical reasoning approach that represents properties of software as a mathematical theorem such as Hoare logic or predicate calculus. The logical reasoning verifies software using a tool such as theorem provers. It is, however, difficult for the provers to verify software in completely automatic manner, and therefore, they require some interactions with the users.

The other one is Model Checking, which is proposed by Clarke et al [1, 11] and known as one of the most successful research topics in Software Engineering. The model checking was initially applied for the verification of communication protocols [12] and hardware circuits. Model checking is currently used for verifying software without any support from users. Model checking consists of the following steps: 1) representing the model of a system as a state transition system such as an automaton, 2) describing a specification representing required property with temporal logic such as Linear Temporal Logic (LTL) [13] or Computation Tree Logic (CTL) [11], and 3) checking whether the state transition system satisfies the specification. The final step is automatically performed by a model checker. For example, SPIN [10, 14] is one of the most popular model checkers. It checks whether a model described in Promela satisfies the specification described in LTL. Promela is the description language specifically designed for SPIN. At this time, SPIN converts the model and the negation of the specification into Büchi automata, then builds their intersection to exhaustively search for its accepting paths on it. If some accepting paths are found, it means the model does not hold the specification, and the corresponding paths are shown as the counter examples. Otherwise the fact of satisfaction is notified.

In the case of safety checking, the Büchi automaton of the given specification has the property that every path from its start state to its accepting state is accepting. Thus, its accepting states are considered to be final error states. Owing to the property, the accepting states of the intersection are also final error states, to which paths show counter examples. In other words, in order to find counter examples, it is sufficient to search for the accepting states on the intersection.

2.2. Challenges and Related Work

In this article, we tackle with two problems of model checking: *state explosion problem* and *incomprehensive counter examples*.

In model checking, the automata tend to be very large. Actually, the size of an automaton increases exponentially as the size of the corresponding model becomes large. The exponential increase is called state explosion, which may cause exhaustion of resources and may lead to system failure. In order to mitigate the state explosion, techniques such as Partial Order Reduction that decreases the number of states [15], and Bitstate Hashing that reduces the memory area occupied by each state [10] have been proposed. Also, Symbolic Model Checking is known that it does not consume too much memory [16]. They are, however, are symptomatic treatments, and therefore, do not essentially solve the problem.

The other problem is related to the length of counter examples. Because a counter example is presented to the user as a diagnosis of specification violation, it is highly desirable to make it comprehensible for the human user. As mentioned above, a counter example is represented as the path over the directed graph. It means that the counter example is more understandable if it is small enough in lengthwise. That is to say, we need to aim at the model checking methods that generate as short counter examples as possible.

Traditionally, the search techniques adopted by most model checkers are based on Depth First Search (DFS), such as Nested Depth First Search [10]. However, DFS may find long counter examples because there is no guarantee of the shortness of paths that DFS searches.

Recently, parallel algorithms have been studied as promising techniques to improve the performance of model checkers. Holzmann et al. parallelizes Breadth First Search (BFS) to verify safety properties and implements the proposed algorithms on SPIN [17, 18]. Their technique can be used for the detection of the shortest counter examples, because BFS is guaranteed to find shortest counter examples unlike DFS. They also extend the proposed algorithm to handle the subset of liveness properties.

Apart from the improvements for traditional deterministic approaches, some heuristics algorithms have been proposed. They are effective in cases where counter examples are required, although it is difficult for the algorithms to prove that the given model holds the specification because heuristics cannot give exact solutions but quasi-optimal solutions. Edelkamp et al. developed HSF-SPIN [12, 19], which is an extension of SPIN with heuristic search algorithms such as A*, Weighted A*, Iterative A* or Best First Search. The HSF-SPIN gives shorter counter examples and consumes less memory than the deterministic approaches. Groce and

Visser proposed some heuristics for model checking of Java programs, based on the specifications to be checked, the structures of the programs, and users' definition [20]. Their evaluation was conducted with DFS, Best First Search, A* and Beam Search.

Recent researches have shown that various meta-heuristic approaches provide more favorable results than traditional deterministic algorithms do in terms of efficiency. Alba et al. showed the applications of Genetic Algorithm (GA) for detection of deadlock, and unnecessary states and transitions [21]. Godefroid et al. proposed a GA based model checking technique [22]. The GA based approaches were the first applications of meta-heuristics for model checking. Alba et al. later showed the effectiveness of Ant Colony Optimization (ACO) for the model checking [3]. We describe the details of the ACO approaches in the next section. Their approach is extended to the checking of safety with Partial Order Reduction [5] and that of liveness [6]. As another work, Francesca et al. proposed a deadlock detection technique using ACO [23]. They utilize the heuristics based on the structures of models to tell ants estimated directions to food. In the paper [24], Ferreira et al. presented a novel technique based on Particle Swarm Optimization (PSO) that finds safety violations. Chicano et al. compared several deterministic and nondeterministic software model checking algorithms using Java PathFinder [25]. Their target algorithms include DFS, BFS, A*, GA, ACO, PSO, Simulated Annealing, Random Search, and Beam Search. They reported that meta-heuristic techniques effectively found safety violations and short counter examples. Note that the work was the first one that applies Simulated Annealing to software model checking.

In addition to those already mentioned, there are some heuristic or meta-heuristic extensions. Staunton et al. proposed the heuristic search algorithms for model checking based on Estimation of Distribution Algorithm [26, 27]. Yousefian et al. proposed a safety checking technique for graph transformation systems based on GA to deal with the state explosion problem. [28]. Rafe et al. proposed a hybrid algorithm combining PSO with Gravitational Search Algorithm in order to find deadlocks in graph transformation systems [29]. Poulding and Feldt extended a variation of Monte-Carlo Tree Search algorithm for heuristic model checking [30].

It is worth noting that meta-heuristic approaches draw a lot of interest from the viewpoint of Search-Based Software Engineering (SBSE) [31]. SBSE refers to a research area of Software Engineering that uses meta-heuristic optimization methodologies. For example, Shousha et al. used GA for the detection of concurrency problems (i.e., starvation and deadlocks) in design models described in Unified Model Language (UML) [32]. Their method does not adopt model

```
procedure ACO
    Initialization
    while terminationCondition do
        ConstructAntSolutions
        UpdatePheromones
    od
end procedure
```

Figure 1. Pseudo code of ACO

checking and aims at presenting a technique that is suitable to UML models. Our approach can be positioned as part of the verification techniques in SBSE.

3. ACO Based Approach

In this section, we give the basics of ACO, and then, describe ACOhg that is a variant of ACO proposed by Alba et al. [3–5] for model checking with large state spaces.

3.1. ACO

ACO is one of the meta-heuristic search algorithms inspired by the behaviors of ants that discover paths from their nest to food. It is known that ACO is effective for some optimization problems such as routing, assigning and scheduling problems. When ACO is applied to model checking problems, a problem is a model expressed in as a directed graph, where the nest and food are the start and error states respectively. The paths between these nodes represent candidate solutions of the model checking problem, i.e. counter examples.

In ACO, agents corresponding to ants cooperatively search the shortest paths through indirect communications using pheromone. The optimal paths found by ants correspond to the optimal solution in optimization problems. The effect of the pheromones is represented as weight on edges, which are assigned to the paths that ants have visited. The pheromones play a role as guides that induce ants to select shorter paths to error states.

The basic model of ACO was given by Ant System (AS) proposed by Dorigo et al. [33]. In most cases, however, AS was not as powerful as other heuristic methods, and needs extensions for practical use. One of the most powerful extensions is Max-Min Ant System (MMAS) [34]. MMAS, which is a kind of iterative algorithms, not only updates pheromones at each iteration step based on the best solution over the previous iterations, but also gives the upper and lower limits to pheromone value. The extension prevents MMAS going into local minimums.

Figure 1 shows how a typical ACO metaheuristic algorithm works. Basically, ACO is the repetition of

ConstructAntSolutions step for searching paths, and *UpdatePheromones* step for updating the distribution of pheromone. Also, *terminationCondition* is satisfied when some solutions are found or the number of the repetition exceeds a fixed number. In the following, we discuss each step in more detail.

Initialization step initializes pheromones on edges for preparation of searching by ants. While regarding the start state and final states as the nest and food respectively, pheromones with random strength are randomly located between these states.

ConstructAntSolutions step makes each ant probabilistically transit states starting from the start state to find candidate solutions. At this time, a transition to the next state is selected using the following equation:

$$p_{ij}^k = \frac{[\tau_{ij}]^\alpha [\eta_{ij}]^\beta}{\Sigma_{l \in N_i}[\tau_{il}]^\alpha [\eta_{il}]^\beta}, \quad if \ j \in N_i \qquad (1)$$

In the equation, N_i is the set of states to which an ant can move from state i; j is the destination state of one step movement of the ant; τ_{ij} is the value of pheromone on the edge (i, j); and η is heuristic value representing the number of transitions to a final state, which is set to a smaller value than actual one. The heuristic value is estimated based on the locations of final states, or the length and property of a specification that are described in LTL. Also, α and β are empirically determined values in order to adjust the effects of the heuristic value and pheromone value, respectively. When ants have moved on edges in the fixed number of times, or some candidates of solutions are found, *UpdatePheromones* step follows.

UpdatePheromones step updates the pheromone value on each edge. The pheromone strengths on selected edges are increased according to the appropriateness of the edges. At the same time, the pheromones on the other edges are updated as follows:

$$\tau_{ij} \leftarrow (1 - x_i)\tau_{ij} \qquad (2)$$

In the equation, x_i is set to a value between 0 and 1. This is the value representing the degree of evaporation of pheromones. Through the update process, the priorities of previously selected edges are decreased step by step until some ants select the edges again.

3.2. ACOhg

It is difficult for traditional ACOs to handle state transition systems for model checking that have thousands of nodes. Because there can be billions of edges in such systems, they require a number of megabytes in a memory to record pheromone values. Especially, the size of a model of concurrent system is known to be huge. For example, the size of the model of Dining Philosophers with n philosophers is 3^n, which

Whole search space

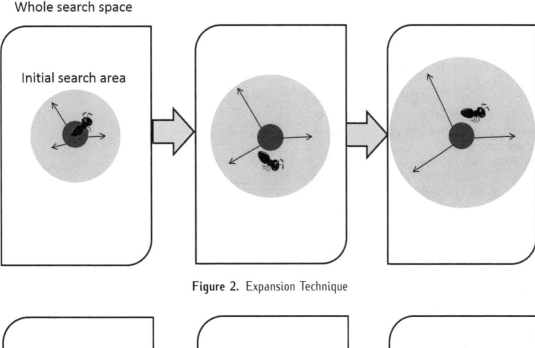

Figure 2. Expansion Technique

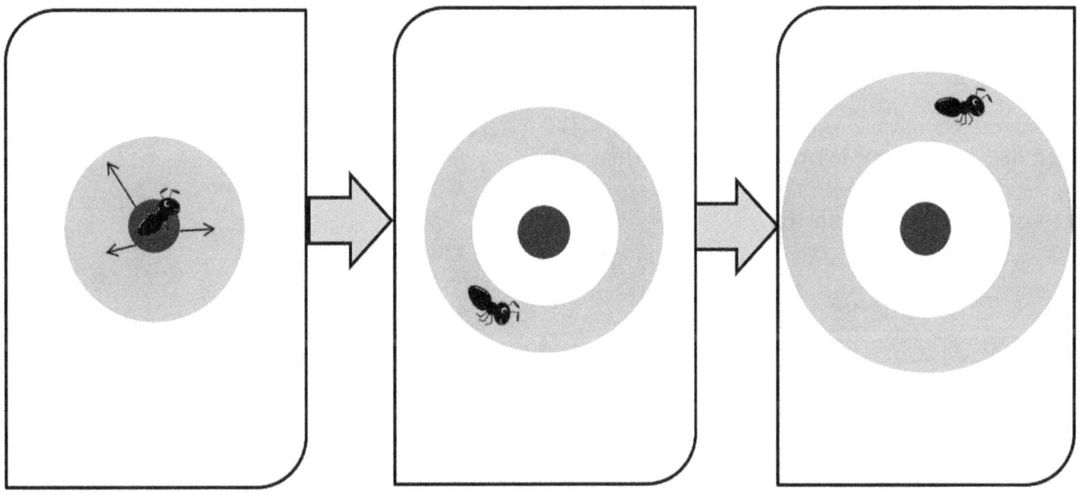

Figure 3. Missionary Technique

increases exponentially. The simple solutions such as prohibiting revisits to the same states are not effective, because some ants may run into brick walls, or may wander from state to state for a long time even if they finally reach the final states. Thus, the behaviors of the traditional ACO in model checking may result in the state explosion without finding any candidates of solutions. In addition, as a more fatal problem, the traditional ACO has to initially set pheromone values to all the transitions. This may also consume too much memory.

In order to mitigate the problems of the traditional ACO, Alba et al. proposed *ACO for huge graphs* (ACOhg), which can perform searching with less memory than the traditional ones [3, 4]. The basic idea of ACOhg is to give the upper limit λ_{ant} to the number of move steps of ants at one stage. This search manner suppresses

the time and memory consumption, but limiting of move steps may prevent ants from reaching the final states. That is, λ_{ant} has to be decided so as to find the final states. ACOhg gives two kinds of techniques for determining λ_{ant}; they are *expansion technique* and *missionary technique*.

In the expansion technique, once the system cannot find a final state in the search for the current λ_{ant}, λ_{ant} is increased by the value given as a parameter, and then the system searches the wider area defined by the new λ_{ant} again as shown in Figure 2. The process starts with small λ_{ant} and repeats until it finds some final states. The expansion technique increases λ_{ant} just enough, so that the memory consumption can be suppressed. Also, it is easy to implement because it is a simple extension of the traditional ACO. On the other hand, its behavior becomes closer to the traditional ACO's as λ_{ant} increases.

The missionary technique is similar to the expansion technique, but searches are performed from not the start state but some states on the edge of the previously searched area, i.e. ignoring old pheromone as shown in Figure 3. The new start state on the edge is selected from the states that ants reach at the previous stage. This search manner enables ACO to gradually extend the search area without changing λ_{ant}, so that it only requires constant time and memory consumption at each stage.

Both approaches decide the strength of pheromones to be assigned based on a *fitness function*. The fitness function returns the degree of penalty for the trail of each ant, which becomes very large in the case where the trail includes some cycles, or no final state. Based on the fitness function f, a^{best} with the lowest penalty $f(a^{best})$ is determined, and then, the pheromone of its trace is strengthened as follows:

$$\tau_{ij} \leftarrow \tau_{ij} + \frac{1}{f(a^{best})}, \forall (i, j) \in a^{best} \qquad (3)$$

ACOhg, which is based on MMAS, also uses the fitness function for calculating the limit values τ_{max} and τ_{min} of the pheromone value for each trail as follows:

$$\tau_{max} = \frac{1}{\rho f(a^{best})}, \qquad (4)$$

$$\tau_{min} = \frac{\tau_{max}}{a} \qquad (5)$$

In the equation, ρ and a are constants that control the range of the pheromone values. Also, the missionary approach uses the fitness function to decide the next start states at each stage.

4. Extended ACOhg

We extend ACOhg by introducing a new kind of pheromones in order to suppress futile movement of ants. We call the extended ACOhg *EACOhg*. This section presents the outline of EACOhg, and then describes the details of the new pheromone guiding ants to the final states.

4.1. Outline of EACOhg

ACOhg can suppress the analysis time and memory consumption, but it searches from the start state in any directions like the traditional ACO. If there is information about the direction, the search area can be localized. We extend ACOhg so as to use the direction information to find the final states. In the real world, the direction information corresponds to smell diffused from food. Indeed, ants can recognize not only

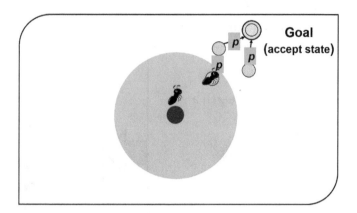

Figure 4. Diffusing of smell

1: $\tau \leftarrow initialize\_pheromone()$;
2: $\gamma \leftarrow \{ node \mid node \in F \}$;
3: **while** $step \leq msteps \wedge \nexists i \in [1..colsize] a_*^i \in F$ **do**
4:     **for** $k = 1$ to $colsize$ **do**
5:         $a^k \leftarrow \emptyset$;
6:         **while** $|a^k| \leq \lambda_{ant} \wedge T(a_*^k) - a^k \neq \emptyset \wedge a_*^k \notin F$ **do**
7:             $node \leftarrow select\_successor(a_*^k, T(a_*^k), \tau, \gamma, \eta)$;
8:             $a^k \leftarrow a^k + node$;
9:             $\tau \leftarrow local\_pheromone\_update(\tau, \xi, (a_*^k, node))$;
10:         **end while**
11:         **if** $f(a^k) < f(a^{best})$ **then**
12:             $a^{best} \leftarrow a^k$;
13:         **end if**
14:     **end for**
15:     $\tau \leftarrow pheromone\_evaporation(\tau, \rho)$;
16:     $\tau \leftarrow pheromone\_update(\tau, a^{best})$;
17:     $\gamma \leftarrow scatter\_goal\_pheromone(\gamma)$;
18:     $\lambda_{ant} \leftarrow \lambda_{ant} + \sigma$;
19: **end while**

Figure 5. Algorithm of EACOhg

pheromones, but also the smell, which is important information to reach unfound food in the early stage.

In our model, we regard the smell as another kind of pheromones. We call this *goal pheromone*. We made the goal pheromone stronger than the normal pheromone. Once the goal pheromones are put on transition edges, the edges are selected in preference to the edges with the normal pheromone as shown in Figure 4. The search manner localizes the search area further, contributing to finding the final states more quickly and generating shorter counter examples, although memory consumption may increase a little to hold the goal pheromones.

Figure 5 shows the pseudo code of EACOhg, where the kth ant is represented by a^k, and a path where a^k traversed is represented by $|a^k|$. Also, a_j^k and a_*^k represent the jth node and the last node on the path respectively. $T(a_*^k)$ represents the set of nodes to which a^k can transit from a_*^k.

The EACOhg starts with randomly assigned pheromone value in $[0 - 1.0]$ to all the edges as shown in line 1. After that, the search step, which consists of movement of ants and update of pheromones, is repeated until the number of repetitions exceeds upper limit *msteps* or some ants reach the final states F in the loop body in lines 3–19.

Each stage performs a movement within λ_{ant} and the movement causes pheromone update. The destination *node* to which to move is probabilistically selected based on the strength of the pheromone value τ through function *select_successor* in line 7. This node is appended to a^k. At this time, the pheromone on the selected edge is enhanced through function *local_pheromone_update* in line 9. Thus, the best path based on the fitness function f in the stage is always held in a^{best}.

Once the operation in the current stage is completed, pheromone values are globally updated for the effect of evaporation and enhancing pheromones on a^{best} through the functions *pheromone_evaporation* and *pheromone_update* respectively in lines 15 and 16. Furthermore, in our algorithm, the goal pheromone is diffused through the function *scatter_goal_pheromone*. Finally, in order to search a wider area in the case where no ant reaches the final states. λ_{ant} is increased in line 18.

4.2. Goal Pheromone

The existence of the goal pheromone shows that there are some paths from the current state to the final states. Therefore, it is enhanced in order to attract ants more strongly through the following properties:

1. Attracting ants more strongly than normal pheromone,

2. Non-volatility, and

3. Defusing from the final states to their peripheries.

Note that the above properties induce ants to select relatively short paths to the final states, which leads to short counter examples.

The normal pheromones behave along with MMAS and hence, have the value less than or equal to τ_{max}. The goal pheromone is set to the value more than τ_{max} in order to attract ants more strongly than normal pheromones. Moreover, while the normal pheromone evaporates, the goal pheromone does not evaporate and has a constant value. It is derived from the fact that the smell is always supplied by the source, i.e. food. Thus, once an ant finds some goal pheromones, it moves to the edges with them with high probability. The behavior of an ant is implemented by *select_successor*.

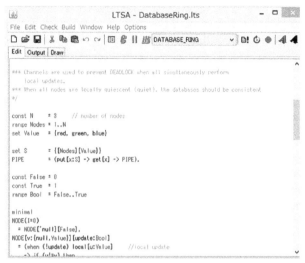

(a) Input model

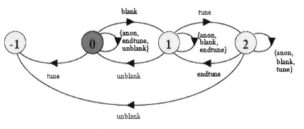

(b) Generated model

Figure 6. Models of LTSA

The goal pheromone is assigned on in-edges of the current states by *scatter_goal_pheromone* in order to make them defuse. At that time, the pheromone is scattered on only some edges that are randomly selected. The scatter manner contributes to suppressing time and memory consumption.

5. Experimental Results

In order to demonstrate the effectiveness of our approach, we have implemented our extended ACO, *EACOhg*, on a practical model checker called LTSA (Labeled Transition System Analyzer) [9, 35]. LTSA is one of the model checkers that can be customized easily, and can handle models that are suitable for our purpose. LTSA supports the checking of Fluent Linear Temporal Logic [35], which is a kind of LTL specialized for event-based systems described as Labeled Transition Systems. For example, we may give a model with several final states as an input of LTSA as shown in Figure 6(a), while LTSA generates models with a single final state, which is an error state corresponding to the final states for checking safety, as shown in Figure 6 (b). The property of single final state of the models makes handling of models easy. In Figure 6 (b), the red state labeled 0 is the initial state, and the state

Table 1. Settings of coefficients

coefficients	values
mstep	100
colsize	10
α	1.0
β	2.0
η	1.0
ρ	0.2
a	5
P_p	70
P_c	70

P_p and P_c are weights of penalties used by the fitness function for no final state and the path with some cycles.

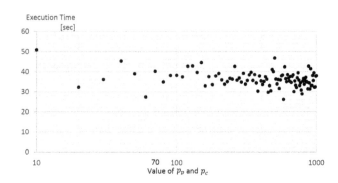

Figure 8. Preliminary execution time on middle model

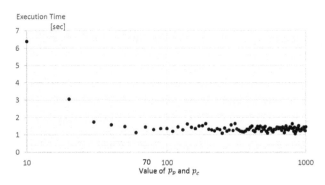

Figure 7. Preliminary execution time on small model

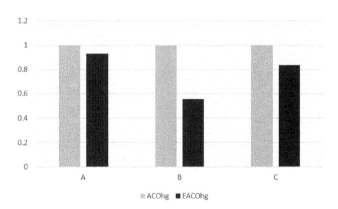

Figure 9. Execution time

−1 is the single final state. LTSA generates the models as directed graphs in Aldebaran form, for which we have extended the checking phase. Also, in the phase, we have implemented goal pheromones in accordance with the description Section 4.2, for which we have chosen random values in tenfold range i.e. [0.0-10.0] so that goal pheromones have much more influence than normal pheromones. Notice that the random setting of each goal pheromone contributes to mitigating local minimum problem as well as normal pheromones.

We used values as shown in Table 1 for the coefficients and constants that appear in equations and algorithms. Most of these values can be basically the same values as ACOhg because EACOhg is a simple extension of ACOhg. However, the values of P_p and P_c have to be empirically decided.

We decided the best settings for P_p and P_c through preliminary experiments. In the preliminary experiments, we generated two models with small and middle sizes based on dinning philosophers problem, checking them for dead lock safety while changing P_p and P_c from 10 to 1000. Figures 7 and 8 show execution time for each experiment, where the small and middle models have 213 and 7,773 states respectively. Note that the figures are semi-logarithmic plots. As shown in the figures, the execution time decreases at first as they increase, regardless of the size of models. Once P_p and P_c

reach 70, the execution time does not decrease. Thus, we decided to adopt 70 as P_p and P_c in main experiments.

In the main experiments, we prepared three models: model A with 3843 states, model B with 31747 states, and model C with 266,218 states adjusting the parameters of two kinds of examples *Mutex_fluent* and *DatabaseRing*. We conducted three experiments in terms of execution time, the length of counter examples, and memory consumption. In each experiment, we compared our approach with ACOhg for models A, B and C, where we show the average of the results of one hundred times applications for each model.

As shown in Figure 9, our approach is more efficient than ACOhg. It shows that goal pheromones guide ants to the final states, suppressing the chances going out their ways. Furthermore, Figure 10 shows that our approach generates much shorter counter examples than ACOhg. The fact also substantiates the efficiency of our approach by the shorter trails of ants.

On the other hand, our approach consumes more memory than ACOhg as shown in Figure 11. The increase of the memory consumption fell within 10% at most, and was 5% in average, though. Considering that our approach have achieved 23% more efficient execution and 50% shorter counter examples in their averages, we can say that the increase is negligible.

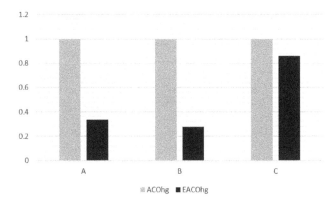

Figure 10. The length of counter examples

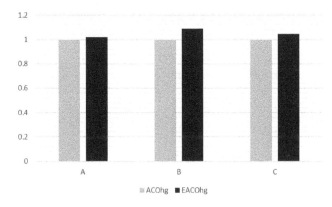

Figure 11. Memory consumption

6. Conclusions and Future Directions

We have proposed a novel ACO based model checking, i.e. EACOhg that further suppresses futile movements of ants while suppressing the resource consumption by introducing smell-like pheromone. The smell-like pheromone diffuses from goals and guides ants to the goals. Thus our approach not only makes the ants reach the goals further more efficiently but also generates much shorter counter examples than the existing best ACO based approach, ACOhg.

In order to show the effectiveness of our approach, we implemented the EACOhg on a practical model checker, and conducted experiments. The results of the experiments show that our approach is effective for improving execution efficiency and the length of counter examples. Future work involves the enhancement of EACOhg and its evaluation based on more realistic case studies.

We have observed that our approach does not achieve effectiveness in the very large model (model C) as shown in Figures 9 and 10. The reason may be that the effect of the smell-like pheromone is compromised in a large model. In order to overcome this problem,

we plan to add directionality in diffusing the smell-like pheromone.

We are pursuing further improvements of EACOhg to make it more practical and complete. We envisage that the improvements should be achieved by the combination of EACOhg with heuristics and the optimization methods of classical model checking. Some researchers showed that appropriate heuristics can improve the efficiency of model checking in the wide range of problem domains [12, 19, 20, 23]. Most heuristics are problem-specific. They depend on the specifications to be checked and the structures of the target system models. Therefore we have to carefully investigate which heuristic methods contribute to the performance improvements of EACOhg.

Traditional model checking researches have proposed various kinds of optimization techniques as noted in Section 2. Although most of the methods aim at optimizing deterministic search, EACOhg can be applicable to some of them such as Partial Order Reduction (POR) [5]. In addition, we plan to extend EACOhg to the checking of liveness, because EACOhg only targets on the safety checking and does not support the check the properties such as Response and Existence [36]. In the case of liveness checking, counter examples may have infinite length and contains cycles. Thus, we have to investigate the effects of goal pheromones on finding paths with cycles. One approach is proposed by Chicano and Alba [6]. As the next phase, we plan to apply our method to safety checking with POR and liveness checking so as to demonstrate the applicability of our approach.

Finally and the most importantly, we have to apply EACOhg to practical models of software systems or communication protocols to evaluate its effectiveness empirically. For example, the recent work by Chicano et al. [25] evaluates several meta-heuristic model checking techniques using communication protocols. Similarly, Shousha et al. [32] uses models of a bank fund transfer problem and a cruise control problem. EACOhg is not built on the specific programming or modeling languages, hence it is possible to adapt to the real world systems. A candidate data set for our empirical research is the Software-artifact Infrastructure Repository [37], which is used for evaluation by Poulding and Feldt [30].

Acknowledgements. This work is supported in part by Japan Society for Promotion of Science (JSPS), with the basic research program (C) (No. 25330089 and 26350456), Grant-in-Aid for Scientific Research. We have received the support and suggestions from Mr. Keiichiro Takada in Department of Information Sciences, Tokyo University of Science.

References

[1] CLARKE, JR., E.M., GRUMBERG, O. and PELED, D.A. (1999) *Model Checking* (MIT Press).

[2] DORIGO, M. and STÜTZLE, T. (2004) *Ant Colony Optimization* (Bradford Company, MIT Press).

[3] ALBA, E. and CHICANO, F. (2007) Finding safety errors with aco. In *Proceedings of the 9th Annual Conference on Genetic and Evolutionary Computation*, GECCO '07: 1066–1073. doi:10.1145/1276958.1277171.

[4] ALBA, E. and CHICANO, F. (2007) Acohg: Dealing with huge graphs. In *Proceedings of the 9th Annual Conference on Genetic and Evolutionary Computation*, GECCO '07: 10–17. doi:10.1145/1276958.1276961.

[5] CHICANO, F. and ALBA, E. (2008) Ant colony optimization with partial order reduction for discovering safety property violations in concurrent models. *Information Processing Letters* **106**(6): 221–231. doi:10.1016/j.ipl.2007.11.015.

[6] CHICANO, F. and ALBA, E. (2008) Finding liveness errors with ACO. In *Proceedings of the IEEE Congress on Evolutionary Computation*, CEC: 2997–3004. doi:10.1109/CEC.2008.4631202.

[7] BOUSSAÏD, I., LEPAGNOT, J. and SIARRY, P. (2013) A survey on optimization metaheuristics. *Inf. Sci.* **237**: 82–117. doi:10.1016/j.ins.2013.02.041.

[8] CLARKE, E.M. (2008) The birth of model checking. In GRUMBERG, O. and VEITH, H. [eds.] *25 Years of Model Checking - History, Achievements, Perspectives*, 1–26. doi:10.1007/978-3-540-69850-0_1.

[9] MAGEE, J. and KRAMER, J. (1999) *Concurrency: State Models & Java Programs* (John Wiley & Sons, Inc.).

[10] HOLZMANN, G. (2004) *The Spin Model Checker: Primer and Reference Manual* (Addison-Wesley).

[11] CLARKE, E.M. and EMERSON, E.A. (1982) Design and synthesis of synchronization skeletons using branching-time temporal logic. In *Logic of Programs, Workshop*: 52–71. doi:10.1007/BFb0025774.

[12] EDELKAMP, S., LEUE, S. and LLUCH-LAFUENTE, A. (2004) Directed explicit-state model checking in the validation of communication protocols. *International Journal on Software Tools for Technology Transfer* **5**(2-3): 247–267. doi:10.1007/s10009-002-0104-3.

[13] MANNA, Z. and PNUELI, A. (1992) *The Temporal Logic of Reactive and Concurrent Systems: Specification* (Springer-Verlag New York, Inc.).

[14] HOLZMANN, G.J. (1997) The model checker spin. *IEEE Transactions on Software Engineering* **23**(5): 279–295. doi:10.1109/32.588521.

[15] LLUCH-LAFUENTE, A., EDELKAMP, S. and LEUE, S. (2002) Partial order reduction in directed model checking. In *Proceedings of the 9th International SPIN Workshop on Model Checking of Software* (Springer-Verlag): 112–127. doi:10.1007/3-540-46017-9_10.

[16] BURCH, J.R., CLARKE, E.M., LONG, D.E., McMILLAN, K.L. and DILL, D.L. (1994) Symbolic model checking for sequential circuit verification. *IEEE Transactions on Computer-Aided Design of Integrated Circuits and Systems* **13**(4): 401–424.

[17] HOLZMANN, G.J. (2012) Parallelizing the spin model checker. In *Proceedings of the 19th International Conference on Model Checking Software*, SPIN'12: 155–171. doi:10.1007/978-3-642-31759-0_12.

[18] FILIPPIDIS, I. and HOLZMANN, G.J. (2014) An improvement of the piggyback algorithm for parallel model checking. In *Proceedings of the 2014 International SPIN Symposium on Model Checking of Software*, SPIN 2014: 48–57. doi:10.1145/2632362.2632375.

[19] EDELKAMP, S., LAFUENTE, A.L. and LEUE, S. (2001) Directed explicit model checking with hsf-spin. In *Proceedings of the 8th International SPIN Workshop on Model Checking of Software*, SPIN '01: 57–79. doi:10.1007/3-540-45139-0_5.

[20] GROCE, A. and VISSER, W. (2004) Heuristics for model checking java programs. *International Journal on Software Tools for Technology Transfer* **6**(4): 260–276. doi:10.1007/s10009-003-0130-9.

[21] ALBA, E. and TROYA, J.M. (1996) Genetic algorithms for protocol validation. In *Proceedings of the 4th International Conference on Parallel Problem Solving from Nature*, PPSN IV: 870–879. doi:10.1007/3-540-61723-X_1050.

[22] GODEFROID, P. and KHURSHID, S. (2004) Exploring very large state spaces using genetic algorithms. *Int. J. Softw. Tools Technol. Transf.* **6**(2): 117–127. doi:10.1007/s10009-004-0141-1.

[23] FRANCESCA, G., SANTONE, A., VAGLINI, G. and VILLANI, M.L. (2011) Ant colony optimization for deadlock detection in concurrent systems. In *Proceedings of IEEE 35th Annual Computer Software and Applications Conference* (IEEE Computer Society): 108–117. doi:10.1109/COMPSAC.2011.22.

[24] FERREIRA, M., CHICANO, F., ALBA, E. and GÓMEZ-PULIDO, J. (2008) Detecting protocol errors using particle swarm optimization with java pathfinder. In *Proceedings of the High Performance Computing & Simulation Conference*, HPCS '08: 319–325.

[25] CHICANO, F., FERREIRA, M. and ALBA, E. (2011) Comparing metaheuristic algorithms for error detection in java programs. In *Proceedings of the Third International Conference on Search Based Software Engineering*, SSBSE'11 (Springer-Verlag): 82–96. doi:10.1007/978-3-642-23716-4_11.

[26] STAUNTON, J. and CLARK, J.A. (2010) Searching for safety violations using estimation of distribution algorithms. In *Proceedings of the 2010 Third International Conference on Software Testing, Verification, and Validation Workshops*, ICSTW '10: 212–221. doi:10.1109/ICSTW.2010.24.

[27] STAUNTON, J. and CLARK, J.A. (2011) Finding short counterexamples in promela models using estimation of distribution algorithms. In *Proceedings of the 13th Annual Conference on Genetic and Evolutionary Computation*, GECCO '11: 1923–1930. doi:10.1145/2001576.2001834.

[28] YOUSEFIAN, R., RAFE, V. and RAHMANI, M. (2014) A heuristic solution for model checking graph transformation systems. *Applied Soft Computing* **24**: 169–180. doi:10.1016/j.asoc.2014.06.055.

[29] RAFE, V., MORADI, M., YOUSEFIAN, R. and NIKANJAM, A. (2015) A meta-heuristic solution for automated refutation of complex software systems specified through graph transformations. *Applied Soft Computing* **33**(C): 136–149. doi:10.1016/j.asoc.2015.04.032.

[30] POULDING, S. and FELDT, R. (2015) Heuristic model checking using a monte-carlo tree search algorithm. In *Proceedings of the 2015 Annual Conference on Genetic and Evolutionary Computation*, GECCO '15: 1359–1366. doi:10.1145/2739480.2754767.

[31] HARMAN, M., MANSOURI, S.A. and ZHANG, Y. (2012) Search-based software engineering: Trends, techniques and applications. *ACM Comput. Surv.* **45**(1): 11:1–11:61. doi:10.1145/2379776.2379787.

[32] SHOUSHA, M., BRIAND, L. and LABICHE, Y. (2012) A uml/marte model analysis method for uncovering scenarios leading to starvation and deadlocks in concurrent systems. *IEEE Trans. Softw. Eng.* **38**(2): 354–374. doi:10.1109/TSE.2010.107.

[33] DORIGO, M., MANIEZZO, V. and COLORNI, A. (1996) The ant system: Optimization by a colony of cooperating agents. *IEEE Transactions on SYSTEMS,Systems, Man, and Cybernetics, Part B: Cybernetics* **26**(1): 29–41. doi:10.1109/3477.484436.

[34] STÜTZLE, T. and Hoos, H.H. (2000) Max-min ant system. *Future Generation Computer System* **16**(9): 889–914.

[35] GIANNAKOPOULOU, D. and MAGEE, J. (2003) Fluent model checking for event-based systems. In *Proceedings of the 9th European Software Engineering Conference Held Jointly with 11th ACM SIGSOFT International Symposium on Foundations of Software Engineering*, ESEC/FSE-11: 257–266. doi:10.1145/940071.940106.

[36] DWYER, M.B., AVRUNIN, G.S. and CORBETT, J.C. (1999) Patterns in property specifications for finite-state verification. In *Proceedings of the 21st International Conference on Software Engineering*, ICSE '99 (ACM): 411–420. doi:10.1145/302405.302672.

[37] Do, H., ELBAUM, S. and ROTHERMEL, G. (2005) Supporting controlled experimentation with testing techniques: An infrastructure and its potential impact. *Empirical Softw. Engg.* **10**(4): 405–435. doi:10.1007/s10664-005-3861-2.

Performance evaluation of composite Web services

Lynda Mokdad[1], Jalel Ben Othman [2] and Abdelkrim Abdelli [3],[*]

[1]Lab. LACL, University of Paris-Est LACL (EA 4219), UPEC F-94010 Créteil, France
[2]Lab. L2TI, University of Paris 13- L2TI (EA 3043), UP13 F-93430 Villetaneuse, France
[3]Lab. LSI, USTHB university of Algiers, Algeria

Abstract

Composite Web service architectures are demanding much guarantee on the Quality of Service (QoS) in order to meet user requirements. Performance evaluation of these architectures has become therefore a very challenging issue, as the task is very complex due to synchronization inside the orchestration of services. We propose in this paper to use stochastic automata networks which a is powerful formalism as it provides semantics to specify synchronization within a very smart formalism. Contrary to previous approaches, the modeling and the performance evaluation of a variable number of remote service invocation become possible. The reported simulation results advocate the use of our approach in the performance evaluation of composite Web service architectures.

Keywords: Stochastic Automata Networks (SAN), Markov Chain, response times, Composite Web services, performance evaluation.

1. Introduction

The use of web services is continuously growing and the technological and economic potential is not yet tapped. The web services have become in recent times by far the technology application integration par excellence as it is now feasible to host basic web services on a smart phone without requiring additional technologies .

Web Services are software components that can be accessed over the Internet using well established web mechanisms. For instance, in the IT domain the impact of XML Web Services has increased during recent years, since the Extensible Markup Language (XML) has been enforced as a meta language for structured information and its representation [1].

Web services are self-descriptive loosely coupled and interact with each other. They are defined and described regardless of their platforms, implementation details. The biggest advantage of Web Services lies in their simplicity in expression, communication and servicing. The componentized architecture of Web Services also makes them reusable, thereby reducing the development time and costs [2].

Unlike its predecessors, such as the Common Request Broker Architecture (CORBA), Remote Method Invocation (RMI) and Distributed Component Object Model (DCOM), web services have responded satisfactorily to interoperability in the context of distributed systems, as well as to the scale of the Internet. Indeed, Web services can be seen as the standardized way to distribute services on the Internet. It uses Internet protocols to communicate and uses a standard language to describe its interface. The success of Web services is in fact due to the use of Internet technology as a communication infrastructure and the availability of a working framework based on a set of standards which are [3]:

- *SOAP* (Simple Object Access Protocol) a communication protocol for structuring the messages exchanged between software components [4]

- *WSDL* (Web Services Description Language) a specification for describing Web services interfaces [6]; and finally

- *UDDI* (Universal Description Discovery and Integration) a specification for publishing and localization of Web services [5].

There are, two key players, in *Web services architecture*: The service provider (which publishes the service), and the service requester. A third actor, the service registry, may be associated with this pair, but its presence is not essential as the service requester needs only to be aware of the address of the service provider. These three participants must be able to interact with each other.

---

[*]Corresponding author. E-mail: akabdelli@gmail.com

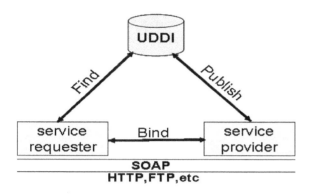

Figure 1. Deployment, research and invocation of web service

Hence, three types of interconnection have defined, as illustrated by the the figure 1.

Living in a competitive world, businesses are naturally interested in information technology supporting them for competitive advantage. As cooperation becomes increasingly important for companies, new challenges arise for the support of business to business scenarios by information technology. The emergence of Web services marks the beginning of a new evolution in this context. This development, a priori technical and architectural introduced a true revolution in how to design and build information systems. Therefore, it became possible to develop an application of high-level by federating some Web services already provided on the Internet by various organizations; hence the concept of *composite Web service.*

In actual fact, available services on the Internet have limited functionalities which do not always meet the user requirements. Therefore, services must often be composed to build more complex services to achieve specific user requirements. In their turn, these new created services are potential candidates for another composition [7]. A composite Web service may be distributed over a network, running on different platforms, implemented in different programming languages and offered by different vendors.

A Web service is said to be composite when its execution involves interactions with other Web services in order to call for their functionalities. The composition of Web services specifies which services need to be invoked, in what order, and how to manage the exceptions. Clearly, it describes a business process, involving different web services.

There are several languages to describe a composition which are classified into two major groups: non-semantic approaches and semantic approaches [8]. Within this context, BPEL4WS (Business Process Execution Language for Web Services), has emerged among non semantic approaches, whereas OWL-S (Web Ontology Language for Services) becomes the representative standard of semantic approaches.

However, existing models have been also used to model and compose web services, such as: workflows graphs, Petri nets and currently programming languages as Java and C.

The composition languages show two levels of abstraction:

The *abstract level* (the abstract process), where the description of a process does not indicate the internal behavior of the parts involved in the process; and the *executable level* (the executable process), where the description is complete and specifies the order of execution of activities, the list of partners, the messages exchanged and treatment of exceptions. These languages provide two methods of execution: orchestration and choreography.

Orchestration: It describes the interaction of services at message level, including the business logics and the order of execution of interactions. The services run independently of the context of business processes. Only the coordinator of the orchestration needs to be aware about the orchestration.

Choreography: Unlike the first way to compose Web services, the choreography has no central coordinator. Each Web services involved in the composition knows the conditions of the execution of its operations and with which other services the interaction have to take place.

The *BPEL4WS* has become a standard composition of business processes. It allows the manipulation of services as activities and processes. A process *BPEL4WS*, is a container where we find a list of external partners, declarations of data exchanged with these partners, managing exceptions and more importantly, the list of activities of the process.

The composition can be made at the time of design of composite Web services, or at runtime. At time of design, the composition is manual, and all the web services that take part, are known as well as their execution order. At runtime, the composition is dynamic and automatically performed and only a specification of the required abstract services is given. Hence, services must first be discovered, then selected and integrated. Microsoft BizTalk Server and BEA WebLogic are examples of platforms of static composition and eFlow and StarWSCoP are platforms for dynamic composition [9].

The composition of web services raises complex problem, being given the multitude of web services on the Internet located at different providers with identical functionalities but however with different qualities. Indeed, for both run time and design time compositions, the choice of concrete services for a particular abstract service may be based on non-functional parameters. Examples of such parameters are availability, throughput, response time, security and cost. In actual fact, web services operate in an environment which is very dynamic (the Web) and thus, their *QoS* values are frequently changing due to updating in elementary services (disappearance of a service for example) or a change in the environment of their execution (a heavy load on the system). This shows the importance of dynamic service composition since services are selected and adapted dynamically at runtime, with services previously discovered to meet user requirements. Consequently, it becomes necessary to integrate, in the web services, such non-functional properties (QoS) in order to distinguish them at runtime [10], [11].

As the market capture of Web services is increasing significantly, in the past years, the applications are quite welcoming the ability to provide secure and reliable communication in the vulnerable and volatile mobile networks. Performance evaluation of these architectures is essential but complex due to synchronization inside the orchestration of services. Consequently, the increasing complexity of such architectures requires the development of methods and tools in order to monitor and evaluate their QoS. In fact, the QoS degradation can lead to serious consequences including a significant economic impact.

We propose in this paper to address this issue. We mainly focus on the composite Web service (CWS) response time computation, where the requests are decomposed into sub-queries to different elementary Web services and then merged into a final result. This includes the following models:

- parallel invocation of a constant number of elementary Web services merged by a federating component;

- parallel invocation of a variable number of elementary Web services merged by a federating component.

To this aim, we consider Stochastic Automata Network (SAN), to model such architectures. Contrarily to other probabilistic models, as Markov's chains for instance, SANs are a very powerful tool as they can specify systems with complex synchronization requirements in a very compact and elegant way. Hence, it becomes possible to specify the composition of a variable number of web services, when it is hard to achieve with other models. To advocate the use of our approach, we provide some empirical studies by simulating the obtained models to compute response times.

This remainder of the paper is organized as follows. In Section 2, we give the related work. In Section 3, we give a brief introduction to SAN model. In section 4, we describe our different models to specify web services composition, where in Section 5, we give some

numerical results. Finally, we conclude and give future research perspectives in Section 6.

2. Related works

In the literature, performance evaluation of Web services have been conducted either by using tests or formal methods.

As concerns testing Web services, XML specification and SOAP protocol have been studied in [13–15] by testing and measuring their response times. In [13] a comparative study of existing protocols, like RMI, RMI/IIOP or CORBA/IIOP, is presented. A critical study of XML-based protocols for Web services is presented and binary encoded protocol has been proposed instead of text XML-based ones in [14]. In [16], information about past workflow executions is collected in a log. Starting from this log a continuous Markov chain is derived, in order to compute the execution response time and the cost of this workflow.

In [11], the composite Web service response time is considered as a response time of fork and join model. This model states that a single Internet application can invoke in parallel a set of elementary Web services and gather their responses from all these launched services in order to return the results to a client. In this considered study, authors analyze the effects of exponential response times based on their earlier work in [17].

An exact analysis of fork and join system is possible when the system is significantly simplified. This is the case for example when the job arrival process in the system follows a Poisson distribution with execution task having exponential distribution and the number of queues is equal to two. The exact computation response time of a such system can be found in [18], [19] and [20]. An approximation technique has been proposed in the case where the number of servers is greater than two and the servers are homogeneous [20]. This last study is extended in [21]. General arrival process and services times are considered in [22]. The most general case is considered in [23]. In this work, upper and lower bounds are proposed by assuming that the response times in each queue are mutually independent. Two approximation techniques are presented: one is based on a decomposition approach and the other is based on an iterative solution method.

In order to overcome the limitations of these studies and particularly the one presented in [11], we have proposed a general model taking into account the fact that elementary Web services are heterogenous and the number of invoked services can be variable (this is the case when we use for example the BPEL multi-choice constructor) [24]. More recently, the problem of computing the distribution of the throughput time in workflow nets has been studied in [25]. In this paper, authors consider workflow with transition execution time having exponential distributions, and formulas have been proposed for each refinement rule (sequence, parallel, synchronization and loop execution pattern).

Response time of a Web service middleware is considered in [26], which follows a fork and join model of execution. The author proposes that while performing a join operation, servers with slow response times can be eliminated to maximize the performances. The work is more oriented towards studying fork and join model in order to understand how to optimally merge the results from various servers. In [27] we have proposed a generic transformation of the studied Markov chain which guarantees that the response time of the new Markov chain is an upper bound of the initial Markov chain response time. We instantiate this transformation in three ways, where each obtained new Markov chain is parameterized by a "quantitative" parameter. By an appropriate choice of the parameter, the recurrence equation systems can be resolved with an algorithm with $O(n)$ and $O(n\sqrt{n})$ respectively space complexity and time complexity, where n is the number of invoked elementary Web services. However, some synchronization in the invocation of a variable number of web services can not be handled by the proposed models.

3. Stochastic Automata Networks

Stochastic Automata Networks have been introduced as an efficient method to represent complex systems with interacting components such as parallel systems or distributed systems [12]. This method automatically provides an analytic derivation of Markov chain generator matrix using tensor algebra. The SAN seems to be more efficient than Queueing Networks or Stochastic Petri Nets to model systems with a large number of states and complex synchronization.

Queueing Networks give a very compact representation of systems with resource contention among independent customers. Analytical methods and well known algorithms may be used to obtain either analytical or numerical results. However, queueing networks are inefficient whenever complex synchronization constraints are to be taken into account. On the other side, stochastic Petri Nets have been defined to represent synchronization constraints of parallel systems or protocols. However, they do not generally yield compact models as they build the transition matrix without any knowledge about its properties.

In the SAN approach, the dynamic behavior of each system component is modeled by an automaton and the interactions between the different components by labels on the directed edges which may represent synchronization events and transition rates [12]. A Stochastic Automata Network is a set of automata.

Each automaton A_i is defined by the tuple (S_i, L, Q_i) where S_i is the set of states of the automaton. Q_i is the transition function of the automaton A_i which associates a label from L to every arc of A_i. Labels describe the rate and the type of the transition. The rate may be dependent of the others automata states. There are 2 types of transitions: *local* and *synchronized*. A local transition occurs only within the automaton, whereas the synchronized transition occurs in several automata at the same time. An automaton itself is not Markovian. The Markovian assumption holds only for the global SAN behavior if we assume exponential distribution and independence for the firing of the transitions.

The transition rate matrix Q is automatically translated from the SAN description. This translation is based on tensor algebra of matrices (see [12] for more details and proofs).

First let us define tensor operators:

Definition 1. Let A be a matrix of order $n \times n$, and B a matrix of order $p \times p$. The **tensor product** of A and B is a matrix C of order $np \times np$ such that C may be decomposed into n^2 blocks of size p.

$$C = A \bigotimes B = \begin{bmatrix} a_{11}B & \cdots & \cdots & a_{1n}B \\ \cdot & \cdot & \cdot & \cdot \\ \cdot & \cdot & \cdot & \cdot \\ \cdot & \cdot & \cdot & \cdot \\ a_{n1}B & \cdots & \cdots & a_{nn}B \end{bmatrix}$$

A and B are matrices of real values but we generalize the definition of tensor product on matrices of functional values (i.e. the elements of A and B are functions using states as arguments). Some properties of the classical tensor product still hold.

Definition 2. Let A be a matrix of order $n \times n$, and B a matrix of order $p \times p$. The **tensor sum** of A and B is defined by :

$$E = A \bigoplus B = A \bigotimes I_B + I_A \bigotimes B$$

where I_D represents the identity matrix with the same size as matrix D.

It has been proved in [12] that, if the states are in a lexicographic order, then the generator matrix Q of the Markov chain associated to a continuous-time SAN is given by:

$$Q = \bigoplus_{i=1}^{n} F_i + \sum_{j=1}^{c} \bigotimes_{i=1}^{n} S_{i,j} + \sum_{j=1}^{c} \bigotimes_{i=1}^{n} R_{i,j}$$

Where:

- n is the total number of automata in the network and c is the number of synchronization.

- F_i is the transition matrix of automaton i without synchronization.

- $S_{i,j}$ is the transition matrix of automaton i due to synchronization j.

- $R_{i,j}$ is a matrix representing the normalization associated to the synchronization j on automaton i.

- $\oplus$ and $\otimes$ denote tensor sum and product, respectively.

The transition matrix P of a Markov chain associated to a discrete-time Stochastic Automata Network can be obtained by a slightly different formula, given by:

$$P = \bigotimes_{i=1}^{n} F_i + \sum_{j=1}^{c} \left(\bigotimes_{i=1}^{n} S_{i,j} - \bigotimes_{i=1}^{n} R_{i,j} \right)$$

The main advantage of this methodology is its ability to represent the Markov chain associated to the SAN model by a compact formula. This point is particularly important since it allows us to deal with systems which may have very large state spaces. In the following section, we show how we model our system using the SAN methodology.

4. Considered composite Web service model

We focus on the composite Web service (CWS) response time computation, where the requests are decomposed into sub-queries to different elementary Web services and then merged into a final result. The control patterns considered here are not directly supported by BPEL [28]:

- parallel invocation of a constant number of elementary Web services merged by a federation component. This model is described in section 4.1.

- parallel invocation of a variable number of elementary Web services merged by a federation component. This model is described in section 4.2.

4.1. Case n is constant

We consider a composite Web service where the data is stored in databases and can be accessed using XML-based protocols noted s_i for $1 \leq i \leq n$. We assume that when a composite Web service is invoked, n elementary Web services are invoked in parallel and the partial responses are then integrated into the global response to provide to the client. We assume that the arrival of the composite Web services follow a Poisson process with rate λ. The response times of the servers s_i for $1 \leq i \leq n$ are also assumed to be of exponential distributions with rate μ_i for $1 \leq i \leq n$. We assume that the merging time of the n elementary Web services is an exponential distribution with rate μ (batch service).

As we have defined the behavior of the system as Markov process, the considered model can be described

by a continuous time Markov chain denoted by $X(t)$. To describe this chain, we define the state x by $(x_1, s_1, s_2, \ldots, s_n, a_1, a_2, \ldots, a_n)$, where:

- x_1 is the number of the composite Web services requests.

- $s_1, s_2, \ldots, s_n$ are the elementary Web services in each queue.

- $a_1, a_2, \ldots, a_n$ are the elementary Web service responses in the related queue waiting to be merged in the global responses to give back to the clients.

Associate queueing model   Hereafter, we define the queueing model when n is constant. Our model can be specified by queuing network. We have one finite buffer for requests with size b. n queues with finite buffers with size b_i for $1 \leq i \leq n$. n others queues with finite buffers with size b_i for $1 \leq i \leq n$ where the elementary Web services waiting for the batch service.

To illustrate the behavior of the system, we give the behavior equations of the considered model in the following:

$x \quad \rightarrow \quad$ CWS arrival

$\quad \rightarrow \quad (x_1 + 1, s_1, s_2, \ldots, s_n, a_1, a_2, \ldots, a_n)$
$\qquad$ *with rate* $\lambda \times \mathbb{1}_{x_1 < b}$

$\quad \rightarrow \quad$ Decomposition of CWC into n elementary WS

$\quad \rightarrow \quad (x_1 - 1, s_1 + 1, s_2 + 1, \ldots, s_n + 1, a_1, a_2, \ldots, a_n)$
$\qquad$ *with rate* $\mu_\lambda \times \mathbb{1}_{x_1 > 0} \times \mathbb{1}_{s_i < b_i}$

$\quad \rightarrow \quad$ End of service of WS1

$\quad \rightarrow \quad (x_1, s_1 - 1, s_2, \ldots, s_n, a_1 + 1, a_2, \ldots, a_n)$
$\qquad$ *with rate* $\mu_1 \times \mathbb{1}_{s_1 > 0} \times \mathbb{1}_{a_1 < b_1}$

$\quad \rightarrow \quad$ End of service of WS2

$\quad \rightarrow \quad (x_1, s_1, s_2 - 1, \ldots, s_n, a_1, a_2 + 1, \ldots, a_n)$
$\qquad$ *with rate* $\mu_2 \times \mathbb{1}_{s_2 > 0} \times \mathbb{1}_{a_2 < b_2}$

$\quad \rightarrow \quad \ldots$

$\quad \rightarrow \quad$ End of service of WSn

$\quad \rightarrow \quad (x_1, s_1, s_2, \ldots, s_n - 1, a_1, a_2, \ldots, a_n + 1)$
$\qquad$ *with rate* $\mu_n \times \mathbb{1}_{s_n > 0} \times \mathbb{1}_{a_n < b_n}$

$\quad \rightarrow \quad$ Synchronization of n WSs, so response of CWS

$\quad \rightarrow \quad (x_1, s_1, s_2, \ldots, s_n, a_1 - 1, a_2 - 1, \ldots, a_n - 1)$
$\qquad$ *with rate* $\mu \times \mathbb{1}_{a_i > 0}$

4.2. Case n is variable

We assume for this model that once a composite Web service (CWS) is requested, it can be decomposed into k Elementary Web Services (EWS) where $1 \leq k \leq n$.

The case is a generalization of the precedent case (n constant).

Thus we define the following probabilities :

- p_1 is the probability that CWB, is decomposed into one elementary Web service

- p_2 is the probability that CWB, is decomposed into two elementary Web services

- p_k is the probability that CWB, is decomposed into k elementary Web services

- p_n is the probability that CWB, is decomposed into n elementary Web services, which is the case of the first model.

Associate queueing model The considered model can also be described by a continuous time Markov chain denoted by $X(t)$. To describe this chain, we define the state x by $(x_1, s_1, s_2, \ldots, s_n, a_1, a_2, \ldots, a_n)$, where:

- x_1 is the number of the composite Web services requests

- $s_1, s_2, \ldots, s_n$ are the elementary Web services in each queue.

- $a_1, a_2, \ldots, a_n)$ are the number elementary Web services responses in each queue waiting for merging and giving the responses to the clients.

As the system is complex, we give the behavior equations only for the case that a CWS can be decomposed into 1, 2 or 3 EWS ($n = 3$). We denote by s_1, s_2 and s_3 the elementary Web service that can compose the CWS denoted by Sw. Thus we have the following combinations:

- Sw is composed only by s_1 with probability p_1

- Sw is composed only by s_2 with probability p_2

- Sw is composed only by s_3 with probability p_3

- Sw is composed by s_1 and s_2 with probability p_{12}

- Sw is composed by s_1 and s_3 with probability p_{13}

- Sw is composed by s_2 and s_3 with probability p_{23}

- Sw is composed by s_1, s_2 and s_3 with probability p_{123}

Thus, the behavior equations are given as follows: x

$\rightarrow$ CWS arrival

$\rightarrow$ $(x_1 + 1, s_1, s_2, s_3, a_1, a_2, a_3)$

  $with\ rate\ \lambda \times\ \mathbb{1}_{x_1 < b}$

$\rightarrow$ Decomposition of CWS into EWS 1

$\rightarrow$ $(x_1 - 1, s_1 + 1, s_2, s_3, a_1, a_2, a_3)$

  $with\ rate\ \mu_\lambda \times p_1 \times\ \mathbb{1}_{x_1 > 0}\ \times \mathbb{1}_{s_1 < b_1}$

$\rightarrow$ Decomposition of CWS into EWS 2

$\rightarrow$ $(x_1 - 1, s_1, s_2 + 1, s_3, a_1, a_2, a_3)$

  $with\ rate\ \mu_\lambda \times p_2 \times\ \mathbb{1}_{x_1 > 0}\ \times \mathbb{1}_{s_2 < b_2}$

$\rightarrow$ Decomposition of CWS into EWS 3

$\rightarrow$ $(x_1 - 1, s_1, s_2, s_3 + 1, a_1, a_2, a_3)$

  $with\ rate\ \mu_\lambda \times p_3 \times\ \mathbb{1}_{x_1 > 0}\ \times \mathbb{1}_{s_3 < b_3}$

$\rightarrow$ Decomposition of CWS into EWS 1 and EWS 2

$\rightarrow$ $(x_1 - 1, s_1 + 1, s_2 + 1, s_3, a_1, a_2, a_3)$

  with rate $\mu_\lambda \times p_{12} \times\ \mathbb{1}_{x_1 > 0} \times$

  $\mathbb{1}_{s_1 < b_1} \times \mathbb{1}_{s_2 < b_2}$

$\rightarrow$ Decomposition of CWS into EWS 1 and EWS 3

$\rightarrow$ $(x_1 - 1, s_1 + 1, s_2, s_3 + 1, a_1, a_2, a_3)$

  with rate $\mu_\lambda \times p_{13} \times$

  $\mathbb{1}_{x_1 > 0} \times \mathbb{1}_{s_1 < b_1} \times \mathbb{1}_{s_3 < b_3}$

$\rightarrow$ Decomposition of CWS into EWS 2 and EWS 3

$\rightarrow$ $(x_1 - 1, s_1, s_2 + 1, s_3 + 1, a_1, a_2, a_3)$

  with rate $\mu_\lambda \times p_{23} \times$

  $\mathbb{1}_{x_1 > 0} \times \mathbb{1}_{s_2 < b_2} \times \mathbb{1}_{s_3 < b_3}$

$\rightarrow$ Decomposition of CWS into EWS 1, EWS 2 and EWS 3

$\rightarrow$ $(x_1 - 1, s_1 + 1, s_2 + 1, s_3 + 1, a_1, a_2, a_3)$

  $with\ rate\ \mu_\lambda \times p_{123} \times$

  $\mathbb{1}_{x_1 > 0} \times \mathbb{1}_{s_1 < b_1} \times \mathbb{1}_{s_2 < b_2} \times \mathbb{1}_{s_3 < b_3}$

$\rightarrow$ End of service EWS1

$\rightarrow$ $(x_1, s_1 - 1, s_2, s_3, a_1 + 1, a_2, a_3)$

  with rate $\mu_1 \times\ \mathbb{1}_{s_1 > 0}\ \times \mathbb{1}_{a_1 < B_1}$

$\rightarrow$ End of service EWS2

$\rightarrow$ $(x_1, s_1, s_2 - 3, s_3, a_1, a_2 + 1, a_3)$

  $with\ rate\ \mu_2 \times\ \mathbb{1}_{s_2 > 0}\ \times \mathbb{1}_{a_2 < B_2}$

$\rightarrow$ End of service EWS3

$\rightarrow$ $(x_1, s_1, s_2, s_3 - 1, a_1, a_2, a_3 + 1)$

  with rate $\mu_3 \times\ \mathbb{1}_{s_3 > 0}\ \times \mathbb{1}_{a_3 < b_3}$

$\rightarrow$ Response to CWS composed only by EWS1

$\rightarrow$ $(x_1, s_1, s_2, s_3, a_1 - 1, a_2, a_3)$

  with rate $\mu \times p_1 \times\ \mathbb{1}_{a_1 > 0}$

$\rightarrow$ Response to CWS composed only by EWS2

$\rightarrow$ $(x_1, s_1, s_2, s_3, a_1, a_2 - 1, a_3)$

  with rate $\mu \times p_2 \times\ \mathbb{1}_{a_2 > 0}$

$\rightarrow$ Response to CWS composed only by EWS3

$\rightarrow \quad (x_1, s_1, s_2, s_3, a_1, a_2, a_3 - 1)$
with rate $\mu \times p_3 \times \mathbb{1}_{a_3>0}$

$\rightarrow \quad$ Response to CWS composed only by EWS1 and EWS2

$\rightarrow \quad (x_1, s_1, s_2, s_3, a_1 - 1, a_2 - 1, a_3)$
with rate $\mu \times p_{12} \times \mathbb{1}_{a_1>0} \times \mathbb{1}_{a_2>0}$

$\rightarrow \quad$ Response to CWS composed only by EWS1 and EWS3

$\rightarrow \quad (x_1, s_1, s_2, s_3, a_1 - 1, a_2, a_3 - 1)$
with rate $\mu \times p_{13} \times \mathbb{1}_{a_1>0} \times \mathbb{1}_{a_3>0}$

$\rightarrow \quad$ Response to CWS composed only by EWS2 and EWS3

$\rightarrow \quad (x_1, s_1, s_2, s_3, a_1, a_2 - 1, a_3 - 1)$
with rate $\mu \times p_{23} \times \mathbb{1}_{a_2>0} \times \mathbb{1}_{a_3>0}$

$\rightarrow \quad$ Response to CWS composed only by EWS1, EWS2 and EWS3

$\rightarrow \quad (x_1, s_1, s_2, s_3, a_1 - 1, a_2 - 1, a_3 - 1)$
with rate $\mu \times p_{123} \times \mathbb{1}_{a_i>0}$

4.3. Associated SAN

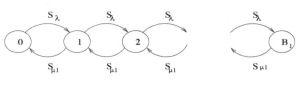

Automaton for EWS 1

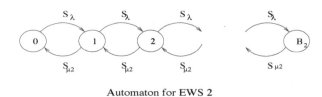

Automaton for EWS 2

Automaton for EWS n

Figure 2. stochastic Automata for elementary service execution

We present in this section how we specify our model using SAN for the both considered models.

4.4. Case n is constant

Before giving the automata, we give the description of the different synchronization in the following.

- S_λ is a synchronization which corresponds to the fork which means that we decompose the request (CWS) into n elementary Web services. Thus, its rate is equal to λ.

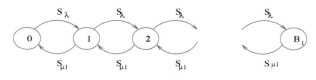

Automaton for EWS 1

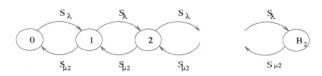

Automaton for EWS 2

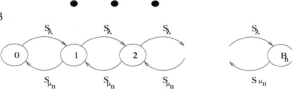

Automaton for EWS n

Figure 3. stochastic Automata for elementary service execution

- S_{μ_1} is a synchronization which corresponds to the service of elementary Web service from server 1. Its rate is equal to μ_1.

- Thus, we can note that S_{μ_i} is the synchronization which corresponds to the service of elementary Web service from server i for $1 \leq i \leq n$. Hence, its rate is equal to μ_i.

- S_ν is a synchronization which corresponds to the batch service of elementary Web service from all servers. Thus, its rate is equal to ν.

For the considered model, we need several automata as described in the following:

- We need one automaton for request arrival which decompose the CWS into n EWS. The action is done by the synchronization S_λ. The considered automaton is given in figure 4.

- We describe one automaton for each servers where are executed the elementary Web services. As we consider that a CWS can be decomposed in n EWS, we need n automata. These automata are described in figure 3.

- We also need one automaton for each EWS waiting for the batch service. The batch service is provided by synchronization S_ν as shown in figure 5.

In the following, we give the associated stochastic automata for the case where n is variable.

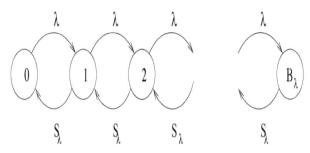

Figure 4. Automaton for request arrival

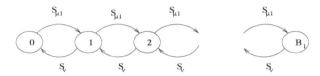

Automaton EWS 1 for batch service

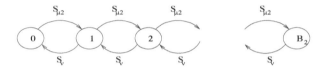

Automaton EWS 2 for batch service

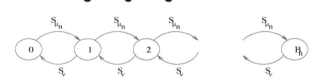

Automaton EWS n for batch service

Figure 5. Automata for batch service

4.5. Case n is variable

For a sake of readability, we represent only the case where a CWS can be decomposed into 1, 2 or 3 EWS ($n = 3$) and where several automata are needed. Before we describe this modeling, we give the used synchronization:

- The synchronization $S_1, S_2, \ldots, S_{123}$ are used for the decompositions of CWS into 1, 2 or 3 EWS ($n = 3$).

- The synchronization $S_{\mu 1}, S_{\mu 2}, S_{\mu 3}$ are used for the service of EWS

- The synchronization $S_{\nu 1}, S_{\nu 2}, \ldots, S_{\nu 123}$ are used for the merge of 1, 2 or 3 EWS.

We present, now, the associated stochastic automata network.

- We need one automaton for request arrival, which decomposes the CWS into n EWS. The action is

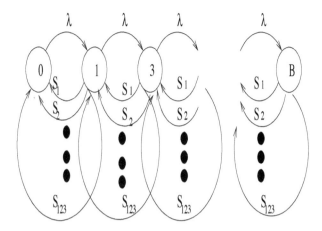

Figure 6. Automaton for request arrival

done by the synchronization S_λ. The considered automaton is given in figure 6.

- We need one automaton for each server where are executed the elementary Web services. As we consider that a CWS can be decomposed in n EWS, where n is variable, we use the corresponding synchronization. These automata are described in figure 7.

- We also need one Automaton for each EWS waiting for the batch service. The batch service is provided by synchronization $S_{\nu 1}, S_{\nu 2}, \ldots, S_{\nu 123}$ as shown in figures 8, 9. and 10.

Once the automata are built, we develop, first, for each automata the local and synchronization matrices. Then we apply the compact formula.

$$Q = \bigoplus_{i=1}^{n} F_i + \sum_{j=1}^{c} \bigotimes_{i=1}^{n} S_{i,j} + \sum_{j=1}^{c} \bigotimes_{i=1}^{n} R_{i,j}$$

The latter makes it possible to compute the rewards as it is discussed in the next section.

5. Numerical results

In this paper, we are interested in assessing the response times as it is most important Qos parameter in the performance evaluation of Web services architecture. We have solved the previous obtained models using the numerical method (Gauss-Seidel) to obtain the steady-state distribution which provides the performance measures. The latter give the response times and the mean requests ratio of the system. In figure 11, we have plotted the response times results according to the system load by considering that a composite Web service can be decompose into n elementary Web services where n is a constant. As we expected, the response times increase when the system load increases. In figure 12, we have considered the basic model (n

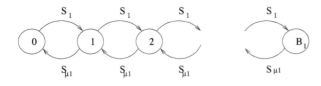

Automaton for EWS 1

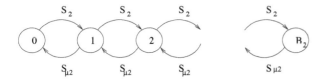

Automaton for EWS 2

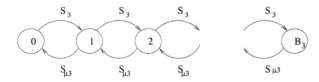

Automaton for EWS 3

Figure 7. Automata for elementary Web services

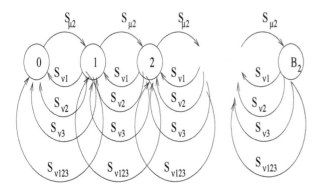

Figure 8. Automate A1

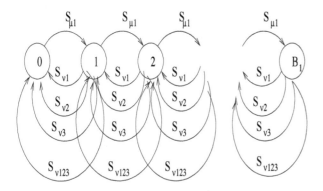

Figure 9. Automate A2

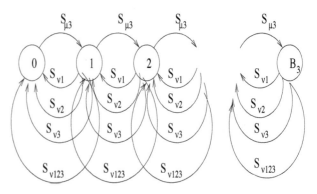

Figure 10. Automate A3

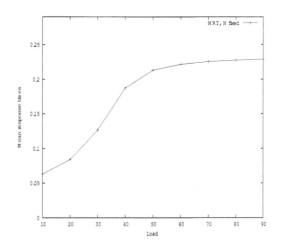

Figure 11. Mean Response times for the case n is constant.

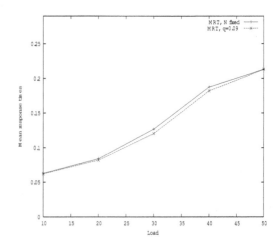

Figure 12. Mean Response times for both cases.

constant) and the general model (n variable); response times according to the system load are reported, thus comparing both models. In figure 13, we compare the performances of both models by computing the mean request ratio of both models. As we can see the variability of the number of composed elementary web services has no effect on the behavior of the system comparing where n is fixed.

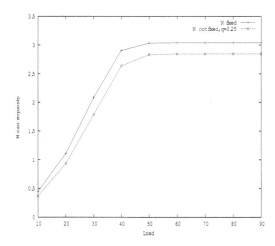

Figure 13. Mean Requests ratio of both cases.

6. Conclusion

The objective of this paper was to present the SAN tool and to show how it can be used to evaluate Web service architectures. Indeed, the proliferation of Web services on the Internet and their interoperable nature have shown very quickly the importance of having the QoS in their operating model. This enables the distinction between them and provides the users with tools to select those which are the most suitable for their needs. The performance evaluation of such systems is therefore crucial to guarantee their reliability and their QoS requirements. Because of the complexity in the modeling of such requirements, new tools and methods are therefore needed to handle complex synchronization as well as variable number of elementary services.

In this paper we have investigated the use of stochastic automata networks and we have shown how we can use this formalism to model and evaluate these systems. The main objective was to compute composite Web services response times when the number of invoked elementary Web services can be variable. Future work will lead us to generalize the study by taking into account more complex patterns (e.g. hierarchical composite Web services). Secondly, we plan to consider time requirements in the modeling as well as in the performance evaluation of Web service architectures.

References

[1] D. Tidwell, "Web services - The Web's next revolution", IBM developerWorks, 2000

[2] David Booth, Hugo Haas, Francis McCabe, Eric Newcomer, Michael Champion, and Chris Ferris David Orchard. Web Service Architecture. Published on the internet, February 2004. URLhttp://www.w3.org/TR/ws-arch/. W3C Recommendation.

[3] M. Hu, "Web Services Composition, Partition, and Quality of Service in Distributed System Integration and Re-engineering", In IEEE, Internet Computing, 2005.

[4] M. Gudgin, and M. Hadley, and N. Mendelsohn, and J. Moreau and H. Nielsen, "Simple Object Access Protocol (SOAP) 1.1", World Wide Web Consortium,

[5] T. Bellwood, and L. Clément, and C. von Riegen, "Universal Description, Discovery and Integration", OASIS UDDI Specification Technical Committee,

[6] E. Christensen, and F. Curbera, and G. Meredith and S. Weerawarana, "Web Services Description Language (WSDL) 1.1", World Wide Web Consortium,

[7] Francisco Curbera and Rania Khalaf and Nirmal Mukhi and Stefan Tai and Sanjiva Weerawarana, The next step in Web services, Commun. ACM journal, volume 46, number 10, pages 29-34, year 2003.

[8] Daniela Claro, Patrick Albers and Jin-Kao Hao, Web services composition, In J. Cardoso, Sheth, Amit (Eds.), Semantic Web Services, Processes and Applications » Chapter 8, 2006.

[9] S. Dustdar, W. Schreiner, A survey on web services composition, International Journal Web and Grid Services 1, pages 1-30, 2005

[10] D.A. Menascé. QoS Issues in Web Services", IEEE Internet Computing, vol. 6, no. 6, pp. 72-74, 2002.

[11] D.A. Menascé et al., Response Time Analysis of Composite Web Services," IEEE Internet Computing, vol. 8, no. 1, pp.90-92, January/February 2004.

[12] B. Plateau and J.M. Fourneau "A Methodology for Solving Complex Markov Models of Parallel Systems", Journal of Parallel and Distributed Computing, Vol. 12, pp. 370-387, 1991.

[13] D. Davis and M. P. Parashar, "Latency performance of soap implementations", In CCGRID '02: Proceedings of the 2nd IEEE/ACM International Symposium on Cluster Computing and the Grid, page 407, Washington, USA, IEEE Computer Society, pp. 407-415, 2002.

[14] C. Kohlhoff and R. Steele, "Evaluating soap for high performance business applications: Real-time trading systems", In Proceedings of WWW, pp. 1-8, 2003.

[15] P. Sandoz, S. Pericas-Geertsen, K. Kawaguchi, M. Hadley, and E. Pelegri-Llopart, "Fast web services", 2009.

[16] J. Klingemann, J. Wäsch, and K. Aberer, "Deriving Service Models in Cross-Organizational Workflows", In proceedings of RIDE -Information Technology for Virtual Enterprises, Sydney, Australia, pp. 100-107, 1999.

[17] D.A. Menascé et al., "Static and Dynamic Processor Scheduling Disciplines in Heterogeneous Parallel Architectures," J. Parallel and Distributed Computing, vol. 28, no. 1, pp. 1-18, 1995.

[18] S. Hahn and L. Fatto, "Two parallel queues created by arrivals with two demands", Applied Mathematics, Vo. 44, pp. 1041-1053, October, 1984.

[19] L. Fatto, "Two parallel queues created by arrivals with two demands II", Applied Mathematics, Vo. 45, pp. 861-878, October, 1985.

[20] R. Nelson and A.N. Tantawi, "Approximate Analysis of Fork/Join Synchronization in Parallel Queues", IEEE Transaction Computer, vol. 37, No. 6, pp. 739-743, 1998.

[21] A. Makawski and S. Verma, "Interpolation approxima-tions for symmetric Fork-Join Queues", Perform. Evalua-tion journal. 20(1-3), pp. 245-265, 1994.

[22] F. Bacelli and A.M. Makowski, "Simple computable bounds for the fork-join queue", Proceeding Information Science, pp. 436-441, March, 1985.

[23] P. Heidlberg and K.S. Trivedi, "Analytic queuing models for programs with internal concurrency", IEEE Trans. Computer, vol. C-32, pp. 73-82, Nov, 1993.

[24] S. Haddad, L. Mokdad and S. Youcef, Response time analysis of composite Web services", Communication Systems, Networks and Digital Signal Processing (CSNDSP), IEEE Computer Society, Graz University of Technology, pp. 42-49, July 2008.

[25] C.W. Piotr, F.Pawel and W. Grzegorz, "Time Distribution in Structural Workflow Nets", Fundam. Inf., vol. 85, n. 1-4, IOS Press, Amsterdam, Netherlands, pp. 67-87, 2008.

[26] M. Sharf, "On the response time of the large-scale composite Web services", Proceedings of the 19th International Teletraffic Congress (ITC 19), Beijing, pp. 1807-1816, 2005.

[27] S. Haddad, L. Mokdad, S. Youcef: Bounding models families for performance evaluation in composite Web services. J. Comput. Science 4(4): 232-241 (2013)

[28] S. Weerawarana and F. Curbera, "Business Process Execution Language for Web Services", IBM Corporation, 2002.

Permissions

List of Contributors

Zhongyi Shen, Xin Zhang, Meng Zhang, Zhihao Chen, Weijia Li and Hongyu Sun
School of Information and Communication Engineering
Beijing University of Posts and Telecommunications
PO Box93, 10 XiTuCheng Rd, HaiDian, Beijing, CHINA

Malla Reddy Sama, Yvon Gourhant and Lucian Suciu
Orange Labs, France

Allan Cook, Helge Janicke, Leandros Maglaras and Richard Smith
Cyber Security Centre, De Montfort University, Leicester, LE1 9BH, UK

Andrew Nicholson
Cyber Security Centre, WMG, University of Warwick, Coventry CV4 7AL, UK

Zhengguo Sheng
Department of Engineering and Design, University of Sussex, UK
Department of Electrical and Computer Engineering, The University of British Columbia, Canada

Chunsheng Zhu and Victor C. M. Leung
Department of Electrical and Computer Engineering, The University of British Columbia, Canada

Marius Georgescu, Hiroaki Hazeyama, Youki Kadobayashi and Suguru Yamaguchi
Nara Institute of Science and Technology, 8916-5 Takayama, Ikoma, Nara 630-0192, JAPAN

Zakaria Maamar
Zayed University, Dubai, U.A.E

Noura Faci
Claude Bernard Lyon 1 University, Lyon, France

Ejub Kajan
State University of Novi Pazar, Novi Pazar, Serbia

Sherif Sakr
University of New South Wales, Sydney, Australia & King Saud bin Abdulaziz University for Health Sciences, Riyadh, Saudi Arabia

Mohamed Boukhebouze
CETIC, Charleroi, Belgium

Ahmed Barnawi
King Abdulaziz University, Jeddah, Saudi Arabia

Dramane Ouattara and Omessaad Hamdi
Univ. Bordeaux, LaBRI, Talence, France

Mohamed Aymen Chalouf
Univ. Rennes 1, IRISA, Lannion, France

Francine Krief
Univ. Bordeaux, LaBRI, Talence, France
IPB, Bordeaux, France

Manabu Tsukada
NRIA Paris - Rocquencourt, Domaine de Voluceau Rocquencourt - B.P. 105 78153 Le Chesnay Cedex, France
The University of Tokyo, 1-1-1, Yayoi, Bunkyo-ku, Tokyo, 113-8656 Japan

José Santa
University Centre of Defence at the Spanish Air Force Academy, MDE-UPCT , Murcia, Spain
University of Murcia, Campus de Espinardo, 30100 Murcia, Spain

Satoshi Matsuura
Tokyo Institute of Technology, 2-12-1, Ookayama, Meguro-ku, Tokyo, 152-8850, Japan

Thierry Ernst
Centre de Robotique, MINES ParisTech, Paris, France

Kazutoshi Fujikawa
Nara Institute of Science and Technology, Nara, Japan

Mohiuddin Ahmed, Adnan Anwar, Abdun Naser Mahmood, Zubair Shah and Michael J. Maher
School of Engineering and Information Technology, UNSW Canberra, ACT 2600, Australia

Fei Gu, Jianwei Niu and Zhenxue He
State Key Laboratory of Virtual Reality Technology and Systems, School of Computer Science and Engineering, Beihang University, Beijing 100191, China

Randa M. Abdelmoneem and Eman Shaaban
Department of Computer Systems, Faculty of Computer and Information Sciences, Ain-Shams University, Egypt

Frédéric Blanchard, Amine Aït-Younes and Michel Herbin
Université de Reims Champagne-Ardenne, CReSTIC, UFR Sciences Exactes et Naturelles, Moulin de la Housse, BP 1039, 51687 Reims CEDEX 2, FRANCE

Paolo Giammatteo, Concettina Buccella and Carlo Cecati
Department of Information Engineering, Computer Science and Mathematics, University of L'Aquila, Via Vetoio, 67100, L'Aquila, Italy

Kui-Ting Chen, Ke Fan, Yijun Dai and Takaaki Baba
Research Center and Graduate School of Information, Production and Systems,Waseda University, 2-7 Hibikino, Kitakyushu, Fukuoka, Japan

Thierno Ahmadou Diallo
Département d'Informatique, LMI, Université Cheikh Anta Diop, 5005 Dakar-Fann, Sénégal
CReSTIC Laboratory - SYSCOM team, University of Reims Champagne-Ardenne, Reims, France

Olivier Flauzac and Luiz-Angelo Steffenel
CReSTIC Laboratory - SYSCOM team, University of Reims Champagne-Ardenne, Reims, France

Samba N'Diaye
Département d'Informatique, LMI, Université Cheikh Anta Diop, 5005 Dakar-Fann, Sénégal

Tsutomu Kumazawa
Software Research Associates, Inc, 2-32-8 Minami-Ikebukuro, Toshima-ku, Tokyo 171-8513, Japan

Chihiro Yokoyama and Munehiro Takimoto
Tokyo University of Science, 2641 Yamazaki, Noda-shi, Chiba 278-8510, Japan

Yasushi Kambayashi
Nippon Institute of Technology, 4-1 Gakuendai, Miyashiro-machi, Minamisaitama-gun, Saitama 345-8501, Japan

Lynda Mokdad
Lab. LACL, University of Paris-Est LACL (EA 4219), UPEC F-94010 Créteil, France

Jalel Ben Othman
Lab. L2TI, University of Paris 13- L2TI (EA 3043), UP13 F-93430 Villetaneuse, France

Abdelkrim Abdelli
Lab. LSI, USTHB university of Algiers, Algeria

Index

Printed in the USA
CPSIA information can be obtained
at www.ICGtesting.com
JSHW051438221024
72173JS00006B/1513

9 781632 406354